POSSIBILITIES

Essays on Hierarchy, Rebellion, and Desire

POSSIBILITIES

Essays on Hierarchy, Rebellion, and Desire

David Graeber

AK Press

Possibilities: Essays on Hierarchy, Rebellion, and Desire
by David Graeber

ISBN 978-1904859-66-6
Library of Congress Number: 2007928387

Earlier versions of essays in this collection appeared in the following publications:

Chapter 1: "Manners, Deference, and Private Property." *Comparative Studies in Society and History* 39/4 (Spring 1997): 694–728.

Chapter 3: "Turning Modes of Production Inside Out: Or, Why Capitalism is a Transformation of Slavery (short version)." *Critique of Anthropology* 26 /1 (March 2006): 61–81.

Chapter 4: "Fetishism and Social Creativity: Or, Fetishes are Gods in Process of Construction." *Anthropological Theory* 5/4 (2005): 407–438.

Chapter 5: "Catastrophe: Magic and History in Rural Madagascar." *Campos: Revista de Antropologia Social* 5/1 (2004): 9–30.

Chapter 6: "Dancing with Corpses Reconsidered: An Interpretation of *Famadihana* in Arivonimamo, (Madagascar)." *American Ethnologist* 22/2 (May 1995): 258–278. Reprinted in *Religion in Culture and Society*, edited by John R. Bowen (Boston: Allyn & Bacon, 1997).

Chapter 7: "Love Magic and Political Morality in Central Madagascar, 1875–1990." *Gender and History* 8/3 (November 1996): 416–439. Special issue on "Gendered Colonialisms in African History," which also appeared as a book of the same (edited by Jean Quataert, et. al., Oxford: Blackwell, 1997).

Chapter 10: "La sociologie comme science et comme utopie." *Revue du MAUSS Semestrielle* 24 (2004), "Une théorie sociologique générale est-elle pensable?" Second Semestre: 205–217.

Chapter 11: "La démocratie des interstices." *Revue du MAUSS Semestrielle* 26 (2005), "Alter-démocratie, alter-économie: chantiers d l'espérance." Second Semestre: 41–89.

AK Press
674-A 23rd Street
Oakland, CA 94612
www.akpress.org
akpress@akpress.org
510.208.1700

AK Press U.K.
PO Box 12766
Edinburgh EH8 9YE
www.akuk.com
ak@akedin.demon.co.uk
0131.555.5165

Cover Design: John Yates
Layout: C. Weigl & Z. Blue
Proofreader: David Brazil

Printed in Canada on 100% recycled, acid-free paper by union labor.

TABLE OF CONTENTS

INTRODUCTION

I decided to call this collection *Possibilities* because the word encompasses much of what originally inspired me to become an anthropologist. I was drawn to the discipline because it opens windows on other possible forms of human social existence; because it served as a constant reminder that most of what we assume to be immutable has been, in other times and places, arranged quite differently, and therefore, that human possibilities are in almost every way greater than we ordinarily imagine. Anthropology also affords us new possible perspectives on familiar problems: ways of thinking about the rise of capitalism from the perspective of West Africa, European manners from the perspective of Amazonia, or, for that matter, West African or Amazonian masquerades from the perspective of Chinese festivals or Medieval European carnival.

One common feature of the essays collected in this book is that they are meant to keep possibilities open. They are not, in any sense, an attempt to create a single grand theory of anything—let alone, a single grand theory of everything. Think of them instead as an attempt to put some of the pluralism I espouse in the later essays into practice.

I often make the argument that (at least as a theoretical problem) incommensurability is greatly overrated. Take any two people, even in the same family or community, and you are likely to find half a dozen incommensurable perspectives. None of us completely understand each other. In practice, the fact that we don't rarely gets in the way of our living together, working together, or loving one another, and it is often an actual advantage when people, say, come together to solve a common, practical problem. It's only when we start imagining that the world is somehow generated by the descriptions we make of it that incommensurability becomes a well-nigh existential dilemma. Of course, the world is not really generated by the descriptions we make of it, as most of us are, occasionally, forced to recognize when some aspect of the world we had not included in our descriptions suddenly contrives to hit us on the head (sometimes figuratively, sometimes not). This book, then, is meant to assemble a series of different and sometimes even incommensurable perspectives on a very real world. They are unified, above all, by a commitment to the idea that that world could possibly look very different than it does—but just as much, perhaps, by the belief that, ultimately, the very combination of anger and curiosity, of intellectual play and creative pleasure that goes into crafting any worthwhile piece of critical social theory also itself partakes of something of the powers that could transform that world into something better. What unites them, then, is a utopian ideal.

The 3-part organization of the volume is broadly autobiographical. Part I, entitled "Some Thoughts on the Origins of Our Current Predicament," represents the kind of work I was doing in the 1980s in graduate school at the University of Chicago. Much of it emerges from research into the origins of capitalism. However, since, as my old mentor Marshall Sahlins has never ceased to point out, capitalism has by now played such a fundamental role in shaping our fundamental assumptions about the nature of human beings, human desires, and the very possibilities for human social relations, all of these essays are by necessity reflections on such larger questions at the same time. I first began trying to puzzle out some of these issues in my Masters paper, submitted in 1987—a much shorter, and updated, version of which appears as Chapter 1. This essay, ostensibly about the history of manners, has a curious history in its own right. Shortly after I finished it, the French sociologist Pierre Bourdieu was visiting the University of Chicago anthropology department. Bourdieu was then at the height of his popularity, and everyone wanted to meet him, but he was much more interested in talking to students than with faculty—since, as he later remarked to a group of us, "with students, you can actually discuss ideas. Your colleagues, all they want to do is kill you." He announced office hours, and for several days beforehand there was a sign-up sheet on the door. I myself was far too timid to actually put my name on it. As it turned out, so was most everyone else. Late on the afternoon of Bourdieu's visit, my friend Becky came down to the student lounge after spending an hour talking to him and assured me that—no, really—Bourdieu was extremely friendly and easy to talk to and, not only that, there was still an empty slot at the end of his schedule. I went up, wrote down my name, and ultimately ended up walking him to his hotel, talking about manners. He was, he explained, quite fascinated by the subject. Bourdieu asked for a copy of my paper, and the next day called me back to announce that he found the argument extremely original and urged me to produce a shorter version for publication in France.

The problem, it soon turned out, was that it proved very difficult to shorten (it was an intricate and tangled argument), and while we both agreed the best thing was for us to sit down together and go over it, I never managed to raise the money to get myself to Paris to do so. Actually, it was an excellent example of the sort of mechanisms of social class reproduction in academia that Bourdieu himself spent so much of his time exposing: it seemed no co-incidence that I, one of the few students in the department from a working class background, always seemed to be the one who—despite endless formal honors—never seemed to be able to get my hands on any of the university or outside funding that magically seemed to appear for those whose parents were doctors, lawyers, or themselves academics. (True, Bourdieu himself did once suggest he could find money for me once I got to Paris, but this turned out to be an example of another of his principles: that intellectual prestige by no means guarantees academic power. Insiders assured me that he was in no position to guarantee the money would actually appear.)

I eventually published a truncated version of the manners essay in *Comparative Studies in Society and History,* more than a decade later. Few seem to have noticed it—largely, I think, since it fell between the cracks, being neither quite anthropology, nor history. I had by then fallen out of contact with Bourdieu. But then, four years later, in the heyday of the global justice movement, we suddenly came very close to establishing contact once again.

Bourdieu had by this time become involved in a project called *Raisons d'Agir,* aimed at creating alliances between scholars, activists, and radical labor unions. Apparently, Bourdieu had been for some time trying to locate scholars in the US engaged in analogous projects, without much success, and had just got word about my work with the New York City Direct Action Network. I had received a message from an intermediary that I was to pre-pare for a phone call from Bourdieu on September 11th. Unfortunately, that was September 11th 2001. I was living in Manhattan at the time, and, of course, owing to the destruction of the Towers, phone lines were down. I was a little confused as to why Bourdieu never ended up calling later on, but eventually learned that he was already quite ill. He died of cancer not long thereafter.

But here I jump ahead.

I have always felt the Manners paper contained important arguments. It is not only a paper about manners and what Bourdieu would no doubt call the "habitus" of possessive individualism—those deeply internalized habits of thinking and feeling about the world that develop when people who be-come accustomed, even without realizing it, to viewing everything around them primarily as actual or potential commercial property. It is also a reflection on the very nature of hierarchy, its most elementary building-blocks, and about how forms of resistance as subtle as foul language, merrymaking, and apparently dubious personal hygiene habits simultaneously challenge and reinforce it. While I did not write it with an explicitly political intention, it always seemed to me that the political implications were clear enough (though also complex and endlessly debatable) and I have tried to highlight them a bit more in the current version.

The other three essays in Part I were written later, but they pursue many of the same themes, with the political implications, usually, far more explicit. The essay on consumption is new, but it was conceived during the lonely days when I was writing my dissertation in the early 1990s. University of Chicago does not provide any support for those at the writing stage, so for several years I was spending much of my daylight hours working for interlibrary loan and at various odd jobs, trying to do my own work at night, and to ignore the fact that my teeth were falling out due to lack of dental care as my faculty advisors (mostly) carefully avoided me. One of the great saving graces of my library job (aside from generally delightful coworkers: Gail and Willie I will always especially remember) was that my supervisor was in a different building, so I managed, periodically, to hide out in the Regenstein stacks and snatch a half hour here and there to absorb unusual books I might never have otherwise encountered. It was there I first discovered Colin Campbell's *The Romantic Ethic and the Spirit of Modern Consumerism*, certainly the most creative and interesting of the generally rather tiresome literature of former counter-culture types turned prosperous middle-class professors trying to demonstrate why, despite their consumption-oriented existence, they had not, in fact, sold out. The book was brilliant, but somehow obviously wrong. This bothered me. I felt there was something important to be said about it, but didn't know what.

It was around the same time, when returning from my library job to my office at the anthropology department in Haskell Hall, that I passed a collection of ambulances and police cars, to learn that Iouan Couliano, a Romanian historian of religions, had been assassinated on the third floor of Swift, the building next to ours. (A man with a silenced pistol had shot him from the adjoining stall in the men's bathroom on the third floor. The next day at my job, I heard that the library, on hearing the news, had immediately leapt into action, sending someone to gather all the library books from his office before they were sequestered by the police as possible evidence.) That was a bad couple years for Romanian-born historians of religion at the U of C: Mircea Eliade had died the year before, after which his library mysteriously caught on fire. At any rate, I decided, as a kind of tribute, to read Couliano's last book, *Eros and Magic in the Renaissance*—and quickly decided that, while shamelessly sensationalistic, it also was somehow important, and formed a complement to Campbell. Understanding the connection, I thought, would surely provide a key to understanding what I had always found so problematic about the cult of "consumption" so prevalent in Cultural Studies and related trendy theory of the time.

Hence the genesis of the idea. It only really came together, however, some years later when I read Agamben's newly translated *Stanzas*, and realized that Couliano must have pirated almost all his central ideas from a then-obscure Italian philosopher who, however, he almost completely failed to cite, except in a couple rather snarky critical footnotes when he happened to disagree with him. (I am not saying, however, that we should add Agamben to the list of suspects—it seems pretty well established that Couliano was murdered by the Romanian secret police.) I ended up putting the pieces together for a panel called "The New Keywords: Unmasking the Terms of an Emerging Orthodoxy," co-organized with Lauren Leve, at the American Anthropology Association meetings of 2003.

The essays in Part I, then, had radically different incubation periods. The piece on capitalism and slavery, for example, was originally inspired by the close relation between slavery and wage-labor I observed in Madagascar, and then noted again in documents about nineteenth-century Madagascar, while writing my dissertation. Over time, I began noticing Madagascar was by no means unique: wage-labor contracts appear to have developed from within the institution of slavery in many times and places, from ancient Greece to the Malay and Swahili mercantile city-states of the Indian Ocean. Historically, I think one can say wage-labor, at least considered as a contractual arrangement, emerged from slavery—a point I intend to explore it in greater detail elsewhere. However, this particular argument only crystallized when I came to know Immanuel Wallerstein at Yale and began to grapple with the finer points of World-Systems analysis. The essay on fetishism, finally, was originally written to be part of the last chapter of my book *Toward an Anthropological Theory of Value*, but had to be cut for space. Again, it traces back to a grad school fascination: in this case with the work of William Pietz, work that instantly struck me as important, even if it took me almost a decade to figure out why. This last essay also is the first to turn from the origins of capitalism in Medieval and Early Modern Europe to begin to look at Africa, and the some of the questions of authority that dominate Part II.

Part II, "Provisional Autonomous Zone: Dilemmas of Authority in Rural Madagascar," consists of essays written and rewritten over the decade or so after I conducted my research in the area surrounding the town of Arivonimamo in the province of Antananarivo between 1989 and 1991.

Most are ostensibly concerned with longstanding anthropological concerns like magic, witchcraft, kinship, and mortuary ritual. Still, I think the political implications are clear enough. What binds all of them together is that they are all ultimately reflections on the nature of authority.

I should explain that I had long considered myself an anarchist. It follows quite naturally, I think, from the way I was brought up. This is not to say that my parents were anarchists themselves. Rather, I say this because it has always seemed to me that almost anyone who believes that anarchism is a viable political philosophy—that it would actually be possible to have a society without states or classes, based on principles of voluntary association, self-organization, and mutual aid—is likely to feel that wouldn't be a bad idea. If most people have a problem with anarchism (that is, those who actually have a clear idea what anarchism is) it's not because they don't think it is an appealing vision, but because they have been taught to assume that such a society would not be possible. I was never taught this. I grew up in a family of 1930s radicals: my father had fought in Spain, my mother had been the female lead in the famous labor musical *Pins & Needles*. Like so many Americans who became radicalized in the 1930s, they were first drawn to the Communist Party, then broke with it. Though we were in no way prosperous (my father worked as a plate stripper, doing photo offset lithography—an occupation never especially lucrative to begin with; then he lost most of his pension when the industry fell apart around the time of his retirement), I grew up in a house full of books and ideas, and even more, in an environment full of the awareness of human possibilities. My father, for example, had been an ambulance driver for the International Brigades in Spain during the war. He was based in Barcelona and had thus had the opportunity to live for some time in a place with no formal government under conditions of worker control. While of course the Internationals were heavily propagandized against the anarchists, he himself was quite impressed with those he knew (including his *sanitario*, the medic assigned to his ambulance, with whom he became good friends), and became deeply indignant over the suppression of the revolution by the Republican government. In later life, he developed a fascination with the emergency paper money issued by local townships and collectives during the war, and even published a scholarly essay on anarchist paper money in Spain—perhaps the only one that exists. (On the desk near me right now is an "honorary mention" plaque from some numismatical society for the essay, dated 1972. They spelled his name wrong.) Anyway, I was never taught to see anarchism as a pipe dream. Among my parents and their friends, it was always seen as at least a viable political philosophy. As a result, I suppose, it was almost inevitable that I would eventually come to embrace it. Still, in the 1980s at least, my commitment remained largely one of principle. I had occasionally made minor efforts to get involved in anarchist politics, but almost invariably ended up disappointed, finding the scene to be dominated largely by squabbling ego-maniacs, each of whom seemed to behave like a sectarian party of one, with almost no feeling of community. In this, I think I was just unlucky: pockets of genuine community did actually exist at that time. I just never happened into one. It was something of an irony, then, that after casting about a while for a likely field site, I eventually wandered into a place where the state had, effectively, ceased to exist, and that, for a long time, I didn't even realize it. The first essay of the second section, "Provisional Autonomous Zone," de-scribes something of this situation.

The other essays in Part II are, as I say, about authority. While the people I knew in Madagascar were for the most part remarkably effective in their resistance to most forms of imposed authority—they had, in fact, so rebelled against those things they found most obnoxious in the former colonial regime that they had reorganized much of their own daily lives to avoid them—one could hardly describe the society I observed as egalitarian. There were ancient divisions of status. The population where I was living was divided between the descendants of *andriana* or "nobles," former free subjects of the Merina kingdom, and the descendants of their former slaves. There were rich and poor. The rich were not, perhaps, so very rich, especially in the countryside, and most people were about equally poor, but divisions were keenly felt. And, of course, there were even more elementary divisions, within families or small communities, though these latter were often curi-ously entangled with what would otherwise seem like egalitarian principles. The old had authority over the young—but, almost everyone would insist, because of all the people in a community, elders were the least inclined to act like what we would consider "leaders." Men, in most contexts, had more authority than women—but largely because they were seen as less inclined to give other people orders. All of the essays in Part II are meant to explore these apparent paradoxes in one way or another, relying on the traditional anthropological assumption that, to truly understand something—in this case, the essential nature of authority—it is best to examine its least familiar manifestations.

The set ends with a previously unpublished essay called "Oppression," that takes the argument about the nature of authority even further, argu-ing that the traditional anthropological concept of cultural relativism, as normally applied, is really a matter of being relativistic about everything *except* structures of authority. In its place, I propose a somewhat clumsily labeled "dialogic relativism": one that begins by observing that, even though what traditional authorities have to say about the nature of truth, beauty, or human nature might vary wildly from culture to culture, there is no place on earth where traditional authorities go completely unchallenged, and the ways people have of challenging them have a lot more in common than most of us would ever have expected.

Part III, "Direct Action, Direct Democracy, and Social Theory," sets off from my involvement in the global justice movement, beginning in 2000. I was employed by Yale University at that time, and still, while an anarchist in theory, almost completely uninvolved in any sort of organizing. My major contribution to American political life at that point in my life was as occasional cultural commentator for the Chicago-based lefty journal *In These Times*, where, my primary accomplishment up to that time had been an essay on the subversive implications of *Buffy the Vampire Slayer*. (Actually, I'm still quite proud of that. That essay was, I believe it has been established, the very first essay ever written by an academic on the subject of *Buffy the Vampire Slayer*. I invented Buffy Studies! It did earn me a brief mention in *Entertainment Weekly*, but it could hardly count as a significant contribution to American political life.)

Then one day, in November 1999, after having just finished the last lecture for a class called "Power, Violence, and Cosmology," I strolled out to pick up a newspaper and saw the headline that martial law had been declared in Seattle.

I was as taken aback as anyone. The next day I received an email from Joe Knowles, my editor at *ITT*. "You're an anarchist," he wrote (or he might not have used exactly those words), "do you think you could figure out who those kids with the black masks breaking all the windows were? What's the deal? Were they agents provocateurs? Or were they really anarchists?" Before long, I was assembling all the information I could get on contemporary anarchism, and discovering that, in those years when I was not paying attention, the movement I always wished existed had actually come into being. Not long after, I was showing up with my friend Stuart for the actions against the IMF in Washington in April 2000, and getting involved in the New York City branch of the Direct Action Network. Soon, I was a regular at DAN meetings, helping to organize actions, and attending endless trainings in the art of facilitation and consensus.

For the first two years or so I was working with the Direct Action Network, I didn't really write anything about it—unless you want to count press releases, calls to action, and reports for *In These Times*. When I first got involved, I never intended to make my involvement part of a research project. Nonetheless, the experience of working in consensus-based groups sparked a kind of intellectual crisis. I should explain here that the fashion at the time was to dismiss the movement, if not as a bunch of stupid kids who did not understand the complexities of modern economics, then as defenders of an incoherent welter of causes in desperate need of a unifying ideology. I quickly realized that such observers simply didn't know, or didn't care to know, what they were looking at. In fact, these groups were rooted, above all, in a commitment to reinventing forms of democratic process; that this was not an abstract ideology, but rooted primarily in developing new forms of practice; that insofar as DAN and other anarchist-inspired groups had an ideology, these new forms of democratic organization and democratic practice *were* its ideology. In this, they were based on a conscious rejection of the older model of Maoist or Leninist or Trotskyist sects that sought first to define the strategic moment, usually according to the teachings of some Great Intellectual Leader, and then to quibble over finer points of doctrine, while leaving the actual fashioning of democratic practice to some hypothetical point far in the future.

The intellectual shock was the result of two near-simultaneous realizations. The first was that the consensus process I was learning in anarchist circles was really an extremely formal, self-conscious version of the very form of decision-making I had witnessed on a day-to-day basis in Madagascar. It had to be formal and self-conscious, of course, because everything was being reinvented—patched together from bits and pieces learned from Quakers and Native Americans, read about in books, or simply invented by trial and error from thirty years of activist experience of trying to organize networks and collectives on anti-authoritarian lines, a tradition that harkened back at least to the days of early feminism. None of it came at all naturally to us. None of us were very good at it, at least at first. But it was obvious that, if we were going to invent a decision-making process that would actually work for a community in which no one had the power to force anyone else to do anything, it was going to have to look like something like the techniques employed by communities that had been living that way for thousands of years. I was trying, then, to actually do what I had observed everyone do in rural Madagascar, and finding it extremely difficult. The second shock, though, was the realization that one reason I found it so difficult was that my intellectual training had inculcated in me habits of thought and argument far more similar to the idiotic sectarian squabbling of Marxist sects than to anything consistent with these new (for us) forms of democracy.

The essays in Part III, starting with the "Twilight of Vanguardism," in which I first began to try to piece together the dimensions of the problem, all grow out of that rather disturbing realization. What would an intellectual practice look like, I began wondering, that would be consonant with genuine democracy? Was "democracy" even the right word to be using? If revolutionary intellectuals were not supposed to come up with the proper grand strategic analysis, the proper definition of reality, in order to lead the masses on the correct path, then what precisely was our role to be? Was it possible to move from the kind of strategic debates in which I actually did find myself embroiled while working with the global justice movement to theoretical reflections of general import? I've wrestled with questions like these at least to some degree in almost everything I've written since: from the diminutive *Fragments of an Anarchist Anthropology* in 2003, to the gargantuan *Direct Action: An Ethnography*, scheduled to appear next year—and even in my ostensibly more conventional work on value theory and theories of debt. I certainly don't claim to have come up with any definitive answers. The final three essays, none of which have previously appeared in English, all represent attempts to engage with one or another aspect of this dilemma, by examining, in turn, the history of social theory, the history of the notion of democracy, and the war of images between police and activists in the early days of the global justice movement. Each is a reflection and an experiment. But most of all, each is meant as a gift and an invitation, and attempt to spark the kind of dialogue between scholars, anyone involved in radical social movements, anyone passionately concerned about the human condition, that Pierre Bourdieu had wanted to discuss with me almost six years ago on September 11th.

That particular conversation never happened. As is so often the case, realities unacknowledged in our description of the situation came and hit us on the head. Still, I like to think this book, written in such a way as to (I hope) be accessible to anyone who finds such questions interesting and important, published outside of the usual academic ghetto, is itself one small step to opening such a dialogue today.

Manhattan
March, 2007

PART I

SOME THOUGHTS ON THE ORIGINS OF OUR CURRENT PREDICAMENT

1

MANNERS, DEFERENCE, AND PRIVATE PROPERTY: OR, ELEMENTS FOR A GENERAL THEORY OF HIERARCHY

This is an essay about the nature of hierarchy. In it, I want to delve into hierarchy's most elementary forms: the way people avert their eyes or stand at attention, the sort of topics they avoid in formal conversation, what it means to treat another human being as somehow abstract, sacred, transcendent, set apart from the endless entanglements and sheer physical messiness of ordinary physical existence—and why something like that always seems to happen when some people claim to be inherently superior to others. It seems to me an investigation like this is important since it is only by beginning to ask such questions that we can begin to think about which of the qualities we ordinarily lump together in a word like "hierarchy" are really inevitable features of human social life, and which might prove dispensable.

This is also an essay about the origins of capitalism. In *The Protestant Ethic and the Spirit of Capitalism* (1930), Max Weber argues that one cannot understand the rise of a commercial economy in Early Modern Europe, let alone the emergence of the near-monastic work discipline and obsessive strategies of accumulation that opened the way to modern capitalism, without understanding the role of religion and, particularly, Puritanism. Weber's argument has been debated endlessly and I have no real interest here in addressing any of his specific arguments about Calvinist doctrine. What really interests me, instead, is the confluence between the kind of Calvinism Weber describes and the spread of Puritanism in what might be called the popular sense of the term: particularly, squeamishness about sex and merrymaking. This was hardly limited to Protestantism. When English Calvinists talked of a "Reformation of Manners" they were referring first and foremost to attempts to reform away what they considered the more scandalous aspects of popular culture. As Peter Burke (1978:207) has noted, at the same time, Catholic authorities on the Continent were doing almost exactly the same thing. Beginning in the sixteenth century, religious authorities began a series of concerted campaigns to eradicate what they considered to be immoral elements in public life and ritual. The result was a great deal of very fractious social conflict. In fact, many of the popular struggles between Puritan and Royalist factions in the years before the English revolution turned precisely on struggles over attacks on the place of festivals in popular life. At the same time though, even more profound changes seemed to be going on, much of it on a level that most people of the time did not seem to be fully aware of. Norbert Elias (1978: 70–84) has pointed out that the sixteenth century also marked the beginning of profound changes in people's immediate physical sensibilities in Western Europe. Specifically, he speaks of a broad "advance of thresholds of shame and embarrassment," an increasing tendency to repress open displays of anger or extreme emotions, but even more, displays of, or references to, bodily functions in everyday interactions. Basic standards of how one was expected to eat, drink, sleep, excrete, make love, shifted almost completely. The transition from the world of Rabelais to that of Queen Victoria was, in historical terms, so remarkably rapid—a mere three centuries—that historians have puzzled over the phenomenon ever since Elias first pointed it out. It seems obvious that all this must have been, in some sense, connected to the rise of Puritanism and the more formal "Reformation of Manners" it brought in its wake, but no one has offered any really plausible suggestion as to what that connection might be.

In this essay, I am going to make a suggestion based on the tools of comparative ethnography. I will start by picking up two hoary ethnographic categories called "joking relations" and "relations of avoidance." These are terms originally coined by European and American anthropologists in the late nineteenth and early twentieth centuries to describe what they considered exotic and extreme forms of behavior prevalent in what they considered "primitive" societies. It strikes me that the logic of joking and avoidance actually provides a very useful means to begin to create both a rudimentary theory of manners and a rudimentary theory of hierarchy. Armed with this theory, I will return to Early Modern Europe, and demonstrate just how all three of the processes described above—Weber's Calvinism, Elias' standards of comportment, and Burke's reform of popular culture—really are part of the same broad historical process—one that also brought about ideologies of absolute private property and the increasing commercialization of everyday life.

Now, I am quite aware that this approach might strike some as a bit idiosyncratic. Certainly, painting with such broad theoretical strokes has fallen out of fashion in recent years. Even anthropologists do not talk much anymore about "joking and avoidance." Such terms evoke memories of large dusty tomes about New Guinea or Nepal, pictures of people who seem to have been intentionally photographed in such a way that you could never imagine having a conversation with them, arcane diagrams, and absurd generalizations ("the Nayar say..."). Like most contemporary anthropologists, I approach most such tomes with a great deal of ambivalence—even find them, in some ways, rather creepy—if only because they are so obviously, and obliviously, products of imperialism. But I also think there are things in them that can be of enormous use to critical social theory. One reason is because the people who wrote them were often confronted with practices they considered so odd and exotic that they lacked any familiar rubric to fit them to. Living among a certain Melanesian group, say, a researcher discovers that a young man who happens onto one of his cross-cousins on the road is expected to insult him; that, in fact, it might even be considered an affront if he does not. The researcher coins a term ("joking relation"). Another, somewhere in Amazonia, discovers that, there, cross-cousins are expected to behave in what seems to be exactly the same way. Even the insults are similar. *Something* was clearly going on here. If nothing else, in using terms like "joking relation," anthropologists were not simply inflicting Euro-American categories, raw, on the people that they studied.

If you look at the early history of anthropology, it was full of such moments of recognition and confusion, and resultant desperate efforts to make sense of what seemed utterly alien ways of defining material and social reality. The theoretical vocabulary of the day was full of peculiar-sounding terms like "joking partners" or "relations of avoidance" or outright borrowings from non-European languages: shamanism, mana, totem, and taboo. The next step was usually to discover that what seemed most alien was not actually all that alien after all: that something very much like joking and avoidance relations exist in middle-class households in Europe, that military units in the American Expeditionary Force in World War I ended up practicing forms of totemism around their regimental mascots and symbols—forms effectively indistinguishable from those practiced by Australian aborigines (Linton 1924). Were it not for those aboriginal practices, however, it is likely no one would have thought there was anything worth noticing in the odd practices surrounding the regimental insignia of army units. In a way, that first moment of estrangement, and second moment of back-translation, constitute, between them, the very essence of anthropology—a discipline that, after all, rests on the assumption that if it is possible to say anything true of human beings or human societies in general, then one has to start with the most apparently anomalous cases. It is a little disturbing, then, to observe that in recent years anthropology has largely stopped generating its own technical vocabulary, but has taken to importing buzzwords from Continental theory: biopower, governmentality, the body, or some new technical term borrowed from Martin Heidegger or Gilles Deleuze. One wonders about the implications for the long-term viability of the discipline.

In this essay, then, I wish to return to what I take to be the Grand Tradition. Most of all, I want to show that tradition has an almost infinite capacity to generate new political perspectives—perspectives that are, at their best, radical in the sense of delving to the very roots of forms of power and domination. Hence the emphasis on hierarchy. I frame the issues in the way I do, not just because I think it will help solve a longstanding intellectual problem about the origins of capitalism. but because I also believe a theory of manners opens the possibility of understanding how forms of social domination come to be experienced in the most intimate possible ways—in physical habits, instincts of desire or revulsion—that often seem essential to our very sense of being in the world, so much so that even our instincts for rebellion often appear to reinforce them. I do not claim to have found a clear way out of this dilemma; but in order to do so, it is at least helpful to be able to state clearly what the dilemma is.

Joking and Avoidance, Substance and Property

Let me turn, then, to the ethnographic literature on "joking" and "avoidance."

The first thing to emphasize about "joking relations" is that the name is somewhat deceptive. They are not really about humor.[1] In the anthropological literature, the expression "joking relation" does not really refer to a relation of people who joke with one another so much as it refers more to a relationship marked by playful aggression. "Joking partners" are people who are expected to make fun of one another, tease, harass, even (often) make play of attacking each other. They are relations of extreme, even one might say, compulsory disrespect and informality. Relations of avoidance, on the other hand, are marked by such extreme respect and formality that one party is enjoined never to speak to or even gaze upon the other.

Some ethnographers (e.g., Eggan 1937) use these term more loosely, describing a kind of broad continuum of types of interaction ranging from obligatory joking to relations of indulgent familiarity, then proceeding through relations marked by greater and greater formality and deference to those of extreme or literal avoidance. Used this way, joking and avoidance represent two ideal poles, and almost any relationship between two people could conceivably be placed somewhere on the continuum between them. Whether or not they take this view, anthropologists have always seen joking and avoidance as clearly opposed modes of behavior. In fact, they seem in many ways to be logical inversions of each other. Where joking relations tend to be mutual, an equal exchange of abuse emphasizing an equality of status, avoidance is generally hierarchical, with one party clearly inferior and obliged to pay respect. One often hears the term "joking partners" in the literature, almost never "partners in avoidance."[2] In avoidance relations, contact of any sort between the two parties tends to be discouraged: such relations are full of stipulations about how the inferior party must not speak first or speak much or speak above a whisper, must not look the other in the eye, must never touch the other first or touch them at all, and so forth. Almost always, the inferior party must steer clear of any sort of reference to or display of such bodily functions as eating, excretion, sex, or physical aggression. One often hears of injunctions against seeing the other eat, touching her bed, behaving violently in her presence, making reference to excretion in casual conversation, and so forth. Emphases vary, but the general direction of such prohibitions remain surprisingly uniform throughout the world. And just as regularly, joking relations play up all that avoidance plays down: one hears constantly of joking partners engaging in sham fights and sexual horseplay, of lewd accusations and scatological jokes. In some cases, the aggressive element can become very strong: one hears also of joking partners privileged to throw excrement at one another, or even wax-tipped spears.

The two stand opposed in other ways as well. Almost any description of avoidance, for instance, will make some reference to shame: often it is said the inferior party is expected to have a general sense of shame in the presence of the superior party; if not, they are certainly expected to be ashamed if they break any of the rules. Joking between joking partners is, as the name implies, generally expected to be accompanied by much hilarity on the part of all involved. But it is important to emphasize that what goes on between joking partners is not simply humor; it is humor of a very particular kind, one which might justifiably be called "shameless," an intentional invocation of the very things that would be most likely to cause embarrassment in other circumstances.

(One can also contrast the two on a more abstract level: in terms of what Levi-Strauss calls "universalization and particularization" [1966: 161]. In avoidance, or other relations of great formality, one generally does not use the proper name of a person to be shown respect, but substitutes a kin term or other title. In our own society we do something very similar with first and last names. In either case the subject is, as it were, taken up a rung of the taxonomic ladder, they are spoken of in a way that makes them more universal or abstract. Various bits of evidence confirm that this sort of abstraction is typical of avoidance, and probably of formal deference more generally. Conversely, joking, along with less dramatic forms of familiarity, tends to focus on the particular: references to idiosyncrasies, personal quirks—real or imagined—and so on. This is something that will become important later on, when I turn to the problem of hierarchy.)

Most of what I have said is pretty much taken for granted in the anthropological literature on joking and avoidance. Rarely, though, have anthropologists taken up the question of why all this should be. Why should it be so common, in so many parts of the world, to have to avert one's eyes when in the presence of a king, or of one's mother in law? Why is it that if one meets a person before whom one must avert one's eyes, it is almost always also inappropriate to discuss bowel movements or sexuality? One of the few anthropologists who has even tried to offer a solution to this problem is Edmund Leach, who suggests that it is necessary to hedge areas like sex and excretion with taboo because they tend to obscure the division between self and other, body and external world (1964: 40). This is a promising direction, I think, but hardly a solution in itself. After all, why should it be so important to maintain a clear division between the self and the external world in the first place? Presumably, Leach does not mean to suggest this is some kind of universal psychological need—or anyway, if he does, he would certainly be mistaken, because it is precisely these ambiguities that are emphasized, even celebrated, in joking relations. The joking body—if I may use the term to describe the human person as conceived within joking relations—is imagined, primarily, as a body continuous with the world around it. In this, it is quite similar to what Mikhail Bakhtin has referred to as "the grotesque image of the body." It is

> a body in the act of becoming. It is never finished, never completed; it is continually built, created, and builds and creates another body. Moreover, the body swallows the world and is itself swallowed by the world... This is why the essential role belongs to those parts of the grotesque body in which it outgrows itself, transgressing its own body, in which it conceives a new, second body: the bowels and the phallus... Next to the bowels and the genital organs is the mouth, through which it enters the world to be swallowed up. And next is the anus. All these convexities and orifices have a common characteristic: it is within them that the confines between bodies and between the body and the world are overcome: there is an interchange and an interorientation (1984: 317).

This is why joking relations can draw a parallel between contact between people (looking, touching, speaking, striking, sexual relations...) and such phenomena as eating, excretion, running noses, decomposition, open sores. What these latter all have in common is that they refer to different sorts of stuffs and substances passing in to, and out of, the physical person—that is, to contact between bodies and the world.

Still, it is not enough to simply say that the joking body is continuous with the world. All of the forms of interaction most played up in joking (and by Bakhtin)—eating, sex, excretion and aggression—imply a very specific *kind* of continuity.

Joking partners "tease" or "abuse" one another; they toss insults, even missiles. At the same time, one hears again and again of joking partners privileged to make off with each other's possessions, and this sort of license is considered of a piece with all the others. There is a sort of symbolic equivalence at play: an equivalence, one might say, between the taking of goods, and the giving of bads. I would venture to say that this sort of idiom is a constant feature of joking relations—"relations," in their broadest sense: "between bodies, and between the body and the world." Take, for example, the famous symbolic identification of sex and eating, familiar to any anthropologist. As Levi-Strauss once pointed out (1966: 100, 105–6), if one conflates sex with eating, it's hard to see sex as an especially reciprocal activity. Eating is an inherently one-sided relation. Of course who is seen to be the eater, and who the eaten, can vary with context: sometimes woman can be pictured as devourer (as, for example, in the case of *vagina dentata* motifs). Sometimes it's the man. "In Yoruba," he notes, "'to eat' and 'to marry' are expressed by a single verb the general sense of which is 'to win, to acquire'" (ibid: 105).

Still, if Yoruba treats sexual relations as analogous to consumption, or appropriation, other African languages frame it quite differently. In Kaguru, Thomas Beidelman points out (1966: 366), the term used for sexual intercourse can also mean "to insult," "to abuse," "to behave obscenely before others." It is also the word used to describe the behavior typical of joking partners. On the one hand, a taking of goods. On the other, a giving of bads.

One could continue with this sort of comparison indefinitely. It certainly does seem to apply to all the principal ways in which the joking body interacts with the world (if eating is the taking of goods, excretion is the giving of bads); or between bodies (joking partners threatening cannibalism against one another, or tossing dung, are doing more or less the same thing).

It follows that joking relations are only ultimately egalitarian. Any given instance, from any given point of view, is not egalitarian at all. It is an attack. But since license between joking partners is reciprocal, such attacks can always be expected to more or less balance out in the end.

Here again, avoidance can be seen as an inversion of joking. On the level of avoidance the body is closed, all orifices shut off and nullified; nothing flows either in or out. The body is constituted as a perfect, abstract, and self-sufficient thing unto itself, with no need for exchange either with other bodies, or the world. Now, this sort of separation itself can't imply a relation of hierarchy, simply because separating two things implies that there is no relation between them at all. But avoidance is ultimately hierarchical.

There is, it is true, a certain mutuality in relations of avoidance. If I were standing before the Queen of England, I wouldn't pick my nose or crack a dirty joke, and I would expect the same from her. On the other hand, the burden of avoidance would definitely be on me, and it is appropriate that any sort of contact ought to be initiated by the person of superior rank: conversation, eye contact, and the like. And further, if I *were* to pick my nose at the Queen, or crack a dirty joke, I could fully expect to be excluded from polite society till the end of my days; while if the Queen did so in my presence I would probably take this as a gesture of indulgent familiarity and perhaps reciprocate—though never quite so freely as she. Norbert Elias provides a telling quote from a sixteenth-century manual on manners:

> One should not sit with one's back or posterior turned towards another, nor raise the thigh so high that the members of the human body, which should properly be covered with clothing at all times, might be exposed to view. For this and similar things are not done, except among people before whom one is not ashamed. It is true that a great lord might do so before one of his servants or in the presence of a friend of lower rank; for in this he would not show him arrogance but rather a particular affection and friendship (1978: 138).

By the logic of my argument, picking my nose at the Queen would be much the same as thumbing my nose at the Queen; it would be a sort of joking attack.[3] It's my obligation then, to constitute her on the level of avoidance, as untouchable and self-enclosing; she, in her ability to initiate contact with me, is showing no such compunctions, and constituting me more on the level of joking.

If this seems a tenuous interpretation, there are many other sorts of evidence to back it up. Let me turn to an entirely different cultural milieu. In most Polynesian languages, the term *tabu* or *tapu* is used to describe avoidance relations, whether with one's father-in-law or with a chief. The word also means "set apart," "not to be touched," and, of course, "sacred."[4] However, it is the chief or the father-in-law who "have *tabu*" in relation to an inferior: that is to say, they are set apart, marked off, and separated from the world—a world which includes, as a residual category, everyone else, including their subjects (or affines as the case may be). The term has also had a curious history in modern social theory, because Emile Durkheim, in his work on religion, used the Polynesian concept of *tabu* to come up with a universal definition of "the sacred" as that which is set apart from the mundane world, not to be touched. Later, Erving Goffman (1956) borrowed Durkheim's concept in his analysis of everyday interactions in the modern West, arguing that, in our own society, the human person is ordinarily considered something sacred, because it is hedged about by invisible barriers, that it is off-limits to others, not to be touched. He had, apparently without realizing, come back to something very close to the original Polynesian idea.

The body in the domain of joking, one might say, is constituted mainly of substances—stuff flowing in or flowing out. The same could hardly be true of the body in the domain of avoidance, which is set apart from the world. To a very large extent, the physical body itself is negated, the person translated into some higher or more abstract level. In fact, I would argue that while joking bodies are necessarily apiece with the world (one is almost tempted to say "nature") and made up from the same sort of materials, the body in avoidance is constructed out of something completely different. It is constructed of property.

Now, I realize that this is a somewhat daring assertion. Not least, because what is considered "property" in the first place can vary a great deal from culture to culture. But I think one can make out an elementary logic to the idea of property that can be said to be more or less constant. Interestingly enough, that logic is very similar to the logic of avoidance.

Social scientists are usually content to follow the jurists and define property as a social relation, a bundle of rights and privileges with regard to some object, held by a person or group of persons to the exclusion of all others. It is important to stress that this is not, fundamentally, a relation between a person and a thing. It is a relation between people. Robinson Crusoe (bourgeois individualist though he might have been) would hardly need to worry himself over property rights on his island, since no one else was there.

However, it is hard to find a long, detailed ethnography that does not contain the word "owns" in quotation marks somewhere between its covers—that is, whose authors are forced to place the word in quotes because a word which otherwise refers to ownership of property is also used in other ways that make no sense by this sort of definition. Let me produce one fairly random example. In an ethnographic account of the Lau Islands of Fiji, Laura Thompson (1940: 109–111, 126) notes that every aristocratic clan of those islands is said to "own" one species of animal, one type of fish, and one variety of tree. These species, she says, are *tabu* for them; to harm any member of them would be considered tantamount to harming their own selves. Far from having a right to exclude others from their property, these people are themselves forbidden to touch the things they are said to own. In fact, this is a fairly clear case of identification. A number of authors have pointed out how many languages lack any verb for unilateral ownership: one cannot say "I own that canoe," merely that the canoe and I have a special relation to each other[5]—rather as in English, one uses the same word to say "that's my car" or "that's my boss." It's interesting to note that the English word "property" has two meanings. On the one hand, my property is something I own, that is, some thing that takes on its identity from me. On the other, one can also say "it is a property of fire to be hot"—here "property" is what makes something what it is, that gives it its identity.

One might call the latter sense of property ("it is the property of fire to be hot") property in its semiotic mode, in so far as its serves mainly to convey meaning. But what I want to emphasize is that even here, one finds the same logic of exclusion. To return to the Lau Islands: it was only aristocratic clans that "owned" species of animals or bird. Commoner clans did not; they were referred to collectively as "owners of the land" (L. Thompson, op cit.). And as Marshall Sahlins (1981) has observed, there was a tendency to merge such Fijian "owners of the land" with nature and natural processes, to identify them with what Bakhtin calls "the material bodily lower stratum"—the latter simply being the grotesque image of the body in its social incarnation. In other words, the aristocratic groups are set apart, marked off against a residual category which is more or less merged with the world. This is precisely the logic of avoidance.[6]

It can be much the same with individuals. The word *tabu* again provides a convenient illustration. Ethnographers of the Maori of New Zealand (Firth 1959; Johansen 1954; Shirres 1982; Smith 1984) often note that everyone was thought to have had a certain amount of "*tapu*."[7] Actually, it was not quite everyone. Slaves had none (they were others' property); neither did most women (since most women could not own property). Otherwise, the extent of one's *tapu* varied with social position. The higher up the social scale, the more *tapu* one had. A chief's *tapu* for instance extended to all of his possessions: all of them were set apart, just as he was set apart, from the ordinary world, and it would be as dangerous for a commoner to touch the chief's things as to touch the chief himself. What's more, a great chief's *tapu* was so very powerful, his person was so sacred, we are told, that anything that did touch his person was as it were drawn into the charmed circle of his sanctity. "The pigs that were called by Hongi's name could never be eaten by other persons—such would be tantamount to eating *him*" (Firth 1959: 345). His property was an extension of his person, and his person was set apart from all the world.

If property is so closely related to avoidance, and if these two principles of identification and exclusion really are so consistently at play (and I think they are), then is it really so daring to suggest that the person, in the domain of avoidance, is constructed out of property? Or, at least, of "properties?"

The etymology of the word "person" is itself suggestive. As Marcel Mauss pointed out long ago (1938 [1968]), the Latin *persona* is derived from an Etruscan word meaning mask; even when taken up in legal parlance as a term roughly similar to our word person, it still kept its implication of an abstract social being identified by physical objects: properties and insignia of various sorts. Slaves, and most women, had no *personae* for the same reasons that Maori slaves and women had no *tapu*.

Two important observations follow from all this. The first concerns exchange. Mauss (1925 [1954]) has also argued that in giving a gift, one is giving a part of oneself. If the person is indeed made up of a collection of properties, this would certainly be true. But it's important to bear in mind that the "self" in question is therefore a very particular kind of "self": specifically, that sort which is constituted on the level of avoidance. Gift-giving of the Maussian variety is never, to my knowledge, accompanied by the sort of behavior typical of joking relations; but it often accompanies avoidance.[8]

Second, in so far as it serves to construct a person in this way, a property need not have any practical use.[9] In ways, it is perhaps better that it does not. It simply needs to say something about its owner. This is a topic I have discussed at some length elsewhere (Graeber 1996), but here suffice it to say that the key thing is some larger code of meanings by which objects can do this, by which properties can be compared and contrasted. This need not be one of exchange value, but that it is a salient example, and I would argue that it is no coincidence that the generalization of exchange value as a medium for social relations has been accompanied, in Europe, by a generalization of avoidance. But I will have to return to this argument a little later on.

Before moving on to hierarchy, I should probably throw in a point of clarification. In treating joking and avoidance relations as extreme poles of a continuum that includes everything from playful familiarity to behavior at formal dinners, I do not mean to imply that all behavior must necessarily partake of one or the other. I certainly do not mean to suggest that all relations of respect imply subordination; even less, that all relations of intimacy involve some element of competition or aggression. What I am describing, rather, is a logic that—while it may come into play in some way or another in any social relation—is at best only one aspect of it. There are always other logics. I have said nothing, for example, of what anthropologists call "relations of common substance," where an entirely material idiom of bodily stuffs and substances can be seen as the basis for bonds of caring and mutual responsibility between human beings.[10] Sexual relations, after all, need not be represented as a matter of one partner consuming the other; they can also be imagined as two people sharing food.

On Hierarchy

The term "good," in most Greek thought, connoted above all a certain definite, though still essentially negative, characteristic. This is manifest in nearly all the Greek schools of moral philosophy which descended from Socrates—in the temper of the ideal Cynic, Diogenes, who needed and wanted nothing any other man could give him, in the ataraxy of the Epicureans, in the apathy of the Stoics. The essence of "good," even in ordinary human experience, lay in self-containment, freedom from all dependence upon that which is external to the individual.

(Lovejoy 1936: 42)

Tjaden hasn't finished yet. He thinks for a while and then asks: "And would a King have to stand up stiff to an emperor?"

None of us are quite sure about it, but we don't suppose so. They are both so exalted that standing strictly to attention is probably not insisted on.

"What rot you hatch out," says Kat. "The main point is that you have to stand stiff yourself."

But Tjaden is quite fascinated. His otherwise prosy fancy is blowing bubbles. "But look," he announces, "I simply can't believe that an emperor has to go to the latrine the same as I have."

—Remarque, *All Quiet on the Western Front*

"Hierarchy" has become a very popular term in contemporary social science, though it is often thrown about so casually that when an author uses it, it's very difficult to figure out precisely what they mean. To say that a set of items is organized into a hierarchy, after all, is merely to say that those items ranked in some way. But there are all sorts of ways to rank things.

The notion the term most immediately brings to mind is what might be called a "linear hierarchy," a way of ranking a collection of items, as along a ruler, so that in the case of any two items, one can immediately know which is higher and which is lower than the other. The classic example of such a linear hierarchy is probably the Great Chain of Being, made famous by Arthur Lovejoy (1936). This was a system by which Medieval and Renaissance scholars tried to rank all living creatures from moss to slugs to humans and seraphim, according to the degree to which they were believed to possess a rational soul. Lovejoy points out that it is critical to such a system that there can only be one criterion of ranking; as soon as others are introduced, the whole system will tend to dissolve into confusion (1936: 56–7).

When an anthropologist refers to a "social hierarchy," however, she is likely to be working with a very different implicit model, one that less resembles the Great Chain of Being than the sort of taxonomic hierarchies employed by botanists or zoologists. These are sometimes referred to as hierarchies of inclusion, since each level encompasses those below: lions are a kind of cat, cats are a kind of mammal, mammals are vertebrates, and so on. Levels are higher in so far as they are more encompassing and abstract, that is, insofar as they have a greater level of generality. A taxonomic hierarchy of this sort is obviously quite different than a simple linear hierarchy, but rarely do social scientists make a clear distinction between the two. Some, like the French anthropologist Louis Dumont—who is in fact the man most responsible for popularizing the use of the term hierarchy to begin with— quite consciously argue that no distinction should be made: that when social categories are ranked, it is *always* on the basis of greater generality and inclusiveness.

Let me take up Dumont's arguments about the nature of hierarchy in a little more detail, since it seems to me that they are the source of a great deal of subsequent confusion.

These arguments go back to Dumont's original structural analysis of the caste system in India, and particularly, of the fourfold division of the *varnas*. It might be useful here to take a glance at his formal analysis of this system (Dumont 1970: 67), which is actually quite brief. He begins by describing a simple linear hierarchy. Everything is based on purity. Brahmans (Priests) are considered purer than Kshatriyas (Warriors), Kshatriyas are purer than Vaishyas (Merchants), and Vaishyas are purer than Shudras (Farmers). However, after saying this, he immediately proceeds to explain that this ranking is worked out through "a series of successive dichotomies or inclusions"—thus implying the existence of a taxonomic hierarchy instead:

> The set of the four varnas divides into two: the last category, that of the Shudras, is opposed to the block of the first three, whose members are "twice-born"... These twice-born in turn divide into two: the Vaishyas are opposed to the block formed by the Kshatriyas and the Brahmans, which in turn divides into two (ibid.).

This is a little confusing but the basic idea is simple enough: at any point along the ladder, those on top could be seen as in some sense lumped together, insofar as they are all superior to those immediately below them. This is obviously true in a certain sense—particularly if one looks at things from the perspective of those towards the top of the ladder. Still, framing matters seems to be an intentional effort to sidestep what almost anyone else would think is the single most important feature of any caste system: that from the perspective of those on the bottom, we are dealing with a system not of inclusion, but of exclusion. Actually, not even just from the perspective of those on the bottom. Would it not make more sense to frame things this way: The Brahmans, the group at the top, see themselves as set off from all others as particularly pure and holy. From their perspective, everyone else can even be seen as a kind of undifferentiated mass, shading into each other and even into non-human creatures in so far as all lack the purity of Brahmans. However, from the point of view of the next highest group, the Kshatriyas, the more relevant opposition is that which sets both they and the Brahmans apart against another residual category, which is again relatively impure. Then comes the opposition between twice-born and others—which would include both Shudras and Untouchables, who are so base they fall out of the fourfold scale entirely, and who Dumont therefore ignores entirely. And so on.

Probably it would be best to describe all such linear hierarchies as "exclusive" rather than "inclusive." The logic, it may be observed, would then be much the same as that of avoidance, since the higher group is set apart from a residual category composed of all the others.

If so, however, it may be easier to understand how social scientists can get away with fudging the distinction between two different kinds of hierarchy, or even insisting they are really the same. It is because any actual social hierarchy will tend to combine elements of both. Always, there are higher and higher levels of inclusion (from household to lineage to clan to tribe; or from household to parish to borough to county...), but also there is a series of ascending, increasingly exclusive groups, who gain their exclusive status by being able to make a claim to represent the whole at every level.[11] Linear and taxonomic hierarchies thus tend to be superimposed.

Let me return once more to the traditional lineage system of the Maori. On the one hand, society was ideally organized according to what anthropologists would call a segmentary lineage system—a taxonomic classification of social groups. Every household belonged to a lineage, every lineage to a clan, every clan to a tribe. At each taxonomic level, each of these groups had its representative—called "headman" or "chief" in the literature—and that headman or chief was also said to "own" everything that belonged to his lineage, or clan, or tribe.[12] Needless to say, the higher up in the taxonomic hierarchy the representative, the more *tapu* he was said to have. But it's here that things become interesting, because (as I have pointed out) it is precisely in the notion of *tapu* that the element of exclusion comes back in.

What this means is that the greater the purview of any given representative, the more inclusive the group he was seen to represent, the more he himself was set apart from everyone else, including other members of his own clan or lineage.[13] As the head of clan, I stand for everyone else in the clan—especially, in dealings with outsiders. They are thus in a sense "included" in my political persona. But this in turn makes me a higher, more "exclusive" sort of person, fit to interact on an equal footing with other clan chiefs like myself, perhaps, but not with those included in me. And of course the status of the head of a tribe is even more exclusive.

A moment's reflection will make it clear that something along these lines happens almost everywhere society is organized into more and more inclusive groups. If those groups have representatives (barons, dukes and kings; mayors, governors, and presidents), then those representatives will also be set off against those they represent as members of more and more exclusive categories of people. The higher the group they represent in the taxonomic hierarchy, the more abstract and universal they themselves are seen to be; hence, the more they are set off against the world—including those they represent.

It is easy to see how this logic could eventually lead to something like an ideology of social class. But it might also help explain some otherwise rather odd consistencies in the way people think about class. How often, for instance, does one hear the upper classes of some society or other described as more refined and elegant than those below them, finer in features, more tactful and disciplined in their emotions? Or hear that the lower orders are cruder, coarser in features as in manners—but at the same time more free with their feelings, more spontaneous? Most people seem to consider it a matter of course that upper and lower stratum of society should differ in this way (if they think about it at all, perhaps they write if off to conditions of health, work, and leisure), or at least, that they should be represented so. In fact, such stereotypes even recur in times and places—say, much of early Medieval Europe—where the upper stratum could equally well be represented as a gang of heavily armed thugs extorting protection from a population of helpless farmers.

It's here one has to move from the role played by joking and avoidance in the dynamics of personal relations, to the way a whole social class or stratum marks itself off from those it considers below it by the way its members conduct themselves towards one another. Norbert Elias (1978) has written at some length about the courtesy manuals Medieval lords and ladies used to set themselves off against their subjects. They are, he argues, primarily concerned with encouraging their readers to repress bodily functions (at least in the presence of their fellows), the control of both natural impulses and violent emotions, and, as I've mentioned, the maintenance of a certain "threshold of embarrassment or shame." In other words, we are dealing with something along the lines of avoidance behavior, or anyway, behavior expected in situations of formal deference. The difference of course is that these standards were expected to be, at a certain level, mutual; in observing them, one was not setting the other person off against the world (a world which included one's own deferential self), so much as setting both off against those whose interactions were assumed to lack such refinement. And all this is quite explicit in the manuals, which constantly warned: one should not behave like a peasant or an animal.

The tendency to see the common people as bestial was itself perfectly in keeping with the notion that standards of comportment were a way for the aristocracy to constitute themselves on a level of avoidance, over and against "a residual category more or less merged with the world." The same attitude was to be seen in literary stereotypes of the peasant as "barely human monster" (LeGoff 1978: 93) and in Medieval art, where

> Man was frequently depicted as part of nature: images of animal-men and plant-men, trees with human heads, anthropomorphic mountains, beings with many hands and many legs, recur over and over all through antiquity and the Middle Ages, and find their most complete expression in the works of Brueghel and Bosch (Gurevich 1985: 53).

The author doesn't note this—it hardly needs be said—but the "Man" he is referring to is Common Man; bishops and duchesses were not depicted as half tree.[14]

However, what's really interesting about these images of an undifferentiated material world of bodies and substances is that it did not simply represent the point of view of the aristocracy. Mikhail Bakhtin (1984) for instance, in his famous study of Rabelais, has shown that there was a powerful strain in Medieval and Early Modern popular culture and popular imagery which took all of the qualities typically invoked by the elite and their representatives to denounce the lower stratum of society—lust and drunkenness, bodily functions, the monstrous and grotesque—and affirmed and celebrated them instead. Since this tendency found its highest elaboration in festivals like Carnival, Bakhtin calls it "the carnivalesque"; but he also argues it pervaded popular culture, setting the tone for everything from charivaris to folk tales, miracle-plays, and the spiels of itinerant quacks and medicine-peddlers, or the remarkably intricate idiom of obscenity and verbal abuse typical of the Medieval market place. Bakhtin sees grotesque imagery of this sort as, often, posed in direct opposition to the stuffy, overbearing and hierarchical "official culture" of the time; a form of resistance against the static, lifeless asceticism foisted on the masses by the church and civil authorities.

Bakhtin was clearly on to something. But it seems to me that he drew the lines between what we now call high and low culture a bit too sharply. One of the virtues of the view of hierarchy I've been trying to develop is that no such sharp line need be drawn. Were the grotesque elements in the work of Bosch or Brueghel derived from popular culture, or from the elite's notions of what the common people were like? Is there any real need to ask? After all, it was not only peasants and journeymen, but merchants, monks, and barons who took part in Carnival. If the emphasis in Carnival was quite clearly on the joking body—on sex, gluttony, violence, and gay abuse—perhaps what we should really be asking is what all this meant to the different participants, and whether it was always the same thing.

What evidence there is implies there was a fairly wide continuum between two extreme points of view. For the loftiest, Carnival was an indulgence for the masses, a chance for them to play the fool and give vent to their base and sinful natures. Some of the more reflective developed a kind of functionalist theory: let the commoners work off a bit of steam, even play at turning the world upside down for a day or two, and it will make it easier for them to endure their lot during the rest of the year.[15] Even a minor knight or master craftsmen might often have taken part, half with a feeling for fun, and half with one of veiled contempt.

To the lowliest, however—and even many of the not so very lowly—the joking element could seem genuinely subversive. And this is apparently true of the "carnivalesque" as a whole.

Given the argument I've been developing, it is easy to see at least two different ways how this might be. The first is quite simple. Joking relations are played out in an idiom of attack: the taking of goods and giving of bads. In the popular culture of the time, this idiom was often used to implicitly political effects: a good example are the folk tales in which young peasant lads so often outwit their superiors, always (as Robert Darnton points out: 1984: 59) making a point of both getting whatever goods they are after and humiliating his adversary: "the clever weakling makes a fool of the strong oppressor by raising a chorus of laughter at his expense, preferably by some bawdy stratagem. He forces the king to lose face by exposing his backside." So it was too with satiric charivaris and other varieties of "rough music." Bakhtin (1984: 197, etc.) sees the uncrowning and debasement of the Carnival King as a more universal attack, one directed against the very principle of hierarchy itself.

This last instance moves closer to the second subversive element in joking—which I think is also by far the more profound. In Carnival, not only was hierarchy temporarily suspended or reversed, but the whole world was reconstructed as a "Land of Cockaigne," as the saying went, a domain in which there was nothing but bodies happily partaking of the world and of each other. Bakhtin implies that the grotesque, that joking and laughter, was a sort of universal solvent of hierarchy: that by representing a world of joking bodies and nothing more, the very fiber was stripped out of the structures of official culture so that even its loftiest pinnacles inevitably came crashing to the earth. Given the categories I've been using in this paper, this makes perfect sense. If one rejects the principle of avoidance altogether, if nothing is set apart or sacred, hierarchy cannot exist. In a joking world, there are only bodies, and the only possible difference between them is that some are bigger and stronger than others; they can take more goods and give more bads. And the implications of that for a view of the contemporary social order, and particularly for the moral standing of the high and mighty of the world, need hardly be mentioned.

As always, I must point out that I am aware that things are more complicated than this; I am dwelling on one particular aspect. For instance, there was an element in Carnival which stressed not joking struggle but an idyllic Golden Age: this was an important element in social criticism both among Church thinkers and popular rebels, and harked back to Classical themes (cf. Cohn 1970). Still, the analogy with joking relations is a useful analytic tool, if for no other reason than because it opens up all sorts of interesting possibilities.[16] This is especially true when one moves from public ritual to everyday practices. Bakhtin himself drew attention to the language of the marketplace (1984: 145–195) and popular idioms of abuse and obscenity in Medieval and Early Modern culture. Would it really be going too far to suggest that this involves something very similar to the reconstruction of the world on the bodily level that occurs in Carnival? If it does, this would be a perfect example of the practices of the lower strata apparently reinforcing the images and stereotypes entertained by the upper, though with diametrically opposed intent. And finally, this would not seem to be an isolated phenomena. There are societies aplenty in which the lower classes do seem to employ obscene language more freely, or at least more openly and consistently, than the more privileged ones. It is hard to escape the impression that this is, in effect, a kind of subversion—at least to the extent that it asserts an intrinsically subversive view of the conditions of human existence.

The Generalization of Avoidance

So far, I have been describing two different ways of looking at the human person: either as a collection of bodily substances ultimately continuous with the world surrounding it, or as an abstract set of properties set apart from that world.[17] These are certainly not the only possible ways of conceiving the human person, but they can always, it seems, be expected to emerge in situations of hierarchy and formal deference.

At this point, I can return to Norbert Elias' argument about the "civilizing process" in Europe (1978 [1939]), and Peter Burke's notion of the reform of popular culture (1978: 207–243).

Elias' observations are mainly based on comparing primers used to instruct children in different periods of European history, beginning in the twelfth century, and ending in the eighteenth and nineteenth. What he discovers is a continual "advance in thresholds of embarrassment and shame" over time, an increasing demand to suppress any public acknowledgment of bodily functions, excretion, aggressiveness, death, decay—in fact, any or all of those things which are typically thought to be embarrassing or shameful within relations of avoidance. The most interesting aspect of Elias' material, from my own perspective, is how behavior which Medieval courtesy books represented as shameful only if done before superiors (say, blowing one's nose in the tablecloth), gradually came to be represented as embarrassing even if done before equals, then inferiors, and finally, as behavior to be avoided on principle, even if no one else is there.[18] In my terms, one might say that avoidance became generalized: in the sense that principles of behavior which once applied mainly to relations of formal deference gradually came to set the terms for all social relations, until they became so thoroughly internalized they ended up transforming people's most basic relations with the world around them.

Now, Elias himself is mainly concerned with feudal courts and the courtly aristocracy. If there was any motor driving the change, he suggests, it was the state's increasing monopoly on the legitimate use of coercive force, which compelled courtiers to contain their aggressive impulses, and thus introduced a general principle of self-control. But he also suggests that it was, in fact, when these new ideals expanded outside the courts, to affect the nascent bourgeoisie, that they began to be fully internalized psychologically. This expansion was something that largely occurred in the sixteenth, seventeenth, and eighteenth centuries, when one first finds middle-class reformers denouncing the polished artificiality of courtly manners, claiming they act mainly to make invidious distinctions and place some people above others, and holding up their own standards of comportment as more honest, moral and spontaneous—and therefore, as fit to be adopted by society as a whole (Elias 1978: 42–50).[19]

Burke's "reform of popular culture" was part of this same movement. Essentially it came down to the attempt, largely on the part of middle class religious authorities, to improve the manners of those below: most of all, by eliminating all traces of the carnivalesque from popular life. Burke lists among their targets "actors, ballads, bear-baiting, bull-fights, cards, chap-books, charivaris, charlatans, dancing, dicing, divining, fairs, folktales, fortune-telling, magic, masks, minstrels, puppets, taverns and witchcraft" (Burke 1978: 208), to name a few. In England, Puritans actually called their campaign a "reformation of manners"; in its name they went about shutting down ale-houses, enforcing laws concerning sexual morality, and most of all, outlawing popular modes of entertainment like May poles, morris dancing, and Christmas revels. In Catholic Europe, counter-reformation authorities were conducting analogous campaigns. Such campaigns almost always generated a great deal of opposition, but overall, they were remarkably successful.

The role of the middle classes, I think, is crucial. "Middle classes," in this period, essentially means "those sections of the population most thoroughly caught up in the commercial life of the times": not only merchants and shopkeepers, but prosperous farmers and urban craftsmen. It is notorious, for instance, that this was the stratum most attracted to English Puritanism (Tawney 1937: 20; Hill 1964; Wrightson 1984). They were also the people whose lives were most dominated by relations of private property, which is also crucial: since according to the terms I have been developing here, a generalization of avoidance would be a process in which everyone in society came increasingly to be defined by the logic of abstract, exclusive properties. One might well imagine that, as social life among all classes of society came to be shaped, more and more, by the logic of the market, the manners once typical of the commercial classes would tend to be generally adopted too.

The question, then, is: are there any ethnographic precedents for something like this happening? Have there been cases where spread of exchange relations led to different standards of daily comportment? Let me try to answer this briefly before returning to concepts of the person in Early Modern Europe.

One thing the ethnographic evidence makes abundantly clear is that, when relationships between two people, or two groups, are defined primarily around exchange (and not, say, by idioms of common substance), they have a strong tendency to also be marked by rules of avoidance. The classic example is relations between affines: particularly when two families are locked in extended cycles of marriage payments.

Where rules of avoidance do exist, and have been broken, very often some sort of formal exchange is required to set things straight. Sometimes these take the form of fines, but they do not need to. MacAllister (1937: 131) recalls the case of a Kiowa-Apache man who accidentally bumped into his mother-in-law, a person he was forbidden ever to touch. To make up for it, it was arranged for the two of them to exchange horses. According to Roy Wagner (1967: 176), something similar is common practice among the Daribi of New Guinea, where a man should never even cast eyes on his wife's mother. Should he happen to do so by accident, the two have to meet and exchange male and female goods of equal value before they can go back to their former situation. Clearly, in neither case are we talking about a punishment or compensation; both parties ended up with things of exactly the same value as they had before. Rather than being a matter of reparations, it appears to be a simple matter of repair. Two people have come into contact who should not have done so. The resulting rift in the shell of avoidance can only be patched up by means of an exchange, because the act of exchanging goods itself transposes relations from the level of bodies and substances and back to that of abstract properties again.[20]

More often, if there's been a violation of the rules of avoidance, a minor fine is levied on the lower-status party (the one on whom the burden of avoidance lies). But even here, the fines are more than simple recompense; the very act of giving them also acts to restore relations to their appropriate level of abstraction. And the same goes for fines levied for actual damage to the person or property of others, or for that matter, affinal payments—in fact, for all those varied kinds of transaction which typically knit together to form what anthropologists refer to as a "gift economy."

Even more interesting for present purposes is what happens to a society when such networks of formal exchange become so important that they could be said to be the main institution setting the terms of social life. In such societies, everyday standards of interaction often begin to resemble what would in other societies be considered mild avoidance.

I am not the first to make note of this phenomena, but earlier anthropologists seem to have lacked a language with which to describe it. Some appealed to Weber. Margaret Mead, for instance, saw the Manus of the Admiralty Islands of New Guinea as practicing "a kind of capitalism," which, she said, was rooted in an ethos of asceticism and self-denial (1930, 1934, 1937). Alfred Kroeber spoke of the "entrepreneurial spirit" of the Yurok Indians of California, which he said arose from something like a Puritan ethic (1925, 1928). To the modern ear, such terms really don't seem appropriate. If New Guinea fishermen can be capitalists, the word "capitalism" loses most of its explanatory power, and one would have to come up with an entirely new term for the heads of joint-stock corporations employing large numbers of clock-punching wage-laborers. But I don't think it would be wise to dismiss such authors' insights out of hand. What the Manus and Yurok did share was something quite reminiscent of Euro-American ideas of private property, and shell money which functioned as a kind of currency. Property could be bought and sold according to an abstract medium of value. Both were also societies in which the exchange of property was one of the main ways in which relations between people worked themselves out: even, sometimes, relations between the closest kin. Much of the commonplace drama of daily life seems to have turned largely on who had been given what, who owed what, who accepted what from whom. And, significantly enough, it is within relations most mediated by exchange that "asceticism" was most in evidence. "Sex," the Yurok dictum had it, "drives away money."[21] It was as if within such relations, the human person itself had to be hedged around with exclusive restrictions as severe as those surrounding property.

All these examples suggest that there can, indeed, be relations of avoidance that are not immediately concerned with constructing hierarchical relations between people, or even with setting one class off against the rest of society. When two people exchange horses with one another, they are marking their equivalence, as persons, by identifying themselves with two possessions of equivalent value. Similarly, in the Manus or Yurok cases, it was the existence of money—an abstract system by which the value of just about any piece of property could be compared—that made all persons comparable as well. In contexts involving exchange, persons were defined by what they had; since money made all property at least potentially equivalent, then people were as well. And the actual process of exchange meant that in practice, people were constantly establishing such temporary equivalences.[22]

All this tends to confirm that the most important area to look at in Early Modern Europe is not so much Elias' court society—which was always mainly interested in setting itself off from the rest of society—as the emergence of regimes of private property, commercial exchange, and of a class of people whose lives were so organized around it that they had begun to internalize its logic of exclusion as a way of defining their own social persons.

In fact, ideals of private property emerged slowly and unevenly. This was true particularly of property in land. Under a feudal regime, almost any plot of land had more than one "owner." Usually, there were different levels of ownership, when those came into conflict, legal theory of the time almost always recognized the most inclusive level to have the ultimate claim. The claims of a village community, for instance, took precedence over those of a plot's actual holder. Feudal tenure meant title to a piece of land tended to be parceled out along a graded hierarchy of owners; while a simple husbandman might have had effective possession of a plot, and a local knight or baron effective control over its disposition, jurists still insisted that true *dominium,* or absolute ownership, belonged only to the King—who represented the highest and most inclusive level of all.

All this might have been in keeping with the hierarchical principles of the time, but it was little conducive to the development of a market in land. In England, most land only became freely disposable after the first great wave of enclosure movements of the sixteenth and seventeenth centuries. In an open field system, a farmer might have exclusive right to grow wheat on a given plot, but would have to open their own fields, after the harvest, to anyone in the village with sheep who wished to graze them on the stubble; fences had to be taken down during the agricultural off-season. With enclosure, fences were replaced by hedges and walls that make clear the owner's right to exclude other members of the community from it at any time. In other cases enclosures involved bounding off stretches of meadow or forest that had always been considered part of the village common—the exploitation of such common lands, one might add, having long been the key to the survival of the landless or poorer villagers. Ownership of enclosed land did not depend on membership in any larger group; it was an exclusive right of access held by a single owner "against all the world" (Thrupp 1977; E. P. Thompson 1976); hence, it could be freely bought and sold. Such land was, effectively, private property—even if it took the law some time to fully recognize this: since it was only around the time of the Restoration that jurists were willing to officially recognize a *dominium* belonging to anyone but the King (Alymer 1980).

The phrasing here—"enclosure," "against all the world"—is certainly suggestive of the logic of avoidance. It is much harder to determine the degree to which these new definitions affected people's common sense about the nature of the individual, society, or the relation between the two. But not, perhaps, impossible. At least one historian, C.B. MacPherson (1962), has suggested that by the seventeenth century the principle of individual, exclusive private property had become so broadly accepted among ordinary English people that popular politicians could invoke it as the basis for making claims of natural rights and political liberties. MacPherson is most famous, perhaps, for his arguments about assumptions about property underlying the political theories of Hobbes and Locke, but his most interesting material is drawn from the Levellers, a radical political faction in Cromwell's New Model Army during the English Revolution. In 1646, for instance, Leveller Richard Overton wrote in his tract *An Arrow Against All Tyrants* that:

> To every Individual in nature is given an individual property by nature, not to be invaded or usurped by any: for every one as he is himself, so he hath a self propriety, else could he not be himself, and on this no second may presume to deprive any of, without manifest violation and affront to the very principles of nature, and of the Rules of equity

and justice between man and man... Every man [is] by nature a King, Priest and Prophet in his own natural circuit and compass, whereof no second may partake, but by deputation, commission, and free consent from him whose natural right and freedom it is. (in MacPherson 1962: 140–141).

In other words, a man's person—his body, like his chattels—were his exclusive property, and therefore he had the absolute right to exclude "all things hurtful and obnoxious" from it.[23] Even the king could not trespass on this right. This was perhaps the first political evocation of the principle that (as Goffman put it) the human person was sacred. The fact that, by the time of the English revolution, such an argument could make sense to an audience of common soldiers does show that concepts of private property had indeed played a large role in reshaping popular conceptions of the person. And, as MacPherson notes, this doctrine—he calls it "possessive individualism"—became the basis of notions of political freedom that emerged at the time, and which have remained the foundation of prevailing theories of the rights of man to the present day (ibid.: 142–159).

MacPherson's arguments inspired a lively debate (e.g., Laslett 1963, MacPherson 1964, Arblaster 1981), but this fundamental insight has never been seriously challenged. Modern individualism was not only an ideology which developed through the rise of the bourgeoisie, it emerged first and foremost through metaphors of property. The assumptions already implicit in authors like Hobbes and Locke became more explicit in the doctrines of British Mercantilists and French Physiocrats, and eventually became the basis of political economy: that private property was a natural institution, in that its logic predated the emergence of any larger human society—that, in fact, society itself had to be created because of people's need to safeguard their property and regulate its exchange. Where an earlier, hierarchical view assumed that people's identities (their properties, if you will) were defined by their place in society, the assumption was now that who one was was based on what one had, rather than the other way around.[24]

One is ultimately left with the view of the world presented by economics, which takes it for granted that humans are bounded, autonomous beings whose identity is determined by what they possess, and whose mutual intercourse is assumed to consist primarily of exchanging such possessions with one another according to the principles of rational calculation. It is the view of human society which has formed the backbone of most subsequent social theory, which has developed either on its basis or in reaction to it. It is also based on a way of imagining the human person that is in almost every way analogous to how the person is imagined in avoidance.

Education and the Fate of Youth

So far, I have been trying to make a case that it was the emerging commercial classes of Early Modern Europe that first embraced the notion of reforming society by reforming its manners, and that the standards of propriety they embraced were ultimately rooted in ideologies of private property. I also suggested that, in so far as projects of reform were successful, it was largely because the market and commercial logic was increasingly setting the terms of social life among all classes of people. Attempts to close down ale-houses or ban mummers' plays, after all, could only achieve so much, and they tended to create a determined and resentful opposition. The more lasting changes were on a much more deeply internalized level. Here some of Elias' material is particularly revealing. In 1558, for example, an Italian courtier could still write:

> For the same reason it is not a refined habit, when coming across something disgusting in the street, as sometimes happens, to turn at once to one's companion and point it out to him.
>
> It is far less proper to hold out the stinking thing for the other to smell, as some are wont, who even urge the other to do so, lifting the foul-smelling thing to his nostrils and saying, "I should like to know how much that stinks," when it would be better to say, "Because it stinks I do not smell it" (Della Caso, *Galateo*, in Elias 1978: 131).

A hundred years later, most readers would probably have found the very notion of behaving this way about as revolting as people would today. But how does one go about explaining changes on this level—in people's most spontaneous, visceral reactions to the world around them? It is one thing to say that there is a logical connection between manners and regimes of property; quite another to understand how such changes actually took place.

The obvious place to look is in the education of children. Elias' material, for example, is almost exclusively drawn from manuals meant to instruct youth. What I am going to do in this section, then, is provide a very brief sketch of ideas of education and the public role of youth in Medieval and Early Modern societies: one which I think makes clear why the emergence of a regime of wage labor should almost inevitably have led to projects of social reform. It is not exactly an explanation; but it does lay out the outlines of what a full explanation might be like.

In the Middle Ages, just about everyone who did know how to read had learned their letters at least partly from "courtesy books"—books which were produced in remarkable numbers. The first were in Latin, and meant for the education of the clergy and perhaps the higher nobility. By the fourteenth century, however, vernacular courtesy books, catering to an increasing demand for literacy among the less exalted nobility, and many of the merchants and tradesmen in the cities, had become common (Nicholls 1985: 57–74).[25] As Philippe Aries (1962: 381–383) remarks, these books often covered a wide variety of topics—ranging from advice on cutting one's fingernails to advice on choosing a suitable wife. They also had a strong tendency to mix precepts on how to eat at table with precepts on how to wait at table. This latter is significant: because the period when young people were learning manners was almost always the one in which they were also expected to be in domestic service.

Aries cites a late-fourteenth century account of England, written by a traveler from Italy:

> The want of affection in the English is strongly manifested towards their children; for after having kept them at home till they arrive at the age of seven or nine years at the utmost, they put them out, both males and females, to hard service in the households of other people, binding them generally for seven or nine years. And these are called apprentices, and during that time they perform all the most menial offices; and few are born who are exempted from this fate, for everyone, however rich he may be, sends away his children into the houses of others, whilst he, in return, receives those of strangers into his own (from *A Relation of the Island of England* [apparently anonymous], cited in Aries 1962: 365).

Though "the Italian considers this custom cruel...insinuating that the English took in each other's children because they thought that in that way they would obtain better service than they would from their own offspring," Aries suggests, realistically enough, that "the explanation which the English themselves gave to the Italian observer was probably the real one: "In order that their children might learn better manners" (op cit.).

This particular Italian observer seems to have spent most of his time in large towns, but this picture appears, in its broad outlines, to have been true of the countryside as well, not only in England but across much of Northern Europe, from the High Middle Ages onwards. Young men and women were expected to leave home at a fairly early age—if not by nine, then certainly by their early teens—and spend the next ten or fifteen years in "service"—which basically meant as wage-laborers living under the roof of their employers. Rural youths, for instance, were usually hired at local fairs and worked for a year's term before receiving their wages. Others were placed by their parents, though most often with masters whose social position was somewhat higher than their own: a husbandman's son in the family of a yeoman, a yeoman's daughter as a maid for a minor member of the local gentry, and so on (Laslett 1972, 1977, 1983; Wall 1983; Kussmaul 1981).

This condition was expected to last until the age of twenty-five or even thirty: in part, because no one was expected to marry until they had accumulated enough resources to set up an independent household of their own. Wage-labor, in other words, was basically a life-cycle phenomena, and "youth" or adolescence, the period during which one accumulated the resources to establish oneself as a fully mature, autonomous being. It was also the period during which one learned one's future trade. Even farm service was, in effect, a form of apprenticeship.[26] Servants in husbandry—no less than dyer's or draper's apprentices, or, for that matter, knight's pages—were in training, and though the technical know-how one picked up in such circumstances was undoubtedly distinguished, in the abstract, from more commonplace matters of deportment and propriety, in practice the process of learning them was more or less the same.[27]

In the Middle Ages and, if anything, even more in the Early Modern period, idioms of youth and age were the most common way people had of talking about authority. It was a commonplace of Renaissance theory that aging was a long process of the drying-out of the body; that young people were as a result dominated by their "animal spirits," and hence prone to violent lusts and passions and every manner of excess; and that it was only when a man reached about the age of thirty, when physical strength began to decline, that his soul or powers of reason (the two were considered more or less the same thing) was deemed capable of overcoming them (Thomas 1971: 208–210, 1976). Thirty was also the age at which his first child should be born, thus establishing once and for all his social persona as a settled householder and full member of the community, with all the responsibility that entailed. "For young men to command," on the other hand, "was against the 'law of nature': they must obey until they had achieved mastery of their baser desires" (Brigden 1982: 37–38). Incapable of autonomy, they had to be kept under the watchful eye and firm hand of some mature master—one, ideally, who was not a kinsman, since kinship was thought to somewhat compromise authority—for their energies to be put to proper use.

It should be clear enough how all this relates to the logic of joking and avoidance. It's not just that youth were considered unformed: their typical vices were the carnal ones of violence and debauchery. They were by nature riotous, rebellious against the legitimate authority of their elders. Mature men, on the other hand, were rational and self-contained; they were the masters of autonomous, bounded, self-sufficient households. But the notion that service had an educational value added a complex play of theory against practice to this relatively straightforward way of representing things. In any

relation of avoidance, the burden of avoidance is always on the inferior party. Masters may have had been seen as more refined or disciplined in their
spontaneous comportment (they had better manners), but, still, it was their
servants who had to perform the acts of formal deference.[28] In practice, it
was by such acts, and by respectful obedience before their masters, that they
constructed the latter as higher, more abstract beings—*at the same time as*
they gradually internalized those same disciplined comportments so as to be
able to ultimately pass on to the status of master themselves.

On the other hand, it is equally important to stress that, in the Middle
Ages, the manners of youth were not utterly rejected. They had their place,
which corresponded almost exactly to the place of the carnivalesque. Natalie
Zemon Davis (1975) goes so far as saying that young men were considered
to have a kind of communal "jurisdiction" over the domains of sex and violence which were considered their natural spheres of activity. In France, every village or urban quarter had its "youth abbeys" which were not only the
basis of the local militia but responsible for putting on satirical charivaris
to mock immoral villagers, as well as organizing celebrations like Carnival.
In England, the organization was less formalized (Capp 1977), and youth
leaders—like the famous Lords of Misrule who presided over Christmas revels—tended to emerge only during certain moments of the ritual calendar,
but the principle was much the same.

The existence of this ideology of youth and age had a profound effect on
how changes in the organization of production, in the Early Modern period,
were perceived. In a typical Medieval town, the majority of young men were
apprentices and journeymen in the employ of an older master craftsman.
Ideally, any apprentice could expect to someday become a master himself,
and full member of the guild—it was for this reason guild regulations limited the number of apprentices a master was permitted to take on. But the
more capitalist relations came to dominate a given industry, the longer a
journeyman would have to wait before being able to achieve full adult status, a wife, a household, and a shop of his own. In the meantime, he would
continue working for wages for his master. The result was that a large part of
the work force, men in their thirties and forties, found themselves living in
a sort of suspended social adolescence. In the end, many began to abandon
the ideal of autonomy entirely, to marry young and resign themselves to the
status of permanent wage laborers. With the enclosure movements and rise
of commercial agriculture of the sixteenth and seventeenth centuries, many
of the rural poor were left in much the same position.

All of this happened so gradually, though, that the underlying assumptions people had about the meaning of wage-labor need never have been
seriously called into question. Traditionally, wage-labor had been no more a

permanent state than was adolescence—it was, in fact, the means by which adolescence was overcome. Even after it had become a permanent status, it was still imagined as a process of transformation. In the eyes of their employers, the laboring classes were not so much undisciplined and carnal by nature (a joking residue, a base stratum whose vices could be held out as a evidence of those employer's own innate superiority) as rambunctious adolescents who needed to be disciplined and reformed through carefully supervised labor.

Casting things in this way at least makes it easier to understand why the actual social struggles which surrounded the commercialization of English society and the emergence of a proto-bourgeoisie took the form that it did: to a large extent, endless quarrels over the place of youth in the community, and struggles over popular festivals and entertainments. Let me return briefly here the Puritan "reformation of manners" in Tudor and Stuart England.

English Puritans

English Calvinists ("Puritans" was, in fact, a term of abuse) were mostly drawn from the "middle stratum" of their communities, the one which, as I've said, was most thoroughly caught up in the emerging national market. They were also the prosperous householders who employed the largest numbers of local youth as servants. The retreat of the aristocracy from rural life, along with much of the gentry (Stone 1965, Laslett 1965: 180–81) left such people in a strategic position in most villages, one which they were quick to take advantage of. Godly reformers circulated pamphlets and bibles, pooled funds to hire preachers, and tried as best they could to win control of both the borough and the parish governments. As churchwardens and magistrates, they began stripping away everything they found distasteful in traditional worship. Bells no longer tolled at funerals, nor was corn thrown at weddings; bagpipers and fiddlers were to have no part in religious ceremonies (Thomas 1971: 66–67). Most of all, their attacks were aimed at calendar festivals, especially carnivalesque rituals like Christmas and May Day, and the ongoing festive life of the village green.

As Keith Thomas points out, such attacks were at the same time attacks on the public place of the young in village culture:

> What were the campaigns for the Reformation of Manners if not attempts to suppress all the great obstacles to the subordination of youth: holidays, when the young people were released from their masters' supervision; theatres, to which they flocked to be corrupted; alehouses, which threw them into disorder, there being "many drunkards short of twenty years old"; gaming, "a pernicious thing and destructive of

youth"; maypoles, which encouraged "the rout" in their insolency towards the "ancient and the honourable" and taught "young people impudency and rebellion": dancing, for "where shall young men and maidens meet, if not at the dancing-place?"; sabbath-breaking, by "servants and...the younger sort"; and all the annual rites of misrule when youth temporarily inverted the social order? (Thomas 1976: 221).

But concerns about youth were already becoming hard to distinguish from those concerning class. One constant complaint in Puritan tracts was the multiplication of impoverished households. The problem, in their view, was that young men and women were abandoning domestic service and marrying early, despite the fact that neither had the resources to support a proper family. This concern was matched with one over "masterless men"—with the independent poor, the murky and disordered world of hawkers, beggars, minstrels and vagabonds. In an ideal society, all these should be assembled under the domestic discipline of the Godly, who would direct them in labor as in prayer (Hill 1979; Wrightson & Levine 1979).[29]

The more radical Calvinists developed a utopian vision in which such authoritarian families were the only hierarchical organization that really needed to exist. The ideal community would be governed by an assembly of "elders," who were simply the heads of larger households. In New England, where Puritans were actually in a position to put some of these ideals into practice, the chief men of a community were given legal authority to place any young man and woman determined to be living alone in an "unruly household" as a servant in the households of more respectable elders—by force if necessary (Morgan 1944: 45–47, 85–89).

In other words, the Puritans did not see any distinction between projects of social reform directed at the lower classes, and the process of educating the youth. The two categories were not fully distinguished: they formed, as it were, a kind of unruly residual; the solution in either case being the imposition of domestic discipline. In their ideal society, anyone without the means or discipline to support a family should be incorporated into a larger household, working under the pay and careful direction of a disciplined master, who would also be responsible for their catechism and moral instruction.

As one might imagine, this vision, or the prospect of reducing collective ritual life to a matter of sermons and bible-reading, did not inspire uniform enthusiasm among parishioners. English villagers seem to have had a particular aversion to being preached at. "When the vicar goeth into the pulpit to read what he himself hath written," observes one Stephen Gardiner in 1547, "then do the multitude goeth straight out of church, and home to drink" (Thomas 1971: 161). And once called so into question, everyday habits like stopping off at the local alehouse after a day's work, or piping on the village green, became overt political issues. May Day celebrations (the English equivalent of the continental Carnival) became perhaps the greatest single particular focus of contention.

> The village maypole, Richard Baxter tells us, was near his father's house at Eaton Constantine, "so that we could not read the Scriptures in our family without the great disturbance of a tabor and pipe and noise in the street." Baxter often wanted to join the revelers, but he was put off by their calling his father a Puritan. The phallic maypole was for the rural lower class almost a symbol of independence of their betters: Baxter's father "could not break the sport," even though the piper was one of his own tenants (Hill 1964: 184).

In some cases they lead to open confrontation:

> A Star Chamber case for 1604 tells how a group in the country parish of Alton, Southam, procured a minstrel and danced on Whitsunday. When the constable and church warden tried to arrest the musician, they were overpowered by his supporters who moved him to another part of the village, locked him in a house and, posting one of their own number on the roof to keep watch, continued to dance merrily on the lawn to the strains of the music that came out through the open window (Wright & Lones 1938: 299).

It's hard to say how often such occasions lead to outright violence (most of our sources were written by Puritans who referred to ordinary church ales as "heathenish rioting"), but riots did occur, and not only over economic issues like enclosure.

Usually, in any community in which a cadre of Calvinist zealots were attempting to reform society, there were also village notables—traditionally minded ministers, minor gentry, prosperous yeoman farmers—who saw them as fanatics and prigs: "precise fellows," "busy controllers," as they were often called, determined to undermine the ancient ways. Such men often found themselves the unofficial leaders of anti-Puritan factions, and were to be found holding court at the local alehouse or hosting a dance in their cottages each Sunday, as surely as the godly themselves would be at their sermons (Hunt 1983: 150–151; Collinson 1983: 408–409).

> The conflict between Puritans and "honest good fellows"—or, from the Puritan point of view, between the godly and the profane—divided vir-

tually every parish in southern England. In Wiltshire and Dorsetshire in the 1630s, it was the custom in many parishes to balance the factions by choosing one Puritan and one "honest man" as churchwardens. This conflict was far more ubiquitous and intense, I would argue, than antagonisms based explicitly on social class or even economic interest (Hunt 1983: 146).

Though one suspects these other issues were usually entangled in the larger one. Hunt also suggests that what was really at issue was a conflict between two very different images of community (ibid.: 130–136). The Puritan one I have already described. The one that rose in opposition to it was less clearly articulated, but it seems to have been largely based on the ethos long implicit in the very popular festivities and rituals which had now been thrown so starkly into question. As a result, opposition to Puritanism followed the same dual nature as Carnival itself: the same combination of joking aggression and idealistic utopias.

At its simplest, opposition to the Puritans might be simple mockery: disruptive catcalls during sermons or catechisms, rude dramas improvised late at night at the local alehouse. If someone could come up with an excuse to carry out a charivari against one of the "Saints," then that was best of all: common suspicion, after all, was that behind their fastidious exteriors, Puritans were really utterly depraved (Hunt 1983: 145). Finally, as festivals like May Day became political issues, their subversive side was played up more and more: it was in the sixteenth century, for instance, that plays and ballads about Robin Hood began appearing in May games throughout England (Wright & Lones 1938 II: 230–231; Hutton 1994: 66–67).

Alongside the abuse there was—here too—a more utopian side. Festivals had once been moments to define a community of equals: now, after they had been pulled out of the fabric of everyday life and challenged from above, that definition began to acquire a whole new meaning. Like Carnivals on the Continent, they came to commemorate a golden age when, it was imagined, equality and physical happiness were not yet things of the past. Festivals were times for merry-making; once, all England had been merry. Note the way in which the expression "merry England" was originally employed: "I perceive you are a Puritan outright, you are one of those new men that would have nothing but preaching. It was never a merry world since that sect first came among us" (Collinson 1983: 1). "The simple sort, which cannot skill of doctrine, speak of the merry world when there was less preaching, and when all things were so cheap, that they might have twenty eggs for a penny" (Hunt 1983: 148). Or even: "It was never merry England since we were impressed to come to the church" (Thomas 1971: 151). In later centuries Tory politicians

would make the maypole and merry England into nostalgic, sentimental images in support of reactionary politics. In the sixteenth century, this imagery
was nostalgic—and even, in a sense, reactionary—but the implications were
very different. It reflected, for instance, the constant complaints over the loss
of "good neighborhood," of the solidarity and mutual aid—seen especially
in the sharing of food, or the collective charity of church-ales, soul-ales, and
the like—that people assured each other had been the universal rule in those
abundant days before greedy yeomen and Calvinist preachers conspired to
destroy it. As time went on, the past came to look more and more like the
Land of Cockaigne.

   In 1647, a group of dissidents and young servants from the newly founded Puritan colony of Plymouth, Massachusetts abandoned their households
to join the local Indians, setting up a sixty foot Maypole to celebrate their
newfound independence. The elders of Plymouth immediately sent out a
military expedition to have the pole ripped down and the ringleaders arrested.

Perspectives

   I began this essay by arguing for the continuing relevance of comparative ethnography. The advantage of terms like joking and avoidance, I suggested, was that they are in no sense projections of existing Euro-American
categories on other cultures; in fact, the people who first coined the terms
were under the impression that they were dealing with something with no
parallel in their own societies. Nonetheless, the implicit logic they reveal can
indeed be applied back to patterns of formal deference and hierarchy anywhere—in Euro-American societies as much as any other. The first section
of the essay was thus largely concerned with developing the outlines of such a
theory. I began by distinguishing two ways of defining the human person, either as a collection of substances intrinsically continuous with the world and
with others, or as a collection of abstract properties set apart from it. In "joking" (by which I mean here, such behavior as is considered typical between
joking partners) relations between bodies are at least playfully hostile; but in
the case of relations of common substance they can take on a more idealistic,
even utopian color. This came out particularly strongly in my analysis of
hierarchy, and its mock-dissolution in the carnivalesque, where it is whole
groups that are set off against the world. I also suggested that carnival is not
simply a matter of inverting hierarchy, but of challenging its very basis by
invoking radically different ways of conceiving the world—even if, from the
perspective of superiors, the very act of challenging hierarchy will often serve
to provide more evidence of their own superiority.

In fact, though, all these perspectives tend to be available to anyone, whatever their social station, and tend to be invoked by the same individuals in different contexts. This is precisely what makes hierarchy such a powerful social principle: though I also think it would be clearly wrong to conclude, as some do, that hierarchy is an immutable, all-encompassing system that will always be able to absorb any challenge thrown at it.[30] Carnivalesque rituals of rebellion might have served, in the eyes of the masters, as means of reinforcing social order, but they had a notorious capacity to spiral out of their control. Rebellions do occur, almost everywhere. Hierarchies have been smashed and uprooted—even if the principle, the potential for their re-emergence, can never perhaps be completely eradicated, rooted as it is in the most fundamental dynamics of social life.

The second half of the essay focused specifically on the question of manners and private property. Rather than rehearse the argument again, let me end with a note of comparison, by comparing my own analysis with the work of Louis Dumont, whose actually has some very interesting things to say on the passage from hierarchical societies to ones based on principles of commercial individualism (Dumont 1981, 1986).

Dumont conceives hierarchical societies, most of all, as holistic ones. A social hierarchy is a system whereby different groups are ranked in relation to a whole.[31] If one group is ranked higher than another, it is always because it is the one that represents the totality to which both of them belong. To return to the Hindu caste system, again, Warriors are exalted because as kings and temporal rulers, they represent society as a whole; Priests rank even higher because they represent humanity before the entire cosmos. By Dumont's logic, everything really is about inclusion (it is just that, in a sort of Orwellian sense, some are a little more included than others). To talk of "exclusion" would be to invoke an entirely alien logic. In fact, Dumont argues, one simply cannot speak of exclusion in a hierarchical system. The term only makes sense where one is dealing with a society based on principles of individualism. This, he argues, is what really destroyed the old hierarchical world of the Middle Ages. The rise of a commercial society brought with it an ideology of individualism. This constituted a fundamental break with everything that had come before. Ideologies of individualism meant that each human being came to be seen as unique, and therefore, of incommensurable value. If the value of humans could not be compared, then no one could be held superior to any other. If no one could be held superior to any other, then there was no plausible reason to why one should have more or less access to the good things in life, to the pursuit of property, or happiness, or however one might care to phrase it, wherever it be found. Ideologies of human equality are thus really side-effects of individualism. Of course, in practice, egalitarian ideals are never fully put into practice. Often even in the most egalitarian societies, such as the United States, there are certain glaring exceptions, where certain categories of people are indeed excluded from the national community. The American "color bar," according to Dumont, is just such an ideology of exclusion, and as such it has nothing in common with hierarchy. It is a fundamentally different type of thing.

Dumont's arguments about individualism are nothing if not insightful, and I would hardly propose they simply be thrown away. Still, the political implications are, as so often in his work (Robbins 1994), profoundly unsettling. My own insistence that social hierarchies are always combinations of inclusion and exclusion has entirely different implications. First of all, one need posit no absolute break between the two periods. Take the ideology of Puritanism as an example. It was clearly hierarchical; only, in place of the endless gradations characteristic of a feudal system, one is left with a minimal hierarchy of two or perhaps three levels. Women, children, and servants were encompassed within the personality of the householder; and, in all but the most radical versions, of householders encompassed by the King or State. Neither was the Puritan concern with "the darker parish" and floating population of "masterless men" notably different than contemporary concerns with an immoral and overly fertile "underclass." In fact, as some historians of the time have noted (Hill 1972; Hunt 1984), Puritan opinions on this subject—that the problem of poverty had nothing to do with real wages, but was really rooted in the poor's own lack of morality and self-control, their unwillingness to create proper families—have an uncanny resemblance to those employed by American conservatives today. Rather than hierarchies being swept away, it is more as if the hierarchical residual was squeezed down, its imagery becoming all the more intense having been so.

This leads to my second point: that any attempt to create a genuinely egalitarian ethos on the basis of principles of formal deference is ultimately impossible. There is a fundamental contradiction here. The logic of setting an abstract being apart necessarily involves setting it off against something; in practice, that always seems to mean creating a residual category of people—if not some racial or ethnic category, then workers, the poor, losers in the economic game—that are seen as chaotic, corporeal, animalistic, dangerous. By this logic, for instance, North American racism is not the great exception to the possessive individualism on which the country is founded—an anomaly for some reason never seems to go away—but something essential to its nature. In the contemporary world, where "the market" is endlessly touted as synonymous with freedom and democracy, and where its proponents have thereby claimed for themselves the right to "reform" everything and everyone on earth, this is a point that even liberals might do well to think about. No hierarchy is ever immutable. Indeed, like capitalism, one could well argue that all hierarchies by their own internal logic must necessarily create images of rebellious disorder—images, indeed, of their own negation—that they then have to exert enormous amounts of energy to contain, so as to ensure that they do not burst out of the level of the imaginary. Such systems are always vulnerable. But by the same token, any genuinely egalitarian system must, it seems, adopt equivalent mechanisms, to stand guard against its own deeply embedded hierarchical possibilities.[32]

Allow me a final word on those hierarchical possibilities. One of the dangers of muddled terms is that they make "hierarchy" (usually defined in two or three different ways at once) seem like an inevitable feature of social life. To a certain degree, of course, it is. There will always be nested sets of categories, and people will always have a tendency to rank some things as better or worse than others, but none of this has any necessary social implications one way or another. What we are used to thinking of as social hierarchies are a particular constellation of these principles, and as Arthur Lovejoy (1936) pointed out, fairly unstable ones, since in order to impose a single all-encompassing hierarchical system, you need to measure everyone on a single scale; the moment one begins to introduce more than one criteria (refinement, rationality, money, grace, etc) into the Great Chain of Being, the whole thing falls apart. Obviously, this alone is not enough to destroy a hierarchical form of social organization. As Dumontians regularly point out, the usual solution is to create a hierarchy of scales: so that in a caste system, for instance, the scale of purity is the highest, which is why Brahmans are the most exalted sort of people, the scale of power second, the scale of wealth comes after that, and so on. This is certainly true to an extent, but—even aside from the fact that it's never clear if the system is really so unified as Dumontians like to make out—there are very real limits to how many different axes of discrimination can be absorbed. Multiply linear hierarchies endlessly, and any such system will, inevitably, fall apart. A million different modes of discrimination is, to all practical intents and purposes, identical to no mode of discrimination at all.

Endnotes

1   Failure to recognize this is the weakness, I think, of much of the existing theoretical literature on the subject. Mary Douglas' essay on "jokes" for instance starts out as an analysis of joking relations. The result is a brilliant reflection on the nature of humor, but, it seems to me, is of little use in understanding the nature of joking relations in the traditional anthropological sense of the term.

2   Though cf. Stasch 2002.

3   Again, I remind the reader that I am using the term "joking" here in a special, technical sense, meaning "along the lines of the sort of construction of human relations typical of joking relations"; hence I do not simply mean "humorous."

4   "Sacred" implies "not to be touched" in most European languages as well—a fact which Durkheim made much of—though I do not know how widespread this is elsewhere.

5   Tikopians for instance identify a man with a canoe by a term Raymond Firth translates as "linked," the same term that is used for, say, bond-friends (1965: 257–8).

6   Claude Levi-Strauss (1962) has made the point that totemic systems are not really about identity but analogy, that is, they are not saying clan X are like bears or clan Y like eagles, but that the relation between clan X and clan Y is like the relation between bears and eagles. This is, of course, a very famous argument. However, in a later work (1966), he also noted that such totemic systems usually develop between groups that all share a roughly equal status; and makes the intriguing suggestion that, when one begins to hear that clan X really do resemble bears, it is usually because some element of hierarchy has entered in. If nothing else, this certainly seems to work for the Lau Islands.

7   And the Maori seem to have been typical of Polynesian societies in this respect.

8   Again, when I say that joking behavior never seems to accompany gift-giving, I do not mean to suggest that it never accompanies *exchange*. It certainly does. The most obvious example is in some very common forms of barter; another, somewhat more obscure, can be found in certain forms of inter-village exchange said to be practiced by the Yanomami of Venezuela (Chagnon 1968): one group enters the village of the other making every sort of mock-threat—threats which the latter are expected to ignore with casual aplomb—and then, begins demanding items of property—demands which the latter cannot refuse. Their demands are only limited by their knowledge that their victims will later have the right to come to their village and do the same. The interesting thing here is that we are dealing with a sort of mirror image of Mauss' formula, not the reciprocal giving, but instead the reciprocal taking of goods. That it should be accompanied by behavior that smacks of joking then should hardly be surprising.

9   When Shakespeare's Henry V refers to France as another jewel for his crown, he is expressing perfectly the equivalence of ornaments or insignia and what we like to call "real property," in terms of signification. Though on this, see also Graeber 1996.

10   Which often accompany what Marshall Sahlins (1972) has called "generalized reciprocity."

11   True, different systems lean more or less heavily to one side or another. The Indian caste system, certainly, presses down very hard on the linear side; the Nuer segmentary system, to take a famous example, lean with equal weight in the opposite

direction. But I doubt one can find any society based entirely on one principle and not the other.

12 "Ownership" in this sense generally had little to do with any kind of rights and duties.

13 In linguistic terminology, one would say the higher up he is, the more he is an unmarked term: standing for not only "man," but "household," "clan," "tribe," and so on. This does fit quite nicely with my observations about avoidance and universalism (moving upwards on the taxonomic hierarchy). But it makes *tapu* a somewhat paradoxical process: the marking of the unmarked.

14 One could go on from here to speak of legal notions, which described peasants as being "owned by the land" as much as the other way around, or for that matter the etymologies of words still in common use today: the *Oxford English Dictionary* for instance, has it that the English word "clown" is derived from an Germanic root meaning both "peasant" and "lump of earth" ("clod" has the same derivation).

15 Burke (1978: 199–204) notes that the metaphor of "letting off steam" began to be employed the moment it was technically possible; before that, the preferred metaphor was letting off pressure in a wine cask. Even at the time, though, many objected that, as safety-valves go, popular festivals made extraordinarily poor ones, considering how many genuine rebellions grew out of them (see Bercé 1976; Burke op cit.; Davis 1980). Bercé provides vivid accounts of preparations for carnival in French cities during the sixteenth and seventeenth centuries, during which the soldiers manning the city walls would systematically turn the cannons on the parapets around so they would face into the town, in case of any serious trouble.

16 Anyway it strikes me that it can be more potentially revealing, for the analysis of rituals such as Carnival, than, say, Victor Turner's notion of liminality and communitas (1969)—terms often thrown around so very casually that their use can stifle further discussion more than encourage it.

17 Each entails its own characteristic notion of exchange: an abusive (or mock-abusive) exchange of substances in one, a benevolent (or mock-benevolent) exchange of properties in the other.

18 Even before medical science was able to produce arguments of "personal hygiene," Erasmus was warning children to restrain their manners even in private, because angels could be watching one unawares.

19 Elias' idea of the "civilizing process" is pretty unabashedly evolutionist and has been widely criticized as such. Many have also pointed to Elias' undue attention to courtly circles and his neglect of Puritan and other middle class ideas as a crucial flaw in his analysis.

20 There are parallel cases which don't involve a breach of avoidance but other kinds of bodily contact considered too intimate for the relation in which it occurred. In the New Hebrides: "Sodomy between two genealogically related men is regarded

as incestuous. However it is not viewed too seriously, as the punishment inflicted is that both parties must kill and exchange two pigs" (Corlette 1935: 486).

21   For Manus parallels, see Mead 1934: 191, 308.

22   Obviously, it was unusual for any two individuals to be exactly equivalent in worth at any given time, but they were inherently capable of being so.

23   Overton clearly did not mean to include women; or for that matter servants. There is some debate as to whether the Levellers even meant to give wage laborers the franchise.

24   Elias himself notes (1978: 42–50) how thoroughly embedded these ideas had become in the common sense of the middle classes most dedicated to the reform of manners.

25   The literate class and the courteous class tended always to be one and the same.

26   It's not so much that "apprenticeship and service were confused" as Aries puts it (ibid.: 366–367) than that they were never really distinguished to begin with.

27   It would be interesting to examine the institution of Medieval and Early Modern service in the light of the anthropological literature on initiation, particularly the kind which involves "fictive kinship" of one sort or another. The study of *compadrazgo* in Latin America provides some obvious parallels: while authors such as Wolf (1966) highlight the way such ties create ties of patronage across class lines, symbolic analyses (e.g., Gudeman 1971; Bloch and Guggenheim 1981) stress the division between the female domestic, and male public domains—which in Western culture have been generally presented in terms of the spirit and the flesh. I've already mentioned that, in Europe, most youths served masters of a marginally higher social class. As for the symbolic aspects, Aries notes that the age of "seven or nine"—the age at which the Italian author of the above-cited account of English habits claims most families sent off their children to the houses of strangers—was "in the old French authors...given as the age when the boys leave the care of the womenfolk to go to school or enter the adult world" (op cit.). The opposition of spirit and flesh—or anyway, something very much like it—was also at play in the very definition of "youth" itself.

28   An obvious parallel is the career military officer who is never obliged to stand as stiffly or salute as smartly as recruits have to do to him, but is still seen as reflecting in his ordinary bearing a more "military" comportment than they.

29   I note in passing that the notion of reforming the lower strata was a bit difficult to reconcile with Calvinist doctrine, which encouraged most heads of household to, at least, the strong suspicion that their charges were predestined from the start to go to hell (cf. Hill 1964). But this merely underlines how much the project itself—of defining a social class in terms of a stage in the life-cycle—was inherently contradictory.

30   Any more than capitalism, about which very similar arguments are often made.

31   He also seems to assume that all holistic systems must be hierarchical; but this is
     another issue.

32   I have elaborated this argument in an earlier work (Graeber 2004: 24–37).

Bibliography

Aries, Philippe
1962 *Centuries of Childhood*. New York: Vintage Press.

Aylmer, G.E.
1980 "The Meaning of Property in Seventeenth-Century England." *Past and Present*
      86: 87–97.

Bakhtin, Mikhail
1984 *Rabelais and his World*. Bloomington: Indiana University Press.

Beidelman, Thomas
1966 "Utani: Kaguru Notions of Sexuality, Death, and Affinity." *Southwestern Journal
      of Anthropology* 20: 354–380.

Bercé, Yves-Marie
1976 *Fête et Révolte*. Paris: Hachette.

Bourdieu, Pierre
1977 *Outline of a Theory of Practice*. Cambridge: Cambridge University Press.

Brigden, Susan
1982 "Youth and the English Reformation." *Past and Present* 95: 37–67.

Burke, Peter
1978 *Popular Culture in Early Modern Europe*. Cambridge: Cambridge University
      Press.

Capp, Bernard
1977 "Communication: English Youth Groups and the Pinder of Wakefield." *Past and
      Present* 76: 111–16.

Chagnon, Napoleon
1968 *Yanomamö, the Fierce People*. New York: Holt, Rinehart & Winston.

Cohn, Norman
1970 *The Pursuit of the Millennium*. Norman: University of Oklahoma Press.

Corlette, Ewan
1935 "Notes on the Natives of the New Hebrides." *Oceania* 5: 474–487.

Darnton, Robert
1984 *The Great Cat Massacre*. New York: Vintage Books.

Davis, Natalie Zemon
1975 *Society and Culture in Early Modern France*. Stanford: Stanford University Press.

Douglas, Mary
1975 "Jokes." *Implicit Meanings: Essays in Anthropology*. London: Routledge.

Dumont, Louis
1970 *Homo Hierarchicus*. Chicago: University of Chicago Press.
1981 *From Mandeville to Marx: the Genesis and Triumph of Economic Ideology*. Chicago:
      University of Chicago Press.

1986 *Essays on Individualism.* Chicago: University of Chicago Press.

Eggan, Fred
1937 "The Cheyenne and Arapaho Kinship System." In *The Social Anthropology of North American Tribes* (F. Eggan, ed.). Chicago: University of Chicago Press.

Elias, Norbert
1978 *The History of Manners.* New York: Pantheon Books.

Firth, Raymond
1959 *Economics of the New Zealand Maori.* Wellington, New Zealand: Owen Press.
1965 *Primitive Polynesian Economy.* London: Routledge & Kegan Paul.

Flandrin, Jean-Louis
1979 *Families in Former Times.* Cambridge: Cambridge University Press.

Goffman, Erving
1956 *The Presentation of the Self in Everyday Life.* Edinburgh: University of Edinburgh Press.

Graeber, David
2004 *Fragments of An Anarchist Anthropology.* Chicago: University of Chicago Press.

Gurevich, A. J.
1985 *Categories of Medieval Culture.* London: Routledge & Kegan Paul.

Hajnal, J.
1965 "European Marriage Patterns in Perspective." In *Population in History* (D.V. Glass & D. E. C. Eversley, eds.) London: Edward Arnold.

Herlihy, David
1985 *Medieval Households.* Cambridge: Harvard University Press.

Hill, Christopher
1964 *Society and Puritanism in England.* London: Routledge & Kegan Paul.
1972 *The World Turned Upside Down.* New York: Penguin Press.
1975 *Change and Continuity in 17th Century England.* Cambridge: Harvard University Press.

Hobbes, Thomas
1968 Leviathan. Harmandsworth: Penguin Press.

Hunt, William
1983 *The Puritan Moment: The Coming of Revolution in an English County.* Cambridge, MA: Harvard University Press.

Hutton, Ronald
1994 *The Rise and Fall of Merry England: The Ritual Year, 1400–1700.* London: Oxford University Press.

Johansen, J. Prytz
1954 *The Maori and His Religion.* Copenhagen: Munksgaard.

Kroeber, Alfred
1925 *Handbook of the Indians of California.* Washington D.C.: Bureau of American Ethnology 78.
1928 "The Law of the Yurok Indians." *Proceedings of the 22nd International Congress of Americanists*: 511–516.

Kussmaul, Ann
1981 *Servants in Husbandry in Early Modern England.* Cambridge: Cambridge University Press.

Laslett, Peter
1972 "Characteristics of the Western Family Considered over Time." In *Household and Family in Past Time* (P. Laslett and R. Wall, eds.). Cambridge: Cambridge University Press.
1977 *Family Life and Illicit Love in Earlier Generations.* Cambridge: Cambridge University Press.
1983 "Family and Household as Work Group and Kin Group." In *Family Forms in Historic Europe* (R. Wall, ed.). Cambridge: Cambridge University Press.

Leach, Edmund
1954 *Political Systems of Highland Burma.* Cambridge: Cambridge University Press.
1964 "Anthropological Aspects of Language: Animal Categories and Verbal Abuse." In *New Directions in the Study of Language* (E. Lennenberg, ed.). Cambridge: MIT Press.

LeGoff, Jacques
1978 *Time, Work and Culture in the Middle Ages.* Cambridge: Cambridge University Press.

Levi-Strauss, Claude
1962 *Totemism.* Boston: Beacon Press.
1966 *The Savage Mind.* Chicago: University of Chicago Press.

Linton, Ralph
1924 "Totemism and the A. E. F." *American Anthropologist* (New Series) Vol. 26 (2): 296–300.

Lovejoy, Arthur
1936 *The Great Chain of Being.* Cambridge: Harvard University Press.

MacAllister, J. Gilbert
1937 "Kiowa-Apache Social Organization." In *The Social Anthropology of North American Tribes* (Fred Eggan, ed.). Chicago: University of Chicago Press.

MacFarlane, Alan
1970 *Witchcraft in Tudor and Stuart England: A Regional and Comparative Study.* London: Routledge & Kegan Paul.
1978 *The Origins of English Individualism.* Oxford: Oxford University Press.

MacPherson, C. B.
1962 *The Political Theory of Possessive Individualism.* Oxford: Oxford University Press.
1973 "Servants and Labourers in Seventeenth Century England." In C.B. MacPherson, *Democratic Theory: Essays in Retrieval.* London: Oxford University Press.

Mauss, Marcel
1954 *The Gift.* Boston: Beacon Press.
1968 "A Category of the Human Spirit." *Psychoanalytic Review* 55: 457–481.

Mead, Margaret
1930 *Growing Up in New Guinea: A Comparative Study of Primitive Education.* New York: Morrow & Co.
1934 *Kinship Organization in the Admiralty Islands.* New York: American Museum of Natural History.
1937 "The Manus of the Admiralty Islands." *Cooperation and Competition among Primitive Peoples.* New York: MacGraw Hill.

Morgan, Edmund Sears
1944 *The Puritan Family.* Boston: Trustees of the Public Library.

Nicholls, Jonathan
1985 *The Matter of Courtesy.* Woodbridge: Brewer Press.

Robbins, Joel
1994 "Equality as a Value: Dumont, Melanesia, and the West." *Social Analysis* 36: 21–70.

Sahlins, Marshall
1972 *Stone Age Economics.* Chicago: University of Chicago Press.
1985 *Islands of History.* Chicago: University of Chicago Press.

Shirres, M. P.
1982 "Tapu." *Journal of the Polynesian Society* 91 (1): 29–51.

Smith, Jean
1974 *Tapu Removal in Maori Religion.* Memoirs of the Polynesian Society no.40. Wellington: Polynesian Society.

Stasch, Rupert
2002 "Joking Avoidance: A Korowai Pragmatics of Being Two." *American Ethnologist* 29 (2): 335–365.

Stone, Laurence
1965 *The Crisis of the Aristocracy, 1558–1641.* Oxford: Clarendon Press.
1968 *The Family, Sex and Marriage in England 1500–1800.* London: Weidenfeld & Nicholson.

Thomas, Keith
1971 *Religion and the Decline of Magic.* New York: Scribner Press.
1976 "Age and Authority in Early Modern England." *Proceedings of the British Academy* 62: 1–46.

Thompson, E. P.
1966 *The Making of the English Working Class.* New York: Vintage Press.
1967 "Time, Labor Discipline, and Industrial Capitalism." *Past and Present* 38: 56–97.
1976 "The Grid of Inheritance." In *Family and Inheritance* (J. Goody, J. Thirsk, and E.P. Thompson, eds.). Cambridge: Cambridge University Press.

Thompson, Laura
1940 *The Southern Lau, Fiji.* Bernice Bishop Museum Bulletin no.162.

Thrupp, Sylvia
1977 *Society & History: Essays.* Ann Arbor: University of Michigan Press.

Turner, Victor
1969 *The Ritual Process: Structure and Anti-Structure.* Ithaca, NY: Cornell University Press.

Wagner, Roy
1967 *The Curse of Souw.* Chicago: University of Chicago Press.

Wall, Richard
1983 *Family Forms in Historic Europe.* Cambridge: Cambridge University Press.

Weber, Max
1930 *The Protestant Ethic and the Spirit of Capitalism.* London: Unwin Press.

Wright, A.R., and T. E. Lones
1938 *British Calendar Customs.* London: William Glaisher for the Folklore Society.

Wrightson, Keith, and David Levine
1979 *Poverty and Piety in an English Village.* Cambridge: Cambridge University Press.

2

THE VERY IDEA OF CONSUMPTION: DESIRE, PHANTASMS, AND THE AESTHETICS OF DESTRUCTION FROM MEDIEVAL TIMES TO THE PRESENT

This essay is not a critique of consumerism. It's not meant to offer yet another exposé of the evils of mass consumption or of contemporary consumer practices. I want to ask instead why it is we talk about "consumption" or "consumer practices" at all. Why is it, when we see someone buying refrigerator magnets, and someone else putting on eye-liner, or cooking dinner, or singing at a karaoke bar, or just sitting around watching TV, we assume that they are on some level doing the same thing, that it can be described as "consumption" or "consumer behavior," and that these are all in some way analogous to eating food? I want to ask where this term came from, why we ever started using it, what it says about our assumptions about property, desire, and social relations that we continue to use it. Finally, I want to suggest that maybe this is not the best way to think about such phenomena and that we might do well to come up with better ones.

To do so necessarily means taking on a whole intellectual industry that has developed, over the last few decades, around the study of consumption. For most scholars, not only is the category of "consumption" self-evident in its importance, one of the greatest sins of past social theorists was their failure to acknowledge it.[1] Since the early 1980s, theoretical discussions of consumption in anthropology (sociology, semiotics, or cultural studies, too, for that matter) almost invariably begin by denouncing past scholars for having refused to give the topic sufficient due. Usually they offer a little morality tale. Once upon a time, it begins, we all used to subscribe to a Marxist view of political economy that saw production as the motor of history, and only truly legitimate field of social struggle. Insofar as we even thought about consumer demand, it was largely written off as an artificial creation, the results of manipulative techniques by advertisers and marketers meant to unload products that nobody really needed. Eventually, the story continues, we began to realize that this view was not only mistaken, it was profoundly elitist and puritanical. Real working people find most of life's pleasures in consumption. They do not simply swallow whatever marketers throw at them like so many mindless automatons; they create their own meanings out of the products with which they chose to surround themselves. In fact, insofar as they fashion identities for themselves, those identities are largely based on the cars they drive, clothes they wear, music they listen to, and videos they watch. In denouncing consumption, we are denouncing what gives meaning to the lives of the very people we claim we wish to liberate.

For me, the interesting question about this story is who the "we" in question is supposed to be. After all, it would be one thing to encounter such arguments coming from someone like Jean Baudrillard, who actually had started out as a Marxist critic of consumerism. It's quite another to hear the story invoked in the 1990s by cultural anthropologists like Daniel Miller (1995) or Jonathan Friedman (1994), members of a discipline that to my knowledge never actually produced any such Situationist or Frankfurt-school-style analysis of consumption to begin with. Why, then, decades later, are we still repeating variations on this same morality tale?

No doubt there are many reasons. Probably one is that it resonates with a common life experience for academics, who often do have to struggle with their own adolescent revulsion against consumer culture as they become older and more established. Still, the real (and rather perverse) effect of this narrative is to import the categories of political economy—the picture of a world divided into two broad spheres—one of industrial production, another of consumption—where it had never existed before. It is no coincidence, here, that this is a view of the world equally dear to Marxist theorists who once wished to challenge the world capitalist system, and to the Neoliberal economists who are currently managing it.

It is precisely this picture I would like to question here. I want to ask how it comes about that we call certain kinds of behavior "consumption," rather than something else. It is a curious fact, for example, that those who write about consumption almost never define the term. I suspect this is, in part, because the tacit definition they are using is so extraordinarily broad. In common academic usage (and to an only slightly less degree, popular usage) "consumption" has come to mean "any activity that involves the purchase, use, or enjoyment of any manufactured or agricultural product for any purpose other than the production or exchange of new commodities." For most wage-laborers, this means nearly anything they do when not working for wages. Imagine, for example, four teenagers who decide to form a band. They scare up some instruments, teach themselves to play; they write songs, come up with an act, practice long hours in the garage. Now, it seems reasonable to see such behavior as production of some sort or another, but in existing social science literature, it would be much more likely to be placed in the sphere of consumption, simply because they did not themselves manufacture the guitars![2] It is precisely by defining "consumption" so broadly, in fact, that one can then turn around and claim that consumption has been falsely portrayed as passive acquiescence, when in fact it is more often an important form of creative self-expression. Perhaps the real question should be: why does the fact that manufactured goods are involved in an activity automatically come to define its very nature?

It seems to me that this theoretical choice—the assumption that the main thing people do when they are not working is "consume" things—carries within it a tacit cosmology, a theory of human desire and fulfillment whose implications we would do well to think about.[3] This is what I want to investigate in the rest of this paper.

Let me begin by looking at the history of the word itself.

Etymologies

The English "to consume" derives from the Latin verb *consumere*, meaning "to seize or take over completely," and hence, by extension, to "eat up, devour, waste, destroy, or spend." To be consumed by fire, or for that matter consumed with rage, still holds the same implications: not just thoroughly taken over, but overwhelmed in a way that dissolves away the autonomy of the object, or even, that destroys the object itself.

"Consumption" first appears in English in the fourteenth century. In early French and English usages, the connotations were almost always negative. To consume something meant to destroy it, to make it burn up, evaporate, or waste away. Hence, wasting diseases "consumed" their victims: a usage that according to the *Oxford English Dictionary* is already documented by 1395. This is why tuberculosis came to be known as "consumption." At first, the now-familiar sense of consumption as eating or drinking was very much a secondary meaning. Rather, when applied to material goods, "consumption" was almost always synonymous with waste: it meant destroying something that did not have to be (at least quite so thoroughly) destroyed.[4]

The contemporary usage, then, is relatively recent. If we were still talking the language of the fourteenth or even seventeenth centuries, a "consumer society" would have meant a society of wastrels and destroyers.

Consumption in the contemporary sense only really appears in the literature of political economy in the late eighteenth century, when authors like Adam Smith and David Ricardo began to use it as the opposite of "production."[5] One of the crucial features of the industrial capitalism emerging at the time was a growing separation between the places in which people—or men, at least—worked and the places where they lived. This in turn made it possible to imagine that the "economy" (itself a very new concept) was divided into two completely separate spheres: the workplace, in which goods were "produced," and the household, in which they were "consumed." That which was created in one sphere is used—ultimately, used up, destroyed—in the other. Vintners produce wine; consumers take it home and drink it; chemical plants produce ink, consumers take it home, put it in pens, and write with it, and so on. Of course, even from the start, it was more difficult to see in what sense consumers were "consuming" silverware or books, since these are not destroyed by use; but since just about anything does, eventually, wear out or have to be replaced, the usage was not entirely implausible.

All this did, certainly, bring home one of the defining features of capitalism: that it is a motor of endless production; one that can only maintain its equilibrium, in fact, by continual growth. Endless cycles of destruction do seem to be, necessarily, the other side of this. To make way for new products, all that old stuff must somehow be cleared away; destroyed, or at least, cast aside as outmoded or irrelevant. And this is indeed the defining feature of "consumer society" as usually described (especially by its critics): one that casts aside any lasting values in the name of an endless cycling of ephemera. It is a society of sacrifice and destruction. And often, what seems to most fascinate Western scholars—and the Western public—about people living in radically different economic circumstances are phenomena that seem to mirror this in one way or another. George Bataille (1937) saw here a clue to the nature of culture itself, whose essence he saw as lying in apparently irrational acts of wild sacrificial destruction, for which he drew on examples such as Aztec human sacrifice or the Kwakiutl potlatch.[6] Or consider the fascination with the potlatch itself. It's hard not to think about Northwest Coast potlatch without immediately evoking images of chiefs setting fire to vast piles of wealth—such images play a central role not only in Bataille, but also in just about every popular essay on "gift economies" since. If one examines the sources, though, it turns out most Kwakiutl potlatches were rarely stately, redistributive affairs, and our image is really based on three or four extremely unusual ones held around 1900, at a time when the Kwakiutl population was simultaneously devastated by disease, and undergoing an enormous economic boom. Clearly, the spectacle of chiefs vying for titles by setting fire to piles of blankets or other valuables strikes our imagination not so much because it reveals some fundamental truth about human nature, largely suppressed in our own society, but because it reflects a barely hidden truth about the nature of our own consumer society.

"Consumption," then, refers to an image of human existence that first appears, in the North Atlantic world, around the time of the industrial revolution: one that sees what humans do outside the workplace largely as a matter of destroying things or using them up. It is especially easy to perceive the impoverishment this introduces into accustomed ways of talking about the basic sources of human desire and gratification by comparing it to the ways earlier Western thinkers had talked about such matters. St. Augustine or Hobbes, for example, both saw human beings as creatures of unlimited desire, and therefore concluded that if left to their own devices, they would always end up locked in competition. As Marshall Sahlins has pointed out (1996), in this they almost exactly anticipated the assumptions of later economic theory. But when they listed *what* humans desired, neither emphasized anything like the modern notion of consumption. In fact, both came up with more or less the same list: humans, they said, desire (1) sensual pleasures, (2) the accumulation of riches (a pursuit assumed to be largely aimed at winning the praise and esteem of others), and (3) power.[7] None were primarily about using anything up.[8] Even Adam Smith, who first introduced the term "consumption" in its modern sense in *The Wealth of Nations*, turned to an entirely different framework in developing a theory of desire in his *Theory of Moral Sentiments*: one that assumed that what most humans want above all is to be the object of others' sympathetic attention.[9] It was only with the growth of economic theory, and its gradual colonization of other disciplines, that desire itself began to be imagined as the desire to consume.

The notion of consumption, then, that assumes that human fulfillment is largely about acts of (more or less ceremonial) material destruction, represents something of a break in the Western tradition. It's hard to find anything written before, say, the eighteenth century that exactly anticipates it. It appears abruptly, mainly in countries like England and France, at exactly the moment when historians of those places begin to talk about the rise of something they call "consumer society," or simply "consumerism" (Berg & Clifford 1999; McKendrick, Brewer & Plum 1982; Stearns 2001; W. Smith 2002). That is, the moment when a significant portion of the population could be said to be organizing their lives around the pursuit of something called "consumer goods," defined as goods they did not see as necessities, but as in some sense objects of desire, chosen from a range of products, subject to the whims of fashion (ephemera again...), and so on. The ideology, and the practice, would seem to emerge as two sides of the same coin.

Theories of Desire

All this makes it sound as if the story should really begin around 1750, or even 1776. But could such basic assumptions about what people thought life is about really change that abruptly? It seems to me there are other ways to tell the story, which reveal much greater continuities. One would be to examine the concept of "desire" itself, as it emerged in the Western philosophical tradition.

Now, this might seem difficult to do because Western thinking on the matter contains a number of apparently contradictory strands. Since Plato, the most common approach has been to see desire as rooted in a feeling of absence or lack. This does makes a certain obvious intuitive sense. One desires what one doesn't have. One feels an absence, imagines how one might like to fill it. This very action of the mind is what we think of as "desire." But there is also an alternative tradition that goes back at least to Spinoza, which starts off not from the yearning for some absent object, but from something even more fundamental: self-preservation, the desire to continue to exist (Nietzsche's "life which desires itself"). Here, desire becomes the fundamental energetic glue that makes individuals what they are over time. Both strands continue to do battle in contemporary social theory. Desire as lack is especially developed in the work of Jacques Lacan. The key notion here is of the "mirror stage," where an infant, who is at first really a bundle of drives and sensations unaware of its own existence as a discrete, bounded entity, manages to construct a sense of self around some external image: for example, an encounter with her own reflection in the mirror. One can generalize from here a much broader theory of desire (or perhaps, merely desire in its more tawdry, narcissistic forms), where the object of desire is always some image of perfection, an imaginary completion for one's own ruptured sense of self (Graeber 2002: 257–58). But then there is also the approach adopted by authors like Deleuze and Guattari (1983), who wrote *Anti-Oedipus*, their famous critique of psychoanalysis, largely as an attack on this kind of thinking. Appealing to the Spinozist/Nietzschean tradition, they deny that desire should be found in any sense of lack at all. Rather, it is something that "flows" between everyone and everything. Much like power in Foucault, it becomes the energy knitting everything together. As such, desire is everything and nothing; there's very little one can actually say about it.

One might be tempted to conclude at this point, that "desire" is not a very useful theoretical concept—that is, one that can be meaningfully distinguished from needs, or urges, or intentions—since even authors working within the same, Western tradition can't make up their minds what it is supposed to mean.[10] But if one goes back to the origins of the alternative tradition in Spinoza, one soon discovers that the two strands are not nearly as different as they appear. When Spinoza refers to the universal driving force of all beings to persist in their being and expand their powers of action, he is really not referring to desire (*cupiditas*) as much as to what he calls *conatus*, usually translated "will." On a bodily level, *conatus* takes the form of a host of appetites: attractions, dispositions, and so forth. Desire is "the idea of an appetite," the imaginative construction one puts on some such attraction or disposition.[11] In other words, the one constant element in all these definitions is that desire (unlike needs, urges, or intentions) necessarily involves the imagination. Objects of desire are always imaginary objects, and usually, imaginary totalities of some sort—since most totalities are themselves imaginary objects.

The other way one might say desire differs from needs, urges, or intentions is that, as Tzvetan Todorov puts it (2001), it always implies the desire for some kind of social relation. There is always some quest for recognition involved. The problem is that, owing to the extreme individualism typical of the Western philosophical tradition, this tends to be occluded; even where it isn't, the desire for recognition is assumed to be the basis for some kind of profound existential conflict. The classic text here is Hegel's "On Lordship and Bondage," the famous "master/slave dialectic" in the *Phenomenology of Spirit*, that has made it difficult for future theorists to think of this kind of desire without also thinking of violence and domination.

If I may be allowed a very abbreviated summary of Hegel's argument: human beings are not animals because they have the capacity for self-consciousness.[12] To be self-conscious means to be able to look at ourselves from an outside perspective—that must necessarily be that of another human being. All these were familiar arguments at the time; Hegel's great innovation was to bring in desire; to point out that to look at ourselves this way, one has to have some reason to *want* to do it. This sort of desire is also inherent to the nature of humanity, according to Hegel, because unlike animals humans desire recognition. Animals experience desire simply as the absence of something: they are hungry, therefore they wish "negate that negation" by obtaining food; they have sexual urges, therefore they seek a mate.[13] Humans go further. They not only wish to have sex—at least, if they are being truly human about the matter—they also wish to be recognized by their partner as someone worthy of having sex with. That is: they wish to be loved. We desire to be the objects of another's desire. So far this seems straightforward enough: human desire implies mutual recognition. The problem is that for Hegel, the quest for mutual recognition inevitably leads to violent conflict, to "life and death struggles" for supremacy. He provides a little parable: two men confront each other at the beginning of history (as in all such stories, they appear to be forty-year-old males who simply rose out of the earth fully formed). Each wishes to be recognized by the other as a free, autonomous, fully human being, but in order for the other's recognition to be meaningful, he must prove to himself the other is fully human, and worthy of recognizing him. The only way to do this is to see if he values his freedom and autonomy so much he's willing to risk his life for it. A battle ensures. But a battle for recognition is inherently unwinnable, since if you kill your opponent, there's no one to recognize you; on the other hand if your opponent surrenders, he proves by that very act that he was not willing to sacrifice his life for recognition after all, and therefore, that his recognition is meaningless. One can of course reduce a defeated opponent to slavery, but even that is self-defeating because once one reduces the other—or, to put it in more Hegelian style, the Other—to slavery, one becomes dependent on one's slave for one's very material survival, while the slave at least produces his own life, and is in fact able to realize himself to some degree through his work.

This is a myth, a parable. Clearly there is something profoundly true in it. Still, it's one thing to say that the quest for mutual recognition is necessarily going to be tricky, full of pitfalls, with a constant danger of descending into attempts to dominate or even obliterate the Other. It's another thing to assume from the start that mutual recognition is impossible. As Majeed Yar has pointed out (2001), this assumption has come to dominate almost all subsequent Western thinking on the subject: especially, since Sartre refigured recognition as "the gaze" that, he argued, necessarily pins down, squashes, and objectifies the Other.[14] As in so much Western theory, when social relations are not simply ignored, they are assumed to be inherently competitive. Todorov notes (2000) that much of this is the result of starting one's examples with a collection of adult males: psychologically, he argues, it is quite possible to argue that the first moment in which we act as fully human beings is when we seek recognition from others; but that's because the first thing a human baby does that an animal baby does not do is to try to catch her mother's eye, an act with rather different implications (ibid: 66–67).

At this point I think we have the elements for a preliminary synthesis. Insofar as it is useful to distinguish something called "desire" from needs, urges, or intentions, then, it is because desire

(a) is always rooted in imagination;
(b) tends to direct itself towards some kind of social relation, real or imaginary;
(c) that social relation generally entails a desire for some kind of recognition and, hence, an imaginative reconstruction of the self; a process fraught with dangers of destroying that social relation, or turning it into some kind of terrible conflict.

Now, all this is more arranging the elements of a possible theory than proposing one; it leaves open the actual mechanics of how these elements interact. But if nothing else, it helps explain why the word "desire" has become so popular with authors who write about modern consumerism—which is, we are told, all about imaginary pleasures, and the construction of identities. Even here, though, the historical connections between ideas are not what one might imagine.

Lovers and Consumers

Let me begin with Colin Campbell's *Romantic Ethic and the Spirit of Modern Consumerism* (1987), one of the more creative essays on the subject. Campbell's book aims to provide a corrective to the usual critique of consumer culture as throwing up all sorts of wonderful fantasies about what you'll get when you purchase some product, and inevitably disappointing you once you get it. It is this constant lack of satisfaction, the argument goes, that then drives consumption, and thus allows the endless expansion of production. If the system delivered on its promises, the whole thing wouldn't work. Campbell isn't denying this happens so much as questioning whether the process itself is really so frustrating or unpleasant as most accounts imply. Really, he says, is not all this is a form of pleasure in itself? In fact, he argues, it is the unique accomplishment of modern consumerism to have assisted in the creation of a genuinely new form of hedonism.

"Traditional hedonism," Campbell argues, was based on the direct experience of pleasure: wine, women and song; sex and drugs and rock 'n' roll; or whatever the local variant. The problem, from a capitalist perspective, is that there are inherent limits to all this. People become sated, bored. There are logistical problems. "Modern self-illusory hedonism," as he calls it, solves this dilemma because here, what one is really consuming are fantasies and day-dreams about what having a certain product *would* be like. The rise of this new kind of hedonism, he argues, can be traced back to certain sensational forms of Puritan religious life, but primarily, to the new interest in pleasure through the vicarious experience of extreme emotions and states, an interest one can see emerging with the popularity of Gothic novels and the like in the eighteenth century and which peaks with Romanticism itself. The result is a social order that has become, in large measure, a vast apparatus for the fashioning of day-dreams. These reveries attach themselves to the promise of pleasure afforded by some particular consumer good, or set of them. They produce the endless desires that drive consumption; but, in the end, the real enjoyment is not in the consumption of the physical objects, but in the reveries themselves.

The problem with this argument (or, one of them—one could find all sorts) is the claim that all of this was something new. It's not just the obvious point that pleasure through vicarious participation in extreme experience did not first become a significant social phenomenon in the seventeenth century. It was accepted wisdom as early the eleventh century that desire was largely about taking pleasure in fantasies.

Here, I turn to the work of the Italian philosopher, Giorgio Agamben (1993), and the Romanian historian of religions, Ioan Couliano (1987), on Medieval and Renaissance theories of love.[15] These theories all turned on the notion of what was called the "pneumatic system." One of the greatest problems in Medieval metaphysics was to explain how it was possible for the soul (or mind) to perceive objects in the material world, since the two were assumed to be of absolutely alien natures. The solution was to posit an intermediate astral substance called *pneuma*, or spirit, that translated sense impressions into phantasmic images. These images then circulated through the body's pneumatic system (which centered on the heart) before they could be comprehended by the intellectual faculties of the soul. Since this was essentially the zone of imagination, all sensations, or even abstract ideas, had to proceed through the imagination—becoming emotionally charged in the process—before they could reach the mind. Hence, erotic theory held that, when a man fell in love with a woman, he was really in love not with the woman herself but with her image; one that, once lodged in his pneumatic system, gradually came to hijack it, vampirizing his imagination and ultimately drawing off all his physical and spiritual energies. Medical writers tended to represent this as a disease that needed to be cured; poets and lovers, a heroic state that combined pleasures (in fantasy, but also, somewhat perversely, in the very experience of frustration and denial) with an intrinsic spiritual or mystical value in itself. The one thing all agreed on, though, is that anyone who got the idea that one could resolve the matter by "embracing" the object of his fantasy was missing the point. The very idea was considered a symptom of a profound mental disorder, a species of *melancholia*.

Agamben on Ficino:

> In the same passage, the specific character of melancholic Eros was identified by Ficino as disjunction and excess. "This tends to occur," he wrote, "to those who, misusing love, transform what rightly belongs to contemplation into the desire of the embrace." The erotic intention that unleashes the melancholic disorder presents itself as that which would possess and touch what ought merely to be the object of contemplation, and the tragic insanity of the saturnine temperament thus finds its root in the intimate contradiction of a gesture that would embrace the unobtainable" (1993a: 17–18).

Agamben goes on to quote the French Scholastic Henry of Ghent, to the effect that melancholics "cannot conceive the incorporeal" as such, because they do not know "how to extend their intelligence beyond space and size." For such depressive characters, lonely brooding is punctuated by frustrated urges to seize what cannot really be seized.[16]

Now, one might quibble over whether anyone was ever quite so consistently pure in their affections as all this might imply. A fair amount of "embracing" certainly did go on in Medieval Europe, as elsewhere. Still, this was the ideal and, critically, it became the model not just for sexual desire, but for desire in general. This leads to the interesting suggestion that, from the perspective of Medieval psychological theory, our entire civilization—as Campbell describes it—is really a form of clinical depression. Which, in some ways, does actually make a lot of sense.[17]

Couliano is more interested in how erotic theory was appropriated by Renaissance magicians like Giordano Bruno, for whom the mechanics of sexual attraction became the paradigm for all forms of attraction or desire, and hence, the key to social power. If human beings tend to become dominated by powerful, emotionally charged images, then anyone who developed a comprehensive, scientific understanding of the mechanics by which such images work could become a master manipulator. It should be possible to develop techniques for "binding" and influencing others' minds: for instance, by fixing certain emotionally charged images in their heads,[18] or even little bits of music (jingles, basically) that could be designed in such a way as to keep coming back into people's minds despite themselves, and pull them in one direction or another. In all of this Couliano sees, not unreasonably, the first self-conscious form of the modern arts of propaganda and advertising. Bruno felt his services should be of great interest to princes and politicians.

It apparently never occurred to Bruno or anyone else, in this early period, to apply such proto-advertising techniques to economic rather than political purposes. Politics, after all, is about relations between people. Manipulating others was, by definition, a political business, which I think brings out the most fundamental difference between the Medieval conception of desire and the sort of thing Campbell describes. If one starts with a model of desire where the object of desire is assumed to be a human being, then it only makes sense that one cannot completely possess the object. ("Embrace" is a nice metaphor, actually, because it is so inherently fleeting.) And one is presumably not intentionally in the business of destroying it either.

One might say, then, as a starting point, that the shift from the kind of model of desire that predominated in the Middle Ages and Renaissance, to the kind of consumerist model described by Campbell—where one can only justify the continued indulgence in the pleasure of fantasies by claiming that the real point is to acquire an endlessly increasing number of consumer products—is a shift from one whose paradigm is erotic, to one in which the primary metaphor is eating food.

Complication 1: Individualism

Still, even if one examines the original Medieval version, the basic conception is already extremely individualistic. This is because it is so passive. Desire is the result of an individual receiving sense impressions from outside. Now, it is certainly true that this is one very common experience of desire: as something that seems to seize us from outside our conscious control, let alone better judgment, and often, causes us to do things for which we would really rather not hold ourselves entirely responsible. But it also allows us to overlook the fact that desire emerges in relations between people.

It's easier to see all this if one compares this Western model of desire, as developed explicitly in Medieval and Renaissance theory and tacitly through the sort of consumer practice Campbell describes, to, say, the kind of value-based approach I have tried to develop elsewhere (Graeber 2001). Money, for example can be considered in Marxian terms as a representation of the value (importance) of productive labor (human creative action), as well as the means by which it's socially measured and coordinated; but it is also a representation that brings into being the very thing it represents, since, after all, in a market economy, people work in order to get money. Arguably, something analogous happens everywhere. Value then could be said to be the way that the importance of one's own actions register in the imagination—always, by translation into some larger social language or system of meaning, by being integrated into some greater social whole. It also always happens through some kind of concrete medium—which can be almost anything: wampum, oratorical performances, sumptuous tableware, kula artifacts, Egyptian pyramids—and these objects, in turn (unless they are utterly generic substances like money that represent sheer potentiality), tend to incorporate in their own structure a kind of schematic model of the forms of creative action that bring them into being, but that also become objects of desire that end up motivating actors to carry out those very actions. Just as the desire for money inspires one to labor; the desire for tokens of honor inspires forms of honorable behavior; the desire for tokens of love inspires romantic behavior; and so on.[19]

By contrast, pneumatic theory begins not from actions but from what might once have been called "passions." Godfrey Lienhardt (1961) long ago pointed out actions and passions form a logical set—either you act on the world, or the world acts on you—but that we have become so uncomfortable with the idea of seeing ourselves as passive recipients that the latter term has almost completely disappeared from the way we talk about experience. Medieval and Renaissance authors did not yet have such qualms. In pneumatic theory, "passions" are not what one does but what is done to one (in which one is not agent but "patient"); at the same time, they referred, as they do now, to strong emotions, that seemed to seize us against our will. The two were linked: emotions like love were in fact seen as being caused by just such impressions on the pneumatic system. Far from being models of action, in fact, the passivity of the situation came to be seen as a virtue in itself: it was those who tried to act on their passions, to seize the object rather than contemplate it, who really missed the point.

Framing things in such passive terms then opened the way for that extreme individualism that appears to be the other side of the peculiarly Western theory of desire. A schema of action is almost of necessity a collective product; the impression of a beautiful image is something that one can imagine involves a relation between only two people, or even (insofar as love became a mystical phenomenon), between the desirer and God. Even with romantic love, the ideal was that it should not really be translated into an ongoing social relation, but remain a matter of contemplation and fantasy.

Complication II: Shifting Lines of Class and Gender

All this makes it easier to understand how it might be possible to shift from erotic fantasies to something more like the modern idea of "consumption." Still, the transition, I would argue, also required a number of other conceptual shifts and displacements, both in terms of class and in terms of gender.

Compare, for example, how images of paradise, in Medieval and Early Modern Europe, varied by social milieu. When peasants, craftsmen, and the urban poor tried to imagine a land in which all desires would be fulfilled, they tended to focus on the abundance of food. Hence the Land of Cockaigne, where bloated people loll about as geese fly fully cooked into their mouths, rivers run with beer, and so forth. Carnival, as Mikhail Bakhtin so richly illustrated, expands on all the same themes, jumbling together every sort of bodily indulgence and enormity, pleasures sexual as well as gastronomic and of every other kind. Still, the predominant imagery always centers on sausages, hogsheads, legs of mutton, lard and tripes and tubs of wine. The emphasis on food is in striking contrast with visions of earthly paradise in other parts of the world at that time (say, those prevalent in Islamic world), which were mostly about sex. Erotic fantasies are usually strikingly absent from the literature on the Land of Cockaigne; or, of if they are present, seem thrown in rather as afterthoughts.

As Herman Pleij has pointed out (2001: 421), the Medieval high culture version of paradise was in many ways conceived in direct opposition to the popular one. Not that it emphasized erotic pleasures either. Instead, it tended to fix on what we would now call elite consumables, the exotic commodities of the day that were, primarily, essences: spices above all, but also incense, perfumes, and similar delicate scents and flavors. Instead of the Land of Cockaigne, one finds a hankering after the lost Garden of Eden, thought to exist somewhere in the East, near the fabled kingdom of Prester John; anyway, from somewhere near those fragrant lands whence cardamom, mace, peppers, and cumin (not to mention frankincense and myrrh) were harvested. Rather than a land of complete, fatty indulgences in every sort of food, these were often conceived as lands whose ethereal inhabitants did not have to eat at all, but simply subsisted on beautiful smells (see Schivelbusch 1992; Friedman 1981). This emphasis on refined flavors and fragrances, in turn, opens onto a whole different realm of experience: of "taste," ephemerality, fleeting essences, and ultimately, the familiar elite consumption worlds of fashion, style, the pursuit of ungraspable novelty. Once again, then, the elite—who in reality of course tended to grasp and embrace all sorts of things—constructed their ideal of desire around that which somehow seemed to escape all possibility of permanent embrace. One might argue, then, that the modern consumer ethos is built on a kind of fusion between these two class ideals. The shift from a conception of desire modeled on erotic love to one based on the desire for food ("consumption") was clearly a shift in the direction of popular discourse. At the same time, though, one might say the innovative aspect of modern, consumerist theories of desire is to combine the popular materialist emphasis on consumption with the notion of the ephemeral, ungraspable image as the driving force of maximization of production.

This might at least suggest a solution to what has always struck me as a profound paradox in Western social theory. As I've already noted, the idea of human beings as creatures tainted by original sin, and therefore, cursed with infinite wants—beings who living in a finite universe were inevitably in an state of generalized competition—was already fully developed in authors like St. Augustine, and therefore formed an accepted part of Christian doctrine throughout the Middle Ages. At the same time, very few people actually seemed to behave like this. Economically, the Middle Ages were still the time of "target incomes," in which the typical reaction to economic good times, even among urban craftsmen and most of the proto-bourgeoisie, was to take more days off. It's as if the notion of the maximizing individual existed in theory long before it emerged in practice. One explanation might be that at least until the Early Modern period, high culture (whether in its most Christian or most courtly versions) tended to devalue any open display of greed, appetite, or acquisitiveness, while popular culture—which could sometimes heartily embrace such impulses—did so in forms that were inherently collective. When the Land of Cockaigne was translated into reality, it was in the form of popular festivals like Carnival; almost any increase in popular wealth was immediately diverted into communal feasts, parades, and collective indulgences. One of the processes that made capitalism possible, then, was what might be termed the privatization of desire. The highly individualistic perspectives of the elite had to be combined with the materialistic indulgences of what Bakhtin liked to call the "material lower stratum."

Getting from there to anything like the capitalist notion of consumption required, I think, one further shift: this time, not along lines of class, but of gender. The courtly love literature, and related theories of desire, represent a purely male perspective, and this no doubt was true of fantasies about the Land of Cockaigne and similar idealized worlds of gastronomic fulfillment, too.[20] Though here it was complicated by the fact that, in the folk psychology of the day, women were widely considered more lustful, greedy, and generally desirous than men. Insofar as anyone was represented as insatiable, then, it was women: the image of woman as a ravenous belly, demanding ever more sex and food, and men as haplessly laboring in an endless, but ultimately impossible, effort to satisfy them, is a standard misogynist *topos* going back at least to Hesiod. Christian doctrine only reinforced it saddling women with the primary blame for original sin, and thus insisting that they bore the brunt of the punishment. It was only around the time of the industrial revolution, and the full split between workplace and household, that this sort of rhetoric was largely set aside; curiously, at just the same time as consumption came to be seen as an essentially feminine business (Thomas 1971: 568–569; Davis 1975: 125–151; Graeber 1997).

On Having Your Cake and Eating It Too, and Certain Problems Incumbent Therein

What I am suggesting, then, is that while Medieval moralists accepted, in the abstract, that humans were cursed with limitless desires (that, as Augustine put it, their natures rebelled against them just as they had rebelled against God), few saw this was an existential dilemma which affected them personally. Rather, they tended to attribute such sinful predilections mainly to people they saw as social, and therefore moral, inferiors. Men saw women as insatiable; the prosperous saw the poor as grasping and material-

istic, and so on. It was really in the Early Modern period that all this began
to change.

Agamben has a theory as to why. He suggests that the idea that all humans are driven by infinite, unquenchable desires is only really possible when
one severs imagination and experience. In the world posited by Medieval
psychology, desires really could be satisfied for the very reason that they were
really directed at phantasms: imagination was the zone in which subject and
object, lover and beloved, really could genuinely meet and partake of one
another. With Descartes, he argues, this began to change. Imagination was
redefined as something inherently separate from experience—as, in fact, a
compendium of all those things (dreams, flights of fancy, pictures in the
mind) that one feels one has experienced but really hasn't. It was at this
point, once one was expected to try to satisfy one's desires in what we have
come to think of as "the real world," that the ephemeral nature of experience,
and therefore of any "embrace," becomes an impossible dilemma (1993b:
25–28). One is already seeing such dilemmas worked out in De Sade, he
argues: again, around same the time as the dawn of consumer culture.

This is pretty much the argument one would have to make, if one were
to confine oneself, as Agamben does, entirely to literary and philosophical
texts. In the last couple sections, I've been trying to develop a more socially
nuanced approach, which argues, among other things, that the modern concept of "consumption," which carries in it the tacit assumption that there's
no end to what anyone might want, could really only take form once certain
elite concepts of desire—as the pursuit of ephemera and phantasms—fused,
effectively, with the popular emphasis on food. Still, I don't think this is
quite a complete or adequate explanation. There is, I believe, another element, which made all this possible; perhaps, inevitable. This was the rise,
in the sixteenth and seventeenth centuries, of what C.B. MacPherson first
called "possessive individualism" (1962), by which he means the fact that
people increasingly came to see themselves as isolated beings who define
their relation with the world not in terms of social relations but in terms of
property rights. It was only then that the problem of how one could "have"
things, or for that matter experiences ("we'll always have Paris") could really
become a crisis.[21]

The very notion of private property in the modern sense was fairly new.
The notion of "consumption," I would suggest, resolves a certain contradiction inherent in it. From an analytical perspective, of course, property is
simply a social relation: an arrangement between persons and collectivities
concerning the disposition of valuable goods. Private property is a particular form that entails one individual's right to exclude all others—"all the
world"—from access to a certain house, or shirt, piece of land, etc. A relation

so broad is difficult to imagine, however, so people tend to treat it as if it were a relation between a person and an object. But what could a relation between a person and an object actually consist of?

In English law, such relations are still described according to the logic of sovereignty—that is, in terms of *dominium*. The power a citizen has over his own possessions is exactly the same power once held by kings and princes, and that is still retained by states in the form of "eminent domain." This is why private property rights took so long to enshrine in law: even in England, which led the way in such matters, it was almost the eighteenth century before jurists were willing to recognize a dominium belonging to anyone other than the king.

What would it mean, then, to establish "sovereignty" over an object? In legal terms, a king's dominium extended to his land, his subjects, and their possessions; the subjects were "included in" the person of the king, who represented them in dealing with other kingdoms, in a similar fashion to that by which the father of a family represented his wife, children, and servants before the law. The wife, children, and servants of a head of household were likewise "included in" his legal personality, in much in the same way as his possessions. And, in fact, the power of kings was always being likened to that of fathers; the only real difference (aside from the fact that in any conflict, the king was seen to have a higher claim) was that, unlike fathers, kings wielded the power of life and death over their subjects. These were the ultimate stakes of sovereignty. Certainly, it was the one power kings were least willing to delegate or share.[22] The ultimate proof that one has sovereign power over another human being is one's ability to have them executed. In a similar fashion, one might argue, the ultimate proof of possession, of one's personal *dominium* over a thing, is one's ability to destroy it—and indeed this remains one of the key legal ways of defining *dominium*, as a property right, to this day. But there's an obvious problem here. If one does destroy the object, one may have definitively proved that one owns it; but, as a result, one does not own it any more.

We end up, then, with what might seem a particularly perverse variation on Hegel's master/slave dialectic, in which the actor, seeking some sort of impossible recognition of his absolute mastery of an inanimate object, can only achieve this recognition by destroying it. Still, I don't really think this is a variation on the master/slave dilemma. I think a better case could probably be made that the dilemma described by Hegel actually derives from this. After all, the one thing least explained in Hegel's account is where the necessity of conflict comes from (after all, there *are* ways to risk one's life to impress another person that do not involve trying to murder them). The quest for recognition, in Hegel, does not lead to the destruction of property: but it does lead to a choice of either destroying the Other, or reducing the Other to property. Relations which are not based on property—or more precisely, on that very ambiguous synthesis between the two types of sovereignty—suddenly become impossible to imagine, and I think this is true because Hegel is starting from a model of possessive individualism.

At any rate, the paradox exists, and it is precisely here where the metaphor of "consumption" gains its appeal.[23] Because it is the perfect resolution of this paradox—or at least, about as perfect a resolution as one is going to get. When you eat something, you do indeed destroy it (as an autonomous entity), but at the same time, it remains "included in" you in the most material of senses.[24] Eating food, then, became the perfect idiom for talking about desire and gratification in a world in which everything, all human relations, were being re-imagined as questions of property.

Sacrifice

What we have documented so far is a conception of human fulfillment as a form of destruction and incorporation; a reconception of human beings as eating machines, absorbing elements of the world around them, burning them up or spitting them out, in a never-ending pursuit of phantasms. Probably, in the final analysis, the only way to understand all this is, as authors like Bataille have suggested, in relation to some kind of sacrificial ideology. If one were to write a complete genealogy of the idea, I suspect, one would probably best begin with the anthropological and historical literature on animal sacrifice.

Certainly, much of that literature (e.g., Lienhardt 1964; Valeri 1985) is very suggestive: at least insofar as it tends to argue that such rituals are ultimately about the creation of transcendental images of desired states through the destruction of desirable goods—goods that were also, usually, living beings. It is the act of destruction, of killing the animal, burning the spirit money, or otherwise effacing the object, that purges that presumably permanent transcendental image from the profane, temporal, material element—for example, those parts of the animal's flesh that can now be eaten. Only then can it end in an act of collective consumption, a feast. One might then go on to observe that Eurasian world religions from Zoroaster onwards ("Axial Age" religions as they're often called) almost invariably seem to have arisen, in large part, in opposition to this sort of sacrificial ritual and all it represents. They were veritable anti-sacrificial ideologies. In practice, this could mean anything from utterly negating one classic form of animal sacrifice (as in Hinduism, where one was forbidden to kill cows) to inverting its logic (as in Christianity, where it was now God, as paschal lamb, who had sacrificed himself), or endless variations in between. Each tradition tended to maintain certain elements of the classic sacrificial scene for continued emphasis—the fire in Zoroastrianism, the incense in Confucianism, the altar in Christianity (Heesterman 1993)—each, significantly, was confronted in doing so with the need to develop some kind of philosophical understanding of human desire. The Medieval European one we have been exploring in this essay, however superficially, might be considered one particular variation, developed in dialogue between the Jewish, Christian, and Muslim intellectual cultures of the time;[25] a rather different, but in many ways more sophisticated, approach to the same existential problems developed in a parallel dialogue between Buddhism, Hinduism, and Taoism; or more interestingly, even, between different strains of Buddhism or, otherwise, within those traditions themselves.

Conclusions: But What About Consumerism?

What does all this imply about the current use of the term "consumption"? For one thing, I think it suggests we should think about how far we really want to extend the metaphor—since a metaphor is, after all, all this is. It makes perfect sense to talk about the "consumption" of fossil fuels. It is quite another thing to talk about the "consumption" of television programming—much though this has been the topic of endless books and essays. Why, exactly, are we calling this "consumption?" About the only reason I can see is that TV programming is created by people paid wages and salaries somewhere other than where viewers are watching it. Otherwise, there appears to be no reason at all. Programming is not even a commodity, since viewers don't usually pay for it; it is not in any direct sense "consumed" by its viewers. It is hardly something one fantasizes about acquiring, and one cannot, in fact, acquire it. It is in no sense destroyed by use. Rather, we are dealing with a continual stream of potential fantasy material, some intended to market particular commodities, some not. Cultural studies scholars, and anthropologists writing in the same vein, tend to insist that these images are not simply passively absorbed by "consumers," but actively interpreted and appropriated, in ways the producers would probably never have suspected, and employed as ways of fashioning identities—the "creative consumption" model again. But to how much TV watching does this really apply? Certainly, there's some. There are people who organize much of their imaginative life around one particular show, Trekkies for instance, who participate in a subculture of fans who write stories or comic zines around their favorite characters, attend conventions, design costumes, and the like. But when a sixteen year old girl writes a short story about forbidden love between Kirk and Spock, this is hardly consumption any more; we are talk-ing about people engaging in a complex community organized around forms of (relatively unalienated) production. Such behavior tends to be especially typical of young people who have a good deal of time on their hands, and a great deal of energy.[26] At the other extreme, we have the vast majority of TV viewing, which is by people who spend most of their waking hours en-gaged in extremely alienated forms of production—who work forty or fifty hours a week at a job that is likely as not mind-numbingly boring, extremely stressful, or both; commute; come home far too exhausted and emotionally drained to be able to engage in any of the activities they would consider truly rewarding, pleasurable or meaningful, but just plop down in from the of the tube because it's the easiest thing to do. As some have noted (e.g. Lodziak 2002), those who analyze consumption as an autonomous domain of mean-ing-creation almost never take the effects of work into account.

In other words, when "creative consumption" is at its most creative, it's not consumption; when it's most obviously a form of consumption, it is not creative.

Above all, I think we should be careful about importing the political economy habit of seeing society as divided into two spheres, of production and consumption into cultural analysis (or at best three: production, con-sumption, and exchange.) Doing so almost inevitably forces us to view al-most all forms of non-alienated production as "consumer behavior":

> Cooking, playing sports, gardening, DIY (Do-It-Yourself), home deco-ration, dancing and music-making are all examples of consumer ac-tivities which involve some participation, but they cannot of themselves transform the major invasion by commercial interest groups into con-sumption which has occurred since the 1950s (Bocock 1993: 51).

According to the logic of the quote above, if I bought some vegetables and prepared a gazpacho to share with some friends, that's actually consum-erism. In fact, it would be even if I grew the vegetables myself (presumably, because I bought the seeds). We are back to the teenagers with the rock band. Any production not for the market is treated as a form of consump-tion, which has the incredibly reactionary political effect of treating almost every form of unalienated experience we do engage in as somehow a gift granted us by the captains of industry.

How to think our way out of this box? No doubt there are many ways. This paper is meant more to raise issues, trace a history, and expose dilem-mas, than to dictate solutions. Still, one or two suggestions might be in order. The obvious one is to treat consumption not as an analytical term but as an ideology to be investigated. Clearly, there are people in the world who do base key aspects of their identity around what they see as the destructive encompassment of manufactured products. Let us find out who these people really are, when they think of themselves this way and when they don't, and how they relate to others who conceive their relations to the material world differently. If we wish to continue applying terms borrowed from political economy—as I have certainly done elsewhere (e.g., 2001, 2006)—it might be more enlightening to start looking at what we've been calling the "consumption" sphere rather as the sphere of the production of human beings, not just as labor power but as persons, internalized nexuses of meaningful social relations. After all, this is what social life is actually about: the production of people (of which the production of things is simply a subordinate moment), and it's only the very unusual organization of capitalism that makes it even possible for us to imagine otherwise.

This is not to say that everything has to be considered either a form of production or of consumption (consider for example a softball game; it's clearly neither), but it at least allows us to open up some neglected questions, such as that of alienated and nonalienated forms of labor, terms which have fallen somewhat into abeyance and therefore remain radically undertheorized. What exactly does engaging in nonalienated production actually mean? Such questions become all the more important when we start thinking about capitalist globalization and resistance. Rather than looking at people in Zambia or Brazil and saying "look! they are using consumption to construct identities!" (implying they are willingly, or perhaps unknowingly, submitting to the logic of neoliberal capitalism), perhaps we should consider that in many of the societies we study, the production of material products has always been subordinate to the mutual construction of human beings. What they are doing, at least in part, is simply insisting on continuing to act as if this were the case, even when using objects manufactured elsewhere. In other words, maybe it is the very opposite of acquiescence.

One thing, I think, we can certainly assert. Insofar as social life is and always has been mainly about the mutual construction of human beings, the ideology of consumption has been endlessly effective in helping us forget this. Most of all it does so by suggesting:

a) that human desire is not essentially a matter of relations between people but of relations between individuals and phantasms;
b) that our primary relation with other individuals is an endless struggle to establish our sovereignty, or autonomy, by incorporating and destroying aspects of the world around them;

c) that for this reason any genuine relation with other people is problematic (the problem of "the Other");

d) that society can thus be seen as a gigantic engine of production and destruction in which the only significant human activity is either manufacturing things, or engaging in acts of ceremonial destruction so as to make way for more: a vision which, in fact, sidelines most things that real people actually do and, insofar as it is translated into actual economic behavior, is obviously unsustainable.

Even as anthropologists and other social theorists directly challenge this view of the world, the unreflective use—and indeed self-righteous propagation—of terms like "consumption" ends up completely undercutting their efforts and reproducing the very tacit ideological logic we would wish to call into question.

Endnotes

1   To take one example, a little while ago a book came out called *The Consumer Society Reader* (Schor & Holt 2000), which contains essays by twenty eight authors ranging from Thorsten Veblen to Tom Frank about consumption and consumerism. Not a single essay offers a definition of either term, or asks why these terms are being used rather than others.

2   Especially if the band had not yet received a record contract or many professional gigs. If they were able to market some kind of product, it might be considered production again.

3   Here, I also want to answer some of the questions rather left dangling at the end of my book on value theory (Graeber 2001: 257–261).

4   In French the word *consummation*, which is from a different root, eventually displaced consumption. But the idea of taking possession of an object seems to remain; and any number of authors have remarked on the implied parallel between sexual appropriation and eating food.

5   "Produce" is derived from a Latin word meaning to "bring out" (a usage still preserved in phrases like "the defense produced a witness..." or "he produced a flashlight from under his cloak") or "to put out" (as from a factory).

6   Bataille's argument was that production, which Marx saw as quintessentially human, is also the domain of activity most constrained by practical considerations; consumption, the least so. To discover what is really important to a culture, therefore, one should look not at how they make things, but how they destroy them.

7   Similar lists appear throughout the Western tradition. Kant also had three—wealth, power, and prestige—interestingly, skipping pleasure.

8   The sensual pleasures they had in mind seem to have centered as much on having sex as on eating food, on lounging on silk pillows as burning incense or hashish; and by "wealth" both seemed to have in mind, first and foremost, permanent things like mansions, landed estates, and magnificent jewelry than consumables.

9   One could even argue that Smith's approach to questions of desire and fulfillment is so one-sided, centering almost entirely on social recognition and immaterial rewards (wealth, in his system, was only really desirable insofar as wealthy people were more likely to be the object of others' attention and spontaneous sympathetic concern) that it is meant to head off the very possibility of the consumption model that was to develop from his economic work.

10   Working here on the assumption that, if one examines any intellectual tradition carefully enough, one could find the materials for a genuinely insightful analysis of such "big questions"—i.e., sufficient perusal of the Buddhist tradition would also have yielded useful results, had I been competent to do it, which I'm not.

11   For the best collection of essays on Spinoza's theory of desire, see Yovel 1999. On his theory of imagination, see Gates & Lloyd 1999.

12   I am especially drawing on the famous "strong reading" of this passage by Alexander Kojéve (1969) that had such an influence on Sartre, and through him, de Beauvoir, Fanon, etc.

13   In Hegel's language, they construct themselves as a negation, therefore they seek to negate that negation by negating something else—i.e., by eating it.

14   Lacan's "mirror phase" itself actually draws directly on Hegel's master-slave dialectic (Casey & Woody 1983). I might note too that it's the Hegel-Kojéve-Sartre connection which is responsible for the habit of writing about "the Other" with a capital "O," as an inherently unknowable creature.

15   It would appear that much of Couliano's work draws on Agamben for inspiration, though Couliano only cites Agamben occasionally, and always to attack him on minor points.

16   "That is the incapacity of conceiving the incorporeal and the desire to make of it the object of an embrace are two faces of the same coin, of the process in whose course the traditional contemplative vocation of the melancholic reveals itself vulnerable to the violent disturbance of desire menacing it from within" (1993a: 18).

17   There is a lot of evidence which suggests that levels of clinical depression do in fact rise sharply in consumer-oriented societies. They have certainly been rising steadily in the US for most of the century. I should emphasize, by the way, that while Agamben and Couliano draw exclusively on European sources, these ideas were very likely developed earlier and more extensively in the Islamic world, and what they could in the European sources are ultimately derivative from them. Unfortunately little of this work has been translated, nor the history of Arabic and Persian theories of the imagination discussed in contemporary work in European languages. But I would underline that this is yet another way in which when one

refers to the "Western tradition," one should think of oneself, especially in this period, referring equally or even primarily to Islam.

18 These images were seen to act on the imagination in ways already developed by the contemporary Art of Memory: see Yates 1964.

19 Almost always, this also ends up involving a certain degree of fetishization, where the objects end up appearing, from the actors' perspective, to be the source of the very powers by which they are in fact created; because, from the actors' position, this might as well be true. Often, too, these objects become imaginary micro-totalities which play a similar role to Lacan's mirror-objects or similar critiques of the commodity as capturing an illusory sense of wholeness in a society fragmented by capitalism itself (Graeber 1996a; Debord 1994).

20 Even women, when they wrote love poems, tended to adopt a male point of view.

21 In other words, rather than asking how is it possible to truly "have" or possess some object or experience, perhaps we should be asking why anyone should develop a desire to do so to begin with.

22 Supposedly, in early Roman law the paterfamilias did have the power to execute his children, as well as his slaves; both rights, if they really did exist in practice, were stripped away extremely early.

23 Or more technically, I suppose, synecdoche.

24 And it has the additional attraction of being almost the only power which kings do not have over their subjects: as one sixteenth century Spanish jurist wrote, in arguing that American cannibalism violated natural law, "no man may possess another so absolutely that he may make use of him as a foodstuff" (in Pagden 1984: 86).

25 As noted above, much of the Medieval philosophy Agamben and others discuss was probably first developed in the Arabic and Persian literatures and only later adopted in Europe.

26 As, incidentally, do those people from other cultures who radically reinterpret TV shows, so much beloved of anthropological media theorists (e.g., Graburn 1982).

Bibliography

Agamben, Giorgio
1993a *Stanzas: Word and Phantasm in Western Culture.* Minneapolis: University of Minnesota Press.
1993b *Infancy and History: Essays on the Destruction of Experience.* (Liz Heron, trans.) London: Verso Press.

Bakhtin, Mikhail
1984 *Rabelais and his World.* Indiana U. Press, Bloomington.

Bataille, Georges
1937 "The Notion of Expenditure." *Visions of Excess, Selected Writings, 1927–1939.* Minneapolis: University of Minnesota Press.

Baudrillard, Jean
1972 *Pour un critique de l'economie du Signe*. Paris: Gallimard.

Benedict, Ruth
1934 "The Northwest Coast of America," chapter 6 of *Patterns of Culture* (New York: Penguin): 160–205

Berg, Maxine, and Helen Clifford, editors
1999 *Consumers and Luxury: Consumer Culture in Europe, 1650–1850*. Manchester: Manchester University Press.

Bocock, Robert
1993 *Consumption*. London: Routledge.

Campbell, Colin
1987 *The Romantic Ethic and the Spirit of Modern Consumerism*. Oxford: Blackwell.

Casey, Edward S. and J. Melvin Woody
1983 "Hegel and Lacan: the Dialectic of Desire." In *Interpreting Lacan* (Joseph Smith and William Kerrigan, eds.). New Haven: Yale University Press.

Couliano, Ioan
1987 *Eros and Magic in the Renaissance*. (Margaret Cook, trans.) Chicago: University of Chicago Press.

Davis, Natalie Zemon
1975 *Society and Culture in Early Modern France*. Stanford: Stanford University Press.

Debord, Guy
1994 *Society of the Spectacle*. New York: Zone Books.

Delumeau, Jean
2000 *History of Paradise: The Garden of Eden in Myth and Tradition*. (Matthew O'Connell, trans.) Chicago: University of Illinois Press.

Deleuze, Gilles, and Felix Guattari
1983 *Anti-Oedipus: Capitalism and Schizophrenia*. Minneapolis: University of Minnesota Press.

Friedman, John Block
1981 *The Monstrous Races in Medieval Art and Thought*. Cambridge, MA: Harvard University Press.

Friedman, Jonathan
1994 "Introduction" to *Consumption and Identity*. Amsterdam: Harwood Academic Publishers.

Gates, Moira and Genevieve Lloyd
1999 *Collective Imaginings: Spinoza, Past and Present*. London: Routledge.

Graburn, Nelson
1982. Television and the Canadian Inuit. *Études Inuit Studies* 6(2): 7–24

Graeber, David
1997 "Manners, Deference and Private Property: The Generalization of Avoidance in Early Modern Europe." *Comparative Studies in Society and History* 39(4): 694–728.
2001 *Towards an Anthropological Theory of Value: The False Coin of Our Own Dreams*. New York: Palgrave.
2006 "Turning Modes of Production Inside Out: Or, Why Capitalism is a Transformation of Slavery (short version)." *Critique of Anthropology* Volume 26 no 1: 61–81.

Heesterman, J. C.
1993 *The Broken World of Sacrifice: An Essay in Ancient Indian Ritual*. Chicago: University of Chicago Press.

Hegel, Georg Wilhelm Friedrich
1997 *Phenomenology of Spirit* (A.V. Miller, trans.). Oxford: Clarendon Press.

Hobbes, Thomas
1968 *Leviathan*. Harmandsworth: Penguin Press.

Kojéve, Alexandre
1969 *Introduction to the Reading of Hegel*. New York: Basic Books.

Lacan, Jacques
1977 *Écrits: A Selection*. New York: Norton Press.

Lienhardt, Godfrey
1961 *Divinity and Experience*. Oxford: Oxford University Press.

Lodziak, Conrad
2002 *The Myth of Consumerism*. London: Pluto Press.

Mauss, Marcel
1954 *The Gift*. Beacon Press, Boston.

McKendrick, Neil, John Brewer, and J.H. Plumb
1982 *Birth of a Consumer Society: The Commercialization of Eighteenth-Century England*. London: Europa.

Miller, Daniel
1987 *Material Culture and Mass Consumption*. London: Basil Blackwell.
1995 *Acknowledging Consumption: A Review of New Studies* (D. Miller, ed.). London: Routledge.

Negri, Antonio
1991 *The Savage Anomaly: The Power of Spinoza's Metaphysics and Politics*. (Michael Hardt, trans.) Minnesota: University of Minnesota Press.

Pleij, Herman
2001 *Dreaming of Cockaigne: Medieval Fantasies of the Perfect Life* (Diane Webb, trans.) New York: Columbia University Press.

Sahlins, Marshall
1972 *Stone Age Economics*, Chicago: University of Chicago Press.
1996. "The Sadness of Sweetness: or, The Native Anthropology of Western Cosmology?" *Current Anthropology* 37 no. 3: 395–428.

Scarry, Elaine
1985 *The Body in Pain: The Making and Unmaking of the World*. (Oxford: Oxford University Press).

Schivelbusch, Wolfgang
1992 *Tastes of Paradise: A Social History of Spices, Stimulants and Intoxicants*. New York: Vintage Press.

Schor, Juliet B. and Douglas B. Holt, eds.
2000 *The Consumer Society Reader*. New York: The New Press.

Scott, James
1992 *Domination and the Arts of Resistance*. New Haven: Yale University Press.

Silverman, Hugh
2000 "Twentieth-Century Desire and the Histories of Philosophy." *Philosophy & Desire.* New York: Routledge.

Smith, Adam
1776 *An Inquiry Into the Nature and Causes of the Wealth Of Nations.* Oxford: Clarendon Press.
1761 *Theory of Moral Sentiments.* Cambridge, U.K: Cambridge University Press (2002).

Smith, Woodruff D.
2002 *Consumption and the Making of Respectability: 1600–1800.* London: Routledge.

Spinoza, Baruch
2000 *Ethics.* (G.H.R. Parkinson, ed. and trans.). Oxford: Oxford University Press.

Stearns, Peter
2001 *Consumerism in World History: The Global Transformation of Desire.* London: Routledge.

Thomas, Keith
1971 *Religion and the Decline of Magic.* New York: Scribner.

Thompson, E.P.
1966 *The Making of the English Working Class.* New York: Vintage.
1967 "Time, Work-Discipline and Industrial Capitalism," *Past and Present* no. 38 (Dec. 1967), 56–97.

Todorov, Tzvetan
2001 *Life in Common: An Essay in General Anthropology.* (Katherine Golsan & Lucy Golsan, trans.). Lincoln: University of Nebraska Press.

Turner, Terence
1979 "Anthropology and the Politics of Indigenous Peoples' Struggles." *Cambridge Anthropology* 5: 1–43.
1980 "The Social Skin." In *Not Work Alone* (Jeremy Cherfas and R. Lewas, eds.). Beverly Hills: Sage Productions.
1984 "Value, Production and Exploitation in Non-Capitalist societies." Unpublished essay based on a paper presented at the AAA 82nd Annual Meeting, Denver, Colorado. To appear in *Whose Creative Energy?: Action and Reflection in the Creation of Society* (ed. David Graeber and Setsuko Nakayama, Berghahn Press.)

Valeri, Valerio
1985 *Kingship and Sacrifice: Ritual and Society in Ancient Hawaii* (Paula Wissing, trans.). Chicago: University of Chicago Press.

Wagner, Roy
1995 "If You Have the Advertisement You Don't Need the Product." In *Rhetorics of Self-Making* (D. Battaglia, ed.). Berkeley: University of California Press.

Williams, Raymond
1983 *Keywords: A Vocabulary of Culture and Society* (revised edition). New York: Oxford University Press.

Yar, Majeed
2001 "Recognition and the Politics of Human(e) Desire." *Theory, Culture and Society* 18 (2–3): 57–76.

Yates, Frances
1964 *Giordano Bruno and the Hermetic tradition*. Chicago: University of Chicago Press.
1966 *The Art of Memory*. Chicago: University of Chicago Press.

Yovel, Yirmiyahu (ed.)
1999 *Desire and Affect: Spinoza as Psychologist*. New York: Little Room Press.

3

TURNING MODES OF PRODUCTION INSIDE OUT: OR, WHY CAPITALISM IS A TRANSFORMATION OF SLAVERY

(SHORT VERSION)

What follows is really just the summary of a much longer argument I hope to develop elsewhere at greater length. A lot of the issues it addresses—the state of Marxist theory, the notion of the mode of production, World-Systems analysis—are ones most anthropologists in the United States (or for that matter, most political activists) have come to think of as tiresome and passé. However, I think that, if well employed, these concepts can still tell us new and surprising things about the world we inhabit. The problem is that they haven't always been employed particularly well.

This is particularly true of the term "mode of production," which in Classical Marxist theory, was in certain ways theoretically quite undeveloped. The concept was, I think, always somewhat jerry-built. As a result, when world-systems analysis came along and changed the frame of reference, it simply collapsed. One might argue this wasn't such an entirely bad thing. Perhaps not. Perhaps it was never that useful a concept to begin with. But the results of its collapse were quite disturbing. Almost immediately upon jettisoning the modes of production model, and with it, the notion that slavery or feudalism constituted distinct economic systems, formerly die-hard Marxists began seeing capitalism everywhere. It's always struck me that there is something very arbitrary about such arguments. After all, if an anthropologist like Jonathan Friedman assembles evidence that Greek and Roman slavery shared many features in common with what we have come to call "capitalism," one could interpret that to mean that modern capitalism is really just a variation of slavery. But it never seems to occur to contemporary authors to make such an argument. Instead the argument is always that ancient slavery, or Ming pottery production, or Mesopotamian tax farming, was really a form of capitalism. When even Marxists are naturalizing capitalism, you know there's a serious problem.

In this essay, I want to go back and see what might have happened had scholars taken a radically different tack. What if instead of throwing out the concept of "modes of production," they had tried to fix it? What if they had re-imagined "modes of production" not as simply ways in which people produce and struggle over some kind of material surplus, but as, equally, about the mutual fashioning of human beings? I am not saying that this is the "correct" way to use the concept, or even that others should necessarily employ it. Still, the point of any theoretical concept is to allow one to see things one would not be able to see otherwise, and it seems to me that the moment one redefines modes of production in this way, all sorts of things leap into focus that might have otherwise remained obscure. For example, one of the most striking things about capitalism is that it is the only mode of production to systematically divide homes and workplaces. It assumes that the making of people and the manufacture of things should properly operate by an entirely different logic in places that have nothing to do with each other. In this, it is actually does have certain striking similarities with slavery, so much so, in fact, that we could say that one is, in a certain sense, a transformation of the other. When we talk about "wage slavery," then, this is, I would suggest, less of a metaphor than we usually think. The genetic links between capitalism and slavery are actually quite profound.

Observation 1: The concept of the "mode of production" was distinctly under-formulated.

As others have noted (e.g., Wolf 1982: 75), Marx himself was never particularly rigorous in his use of the term "mode of production." Often, he threw the term about quite casually, speaking not only of the capitalist or feudal modes of production, but "primitive," "patriarchal," or "slavonic" ones. It only became a rigorous theoretical concept when, in the 1950s, Louis Althusser seized on the term as a way of breaking out of the official, evolutionist model that had dominated official Marxism up to his day—one that saw history everywhere as proceeding, mechanically, from slavery to feudalism to capitalism—without entirely alienating the very dogmatic French Communist party of his day.

The resulting formulation, later developed by anthropologists like Meillassoux (1981) and Terray (1969), or historians like Perry Anderson (1974a; 1974b), runs something like this:

A mode of production (MoP) is born of the relation between two factors: the forces of production (FoP) and the relations of production (RoP). The former is largely concerned with factors like the quality of land, level of technological knowledge, availability of machinery, and so on. The latter are marked by a relation between two classes, one a class of primary produc-ers, the other an exploiting class. The relation between them is exploitative because while the primary producers do in fact create enough to reproduce their own lives through their labors, and more to spare, the exploiting class does not, but rather lives at least in part on the surplus extracted from the primary producers. This extraction, in turn, is carried out through one or another form of property arrangement: in the case of the slave mode of pro-duction, the exploiters directly own the primary producers; in feudalism, both have complex relations to the land, but the lords use direct jural-politi-cal means to extract a surplus; in capitalism, the exploiters own the means of production and the primary producers are thus reduced to selling their labor power. The state, in each case, is essentially an apparatus of coercion that backs up these property arrangements by force.

A society, or "social formation" as the term went, rarely involves just one MoP. There tends to be a mix, however, one will be predominant. And that exploiting class will be the ruling class, which dominates the state.

Finally, all MoPs are assumed to be inherently unstable. Owing to their internal contradictions, they will eventually destroy themselves and turn into something else.

When one looks at actual analyses, however, what one finds is slightly different. For one thing, the "forces of production" are rarely much invoked. Roman slavery and Haitian slavery involved completely different crops, cli-mates, technologies, and so on; but no one has ever suggested that they could not, for that reason, both be considered slavery. In fact, the "forces" really only seem to be there at all as a gesture to certain passages in Marx, such as his famous claim in *The Poverty of Philosophy* that "the hand-mill gives you society with the feudal lord; the steam-mill, society with the industrial capitalist" (1847: 91). So, in effect, the MoP was just a theory of the social relations through which surpluses were extracted. Second, it proved quite difficult to break out of Marxism's earlier, evolutionary, Eurocentric mold. Clearly, the division between slavery, feudalism, and capitalism was origi-nally designed to describe class relations in ancient, medieval, and modern Europe, respectively. It was never clear how to apply the approach to other parts of the world. Anthropologists found it especially difficult to figure out how to apply the model to stateless societies. While some coined phrases like the "lineage" or "domestic" mode of production, they never quite seemed to fit. Then there was the question of non-Western states. Marx's had ar-gued that empires like China or Mughal India were locked in a timeless "Asiatic" mode of production that lacked the internal dynamism of Western states; aside from being extremely condescending, the way he formulated the concept turned out to be hopelessly contradictory (Anderson 1974b).

Attempts to create alternatives, like the "African MoP" (Coquery-Vidrovitch 1978) never really caught on. Were all these states simply variations on feudalism, as so many Communist Parties insisted? Samir Amin (1973; 1985) tried to salvage the situation by proposing that pretty much all non-capitalist states be subsumed in a single, much broader category, which he called the "tributary mode of production." This, he suggested, would include any system in which the surplus was extracted through political-coercive means. Centralized states like Sung China or the Sassanian empire could be considered highly organized examples; feudalism, as practiced in Europe and perhaps Japan, one particularly disorganized variant. In *Europe and the People Without History* (1982), Eric Wolf took this further, proposing three broad MoPs: the kinship mode of production, which encompassed those stateless societies which were the traditional stomping-grounds of anthropologists; the tributary mode; and finally capitalism itself. But at this point the concepts had become so diffuse that it became impossible to think of a social formation as a complex mix of different modes of production, except insofar as each new stage incorporated the previous ones (i.e., under tributary states there was still kinship, and under capitalism, state apparatuses that made war and levied taxes).

Observation 2: The concept of the "mode of production" largely dissolved when removed from the framework of the state.

Back in 1974, when Perry Anderson sounded the death-knell of the "Asiatic mode," he called for work to create new concepts to describe states like India or China. One might have imagined this would have been answered by an outpouring of proposals for new modes of production. Instead, what happened was almost exactly the opposite. The list kept getting shorter. By the early 1980s, in Wolf, we were back to exactly the kind of three-part evolutionary sequence Althusser originally invented the concept in order to escape—the main difference being that "slavery" had been replaced by "kinship." How could this happen?

Wolf's book was the first major work of anthropology to try to come to grips with the kind of World-Systems analysis being developed by Immanuel Wallerstein and others at the time, and I don't think this is insignificant. One reason for the collapse of the MoP approach was that it was essentially a theory of the state. For all the fancy terminology, "social formations" just about always turned out to be kingdoms or empires of one sort or another. Hence the theory was thrown into a profound crisis when the World-Systems approach completely transformed the unit of analysis. At first this was not entirely clear, because the arguments were mainly about capitalism.

Proponents of the mode of production approach insisted that capitalism first emerged from the internal class dynamics of individual states, as wage-labor relations gradually became predominant, ultimately leading to a point where the bourgeoisie could seize control of the state apparatus (as in the English or French revolutions). Wallerstein argued it emerged in the form of a "capitalist world-economy," a broader system of market relations that created an overall division of labor between regions (differentiating a core, periphery and semi-periphery). According to the World-Systems approach, what went on within any particular "society"—for example, the rise of wage-labor—could only be explained with reference to that larger system.

In principle, this is true of all world-systems—called this not because they encompassed the entire globe, since only capitalism has done that, but because they were spheres of regional interaction that were, in effect, worlds unto themselves.

The holistic emphasis made it impossible to simply substitute "world-system" for "social formation" and still argue that any world-system contains a number of different modes of production, of which only one will be dominant. World-systems are assumed to be coherent wholes. As a result, "capitalism" or "feudalism" came to be seen as overall modes of organization for these new, larger units.

Wallerstein originally proposed three different sorts of world-system, in a formulation that looked suspiciously like yet another of those three-part evolutionary sequences: "mini-systems" (self-sufficient, egalitarian societies), "world-empires" (such as the Achaemenid or Chinese), and "world-systems" linked by trade (which prior to capitalism, tended to eventually transform into empires, then dissolve). In part, the categories were inspired by the Hungarian economist Karl Polanyi's distinction between three modes of distribution of wealth: reciprocity (typical of mini-systems), redistribution (typical of empires), and the market (typical of world-systems). Wallerstein was careful to note that all this was meant as a mere first approximation, to stand as a basis for research until better terms were found, so perhaps it's not right to make too much of these terms. But one thing stands out. Each was distinguished not by a form of production, but a form of distribution. And it was this larger organization of distribution which gave shape to everything else within each particular universe. This actually suggested a very daunting project of cultural comparison, since Wallerstein argued that almost all our familiar categories of analysis—class, state, household, and so on—are really only meaningful within the existing capitalist world-system, then presumably, entirely new terms would have to be invented to look at other ones. If so, then what did different world-systems have in common? What was the basis for comparison?

Subsequent divisions turn largely on this question. One school of World-Systems theorists—the "Comparativists," whose most prominent exponents are Chase-Dunn and Hall (1997)—have tried to refine the terms so as to be able to do so. First of all, they had to ditch the notion of mini-systems (basically "tribes"), by demonstrating that even in the case of extremely egalitarian societies like the Wintu of Southern California, there were always regional spheres of interaction, "very small world-systems" as they call them. These smaller systems though seemed to lack the cycles of growth and collapse typical of larger, more hierarchical systems like markets and empires. Larger world-systems, they proposed, tended to be made up of a complex series of overlapping networks. In the end, though, the overall organization of all these systems still ends up falling into Wolf's three categories: kinship, tributary, and capitalist (plus one hypothetical socialist one that does not yet exist, but might someday). The main difference with Wolf is that they tend to refer to these, not as "modes of production," but as "modes of accumulation," which they define as "the deep structural logic of production, distribution, exchange, and accumulation" (1997: 29). This seems a reasonable change in terminology from a world-systems perspective. But it lays bare just how far the term "mode of production" had drifted from its supposed original focus on people making things.

Once the terms of comparison have been made this broad, it's really just a short hop to arguing that we are not dealing with terms of comparison at all, but different functions that one would expect to find in any complex social order. This was the move taken by the "Continuationists." The prominent names here are Andre Gunder Frank and Barry Gills (Frank 1993, 1998; Frank & Gills 1993), Jonathan Friedman, and Kajsa Eckholm (Eckholm and Friedman 1982; Friedman 1982, 2000)—who argue that just as any complex society will still have families ("kinship"), they will also tend to have some sort of government, which means taxes ("tribute") and some sort of market system ("capitalism"). Having done so, it's easy enough to conclude that very project of comparison is pointless. In fact, there is only one world system. It began in the Middle East some five thousand years ago and fairly quickly came to dominate Afro-Eurasia. For the last couple thousand years, at least, its center of gravity has been China. According to Gunder Frank, this "World System" (note, no hyphens now) has seen broad but regular cycles of growth and expansion. This is the basis for his notoriously provocative claim that not only was Europe for a long time a barbarous periphery to the dominant world system—in itself actually a fairly uncontroversial observation by now—but that European dominance in recent centuries was really only the result of a successful campaign of import substitution during a time when the rest of the World System was in its periodic downswing, and that now that it's time for the boom end of the cycle to reassert itself, the dominance of "the West" may well prove a merely passing phase in a very long history (Frank 1998).

Observation 3: The main result of the eclipse of the mode of production concept has been a naturalization of capitalism. This becomes particularly evident when looking at the way "continuationists" treat wage-labor and slavery.

Friedman, Eckholm, and others now openly talk of a capitalist world system that has existed for five thousand years. Andre Gunder Frank (1991) would prefer to discard the term "capitalism" entirely, along with all other "modes of production," but what he describes comes down to pretty much the same thing. The idea that capitalism is as old as civilization is of course a position long since popular amongst capitalists. What now makes it palatable on the Left is largely that it can be seen as an attack on Eurocentrism: if capitalism is now to be considered an accomplishment, then it is deeply arrogant of Euro-American scholars to assume Europeans had invented it a mere five hundred years ago. Alternately, one might see this as a position appropriate for Marxist scholars working in an age when anarchism is rapidly replacing statist ideologies as the standard-bearer of revolutionary struggle: if capitalism appeared together with the state, it would be hard to imagine eliminating one without the other. The problem of course is that in doing so, most Marxist scholars have come to define capitalism so broadly—for example, as any form of economic organization where some important actors are using money to make more money—it is hard to imagine eliminating capitalism at all.

Neither does this position eliminate the privileged position of Europe—at least not if you really think about it. Even if the Continuationists argue that seventeenth and eighteenth centuries did not witness the birth of capitalism in Western Europe, and thus did not mark some great economic breakthrough, they are still arguing that it marked an equally momentous intellectual breakthrough, with Europeans like Adam Smith discovering the existence of economic laws that (we are now supposed to believe) had existed for thousands of years in Asia and Africa, but that no one there had previously been able to describe or even, really, notice.

This is actually a more important point than it may seem. The Continuationists find their great intellectual nemeses mid-century scholars like Moses Finley and Karl Polanyi, who had argued that authors in ancient and non-Western societies really did understand what was going on in their own societies, and that, if they did not speak of something that could be labeled "the economy," it was because nothing exactly parallel to capitalist economic institutions existed. Both come in for particular denunciation and abuse by the Continuationists: apparently, for that very reason.

Let me illustrate something of what's at stake here. Typically, definitions of capitalism focus on one of two features. Some, like exponents of the MoP approach, focus on wage-labor. The Continuationists, predictably, prefer the other, which looks for the existence of capital: that is, concentrations of wealth employed simply to create more wealth and, in particular, an open-ended process of endless reinvestment and expansion. If one chose the first, it would be hard to say capitalism has always existed, since for most of human history, it's rather difficult to find much evidence of wage-labor. This is not for lack of trying. Continuationists—like most economic historians, actually—tend to define "wages" as broadly as possible: essentially, as any money given anyone in exchange for services. If you spell it out, the formulation is obviously absurd: if so, kings are wage-laborers insofar as they claim to provide protection in exchange for tribute, and the Agha Khan is currently a wage-laborer in the employ of the Ismaili community, because every year they present him with his weight in gold or diamonds to reward him for his prayers on their behalf. Clearly, "wage-labor" (as opposed to, say, receiving fees for professional services) involves a degree of subordination: a laborer has to be to some degree at the command of his or her employer. This is exactly why, through most of history, free men and women tended to avoid wage-labor, and why, for most of history, capitalism according to the first definition never emerged.

As Moses Finley noted (1973), the ancient Mediterranean world was marked by a strong feeling of contradiction between political and commercial life. In Rome, most bankers were freed slaves; in Athens, almost all commercial and industrial pursuits were in the hands of non-citizens. The existence of a huge population of chattel slaves—in most ancient cities apparently at least a third of the total population—had a profound effect on labor arrangements. While one does periodically run into evidence of arrangements which to the modern eye look like wage-labor contracts, on closer examination they almost always actually turn out to be contracts to rent slaves (the slave, in such cases, often received a fixed per diem for food). Free men and women thus avoided anything remotely like wage-labor, seeing it as a matter, effectively, of slavery, of renting themselves out (Humphries 1978: 147, 297n37–38.) Working for the city itself was sometimes considered acceptable, since one was effectively in the employ of a community of which one was a member, but even this was normally kept to a temporary contract basis. In fifth-century Athens, permanent employees, even state employees such as police, were invariably slaves.

All this was hardly unique. Remarkably similar things have been docu-mented in, say, nineteenth-century Madagascar or Brazil, and similar insti-tutions often seem to develop in mercantile city states, such as the Swahili or Malay cities in the Indian Ocean. Reflection on the implications of the idea of renting persons might yield all sorts of insights. Similarly, one could consider how institutions that might look to us remarkably like wage-la-bor relations—in that one party worked and another compensated them in some way—might really have had a completely different basis: extended ties of patronage and dependency, for example, those complicated statuses that Finley (1964) described as hovering "between slave and free." But for the Continuationists, as for most economic historians, all this is brushed aside. Friedman for example accuses Polanyi, Finley, and their followers of being driven by "ideological" motivations in denying the importance of capital and markets in the ancient world. After all, what the actors *thought* they were doing is largely irrelevant. Capitalism is not a state of mind but a matter of objective structures, which allow wealth and power to be translated into abstract forms in which they can be endlessly expanded and reproduced. If one were to make an objective analysis, says Friedman, one would have to start from the fact that wage-laborers, even if they were of servile status, did exist, that they produced objects for sale on the market, and that the whole system evinced just the sort of boom-bust cycle we're used to seeing in con-temporary capitalism. He concludes "slavery in Classical Greece is a complex affair involving wage, interest and profit in an elaborate market system that appears to have had cyclical properties of expansion and contraction. This was, in other words, a form of capitalism that is not so different from the more obvious varieties in the modern world" (2000: 152).

For all the pretensions of objectivity, though, it's hard to see this choice as any less ideological than Finley's. After all, one can define "capitalism" as broadly or narrowly as one likes. It would be easy enough to play the same trick with terms like socialism, communism, or fascism, and define them so broadly one could discover them all over ancient Greece or Safavid Persia. Yet somehow no one ever does. Alternately, one could just as easily turn Friedman's own example around, define "capitalism" as necessarily a matter of free wage-labor, but define "slavery" in the broadest terms possible: say, as any form of labor in which one party is effectively coerced. One could thereby conclude that modern capitalism is really a form of slavery. One could then go on to argue that the fact that modern capitalists don't see themselves as coercing others is irrelevant, since we are talking about objec-tive constraining structures and not what the actors think is going on. Such an argument would not be entirely unprecedented: there's a reason why so many workers in modern capitalist countries have chosen to refer to themselves as "wage slaves." But no economic historian has ever, to my knowledge, even suggested such a thing. The ideological biases become clearest when one considers not just what's being argued, but the arguments it never occurs to anyone to make.

Thesis 1: The key mistake of the mode of production model was to define "production" simply as the production of material objects. Any adequate theory of "production" would have to give at least equal place to the production of people and social relations.

The ultimate weakness of MoP approaches, it seems to me, is that they set out from a very naïve sort of materialism. "Material production" is assumed to be the production of valuable material *objects* like food, clothing, or gold bullion; all the important business of life is assumed to be moving such objects around and transferring them from one person or class to another.

The approach is usually attributed to Marx—indeed, "historical materialism" of this sort is about the only aspect of Marx's thought scholars like Gunder Frank claim is really salvageable (e.g., Gills & Frank 1993: 106–109). Now, I really don't see the point of entering into some prolonged debate about whether this represents what Marx "really" meant when he talked about "materialism." Marx's work pulls in any number of different directions. But some are decidedly more interesting. Consider this passage from his ethnographic notebooks:

> Among the ancients we discover no single inquiry as to which form of landed property. etc., is the most productive, which creates maximum wealth. Wealth does not appear as the aim of production, although Cato may well investigate the most profitable cultivation of fields, or Brutus may even lend money at the most favorable rate of interest. The inquiry is always about what kind of property creates the best citizens. Wealth as an end in itself appears only among a few trading peoples—monopolists of the carrying trade—who live in the pores of the ancient world like the Jews in medieval society....
>
> Thus the ancient conception, in which man always appears (in however narrowly national, religious or political a definition) as the aim of production, seems very much more exalted than the modern world, in which production is the aim of man and wealth the aim of production. In fact, however, when the narrow bourgeois form has been peeled away, what is wealth, if not the universality of needs, capacities, enjoyments, productive powers, etc., of individuals, produced in universal exchange? (1854 [1965: 84])

What Marx says here of the ancient Greeks and Romans could, clearly, apply equally well to the BaKongo, or to the inhabitants of medieval Samarkand, or to pretty much any non-capitalist society. Always, the production of wealth was seen not as an end in itself, but as one subordinate moment in a larger process that ultimately aimed at the production of people. Neither does he suggest that this was just a subjective illusion that we have only now learned to see through now that we have developed the science of economics; rather, it is quite the other way around. The ancients had it right. In *The German Ideology*, Marx had already suggested that the production of objects is always simultaneously the production of people and social relations (as well as new needs: 1846 [1970]: 42). Here, he observes that the objects are not ultimately the point. Capitalism and "economic science" might confuse us into thinking that the ultimate goal of society is simply the increase of national GDP, the production of more and more wealth, but in reality wealth has no meaning except as a medium for the growth and self-realization of human beings.

The question then becomes: what would a "mode of production" be like if we started from this Marx, rather than, say, the Marx of the *Contribution to a Critique of Political Economy*? If non-capitalist modes of production are not ultimately about the production of wealth but of people—or, as Marx emphasizes, of certain specific kinds of people—then it's pretty clear that existing approaches have taken entirely the wrong track. Should we not be examining relations of service, domestic arrangements, educational practices, at least as much as the disposition of wheat harvests and the flow of trade?

I would go even further. What has passed for "materialism" in traditional Marxism—the division between material "infrastructure" and ideal "superstructure," is itself a perverse form of idealism. Granted, those who practice law, or music, or religion, or finance, or social theory, always do tend to claim that they are dealing with something higher and more abstract than those who plant onions, blow glass, or operate sewing machines. But it's not really true. The *actions* involved in the production of law, poetry, etc., are just as much material as any other. Once you acknowledge the simple dialectical point that what we take to be self-identical objects are really processes of action, then it becomes pretty obvious that such actions are (a) always motivated by meanings (ideas); and (b) always proceed through a concrete medium (material). Further, that while all systems of domination seem to propose that "no, this is not true, really there is some pure domain of law, or truth, or grace, or theory, or finance capital, that floats above it all," such claims are, to use an appropriately earthy metaphor, bullshit. As John Holloway (2003) has recently reminded us, it is in the nature of systems of domination to take what are really complex interwoven processes of action and chop them up and redefine them as discrete, self-identical objects—a song, a school, a meal, etc. There's a simple reason for it. It's only by chopping and freezing them in this way that one can reduce them to property and be able to say one owns them.

A genuine materialism then would not simply privilege a "material" sphere over an ideal one. It would begin by acknowledging that no such ideal sphere actually exists. This, in turn, would make it possible to stop focusing so obsessively on the production of material *objects*—discrete, self-identical things that one can own—and start the more difficult work of trying to understand the (equally material) processes by which people create and shape one another.

Thesis 2: If one applies Marx's analysis of value in *Capital* to the production of people and social relations, one can more easily see some of the mechanisms which obscure the most important forms of labor that exist in most societies. By obscuring the real stakes of human existence, which always have to do with human ends and human relations, these mechanisms are precisely what allow "scientific" observers to treat human beings as if they were mere automatons competing over abstractions like "wealth" or "power."

It might be easier to understand what I'm getting at here by considering the work of some anthropologists who have taken roughly the approach I'm endorsing.

I'm referring here to the tradition of what I'll call "anthropological value theory." Such theory was made possible first and foremost by the insights of feminist social science, which has made it impossible to simply ignore the endless labor of care, maintenance, education, and so on, which actually keeps societies running and which has tended to be carried out overwhelmingly by women. Recognizing such forms of action as productive labor, in the Marxian sense, made it easier to see how Marx's insights might be applied to many of the more egalitarian, stateless societies that the MoP approach finds so difficult to deal with. The real pioneer here is Terry Turner (1979, 1984, 1987), with his work on the Kayapo, though there are a number of others working along similar lines (e.g., Myers on the Pintupi [1986], Munn on Gawa [1986], Fajans on the Baining [1997], Sangren on rural Taiwan [1987, 2000], etc.). I have tried to systematize some of their insights myself in a book called *Toward An Anthropological Theory of Value* (Graeber 2001).

This approach does, indeed, take it for granted that while any society has to produce food, clothing, shelter, and so forth, in most societies, the production of such things as houses, manioc, and canoes is very much seen as a subordinate moment in larger productive processes aimed at the fashioning of humans. True, the former varieties of production tend to involve physical constraints that are very real and important to take into account. But that doesn't mean they are simply matters of technical activity. Anthropologists have demonstrated time and time again that even such apparently mundane activities as building or moving about in a house (Bourdieu 1979) or producing manioc flour (Hugh-Jones 1979) encode symbolic structures—hot/cold, dry/wet, heaven/earth, male/female—which tend to recur as well in complex rituals, forms of artistic expression, or conceptions of the nature of cosmos as a whole, but which are, ultimately, embedded in those very structures of action themselves. In other words, we are never dealing with pure, abstract ideas, any more than we are ever dealing with purely mechanical production. Rather, the very idea that either pure ideas or mindless material action exist is an ideology whose operations need to be investigated.

The latter is an important point because many such societies do make this sort of ideal/material distinction, even if it rarely takes exactly the form we are used to. This seems directly related to the fact that, just about invariably, some form of exploitation does occur in such societies; and where it does, much as in capitalism, the mechanisms of exploitation tend to be made subtly invisible.

In Marx's account of capitalism, this happens mainly through the mechanism of wage-labor. Money is in fact a representation of abstract labor—the worker's capacity to produce, which is what his employer buys when he hires him. It is a kind of symbol. In the form of a wage, it becomes a very powerful sort of symbol: a representation which in fact plays a crucial role in bringing into being what it represents—since, after all, laborers are only working in order to get paid. It's also in precisely this transaction that the actual sleight-of-hand on which exploitation is based takes place, since Marx argues that what the capitalist ends up paying for is simply the cost of abstract labor (the cost of reproducing the worker's capacity to work), which is always going to be less than the value of what the worker can actually produce.

The point Turner makes is that even where there is no single market in labor—as there has not been in most societies in human history—something similar tends to happen. Different kinds of labor still tend to get reflected back in the form of a concrete, material medium which, like money, is both a representation of the importance of our own actions to ourselves, and simultaneously seen as valuable in itself, and which thus ends up becoming the actual end for which action takes place. Tokens of honor inspire honorable behavior. Really, their value is just that of the actions they represent, but the actors see them as valuable in themselves. Similarly, tokens of piety inspire religious devotion, tokens of wisdom inspire learning, and so on. Actually, it's quite the same in our own society: it's precisely in those domains of activity where labor is not commodified where we talk not of abstract "value" but concrete "values": i.e., housework and childcare become matters of "family values"; work for the church, a matter of religious values; political activism is inspired by the values of idealism; and so on. In either case, certain basic principles seem to apply:

1) value is the way actors represent the importance of their own actions to themselves as part of some larger whole (or "concrete totality," as Marx liked to put it);

2) this importance is always seen in comparative terms: some forms of value are considered equivalent because they are unique, but normally there are systems of ranking or measurement;

3) values are always realized through some kind of material token, and generally, in someplace other than the place it is primarily produced. In non-capitalist societies, this most often involves a distinction between a domestic sphere, in which most of the primary work of people-creation takes place, and some kind of public, political sphere, in which it is realized, but usually in ways which exclude the women and younger people who do the bulk of the work and allow tokens of value to be realized.

The Kayapo of central Brazil organized their communities as circles, with a ring of households surrounding a public, political space in the center. Forms of value produced largely in the domestic units through the work of producing and socializing people comes to be realized through certain forms of public performance (chanting, oratory, keening). These can be performed only by elders, who are themselves only "elders" because they are the peak of a domestic process of creating and socializing children that takes place just offstage.

This emphasizes that this process of realization of value almost always involves some form of public recognition, but this is not to say that people are simply battling over "prestige." Instead, the range of people who are willing to recognize certain forms of value constitutes the extent of what an actor considers "society," in any meaningful sense of the term, to consist of (Graeber 2001).

What I especially want to stress here, though, is that, when value is about the production of people, it is always entirely implicated in processes of transformation: families are created, grow, and break apart; people are born, mature, reproduce, grow old, and die. They are constantly being socialized, trained, educated, mentored towards new roles (a process which is not limited to childhood, but lasts until death). They are constantly being attended to and cared for. This is what human life is mainly about, what most people have always spent most of their time worrying about, what our passions, obsessions, loves, and intrigues tend to center on, what great novelists and playwrights become famous for describing, what poetry and myth struggle to come to terms with, but which most economic and political theory essentially makes to disappear.

Why? It seems to happen, at least in part, because of the very mechanics of value realization. Value tends to be realized in a more public—or anyway political and, hence, universalized—domain than the domestic one in which it is (largely) created. That sphere is usually treated as if it is to some degree transcendent, that is, as floating above and unaffected by the mundane details of human life (the special domain of women), having to do with timeless verities, eternal principles, absolute power—in a word, of something very like idealist abstractions. Most anthropological value analyses end up tracing out something of the sort: so Kayapo value tokens end up embodying the abstract value of "beauty," a profound higher unity and completion especially embodied in perfect performances and communal ritual (Turner 1987 etc.); people practicing kula exchange seek "fame" (Munn 1986); Berbers of the Morroccan Rif, with their complex exchanges of gifts and blood-feud, pursue the values of honor and *baraka*, or divine grace (Jamous 1981), and so on. All of these are principles which, even when they are not identified with superhuman powers like gods or ancestors, even when they are not seen as literally transcendental principles, are seen as standing above and symbolically opposed to the messiness of ordinary human life and transformation. The same is usually true of the most valued objects, whose power to enchant and attract usually comes from the fact that they represent frozen processes. If one conducts a sufficiently subtle analysis, one tends to discover that the objects that are the ultimate stakes of some field of human endeavor are, in fact, symbolic templates which compress into themselves those patterns of human action which create them.

It seems to me that even beyond the labor that is constantly creating and reshaping human beings, a key unacknowledged form of labor in human societies is precisely that which creates and maintains that illusion of transcendence. In most, both are performed overwhelmingly by women. A nice way to illustrate what I'm talking about here might be to consider the phenomenon of mourning. Rarely do the political careers of important individuals end in death. Often political figure, as ancestors, martyrs, founders of institutions, can be far more important after their death than when they were alive. Mourning, and other acts of memorialization, could then be seen as an essential part of the labor of people-making—with the fact that the dead person is no longer himself playing an active role simply underlining how much of the work of making and maintaining a career is always done by others. Even the most cursory glance at the literature shows that the burden of such labor, here, tends to be very unevenly distributed. This is especially true of the most dramatic forms—cutting off one's hair, self-mutilation, fasting, wearing drab clothes, sackcloth and ashes, or whatever is considered the culturally appropriate way to make oneself an embodiment of grief—to, essentially, negate oneself to express anguish over the loss of another. Social subordinates mourn their superiors and not the other way around. And pretty much everywhere, the burden of mourning falls disproportionately, and usually overwhelmingly, on women. In many parts of the world, women of a certain age are expected to exist largely as living memorials to some dead male: whether it be Hindu widows who must renounce all the tastiest foods, or Catholic women in the rural Mediterranean who are likely to spend at least half their lives wearing black. Needless to say these women almost never receive the same recognition when they die, and least of all from men.

The point though is that symbolic distinctions between high and low do not come from some pre-existing "symbolic system," they are continually constructed in action, and the work of doing so is done disproportionably by those who are effectively defining themselves as lower. So with mourning. As Bloch and Parry (1982) have emphasized, mourning is also about creating dramatic contrasts between what is considered truly permanent, and everything that is corporeal, transitory, afflicted with the possibility of grief and pain, subject to corruption and decay. Mourners when they cover themselves in dirt or ashes, or engage in other practices of self-negation that seem surprisingly similar across cultures, are also making themselves the embodiment of the transitory, bodily sphere as against another, transcendental one which is, in fact, created in large part through their doing so. The dead themselves have become spirits, ethereal beings or bodiless abstractions. Or perhaps they are embodied in permanent monuments like tombs or beautiful heirlooms, or buildings left in their memory (usually, in fact, it's a bit of both), but it's the actions of the mourners, mainly by the dramatic negation of their own bodies and pleasures, that constantly recreate that extremely hierarchical contrast between pure and impure, higher and lower, heaven and earth.

It is sometimes said that the central notion of modernism is that human beings are projects of self-creation. What I am arguing here is that we are indeed processes of creation, but that most of the creation is normally carried out by others. I am also arguing that almost all the most intense desires, passions, commitments, and experiences in most people's lives—family dramas, sexual intrigue, educational accomplishment, honor and public recognition, one's hopes for one's children and grandchildren, one's dreams of posterity after one is dead—have revolved precisely around these processes of the mutual creation of human beings, but that the mechanics of value-creation tend to disguise this by positing some higher sphere, of economic values, or idealist abstractions. This is essential to the nature of hierarchy (Graeber 1997) and the more hierarchical the society, the more this tends to happen. Finally, I am suggesting that it is precisely these mechanisms that make it possible for historians and social scientists to create such odd simplifications of human life and human motivations. The labor of creating and maintaining people and social relations (and people are, in large measure, simply the internalized accretion of their relations with others) ends up being relegated, at least tacitly, to the domain of nature—it becomes a matter of demographics or "reproduction"—and the creation of valuable physical objects becomes the be-all and end-all of human existence.

Thesis 3: One of the great insights of World-Systems analysis is to show how very simple forms of social relation most typical of long-distance relations between people who do not know much about each other are continually introjected within those societies to simplify social relations that need not be that way.

Unfortunately, this thesis can't really be adequately explained, let alone defended, in the space available, so let me just summarize it.

Marx was already noting in the passage cited above that commercial relations, in which wealth was the main aim of human activity, appear "in the pores of the ancient world," among those who carry out the trade *between* societies. This is an insight developed in world-systems analysis, where capitalism is often seen as developing first in long-distance trading and then gradually worming its way into ever-more-intimate aspects of communities' daily life. I would suggest we are dealing here with a much more general principle. One could name a whole series of highly schematic, simplified forms of action, that might be inevitable in dealings between people who don't understand each other very well, that become introjected in a similar way. The first is probably violence. Violence is veritably unique among forms of action because it is pretty much the only way one can have relatively predictable effects on others' actions without understanding anything about them. Any other way one might wish to influence others requires that one has to at least know or figure out who they think they are, what they want or find objectionable, etc. Hit them over the head hard enough and all this becomes irrelevant. Hence, it is common to relations between societies, even those not marked by elaborate internal structural violence. However, the existence of structural violence—social hierarchies backed up by a systematic threat of force—almost invariably creates forms of ignorance internally: it is no longer necessary to carry out this sort of interpretive work and, generally speaking, those on the top know remarkably little about what those on the bottom think is going on. Here, again, gender relations are probably the most revealing example: with remarkable consistency, across a very wide range of societies, men tend to know almost nothing about women's lives, work, or perspectives, while women tend to know a great deal about men's—in fact, they are expected to, since a large share of that interpretive labor (if one may call it that) always seems to fall to women, which in turn helps explain why it is not generally considered "labor" at all. And the same tends to apply to relations of caste, class, and other forms of social inequality.

Market exchange is another case in point. It's enough to take a glance at the rich anthropological literature on "gift exchange," or even consider the way objects move within families or circles of friends, to realize how incredibly stripped-down and simplified is a standard commodity transaction in comparison. One need know almost nothing about the other party; all one needs to know is a single thing they want to acquire: gold, or fish, or calicoes. Hence, the popularity, in early Greek or Arab travelers' accounts, of the idea of the "the silent trade": in theory, it sould be possible to engage in commercial exchange with people about whom one knew nothing at all, who one had never even met, by alternately leaving goods on a beach. The point is again that commercial relations were in many societies typical of relations with foreigners, since it required minimal interpretive work. In dealing with those one knew better, other, more complex forms of exchange usually applied; however, here too, the introjection of commercial relations into dealings with one's neighbors made it possible to treat them, effectively, like foreigners. Marx's analysis of capitalism actually gives a central role to this phenomenon: it is a peculiar effect of the market to erase the memory of previous transactions and create, effectively a veil of ignorance between sellers and buyers, producers and consumers. Those who purchase a commodity usually have no idea who made it and under what conditions it was made. This is of course what results in "commodity fetishism."

Thesis 4: If one reinterprets a "mode of production" to mean a relation between surplus extraction and the creation of human beings, then it is possible to see industrial capitalism as an introjected form of the slave mode of production, with a structurally analogous relation between workplace and domestic sphere.

If the notion of "mode of production" can be salvaged, it has to be seen not merely as a structure for the extraction of some kind of material surplus between classes, but as the way in which such a structure articulates with structures for the creation of people and social relations.

We might start here with the capitalist mode of production, since this was always the case from which the others were extrapolated. As I've mentioned, definitions of capitalism tend to start either from exchange or production. In the first case, one tends see to what makes capitalism unique as lying in the unlimited need for growth: where most systems of market exchange involve actors trying to get what they feel they want or need, capitalism occurs when profit becomes an end in itself, and "capital" becomes like a living entity, which constantly seeks to expand. Indeed, capitalist firms cannot remain competitive unless they are continually expanding. In the second, the emphasis is on wage-labor: capitalism occurs when a significant number of firms are owned or managed by people who hire others to do their bidding in exchange for a direct payment of money, but otherwise have no stake in the enterprise. In the industrial capitalism described by Marx, the two appear together, and are assumed to be connected. I would propose a third. The industrial revolution also introduced the first form of economic organization to make a systematic distinction between homes and workplaces, between domestic and economic spheres. This is what made it possible to begin talking about "the economy" in the first place: the production of people, and of commodities, were to take place in different spaces by entirely different logics. This split plays a central role in Marx's analysis as well. For one thing, the market's veil of ignorance falls precisely between the two. All this was in dramatic contrast to what had existed previously in most of Europe, where very complex systems of "life-cycle service" (Hajnal 1965, 1982; Laslett 1972, Wall 1983) ensured the majority of young people spent years as apprentices or servants in the households of their social superiors. Once one recognizes this, the similarities with slavery become much easier to see.

I should explain here that the conventional Marxian interpretation of slavery as a mode of production is that slavery makes it possible for one society to effectively steal the productive labor that another society has invested in producing human beings (Meillassoux 1975, 1979, 1991; Terray 1975, Lovejoy 2000). That's why slaves always have to come from someplace else (it is only under extraordinary conditions, such as the Southern cotton boom created by the British industrial revolution, that it is economically viable to breed slaves, and even there it was not really sustainable). Human beings, after all, are largely useless as laborers for the first ten or fifteen years of their existence. A slave-owning society is effectively appropriating the years of care and nurture that some other society has invested in creating young men and women capable of work, by kidnapping the products—and then, often as not, working them fairly rapidly to death.

In a way, then, one could say that slavery too involves a separation of domestic sphere and workplace—except in this case, the separation is geographic. Human labor produced in Anatolia is realized in a plantation in Italy; human labor produced in what's now Gabon is realized in Brazil or Jamaica. In this sense, capitalism could be seen as yet another case of introjection. This might seem far-fetched, but in fact the structural similarities are quite striking.

In most times and places, the institution of slavery is seen to derive from war. If the victor in war spares the life of a captive, he thereby acquires an absolute right to it. The result is often described as a "social death" (e.g., Patterson 1982): the new slaves are spared literal execution, but henceforth, they are also shorn of all previous status within their former communities, they have no right to social relations, kinship, citizenship, or any social relation other than their relation of dependence to a master who thus has the right to order them to do pretty much anything he wants. Now, there have been cases where this is all there is to it, but in the overwhelming majority of known historical cases, this process is mediated by the market. Normally, one is first captured, kidnapped, or perhaps reduced to slavery by judicial decision; and then one is sold to foreigners; or perhaps one's impoverished or debt-ridden parents sell one off directly, but at any rate, money changes hand. Afterwards, slaves remain marketable commodities that can be sold again and again. Once purchased, they are entirely at the orders of their employers. In this sense, as historian Yann Moulier-Boutang (1998) has recently pointed out, they represent precisely what Marx called "abstract labor": what one buys when one buys a slave is the sheer capacity to work, which is also what an employer acquires when he hires a laborer. It's of course this relation of command which causes free people in most societies to see wage-labor as analogous to slavery, and hence, to try as much as possible to avoid it.

We can observe the following traits shared by slavery and capitalism:

1) Both rely on a *separation of the place of social (re)production of the labor force, and the place where that labor-power is realized in production.* In the case of slavery, this is effected by transporting laborers bought or stolen from one society into another one; in capitalism, by separating the domestic sphere (the sphere of social production) from the workplace. In other words, what is effected by physical distance, in one, is effected by the anonymity of the market in the other.

2) The transfer is effected through *exchanging human powers for money*: either by selling workers, or hiring them (essentially, allowing them to rent themselves).

3) One effect of that transfer is "*social death*," in the sense that the community ties, kinship relations, and so forth which shaped that worker are, in principle, supposed to have no relevance in the workplace. This is true in capitalism too, at least in principle: a worker's ethnic identity, social networks, kin ties, and the rest should not have any effect on hiring or how one is treated in the office or shop floor, though of course in reality this isn't true.

4) Most critically, the financial transaction in both cases produces *abstract labor*, which is pure creative potential. This is created by the effects of command. Abstract labor is the sheer power of creation, to do anything at all. Everyone might be said to control abstract labor in their own person, but in order to extend it further, one has to place others in a position where they will be effectively an extension of one's will, to be completely at one's orders. Slavery, military service, and various forms of corvée, are the main forms in which this has manifested itself historically. Obviously, this too is something of an unrealized ideal: the struggle against overbearing forms of control has always been one of the key areas of labor struggle. But it's worth noting that feudalism (or manorialism if you prefer) tends towards exactly the opposite principle: the duties owed by liege to lord tended to be very specific and intricately mapped out.

5) A constant ideological accompaniment of this sort of arrangement is an *ideology of freedom*. As Moses Finley first pointed (1980), most societies take it for granted that no human is completely free or completely dependent. Rather, all have different degrees of rights and obligations. The modern ideal of political liberty, in fact, has historically tended to emerge from societies with extreme forms of chattel slavery (Pericles' Athens, Jefferson's Virginia), essentially, as a point of contrast. Medieval jurists, for example, assumed every right was someone else's obligation and vice versa. The modern doctrine of liberty as a property humans could possess was developed, significantly, in Lisbon and Antwerp, cities that were at the center of the slave trade at the time; and the most common objection to this new notion of liberty was that, if one owns one's freedom, it should then also be possible to sell it (Tuck 1979). Hence, the doctrine of personal liberty—*outside of the workplace*—or even the notion of freedom of contract that one so often encounters in societies dominated by wage-labor does not really mean we are dealing with a fundamentally different sort of system. It means we are dealing

with a transformation. We are dealing with the same terms, differently arranged: so that rather than one class of people being able to imagine themselves as absolutely "free" because others are absolutely unfree, we have the same individuals moving back and forth between these two positions over the course of the week and working day.

So, in effect, a transfer effected just once, by sale, under a regime of slavery is transformed under capitalism into one repeated over and over again.

Now, it might seem a bit impertinent to compare the morning commute to the Middle Passage, but structurally, they do seem to play exactly the same role. What is accomplished once, violently and catastrophically, in one variant, is repeated with endless mind-numbing drudgery in the other.

I should emphasize that when I say one mode of production is a transformation of the other, I am talking about the permutation of logical terms. It doesn't necessarily imply one grew out of the other, or even that there was any historical connection at all. I am not, for example, necessarily taking issue with the historical argument that capitalism first emerged within the English agricultural sector in the sixteenth and seventeenth centuries, rather than from long-distance trade (Dobb 1947; Brenner 1976, 1979; Wood 2002). Or, perhaps I should be more specific. It seems to me that the "Brenner hypothesis," as it's called, can account for the first two of the three features that define industrial capitalism as a mode of production: it demonstrates that the emergence of wage-labor in the agricultural sector developed hand in hand with structural forces that demanded ever-expanding profits. However, it doesn't explain the third: the emerging rural proletariat were, in legal principle and usually in practice, servants resident in their employers' households (see, e.g., Kussmaul 1981). Note, too, this same age of "merchant capitalism" *did* see a sudden and spectacular revival of the institution of chattel slavery, and other forms of forced labor, which had largely vanished in Europe during the late Middle Ages—even though these were legally confined to the colonies. As C.L.R. James argued long ago, rationalized industrial techniques were largely developed on slave plantations, and much of the wealth which funded the industrial revolution emerged from the slave trade and even more from industries with servile work forces (James 1938, Williams 1944, Blaut 1993: 203–205). This makes sense. Wage-labor relations might have emerged among "improving" landlords during that first period, but the wealthy traders of the time were after "abstract labor" in the easiest form possible. They wanted workers who would do anything they told them to do, so their first impulse was to use slaves. Full, industrial capitalism might then to be said to have emerged only when the two fused. One might speculate that one reason large-scale merchants eventually came to apply wage-labor at home, even within the industrial sector, was not because slavery or other forms of forced labor proved inefficient as a form of production, but rather, because it did not create efficient markets for consumption: one cannot sell much of anything to slaves; and, at least at that time, it was difficult to keep one's population of producers and consumers on entirely different continents.

None of this, perhaps, explains the exact connection between wage-labor, separation of household and workplace, or the capitalist's need for unlimited growth. But the theoretical terms I've been developing might suggest some directions. The main difference between European firms of this period and commercial enterprises in the Islamic world, or East Asia, seems to have been that they were not for the most part family firms. Especially with the development of the corporate form—the idea that capitalist enterprises were immortal persons free of the need to be born, marry, or die—the economic domain was effectively excised from the domain of transformation and the mutual shaping of human beings and came to be seen as something transcendent. It was an uneven path (the nineteenth century, for example, after the dissolution of the great East Indies Companies, seems like something of an anomaly in this regard), but it is a direction well worth further investigation. This might suggest:

Thesis 5: Capitalism's unlimited demand for growth and profit is related to the transcendent abstraction of the corporate form. In any society, the dominant forms are considered transcendent from reality in much the way value forms tend to be and, when these transcendent forms encounter "material" reality, their demands are absolute.

This one, though, I will have to leave as a possible direction for future research.

Bibliography

Abu-Lughod, Janet
1989   *Before European Hegemony: The World System AD 1250–1350.* New York: Oxford University Press.

Amin, Samir
1988   *L'Eurocentrisme. Critique d'une idéologie.* Paris: Anthropos.
1991   "The Ancient World-Systems Versus the Modern Capitalist World-System." *Review* 14: 3 (Summer): 349–385.

Anderson, Perry
1974a   *Passages from Antiquity to Feudalism.* New York: Verso Press.

1974b *Lineages of the Absolutist State*. New York: Verso Press.

Barraud, Cecile, Daniel de Coppet, André Iteanu, and Raymond Jamous
1994 *Of Relations and the Dead: Four Societies Viewed from the Angle of Their Exchanges*. (Stephen J. Suffern, trans.). Oxford: Berg Press.

Battaglia, Debbora
1983 "Projecting Personhood in Melanesia: the Dialectics of Artefact Symbolism on Sabarl Island." *Man* n.s. 18: 289–304.
1990 *On the Bones of the Serpent: Person, Memory and Mortality in Sabarl Island Society*. Chicago: University of Chicago Press.

Blaut, James
1993 *The Colonizer's Model of the World: Geographical Diffusion and Eurocentric History*. New York: Guilford.

Bloch, Marc
1961 *Feudal Society*. 2 vols. Cambridge University Press, Cambridge.

Bloch, Maurice
1982 "Death, Women and Power." In *Death and the Regeneration of Life* (M. Bloch and J. Parry, eds.). Cambridge: Cambridge University Press.

Bourdieu, Pierre
1979 *Outline of a Theory of Practice* (Richard Nice, trans.). Cambridge: Cambridge University Press.

Brenner, Robert
1976 "Agrarian Economic Development and Pre-Capitalist Class Structure in Pre-Industrial Europe." *Past and Present* 70: 30–75.
1982 "The Agrarian Roots of Modern Capitalism." *Past and Present* 97: 16–113.

Caillé, Alain
1984 "Deux mythes modernes: la rareté et la rationalité économiques." *Bulletin du MAUSS* 12: 9–37.
1989 *Critique de la raison utilitaire: Manifeste du MAUSS*. Paris: Editions la Découverte/MAUSS.
1994 *Don, intérêt et désintéressement: Bourdieu, Mauss, Platon et quelques autres*. Paris: Editions la Découverte/MAUSS.

Chase-Dunn, Christopher, and Thomas D. Hall
1997 *Rise and Demise: Comparing World-Systems*. Boulder: Westview Press.

Chaudhuri, K.
1985 *Trade and Civilization in the Indian Ocean: an Economic History from the Rise of Islam to 1750*. Cambridge: Cambridge University Press.
1990 *Asia Before Europe: Economy and Civilization in the Indian Ocean from the Rise of Islam to 1750*. Cambridge: Cambridge University Press.

Coquery-Vidrovitch, C.
1978 "Research on an African Mode of Production." In *Relations of Production* (D. Seddon, ed.). London: Frank Cass.

Dobb, Maurice
1947 *Studies in the Development of Capitalism*. London: International Publishers.

Duby, Georges
1982 *Rural Economy and the Country Life in the Medieval West*. Routledge and Kegan Paul, New York.

Ekholm, Kajsa, and Jonathan Friedman
1982   "'Capital' Imperialism and Exploitation in Ancient World-Systems." *Review* 4: 87–109.

Fajans, Jane
1997   *They Make Themselves: Work and Play among the Baining of Papua New Guinea.* Chicago: University of Chicago Press.

Finley, Moses
1960a "The Servile Statuses of Ancient Greece," *Revue International des droits de l'antiquité*, 7: 165–89.
1960b *Slavery in Classical Antiquity.* Cambridge: Heffer.
1964   "Between Slavery and Freedom." *Comparative Studies in Society and History*, 6: 233–49.
1973   *The Ancient Economy.* Cambridge: Cambridge University Press.

Fortunati, Leopoldini
1995   *The Arcana of Reproduction: Housework, Prostitution, Labor and Capital.* (Hillary Creek, trans.) New York: Autonomedia [1981].

Frank, Andre Gunder
1991   "Transitional Ideological Modes: Feudalism, Capitalism, Socialism." *Critique of Anthropology* 11: 171–188.
1993   "Bronze Age World Systems Cycles." *Current Anthropology* 34: 383–429.
1998   *ReOrient: The Silver Age in Asia and the World Economy.* Berkeley: University of California Press.

Frank, Andre Gunder and Barry K. Gills
1993   *The World System: Five Hundred Years or Five Thousand?* London: Routledge.

Friedman, Jonathan
2000   "Concretizing the continuity argument in global systems analysis." In *World System History: The Social Science of Long-Term Change* (Robert A. Denemark, Jonathan Friedman, Barry K. Gills, George Modelski, eds.). London: Routledge.

Godbout, Jacques T., and Alain Caillé
1998   *The World of the Gift.* Montréal: McGill-Queen's University Press.

Godelier, Maurice
1977   *Perspectives in Marxist Anthropology.* New York: Cambridge University Press.
1978   "'Salt Money' and the Circulation of Commodities among the Baruya of New Guinea." In *Perspectives in Marxist Anthropology* (M. Godelier, ed.). Cambridge: Cambridge University Press.
1986   *The Making of Great Men: Male Domination and Power among the New Guinea Baruya.* Cambridge: Cambridge University Press.

Goody, Jack
1996   *The East in the West.* Cambridge: Cambridge University Press.

Graeber, David
1995   "Dancing with Corpses Reconsidered: An Interpretation of Famadihana (in Arivonimamo, Madagascar)." *American Ethnologist* 22: 258–278.
1997   "Manners, Deference and Private Property: The Generalization of Avoidance in Early Modern Europe." *Comparative Studies in Society and History* 39(4): 694–728.
2001   *Toward an Anthropological Theory of Value: The False Coin of Our Own Dreams.* New York: Palgrave.

Hajnal, John
1965 "European Marriage Patterns in Perspective." In *Population in History*. (D.V. Glass and D.E.C. Eversley, eds.). Chicago: Aldine.
1982 "Two Kinds of Preindustrial Household Formation System." *Population and Development Review* 8: 3 (September): 449–94.

Herlihy, David
1960 "The Carolingian Mansus" *Economic History Review* vol. 13.
1985 *Medieval Households*. Harvard University Press, Cambridge.

Holloway, John
2003 *Change the World Without Taking Power: The Meaning of Revolution Today*. London: Pluto Press.

Humphries, Susan C.
1978 *Anthropology and the Greeks*. London: Routledge and Kegan Paul.

James, C. L. R.
1938 *The Black Jacobins: Toussaint L'Ouverture and the San Domingo Revolution*. London: Secker and Warburg.

Jamous, Raymond
1981 *Honneur et Baraka: les structures sociales traditionelles dans le Rif*. Paris: Atelier d'Anthropologie Sociale, Maison des Sciences de l'Homme.

Kussmaul, Ann
1981 *Servants in Husbandry in Early Modern England*. Cambridge: Camridge University Press.

Laslett, Peter
1972 "Characteristics of the Western Family Considered over Time." In *Household and Family in Past Time* (Laslett and Wall, eds.). Cambridge: Cambridge University Press.

Lovejoy, Paul E.
2000 *Transformations in Slavery: A History of Slavery in Africa*. 2nd edition. Cambridge: Cambridge University Press.

Marx, Karl
1846 *The German Ideology*. New York: International Publishers (1970).
1858 *The Grundrisse*. New York: Harper and Row (1973).
1858 *Pre-Capitalist Economic Formations* (Jack Cohen, trans.). New York: International Publishers (1964).
1859 *Contribution to the Critique of Political Economy*. New York: International Publishers (1970).
1867 *Capital*. 3 volumes. New York: New World Paperbacks (1967).

Meillassoux, Claude
1975 *L'esclavage en Afrique precoloniale*. Paris: Maspero.
1979 "Historical Modalities of the Exploitation and Over-Exploitation of Labor." *Critique of Anthropology* 4: 7–16.
1981 *Maidens, Meal and Money: Capitalism and Domestic Community*. Cambridge: Cambridge University Press.

Moulier-Boutang, Yann
1998 *De l'esclavage au salariat: économie historique du salariat bridé*. Paris: Presses Universitaires de France.

Munn, Nancy
1986   *The Fame of Gawa: A Symbolic Study of Value Transformation in a Massim (Papua New Guinea) Society*. Cambridge: Cambridge University Press.

Myers, Fred
1986   *Pintupi Country, Pintupi Self.* Washington: Smithsonian Press.

Patterson, Orlando
1982   *Slavery and Social Death: A Comparative Study*. Cambridge, MA: Harvard University Press.

Polanyi, Karl
1944   *The Great Transformation*. New York: Rinehart.
1957   "The Economy as an Instituted Process." In *Trade and Market in the Early Empires* (K. Polanyi, C. Arensberg and H. Pearson eds.). Glencoe: The Free Press.
1968   *Primitive, Archaic, and Modern Economies: Essays of Karl Polanyi* (George Dalton, ed.). New York: Anchor.

Pommeranz, Kenneth
2000   *The Great Divergence: China, Europe, and the Making of the Modern World Economy*. Princeton: Princeton University Press.

Sahlins, Marshall
1972   *Stone Age Economics*. Chicago: Aldine.
2001   *Culture in Practice: Selected Essays*. New York: Zone Books.

Sangren, P. Steven
1987   *History and Magical Power in a Chinese Community*. Stanford: Stanford University Press.
2000   *Chinese Sociologics: An Anthropological Approach to the Study of Alienation in Social Reproduction*. London: Athlone Press.

Sherratt, Andrew
2000   "Envisioning Global Change: A Long-Term Perspective." In *World System History: The Social Science of Long-Term Change* (Robert A. Denemark, Jonathan Friedman, Barry K. Gills, George Modelski, eds.). London: Routledge.

Terray, Emmanuel
1969   *Le Marxism devant les sociétés "primitives."* Paris: Maspero.

Tibebu, Tashame
1990   "On the Question of Feudalism, Absolutism, and the Bourgeois Revolution." *Review* 13: 49–152.

Tuck, Richard
1970   *Natural Rights Theories: Their Origin and Development*. Cambridge: Cambridge University Press.

Turner, Terence
1979c "Anthropology and the Politics of Indigenous Peoples' Struggles." *Cambridge Anthropology* 5: 1–43.
1984   "Value, Production and Exploitation in Non-Capitalist societies." Unpublished essay based on a paper presented at the AAA 82nd Annual Meeting, Denver, Colorado. To appear in *Critique of Pure Culture*. New York: Berg Press [forthcoming].
1987   *The Kayapo of Southeastern Para*. Unpublished monograph prepared for CEDI, Povos Indigenas do Brasil, Vol. VIII, Sul do Para, Part II.

1993   "The Poetics of Play: Ritual Clowning, Masking and Performative Mimesis among the Kayapo." Unpublished essay. To appear in Bruce Kapferer and Peter Koepping, eds. *The Ludic: Forces of Generation and Fracture*. Oxford: Berg Press.
1995   "Social body and embodied subject: the production of bodies, actors and society among the Kayapo." *Cultural Anthropology* 10: 2.

Turner, Terence and Jane Fajans
1988   "Where the Action Is: An Anthropological Perspective on 'Activity Theory,' with Ethnographic Implications." Unpublished manuscript, University of Chicago.

Wall, Richard
1972   "Mean Household Size in England from Printed Sources." In *Household and Family in Past Time* (Peter Laslett, ed.). Cambridge: Cambridge University Press.
1983   *Family Forms in Historic Europe*. Cambridge University Press, Cambridge.

Wallerstein, Immanuel
2000   *The Essential Wallerstein*. New York: The New Press.

Warburton, David
2000   "State and Economy in Ancient Egypt." In *World System History: The Social Science of Long-Term Change* (Robert A. Denemark, Jonathan Friedman, Barry K. Gills, George Modelski, eds.). London: Routledge.

Weber, Max
1930   *The Protestant Ethic and the Spirit of Capitalism*. London: Unwin.

Wiedemann, Thomas
1981   *Greek and Roman Slavery*. London: Routledge.

Williams, Eric
1944   *Capitalism and Slavery*. Chapel Hill: University of North Carolina Press.

Wolf, Eric
1982   *Europe and the People without History*. Berkeley: University of California Press.
1999   *Envisioning Power: Ideologies of Dominance and Crisis*. Berkeley: University of California Press.

Wood, Ellen Meiskins
2002   *The Origin of Capitalism: A Larger View*. London: Verso.

4

FETISHISM AS SOCIAL CREATIVITY: OR, FETISHES ARE GODS IN THE PROCESS OF CONSTRUCTION

In this paper, I would like to make a contribution to theories of social creativity. By social creativity, I mean the creation of new social forms and institutional arrangements. Creativity of this sort has been the topic of some discussion in social theory of late, although up to now anthropology has not played much of a role in it. Here, I would like to bring anthropology into an area that has traditionally been seen as its home turf: by looking at the literature on "fetishism" in Africa.

Now one could argue that creativity of this sort has always been one of the great issues of social theory, but it seems to me the current interest can be traced to two impulses. Or perhaps more precisely, the desire to work one's way out of two ongoing dilemmas that have haunted social theory for some time. One, mapped out most clearly, perhaps, by Alain Caillé (2001), French sociologist and *animateur* of the MAUSS group, is the tendency for theory to endlessly bounce back and forth between what he calls "holistic" and "individualistic" models. If one does not wish to look at human beings as simply elements in some larger structure (a "society," a "culture," call it what you will), doomed to endlessly act out or reproduce it, but also does not want to fall back on the economistic "rational-choice" option, which starts from a collection of individuals seeking personal satisfaction of some sort and treats larger institutions as mere side-effects of their choices, then this seems precisely the point at which to begin formulating an alternative. Human beings do create new social and cultural forms all the time, but they rarely do so just in order to further their own personal aims. In fact, often their personal aims come to be formed through the very institutions they create. Caillé proposes that the best way to develop an alternative to the currently dominant, utilitarian, "rational-choice" models is by setting out, not from market relations, but from Marcel Mauss' famous exposition of the gift, which is all about the creation of new social relations. He's not the only one working in this direction. Hans Joas (1993, 1996, 2000) has been trying to do something quite similar, setting out not from Mauss but from the tradition of American pragmatism. I tried to do something along these lines myself in my book *Towards an Anthropological Theory of Value*, where, inspired in part by ideas developed by my old professors Terry Turner and Nancy Munn, I attempted to broaden the Marxian notion of production to include the fashioning of persons and social relations.

The other impulse is more explicitly political, and has to do with the concept of revolution. Here the problematic stems broadly from within Marxism. Marx, perhaps more than any other classic social theorist, saw creativity and imagination as the essence of what it means to be human; but, as Hans Joas among others have remarked, when he got down to cases he tended to write as if all forms of creative action really boiled down to two: the production of material objects and social revolution. For Joas, this makes Marx's approach so limited he prefers to discard it entirely; I prefer to keep what I take to be his most profound insights and apply them to other forms of creativity as well; but what's at issue here is the relation between the two forms of creative action. Because there is a curious disparity. Marx assumes that both the human capacity for creativity and human critical faculties are ultimately rooted in the same source, which one might call our capacity for reflexive imagination. Hence, his famous example of the architect who, unlike the bee, raises her building in her own imagination before it is raised in reality. If we can imagine (as yet non-existent) alternatives, we can see the existing world as inadequate; we can also cause those things to exist. This is the ambiguity, though: while our ability to revolutionize emerges from this very critical faculty, the revolutionary, according to Marx, must never proceed in the same manner as the architect. It was not the task of the revolutionary to come up with blueprints for a future society and then try to bring them into being, or, indeed, to try to imagine details of the future society at all. That would be utopianism, which, for Marx, is a foolish bourgeois mistake. So the two forms of creativity—the creation of houses, or other material objects, and the creation of new social institutions (which is, after all, what revolution actually consists of) should not work in at all the same way.

I have written a little about this paradox before.[1] What I want to emphasize here is how it has contributed to a fundamental problem in revolutionary theory: what precisely is the role of creativity, collective or individual, of the imagination, in radical social change? Unless one wishes to adopt completely absurd formulations (the revolution will come about because of the inexorable logic of history; human agency will have nothing to do with it; afterwards however history will end and we will enter a world of freedom in which human agency will be utterly untrammeled...) this has to be the key question, but it's not at all clear what the answer is supposed to be. The revolutionary theorist who grappled with the problem most explicitly was Cornelius Castoriadis, whose *Socialisme ou Barbarie* group was probably the single most important theoretical influence on the student insurrectionaries of May '68, and who was the effective founder of the Autonomist tradition which has come to be probably the dominant strain of Continental Marxism.[2] Castoriadis ended up taking Marx's starting point—his faith in the critical role of the creative imagination and hence, our capacity to revolutionize—so seriously that he ended up abandoning most other tenets of Marxism entirely. For him, the great question became the emergence of the new.[3] After all, most of the really brilliant moments of human history involve the creation of something unprecedented, something that had never existed before—whether Athenian democracy or Renaissance painting—and this is precisely what we are used to thinking of as "revolutionary" about them. History, then, was a matter of the constant pressure of the imaginary against its social containment and institutionalization. It is in the latter process, he argued, that alienation enters in. Where Marx saw our dilemma in the fact that we create our physical worlds, but are unaware of, and hence not in control of, the process by which we do so (this is why our own deeds seem to come back at us as alien powers), for Castoriadis, the problem was that "all societies are instituted by themselves," but are blind to their own creativity. Whereas a truly "democratic society is a society which is instituted by itself, but in an explicit way" (in Ciaramelli 1998: 134). By the end, Castoriadis abandoned even the term "socialism," substituting "autonomy," defining autonomous institutions as those whose members have themselves, consciously, created the rules by which they operate, and are willing to continually reexamine them.[4]

This does seem a unique point of tension within radical thought. It is probably no coincidence that Roy Bhaskar, founder of Critical Realism, found this exactly the point where he had to break with the Western philosophical tradition entirely. After arguing for the necessity of a dialectical approach to social problems, he found himself asking, when contradictory elements are subsumed in a higher level of integration which are more than the sum of their parts, when apparently intractable problems are resolved by some brilliant new synthesis which takes things to a whole new level, where does that newness actually come from? If the whole is more than the sum of its parts, what is the source of that "more," that transcendent element? In his case he ended up turning to Indian and Chinese philosophical traditions and arguing that the main reason actually existing Marxism has produced such disappointing results has been its refusal to take on such issues, owing to its hostility to anything resembling "spiritual" questions (Bhaskar 2001, 2002).

What's important for present purposes is merely to underline that all these authors are, in one way or another, dealing with the same problem. If one does not wish to see human beings as simply side-effects of some larger structure or system, or as atoms pursuing some inscrutable bliss, but as beings capable of creating their own meaningful worlds, then the ability to create new institutions or social relations does seem just the place to look. Radical thinkers are just dealing with the same issues from a more pragmatic perspective, since, as revolutionaries, what they are interested in is precisely the creation of new social institutions and new forms of social relation. As I say, it is obvious that people do, in fact, create new institutions and new relations all the time. Yet how they do so remains notoriously difficult to theorize.

Can anthropology be of any assistance here? It's not obvious it could. Anthropologists have not exactly been grappling with these grand theoretical issues of late, and have never had much to say about revolution. One could, of course, argue that maybe this is all for the best, that human creativity cannot be, and should not be subjected to anyone's theoretical model. But a case could equally well be made that, if these are questions worth asking, then anthropology is the only discipline really positioned to answer them—since, after all, the overwhelming majority of actual, historical social creativity has, for better or worse, been relegated to our academic domain. Most of the classic issues even of early anthropology—potlatches, Ghost Dances, magic, totemic ritual and the like—are precisely about the creation of new social relations and new social forms.

Alain Caillé would certainly agree with this assessment: that's why he chose Marcel Mauss' essays on the gift as his starting point. Mauss himself saw his work on gifts as part of a much larger project, an investigation into the origins of the notion of the contract and of contractual obligation (that's why the question that really fascinated him was why it was that someone who receives a gift feels the obligation to return one). This has proved a highly fruitful approach, but in this essay I would like to suggest another one, hopefully equally productive, which opens up a slightly different set of questions. This is to begin with the problem of fetishism.

Why Fetishism?

"Fetishism" is, of course, a much debated term. It was originally coined to describe what were considered weird, primitive, and rather scandalous customs. As a result, most of the founders of modern anthropology—Marcel

Mauss prominent among them—felt the term was so loaded it would be better abandoned entirely. It no doubt would have been, had it not been for the fact that it had been so prominently employed—as a somewhat ironic technical term to describe certain Western habits—by both Karl Marx and Sigmund Freud. In recent years, the word has undergone something of a revival, mainly, because of the work of a scholar named William Pietz, who wrote a series of essays called "The Problem of the Fetish" (1985, 1987, 1988), tracing the history of the term's emergence in intercultural enclaves along the West African coast from the sixteenth through eighteenth centuries CE. Pietz is that most unusual of things: an independent scholar who has had an enormous influence on the academy. His essays ended up inspiring a small literature of their own during the 1990s, including one large and well-received interdisciplinary volume in the US (Apter and Pietz 1993), two different collections in the Netherlands (Etnofoor 1990, Spyer 1998), and any number of essays. The overriding theme in all this literature is materiality: how material objects are transformed by becoming objects of desire, or value, often one which seems somehow displaced, inordinate, or inappropriate. My own interest here is slightly different. What is especially interesting to me is Pietz' argument that the idea of the "fetish" was the product neither of African nor of European traditions, but of a confrontation between the two: the product of men and women with very different understandings of the world and what one had a right to wish from it trying to come to terms with one another. The fetish was, according to Pietz, born in a field of endless improvisation, that is, of near pure social creativity.

In what follows, I will first consider Pietz' story of the origin of the fetish, then try to supplement his account (drawn almost exclusively from Western sources) with some that might give insight into what the African characters in the story might have thought was going on, and then, return to our initial problem—and see how all this relates to "fetishism" in the more familiar Marxian sense. To summarize a long and complex argument, basically what I will propose is this:

We are used to seeing fetishism as an illusion. We create things, and then, because we don't understand how we did it, we end up treating our own creations as if they had power over us. We fall down and worship that which we ourselves have made. By this logic, however, the objects European visitors to Africa first labeled "fetishes" were, at least from the African perspective, remarkably little fetishized. They were in fact seen quite explicitly as having been created by human beings; people would "make" a fetish as the means of creating new social responsibilities, of making contracts and agreements, or forming new associations. It was only the Europeans' obsession with issues of value and materiality, and their almost complete lack of interest in social relations as things valuable in themselves, that made it possible for them to miss this. This is not to say they were completely unfetishized. But this is precisely what's most interesting about them.

Pietz on Fetishism

If the reader will allow me a highly simplified version of Pietz's complex and layered argument: the notion of the fetish was not a traditional European concept. Medieval Europeans tended to interpret alien religions through very different rubrics: for example, idolatry, apostasy, and atheism. Instead it seems to have arisen, in the minds of early Italian, Portuguese, and Dutch merchants, sailors, and maritime adventurers doing business in West Africa starting in the fifteenth century, primarily from a confrontation with the threat of relativism. These foreign merchants were operating in an environment which could hardly fail to cast doubt upon their existing assumptions about the nature of the world and of society: primarily concerning the relativity of economic value, but also with regard to the logic of government, the dynamics of sexual attraction, and any number of other things. By describing Africans as "fetishists," they were, first and foremost, trying to avoid some of the most disturbing implications of their own experience.

The first Portuguese merchants who set up "castles" on inlets and river islands along the West African coast were brought there by one thing: the belief that this part of the world was the origin of most—if not all—of the world's gold. In the sixteenth and seventeenth centuries, gold was the main product being extracted from the region (it was only somewhat later that attention shifted to slaves). These were extremely practically minded individuals, entering into a complex world full of an apparently endless variety of unfamiliar languages, religions, and forms of social organization—none of which, however, they had any particular interest in understanding as phenomena in their own right. They were simply after the gold. The very experience of moving between so many cultures, Pietz suggests, encouraged a kind of bare-bones materialism; in their writings, he notes, early merchant explorers tended to describe a world in which they perceived only three categories of significant object: tools, potential dangers, and potential commodities (1985: 8). And, for obvious reasons, they also tended to assess the value of just about everything by the price they thought it could fetch in European markets.

The problem was that in order to conduct their trade, they had to constantly confront the fact that the Africans they met had very different standards of value. Not entirely different. "Gold is much prized by them," wrote an early Venetian merchant named Cadamosto, "in my opinion, more than by us, for they regard it as very precious: nevertheless they traded it cheaply, taking in exchange articles of very little value in our eyes." To some extent this led to the familiar rhetoric of beads and trinkets. Merchants were always going on about how Africans were willing to accept all manner of junk— "trifles," "trash," "toys"—for gold and other valuable commodities. But at the same time, Africans were clearly not willing to accept just anything, and one could never tell in advance what sort of junk a given group would fancy. Anyone who has pored over "traveler's accounts" from this period will likely have noticed how much time and energy merchants had to put into figuring out which particular variety of worthless beads, what color or type of worthless trinkets would be accepted at any given port of call.

Situations like this can very easily lead one to reflect on the arbitrariness of value. After all, it is important to bear in mind that these early merchant adventurers were not only seeking gold, they were doing it at very considerable risk to their own lives. Coastal "castles" were malarial pest-holes: a European who spent a year in one had about a fifty-fifty chance of coming back alive. It would be very easy, in such circumstance, to begin to ask oneself: why are so many of us willing to risk death for the sake of a soft yellow metal, one which isn't even useful for anything except to look pretty? In what way is this really different than desire for beads and trinkets?[5] It was not as if people of the time were incapable of such reflections: the absurdity of such overweening desire for gold became a stock theme for popular satirists, particularly in the age of the *conquistadors*. The merchants in West Africa, however, instead seem to have come to the brink of such a conclusion and then recoiled. Instead of acknowledging the arbitrariness underlying all systems of value, their conclusion was that it was the Africans who were arbitrary. African societies were utterly without order, their philosophies utterly unsystematic, their tastes utterly whimsical and capricious:

> the most numerous Sect [in Guinea] are the Pagans, who trouble themselves about no Religion at all; yet every one of them have some Trifle or other, to which they pay a particular Respect, or Kind of Adoration, believing it can defend them from all Dangers: Some have a Lion's Tail, some a Bird's Feather, some a Pebble, a Bit of Rag, a Dog's Leg; or, in short, any thing they fancy: And this they call their Fetish, which Word not only signifies the Thing worshipped, but sometimes a Spell, Charm, or Inchantment (William Smith 1744, in Pietz 1987: 41).

So Africans were evidently like small children, always picking up little objects because they look odd or gross or brightly colored, and then becoming attached to them, treating them like they had personalities, adoring them, giving them names. The same thing that inspired them to value random objects in the marketplaces caused them to make random objects into gods.

The most common explanation of the origin of fetishes begins something like this. An African intends to set out on some project, to go off trading for example. He heads out in the morning and the first thing he sees that strikes him as in any way unusual or extraordinary, or just that randomly strikes his fancy, he adopts as a charm that will enable him to carry out his project. Pietz calls it the "chance conjuncture of a momentary desire or purpose and some random object brought to the desirer's attention"; Le Maire put it more simply: they "worship the first thing they meet in the Morning." Bosman writes of one of his informants:

> He obliged me with the following Answer, that the Number of their Gods was endless and innumerable: For (said he) any of us being re-solved to undertake any thing of Importance, we first of all search out a God to prosper our designed Undertaking; and going out of Doors with this design, take the first Creature that presents itself to our Eyes, whether Dog, Cat, or the most contemptible Animal in the World, for our God; or perhaps instead of that any Inanimate that fals in our way, whether a Stone, a piece of Wood, or any Thing else of the same Nature (in Pietz 1987: 43).

It was not the "Otherness" of the West Africans that ultimately drove Europeans to such extreme caricatures, then, but rather, the threat of similarity—which required the most radical rejection. So too with aesthetics, particularly the aesthetics of sexual attraction. European sources wrote of the odd practices of the women they encountered in coastal towns, who "fetishized themselves" by making up their faces with different kinds of colored clays, or wore "fetish gold" in their hair, intricately worked ornaments, frogs and birds along with glass beads and similar adornment. The descriptions here are not usually morally condemnatory, but they usually adopt a kind of sneering tone, one of contempt for what seems to pass as beauty in these parts, what Africans found alluring or attractive. But, again, they obviously protest too much. If European sojourners were entirely immune to the charms of women with earth on their faces and frogs in their hair, they would not have fathered hundreds of children with them; indeed, there is no particular reason to assume that the numbers of such children would have been substantially higher had the women in question behaved liked proper European ladies and put grease on their lips and gold rings in their ears instead.

The same dynamic recurs when Europeans talked about African modes of government. First, observers would insist that the basis of African social life was essentially chaotic, that it was utterly lacking in systematic public order; they would usually end up by admitting that laws were, in fact, quite systematically obeyed. According to some, almost miraculously so. The attitude is summed up by a later British administrator, Brodie Cruickshank, Governor General of the Gold Coast in the nineteenth century:

> The local govt of the Gold Coast must have the candor to acknowledge its obligations to Fetish, as a police agent. Without this powerful ally, it would have been found impossible to maintain that order, which characterized the country during the last twenty years, with the physical force of the govt. The extraordinary security afforded to property in the most remote districts, the great safety with which packages of gold of great value are transmitted by single messengers for hundreds of miles, and the facility with which lost or stolen property is generally recovered, have excited the astonishment of Europeans newly arrived in the country (Cruickshank 1853, in Pietz 1995: 25).

The reason, they concluded, boiled down to the most primitive of instincts: fear of death, or the terrible punishments fetishes were thought to bring down on those who violated their (somewhat arbitrary) principles.

Again, the problem was not the picture was so alien, but that it was so familiar. That government was an institution primarily concerned with threatening potential miscreants with violence, was a longstanding assumption in Western political theory; that it existed primarily to protect property was a theme in the process of emerging at this very time. True, the fetish was said to operate by invisible, supernatural means, and hence to fall under the sphere of religion and not government. But these observers were also, overwhelmingly, Christians, and Christians of that time insisted that their religion was morally superior to all others, and particularly to African religions, on the very grounds that their God threatened wrong-doers with the systematic application of torture for all eternity, and other people's gods did not. The parallels were in fact striking, although this was an area in which Europeans found it particularly difficult to be relativistic. It was above all their assumption of the absolute truth of Christian faith that made any broader move to a relativistic attitude impossible. Insofar as Africans were heathens, they had to be fundamentally mistaken about what was important in the world.

On the other hand, this was an area where common understandings made a great deal of practical difference, because especially before Europeans came as conquerors, oaths sworn on fetishes and contracts made by "making" or "drinking" fetishes were the very medium of trust between Europeans and Africans engaged in trade. If it were not for their common participation in such rituals—often newfangled ones improvised for the occasion combining bibles and beads and bits of wood all at the same time—the trade itself would have been impossible. And, of course, this is what especially interests us here.

Fetishes and Social Contracts: Two Case Studies

Now, as the reader might have noticed, Pietz is almost exclusively concerned with how things seemed to Europeans who came to Africa. There is almost no speculation about what any of the Africans with whom they traded might have thought was going on.[6] Of course, in the absence of documentary evidence, there is no way to know for sure. Still, there is a pretty voluminous literature on more recent examples of the sort of objects these Europeans labeled "fetishes," as well as on African cosmological systems more generally, so one can make some pretty good guesses as to what the Africans who owned and used such objects thought they were about. Doing so does not, in fact, invalidate any of Pietz's larger points. Actually, it suggests that the "threat of recognition," if I may call it that, runs deeper still.

Allow me to begin here with some very broad—and therefore, no doubt, overstated—generalizations about the relation between European and African cosmologies. My interest in Pietz, and in fetishism more generally, originally arose as part of a comparative study of beads and other "currencies of trade" (Graeber 1995, 2001), which included cases ranging from Trobriand kula shells or Iroquois wampum to Kwakiutl coppers. For someone such as myself, brought up in a religious environment largely shaped by Christianity, moving from Oceania or native North America to Africa is moving from very alien, to far more familiar, cosmological territory. It is not just that, throughout Africa, one can find mythological *topoi* (the Garden of Eden, the Tower of Babel) that are familiar from the Old Testament and that just do not seem to be present in other traditions. There is a sense that African theologians seem to be asking mostly the same existential questions.[7] Max Weber, for instance, made a famous argument that every religion has to come up with some answer to the question of "theodicy," or the justice of God. How is it, if God is both good and all-powerful, that human beings must suffer? Now, it's pretty obvious that as a universal statement, this is simply untrue. The question probably wouldn't have even made sense to a Maori theologian, let alone, say, an Aztec poet or Trobriand chief. While every tradition does seem to see the human condition as inherently problematic in some way, in most, the reasons for human suffering is just not the issue. The problem lies elsewhere. Mythic speculation in Africa, on the other hand, focuses on the question endlessly (e.g., Abrahamsson 1952)—even many African theologians came up with what were from the Christian perspective very disturbing answers (i.e., who says God is good?).[8]

I said such generalizations are necessarily overstated because, as any number of authors have reminded us, terms like "Africa," "Europe," or "the West," are fuzzy at best, and probably meaningless. I cannot claim to know why so many European and African thinkers seem to have been asking the same existential questions. Perhaps it is because Europe and Africa were, for so much of their history, peripheral zones under the influence of the great urban civilizations of the Middle East. Perhaps there is some even deeper historical connection. I don't know. What I want to stress though is that, here, seventeenth- or eighteenth-century European seafarers found themselves in much more familiar territory than they did when they ventured to places like China or Brazil. It was this underlying affinity, I suspect, which accounted for the common European reaction of shocked revulsion and dismay on being exposed to so many aspects of African ritual: a desperate denial of recognition. Because, in many ways, African cosmological ideas seemed to take the same questions and come up with precisely the conclusions Europeans were most anxious to avoid: i.e., perhaps we suffer because God is not good, or is beyond good and evil and doesn't care; perhaps the state is a violent and exploitative institution and there's nothing can be done about it.

I'll return to this theme in a moment.

Throughout much of Africa, ceremonial life is dominated by what anthropologists have labeled "rituals of affliction." Those Powers considered worthy of recognition are almost invariably those capable of causing human misery, and one comes into contact with them when they attack one in some way. A typical chain of events (I'll use a Malagasy example out of familiarity) might run like this: one offends a Power without knowing it, say by bringing pork into a spot inhabited by a *Vazimba* spirit; the offended spirit causes one to become ill, or to experience nightmares; one goes to a local curer who identifies the spirit and tells one how to propitiate it; doing so, however, causes one to become part of a congregation of former victims all of which now have a special relation with the spirit, which can help one or even direct its powers against one's enemies. Suffering leads to knowledge; knowledge, to power. This is an extremely common pattern. Victor Turner, for instance estimates that among the Ndembu of Zambia, there are essentially only two types of ritual: rituals of affliction, and "life-crisis rituals" such as initiations and funerary rites. He also adds that even the latter always "stressed the

theme of suffering as a means of entry into a superior ritual and social status"
(1968: 15–16); normally, because initiation rituals passed through physical
ordeals (suffering) to the attainment of some kind of ritual knowledge.

Most of the African objects labeled "fetishes" were enmeshed in precisely this ritual logic.

Let me take two representative examples. The first is the Tiv of central
Nigeria, c1900–1950. They are a good place to start because they are both
well-documented, and lived not too far from the region dealt with in Pietz's
texts. The second is the BaKongo of the Central African coast, who have a
much longer history of entanglement with European trade. The Tiv are a
classic example of a "segmentary" society: before they were conquered by
the British, they recognized no centralized authority of any sort, beyond the
confines of a typical extended family compound. Larger society was instead
organized on a genealogical basis, through an elaborate system of patrilineal lineages, which, however, had no permanent officials or ritual officers.
Where the ritual life of most segmentary societies in the region centered on
an elaborate cult of ancestors or of earth shrines, the Tiv lacked these too.
Instead, their ritual life revolves largely around warding off witchcraft, and
the control of objects called *akombo*, or "fetishes."

The names of most *akombo* were also those of diseases. In a certain
sense, the *akombo* quite simply were those diseases,[9] though they were also
embodied in material "emblems." These emblems might be almost anything:
a pot of ashes, a whisk broom, a piece of elephant bone. These existed in certain places, and were owned by "keepers," and they were always surrounded
by a host of rules and regulations indicating what could and could not be
done in the vicinity. One came into relation with an *akombo* when one broke
one of those rules—this is called "piercing" it—and became sick as a result.
The only way to set things straight was to approach its keeper in order to
"repair" the *akombo* or "set it right." After a victim has so freed themselves
from the effects of the fetish, they might also decide to take possession of it
themselves, which involves a further ritual of "agreement" and sacrifice in order to give one the power to operate ("repair") it oneself, so as to help others
so afflicted, and also, gain access to whatever other powers the *akombo* might
have (Bohannan & Bohannan 1969). All this is very much on the model of
a typical "cult of affliction."

What I have said so far applies to minor, or ordinary, *akombo*. There
were also major *akombo*, which had broader powers. Probably the most important of these were those that protected markets. According to Tiv informants of the colonial period, what really distinguished these great *akombo*
from the ordinary variety was, first of all, that they could protect a whole
territory from harm; second, that they could be passed on from father to

son; third, that they "either contain a part of a human body as a portion of their emblems, or they must be repaired by a human sacrifice...or both" (Bohannan & Bohannan 1969 IV: 437).

To understand this, one has understand something, I think, about traditional Tiv conceptions of social power—at least as they stood in the early twentieth century. The Tiv combined very hierarchical domestic arrangements—with household compounds constructed around some important older man, almost invariably with numerous wives, surrounded by a host of frustrated unmarried adult sons—and a fiercely egalitarian ethos which allowed next to nothing in the way of political office outside the compound. Certain older men manage to gain a larger influence in communal affairs, but such accomplishments are viewed with extreme ambivalence. Social power, the ability to impose one's will on others, is referred to as *tsav*; it is seen in quite material terms as a fatty yellow substance that grows on human hearts. Some people have *tsav* naturally. They are what we'd refer to as "natural leadership types." It can also be created, or increased, by eating human flesh. This is "witchcraft," the definition of evil:

> Tiv believe that persons with *tsav* form an organization called the *mbatsav*. This group is said to have a division of labor and a loose organization. The *mbatsav* are said to meet at night, usually for nefarious purposes; they rob graves in order to eat corpses; they bewitch people in order to put corpses into graves which they can rob. There is thought to be a network of "flesh debts" which become established when someone tricks you into eating human flesh and then claims a return in kind; the only thing you can do is to kill your children and your close kinsmen—people over whom you have some sort of power—and finally, because no one can ever win against the organization, you must give yourself to them as a victim because you have no kinsmen left to give (P. Bohannan 1958: 4–5).

As Paul Bohannan succinctly puts it: "men attain power by consuming the substance of others." While one can never be certain that any particular elder is also an evil cannibalistic witch, the classes overlap, and it would seem that, in recorded times at least, every generation or so, a witch-finding movement would sweep through the country unmasking the most prominent figures of local authority (Akiga 1939; P. Bohannan 1958).[10]

This is not quite a system in which political power is seen as intrinsically evil, but it is very close. It only stands to reason, then, that *akombo* that have power over communities should have a similar predilection to absorb human flesh. The information we have about most of these "great *akombo*" is somewhat limited, because most were destroyed during a witch-finding movement in the 1920s, but the one sort that did tend to survive were the *akombo* of markets. Fortunately, these are the most relevant to the issues under consideration here.

Tiv markets are dominated largely by women, who are also the main producers. Over the last few centuries, markets have also been the principal context in which most Tiv come into contact with those with whom they can trace no close genealogical ties and, therefore, towards whom they have no necessary moral obligations. In markets, then, the destructive powers of *akombo* could be used to keep the peace. Every significant market had its own fetish (Bohannan & Bohannan 1968: 149, 158–162), which Tiv of the colonial period, interestingly, often compared to an authorization certificate from the colonial regime. Essentially, they embodied peace agreements between a series of lineages who shared the same market, by which their members undertook to deal fairly with one another, and to abstain from theft, brawling, and profiteering. The agreement was sealed with a sacrifice—nowadays said to be a human sacrifice, though the Bohannans suspect most often it was really just a dog—whose blood was poured over the *akombo's* emblem. This is the sacrifice by day: in addition, the (male) elders, in their capacity as *mbatsav*, kill others of their own lineages "by night"—that is, by witchcraft (ibid.: 159–60). Henceforth, all those who violated the agreement would be struck down by the *akombo's* power. And in fact, the existence of such agreements made it possible for marketplaces to become meeting places for the regulation of local affairs, judgments, and the taking of oaths.

This gives some idea, I think, of the logic by which "fetishes" also came to mediate trade agreements with European merchants in the sixteenth and seventeenth centuries. The similarity with European theories of the social contract, which were developing at precisely this time, need hardly be remarked. I will return to these parallels in a moment.

The Tiv themselves had little to do with Europeans before the British conquest; they came into relation with the trade largely as victims, being raided for slaves by more powerful neighbors. As a result their recorded history is very shallow. On the other hand, the BaKongo, famous for their *minkisi* or "fetishes," many considered brilliant works of art, have one of the longest recorded histories in Africa. In 1483, the Kongo kingdom entered into an alliance with Portugal and the royal family converted to Catholicism. At the time, its capital, Sao Salvador, was the largest city south of the Sahara. Within a century, the kingdom was torn apart by the pressures of the slave trade. In 1678, the capital was destroyed. The kingdom broke down into a series of smaller successor states, most of which officially recognized the authority of a nominal Kongo monarch stripped of almost all real power: a classic hollow center (Thornton 1987). Later centuries witnessed even greater fragmentation, the centers of most of the successor states hollowed out in similar fashion, leaving a highly decentralized social field in which former chiefly titles increasingly became prizes that could be bought and sold by successful merchants and slave-traders. Certainly, this was the case by the nineteenth century, during which power gradually shifted to commercial towns along the coast. This is also the period from which we have most of our information on *minkisi*, as recalled in documents recorded by Christian converts, in the KiKongo language, at the very beginning of the colonial age.

In a lot of ways, the BaKongo might seem as different from Tiv as can be: matrilineal where the Tiv were patrilineal, hierarchical where the Tiv were egalitarian, with a cosmology centering on the ancestral dead which is totally alien to Tiv conceptions. But the basic assumptions about the nature of power in both cases are remarkably similar. First of all, we find the same logic of affliction: here too, one comes into contact with powers largely by offending them; once that power has caused one to suffer, then one has the opportunity to master it and, to an extent, to acquire it for oneself.[11] This was the normal way in which one comes into relation with a *nkisi*: one first appeals to its keeper to cure one of an ailment; as such one becomes a member of what might be broadly called its congregation; later, perhaps, if one is willing to undergo the expensive initiation process, one can eventually become a keeper oneself.

BaKongo and Tiv theories of the relation of political power and witchcraft were also remarkably similar. The power of chiefs was assumed to be rooted in a physical substance in the body—in this case, called *kindoki*. This was also the power of witches. The main difference was that Kongo witches operate on a level that is somewhat more abstract than Tiv witches; while they too become entangled in "flesh debts," they mainly are represented as consuming the spiritual substance of their victims, through invisible means, sucking up their souls rather than literally dining on them. Also, while at first witches feed on their own relatives, those who have sucked up, and thus gained the power of, a large number of souls can eventually become powerful enough to attack almost anyone. It is the responsibility of chiefs to thwart their evil plans, using their own *ndoki*. However, as Wyatt MacGaffey emphasizes (1986, 2000), the difference between a chief and a witch is merely one of motive: witches are simply those who use their nocturnal powers for their own selfish purposes, greed or envy rather than the good of the community. And since the latter is a notoriously slippery concept, while no one without *kindoki* is of any real public account, no one with it is entirely above suspicion.

There are two key differences, though, with Tiv *akombo*, and these appear to be linked. One is that Kongo *minkisi* tend to become personified. They have not only names and histories, but minds and intentions of their own. This is because their powers are really those of ancestral ghosts: most *nkisi* statuettes, in fact, contained in their chests both a series of medicinal ingredients, which gave them their specific capacities for action (cf. Graeber 1995), and grave dirt, which effected their connection with the dead. The second difference is that they tend to act largely when someone intentionally provokes them. While Tiv might say that one who unintentionally offends an *akombo* "pierces" it, with *minkisi* this was no mere metaphor. Those operating a *nkisi* would often quite literally drive nails into the object to provoke it into action. This was not, I should stress, at all like driving pins into a voodoo doll, since the idea was to provoke the *nkisi* to anger (though MacGaffey [1986] stresses that in a larger sense, the figures represented both the aggressor and the victim simultaneously, the assumption that the infliction of suffering creates a kind of unity between the two).

Even chiefly office could be drawn into the same logic. In much of Central Africa, leopards were symbols of royal power. So here. One nineteenth-century Notebook (#45, MacGaffey 1986: 159) describes how, should someone kill a leopard, a man wishing to be invested in an important chiefly title might rush to the scene to "desecrate its tail" by stepping on it. This was a period in which such titles could be acquired by fairly easily by men who had acquired fortunes in trade: after desecrating the object, the man could proceed to acquire the title through what is a kind of "purchase," which might typically involve, for example, the payment of ten lives "by day" (slaves delivered to the current holder), and ten "by night" (members of the chief's own kin group killed by witchcraft; cf. Vansina 1973).

The following gives something of the flavor of their power:

> Lunkanka is a nkisi in a statue and it is extremely fierce and strong. It came from Mongo, where many of our forebears used to go to compose it, but now its keepers have all died out. When it had a keeper it was very strong, and so it destroyed whole villages. Its strength lay in seizing [its victims], crushing their chests, making them bleed from the nose and excrete pus; driving knives into their chests, twisting necks, breaking arms and legs, knotting their intestines, giving them night-mares, discovering witches in the village, stifling a man's breathing and so on. When it was known that Lunkanka was exceedingly powerful, a great many people trusted it for healing, placing oaths and cursing witches and magicians, and so on (in MacGaffey 1991: 127).[12]

The text goes on to explain that if two men make an agreement—say, one agreed to be the other's client, or pawn, and thus bound to his village— they might both drive nails into Lunkanka to seal the agreement; the *nkisi* would then act as its power of enforcement. According to MacGaffey (1987), in the nineteenth century every aspect of BaKongo economic life, from the policing of marketplaces to the protection of property rights to the enforcement of contracts, was carried out through the medium of *minkisi*, and the *nkisi* so employed were, in every case, forms of crystallized violence and affliction.

The underlying logic seems to have a remarkable similarity to social contract theories being created in Europe around the same time: MacGaffey has even found KiKongo texts which celebrate the existence of *minkisi* as a way of preventing a war of all against all.[13] Once again, there is a striking parallelism in underlying assumptions: in this case, the same background of competitive market exchange, the same assumption that (at least outside of kin relations) social peace is therefore a matter of agreements, particular agreements to respect one and other's property, that must be enforced by an overarching power of violence. The main difference seems to lie in the assumed reasons why such violence is necessary. As authors like Sahlins (2001) have much emphasized, the Judeo-Christian tradition, going back at least to Augustine (himself an African), assumes that human desires are in their essence insatiable. Since we can never have enough pleasure, power, or especially material wealth, and since resources are inherently limited, we are all necessarily in a state of competition with one another. The state, according to Augustine, embodies reason, which is divine. It is also a providential institution which, by threatening punishment, turns our own base egoism—especially our fear of pain—against us to maintain order. Hobbes (1651) merely secularized the picture, eliminating the part about the endless desires being a punishment for original sin, but keeping the basic structure. Then Adam Smith, Enlightenment optimist that he was, brought divine providence back in to argue that God had actually arranged things so that even our competitive desires will ultimately work for the benefit of all. In every case, though, the Western tradition seems to combine two features: the assumption that humans are corrupted by limitless desires, and an insistent effort to imagine some form of power or authority (Reason, God, the State) which is not corrupted by desire, and hence inherently benevolent. God must be just (despite all appearances to the contrary); a rational man can rise above bodily passions; it should at least be possible to have rulers who are not interested in their own aggrandizement but only about the public welfare. The result was that the effects of power tend to be endlessly euphemized or explained away. African cosmological systems seemed to lack both features: probably, because they were less inclined to see human motivation as, say, a desire for wealth, or pleasures that could be abstracted from, or imagined independently from, the social relations in which they were realized. They tend to assume what people desired was thus power itself.[14] Thus, it was impossible to imagine a form of political power which was not—at least partly—constituted by the very form of evil which the Western tradition saw it as the means to transcend.[15] Perhaps for this reason, what Europeans nervously euphemized was exactly what Africans seemed to self-consciously exaggerate. One might consider here the difference between the famous "divine" kingships of much of Africa, whose subjects insisted that any ruler who became weak or frail would be promptly killed—but in which, in actual fact, this seems to have happened only rarely—with an institution like Augustine's Roman Empire, which claimed to be the embodiment of rational law and guardian of public order, but whose actual rulers murdered one another with such savage consistency that it's almost impossible to come up with an example of an emperor who died a natural death. Similarly, in seventeenth- and eighteenth-century Europe, African states developed a reputation for being extraordinarily bloodthirsty, since their representatives and subjects never saw any point in disguising the essentially murderous nature of state power. This despite the fact that the actual scale of killing even by the Ganda or Zulu states was negligible in comparison with the devastation wreaked in wars within Europe at the same time—not even to mention what Europeans were prepared to do to anybody else.

The Materiality of Power

Another way to understand the difference is to look at the contrasting ways in which power was seen to take on material substance or tangible form. For Pietz' merchants, of course, the emphasis was on material valuables, beautiful or fascinating objects—or sometimes artificially beautified people—and their powers to enchant or attract. The value of an object was its power. In the African cases we've looked at, at least, power is imagined above all as a material substance inside the body: *tsav, ndoki*. This is entirely in keeping with the distinctions sketched out above, but it also has an interesting corollary, which, in a sense, systematically subverts that principle of representation which is the very logical basis of any system of legitimate authority. Here I can only refer to an argument I've made at greater length in Chapter 1: that any system in which one member of a group can claim to represent the group as a whole necessarily entails setting that member off in a way resembling the Durkheimian notion of the sacred, as set apart from the stuffs and substances of the material world, even, to a certain degree, abstracted from it. Much of the etiquette surrounding figures of authority always tends to center on a denial of the ways in which the body is continuous with the world; the tacit image is always that of an autonomous being who needs nothing. The ideal of the rational, disinterested state seems to be just one particular local variation of this very common theme; inherent, I have argued, to any real notion of hierarchy.

It's not that the logic of hierarchy is not present—one might well argue it always is, in some form or another—but rather that things seem to work in such a way as to constantly subvert it. It seems to me one can't really understand even the famous Tiv system of spheres of exchange without taking this into account. The system, as mapped out by Paul Bohannan in an essay in 1955, is really quite simple. Everything considered worth exchanging, all things of value, fell into one of three categories; things of each category could, ordinarily, be exchanged only for each other. The resulting spheres of exchange formed a hierarchy. At the bottom were everyday goods like food or tools or cooking oil, which could be contributed to kin or friends or sold in local markets. Next up were prestige goods such as brass rods, slaves, a certain white cloth, and magical services such as those provided by owners of *akombo*. The highest consisted in nothing but rights in women, since all marriages, before the colonial period, were considered exchanges of one woman for another—or more exactly, of their reproductive powers—and there was a complicated system of "wards" whereby male heads of household could acquire rights in women seen as owed by them in one way or another and marry them off in exchange for new wives, even if they did not have an unmarried sister or daughter of their own. On the other hand, division between spheres was never absolute. It *was* possible to convert food into valuables, if one found someone sufficiently desperate for food, or, under other circumstances, valuables into additional wives. To do so took a "strong heart," which according to Bohannan was inherently admirable ("morally positive"), though, one has to imagine somewhat ambivalently so, since having a strong heart meant, precisely, that one had that yellow substance on one's heart which also made one a witch.[16]

Obviously, the system is all about male control of women. The sort of goods that are largely produced and marketed by women are relegated to the most humble category; those controlled by men rank higher; the highest sphere consists solely of men's rights in the women themselves. At the same time, one could say as one moves up the spheres, men are increasingly gaining control of the capacity to create social form (households, descent, genealogy); converting upwards from food and tools that can merely keep people alive, to objects with the capacity to assemble clientages, and then finally, to the power to create descent itself. Since, after all, when one assembles wives and wards one is not, technically speaking, trafficking in women so much as in their reproductive capacities. All of this one does by manipulating debt, in its various manifestations, placing others in a position of obligation. This, in turn, makes it easier to understand what's really going on with stories about witchcraft and the flesh debt, what I would propose should really be considered the fourth sphere, since it marks the ultimate fate of those with "strong hearts." This is where the whole system collapses on itself, the direction is utterly reversed: since those who are most successful in manipulating networks of debt to gain such powers over creation are discovered, here, to be in a position of limitless debt themselves, and hence forced to consume the very human substance the system is ostensibly concerned with producing. Or, to put the matter starkly, by manipulating debt, a man with a strong heart can transform food into the stuff of social networks, transform social networks into control over women, and therefore, the power to generate descendants. But the very power to do so constantly threatens to spiral out of control, finally locking those who manage to play the game most successfully into flesh debts that force them to convert descendants back again to food. In striking contrast with the Western version, the insatiable desire for consumption, when it does appear, is not a desire for wealth but for the direct consumption of human beings, indistinguishable from the political power which, in the European version, is usually imagined as the only thing capable of controlling it.

Now, all this might seem appropriate to an egalitarian society like the Tiv, which one would expect to be somewhat ambivalent about the nature of social power and authority. The surprising thing, then, is how much of this is reproduced, almost exactly unchanged, in the BaKongo material, where the political situation was so different. Granted it was not entirely different—this was an area where centralized authority had been being effectively broken down for generations (Ekholm 1991), but the parallels are striking: even down to the small details like the payments "by day" and "by night." The few salient differences do seem to reflect a greater acceptance of social hierarchy among the BaKongo (at least in principle): there is more of an overt willingness to see *kindoki* as capable of serving the common good, and, significantly, I think, also a tendency to treat the whole matter of witchcraft more abstractly: while there is occasional talk of feasting on disinterred bodies, the usual imagery is of a kind of disembodied vampiric power feeding off the soul-stuff of its victims—which, if nothing else, shows a reluctance to challenge the fundamental logic of representation through abstraction on which any system of legitimate rule must, it would seem, rest. Ultimately, though, these are minor differences.

Different Sorts of Social Contract

The first Portuguese and Dutch sources, as I mentioned, seem entirely oblivious to all this. Caught up as they were with their own newfound materialism, questions of economic value—and particular, value in exchange—were the only ones that really concerned them. The result is that, oddly enough, at the moment when Hobbes was writing his famous theory of the social contract (1651), he seems to have been entirely unaware that, in Africa, social contracts not so different from the sort he imagined were still being made, on a regular basis.

This brings us back to the questions with which we began: about the nature of social creativity. The main way of talking about such matters in the Western intellectual tradition, for the last several centuries, has been precisely through the idiom of contracts, social or otherwise. As I mentioned at the start of the essay, Marcel Mauss claimed that his essay on the gift (1925) was really part of a much larger project on the origins of the notion of the contract and contractual obligation. His conclusion—a rather striking one—was that the most elementary form of social contract was, in fact, communism: an open-ended agreement between two groups, or even two individuals, to provide for each other; within which, even access to one another's possessions followed the principle of "from each according to their abilities, to each according to their needs." Originally, he argued, there were two possibilities: total war, or "total reciprocity." The latter informed everything from moiety structures (where those on one side of a village can only marry the daughters of those on the other, or only eat food grown on the other, or only the others can bury their dead...) to relations of individualistic communism such as applied between close friends, or in-laws, or in our own society, husband and wife. This later gets refracted into various more specific forms of gift relation, and then of course eventually you get the market, but "total reciprocity" remains the kind of base-line of sociality, even to the present day. This is why, Mauss suggests, wage-labor contracts seem so unsatisfying to those on the receiving end; there's still that underlying assumption that voluntary agreements (like, say, marriage) should involve an open-ended commitment to respond to one another's needs.

Alain Caillé (2001) sums up the difference between the first sort of contract, and gift relations in general, and the more familiar contract as between "conditional unconditionality" and "unconditional conditionality." The first is an unlimited commitment, but either party is free to break it off at any time; the second specifies precisely what is owed by each party, no more and no less—but within that, each party is absolutely bound. My own work on trade currencies, and in particular what happened to beads or shell currency once they left the circuits of the trade (Graeber 2001), revealed some striking patterns. Everything seemed to turn on the presence or absence of an internal market. In North America, belts of wampum, originally acquired in the fur trade, were never used as money by indigenous people when dealing with each other (in fact there were no market relations between indigenous people of any kind at all); instead they became a key element in the construction of social peace. The Iroquois Confederation, for example, saw themselves as emerging from a kind of Hobbesian period of war of all against all, but it was caused not by competition over wealth and power but by the power of grief and mourning, which twisted humans into monstrous creatures craving vengeance and destruction. Wampum, in comparison, was never seen as causing anyone to hurt anybody else. Wampum was crystallized peace, a substance of light and beauty with the power to heal and open those wounded and cramped by rage; gifts of wampum cleared the way to open-ended relations of mutual responsibility of just the sort Mauss seemed to have in mind. In Madagascar, in contrast, where buying and selling was everywhere, trade beads and, later, ornaments made of melted silver coins, became elements in charms (*ody, sampy...*) that operated very much like West African fetishes: they might not have embodied diseases, quite, but they were capable of being highly punitive in their effects. If anything, in Madagascar, the Hobbesian logic becomes much more explicit, because this was also the way one created sovereign power and the state.

Here again I can only summarize a much more elaborate argument (Graeber 1995, 2001) but the gist goes something like this. Silver coins, which came into Madagascar largely through the slave trade, and which were melted down to create ornaments and broken up to create smaller denominations of currency which people actually used in daily life, were also used, in Imerina, to create the power of kings. Every major event at which the ruler appeared was marked by "giving *hasina*," the presentation of unbroken silver coins by representatives of the people to the king—unbroken to represent the unity of the kingdom created by this act of recognition. The ultimate message was that by doing so, the people created royal power, in exactly the way that one created a charm or fetish. Even more critically, in the Merina kingdom, every time two people came to any sort of business agreement, or for that matter, every time members of a community came to an agreement on the disposal of property or the maintenance of irrigation works, they invariably sealed the contract by "giving *hasina*" to the king (Graeber 1995: 96–109), recreating that power of violence which bound them to their contractual obligations.[17]

It is not that contracts of the more open-ended, Maussian variety did not exist in Madagascar or, for that matter, in West Africa. Most often, they are referred to in the literature under the rubric of "rituals of blood brotherhood." In Malagasy these are called *fatidra*. In nineteenth-century texts gathered by missionaries (Callet 1908: 851; Cousins 1968: 93–94; also Ellis 1835 1: 187–90; Sibree 1897), they are indeed treated as the most basic, even primordial, form of contract (most business partners for instance seem to have been bound together in this way). The two parties would each put a little of their blood together in a piece of liver, eat the liver, and then would swear always to be responsive to one another's needs, never refuse help in a crisis, never refuse food when the other is hungry, and so on. However, the actual body of the oath takes the form of imprecations, invoking an invisible spirit created by the ritual and calling on it to wreak every sort of disaster and havoc upon them should they ever fail to live up to these obligations. The same is true of the creation of communal ties: people insisted (in fact, they still insist) that, even before there were kings, those creating new communities would begin by "giving *hasina*" to some stone or tree or other object which would then have the power to enforce their communal obligations, to punish or at least expel those who did not respect the social contract.

When Mauss described "total reciprocity," he was thinking of the sort of agreements that would be made in the complete absence of market institutions: here, we are dealing with societies deeply entangled in market relations, in fact, often, relations between people had little else in common. It's hard to escape the conclusion that the generic power of money—as the one thing already binding the parties together—itself became the model for that invisible power which was, as it were, turned back against itself to maintain commitments even when it might have been in one party's short-term financial interest not to. Hence, even the "individualistic communism" of blood brotherhood, ends up subsumed under that same logic.

The comparison of North America and Madagascar is telling, I think, because in both cases stuff which is an embodiment of pure value, and which is seen as coming from very far away, becomes the basic medium for the creation of new social ties—for social creativity. The Iroquois of the Six Nations used wampum to create peace, but in fact what we call society *was*, for them, peace: the "League of the Iroquois" was called "The Great Peace," and the presentation of wampum became the medium for creating all sorts of contracts, mutual agreements and new institutional forms (see Graeber 2001: 125–26, 132–34). In the Malagasy—and also African—cases we are looking at the media for the creation of agreements, communities, even kingdoms.

That this should so often involve manipulation of objects of alien, and apparently universal, value should perhaps come as no surprise. No doubt we just dealing with the familiar structural principle that a social field, or logical domain, cannot be constituted except in relation to something which is not part of it—something transcendent or, anyway, alien. A constitution cannot be created by constitutional means; beings capable of establishing a system of justice cannot themselves be bound by that system of justice; always one needs something else. This much is straightforward enough. But it's also important to stress that these objects were, ultimately, only the medium. Hence, what they are is ultimately somewhat arbitrary: one can use valuable objects from faraway lands, or one can, in fact, use pretty much any random object one lays one's hands on, "a Lion's Tail...a Bird's Feather...a Pebble, a Bit of Rag." In this, Pietz' sources had a point, because this is exactly the moment where the arbitrariness of value comes fully into focus. Because, really, creativity is not an aspect of the objects at all, it's a dimension of action. In this sense, the new does in fact emerge from the old, and the numinous, alien nature of the object is really the degree to which it reflects on that aspect of our own actions that is, in a sense, alien to ourselves.

Our Own Actions Coming Back At Us

Here of course is where we start, finally, moving in the direction of the Marxian notion of the fetish: objects which seem to take on human qualities which are, ultimately, really derived from the actors themselves.

Not that we are speaking of pure mystification here. As I have tried to demonstrate in my analysis of the Merina Royal Bath ceremony (2001: 232–39) and *hasina* ritual in general, people were not entirely unaware that it was the ritual that made the king, that what constructed royal power was not the coin, but the action of giving it. This was tacit in the ritual itself, and stated explicitly just off-stage. Similarly, Malagasy charms involved the giving of an oath or pledge by those protected by them, or over whom they had power; without that, it was simply a powerless object. On the other hand, once given, the object was treated as having a power of its own. Something similar seems to have been widely recognized by West African "fetishists." In fact, if one looks over the literature surveyed by Pietz, one sees the exact same emphasis on action: here, taking a collective oath could be called "making" or "drinking" or "eating" fetish, phrases which appear to be direct translations from African languages. A fetish is something one makes, or does:

> Obligatory Swearing they also call, making of Fetiche's; If any Obligation is to be confirmed, their Phrase is, let us as a farther Confirmation make Fetiche's. When they drink the Oath-Draught, 'tis usually accompanied with an Imprecation, that the Fetiche may kill them if they do not perform the Contents of their Obligation (Bosman 1705 [1967: 149]).

The basic sequence here—people create ("make") something; then they act as if that thing has power over them—is of course just the sort of sequence Marx was thinking of when he spoke of "fetishism." There are two curious elements here. One is that those involved seemed not entirely unaware that this was happening: both that these objects were constructed, but at the same time, that they came to have some kind of power over those who constructed them. This is very important, I think, and I will try to consider the full implications in a moment. The other curious thing is that Pietz does not even consider any of this. In fact, even when he turns to look at Marx's own work (1993), Pietz considers every definition of fetishism, every aspect, other than the simplest and most common one: that "fetishism" occurs when human beings end up bowing down before and worshipping that which they have themselves created.[18]

Now, this is a peculiar oversight.

The reason seems to lie in the structure of Pietz' argument: that "the fetish" is a concept that emerged within a peculiar intercultural space in which neither existing European, nor existing African categories really applied. He calls it a "space of cultural revolution," in which the "conceptualities, habits and life forms, and value systems" of a number of radically different social systems (feudal Christianity, proto-capitalist mercantilism, African lineage systems) were suddenly juxtaposed and forced to come to terms with one another. [19] It was therefore a space of continual innovation and cultural creativity: as each side found their existing practices and categories inadequate in dealing with the others, a kind of pidgin culture emerged, particularly among figures like the *tangomaos*, "Portuguese speaking adventurers and traders who made their home on the Guinea mainland, in defiance of the orders of the crown, and who married there and established mulatto families" (Donelha in Pietz 1987: 39).

In this situation, Pietz argues, the standard Christian rubrics for dealing with alien religious practices just didn't seem to work. The most common of these had been "idolatry." Pagans worshipped idols. Idols were material images, made by human beings, that represented invisible powers—conceived as a god or a spirit, though the Christian knew them to really be demons—with whom the worshipper came into relation by some kind of verbal compact. Here was the key difference with fetishism. Fetishes—at least in the descriptions of the first Portuguese and Dutch traders—did not represent anything; they were material objects seen as having power in and of themselves; imaginary products, in effect, of the merchants' own materialistic cosmology. As MacGaffey noted early on (1994), this materialistic emphasis was precisely what was missing from the way Africans talked about these things (making one wonder how much one is really talking about a "pidgin culture" at all). Some of the items labeled "fetishes" took the form of images, many did not; but verbal compacts and invisible spirits were almost invariably involved. The foreign missionaries who were the first to establish themselves in Imerina, for instance, did not hesitate to label their Merina equivalents "idols" instead of "fetishes," even though *sampy* only rarely took representational form. The difference between Malagasy "idols" and West African "fetishes" seems to be quite simply that the former were first named by missionaries and the latter, mainly by merchants, men really only concerned with exchange and questions of material value. Questions of production or creation, let alone the production or creation of social relations, were simply of little interest to those Pietz cites. As a result, what is to me, at least, the most fascinating aspect of the whole complex of ideas drops away from their accounts. Here I am referring to the notion of "making fetish"—that by a form of collective investment one can, in effect, create a new god on the spot. This casual attitude toward divinity also seems to be what most startled European newcomers to Africa, and ultimately caused them to launch into peculiar fantasies about people who worship the first thing they see in the morning. It was the improvisational quality of the ritual surrounding fetishes, which made it appear to them that, in many African societies at least, it was particularly in the domain of religion—what should have been the domain of eternal verities—that everything was up for grabs, precisely because this was also the main locus for social creativity. In this sense, as we'll see, the issue is not so much that these were objects that existed in a "space of revolution," but rather that they were themselves revolutionary objects.

Necessary Illusions?

So what, then, is a fetish?

A fetish is a god under process of construction.

At least, if "fetish" can still be used as a technical term at all in this context—and of course there's no consensus on this point—this is what I would suggest. [20]

Fetishes exist precisely at the point where conventional distinctions between "magic" and "religion" become meaningless, where charms become deities. Frazer of course argued that magic is a technique, a way humans try to shape the world to their will—if only by mistaken means—while religion was instead a matter of submitting to an external authority. [21] For Durkheim, magic was ritual pursued for purely individual ends; it becomes religion when it acquires a church, a congregation; because religion is about society. Fetishism, then, is the point where each slips into the other: where objects we have created or appropriated for our own purposes suddenly come to be seen as powers imposed on us, precisely at the moment when they come to embody some newly created social bond.

This may sound rather abstract, but if one looks carefully at the ethnographic evidence, this is exactly what happens. Ordinary life in rural Madagascar is still full of different sorts of "medicine" (*fanafody*), a term which covers everything from herbal infusions to charms with the power to bring bolts of lightning down on an enemy's head. Most people know how to make or work one or two sorts, or at the very least, are willing to encourage others to speculate that they might. The simplest charms are improvised for a specific occasion; others are more permanent; very important, older charms which affect whole communities—charms which guard the crops against hail, or protect villages from thieves—which have names and histories and keepers, or even have to be renewed (like kings) by periodic sacrifice. In earlier centuries, certain of these went on to take on a more general role as protectors of communities, and these came to be known as "*sampy*." They were ultimately collections of bits of rare wood, beads and silver ornaments, kept hidden under cloth or in boxes, usually with little houses of their own. Sometimes, they spoke through their keepers. They had names and stories, wills and desires. They received homage, gave blessings, imposed taboos. They were, in other words, very much like gods. Especially when they came to be adopted into the royal pantheon: at any given time, the king would choose twelve or so to be the guardians of the kingdom. These would be borne before the royal army during campaigns. They were present at important rituals, their ritual days were national holidays, and their keepers were a de facto priesthood. These were also the "idols"—with names like Kelimalaza, Manjakatsiroa, Ravololona—that so offended the English missionaries in the nineteenth century. Yet, this was also a very unstable pantheon. If these were gods—and in fact they were called "gods" (*Andriamanitra*, the same word used for the Creator, or later the Christian God)—their hold on godhood seemed remarkably tenuous. New *sampy* would appear; older ones might slip into obscurity, or else be exposed as frauds or witchcraft and purged from the pantheon. There literally was no clear line between ordinary "magic" and deities, but for that reason, the deities were a constant process of construction. They were not seen as representing timeless essences, but powers that had proved, at least for the moment, effective and benevolent. [22]

West African "fetishes" were not exactly the same as Merina *sampy*—they tended to be more destructive in their powers, more caught up in the logic of affliction. There were other subtle differences—but there, too, we find the same continuum between casual charms and quasi-deities, the same sense of objects created through human actions, property that could be possessed, inherited, even bought and sold; tools, but at the same time objects of obeisance and adoration, capable of acting with potentially devastating autonomy.

So what does all this strange theology have to do with social creativity per se? Here, I think we can finally return to Marx.

For Marx, the "fetishism of commodities" was one particular instance of a much more general phenomenon of "alienation." Collectively, human beings create their worlds, but owing to the extraordinary complexity of how all this creative activity is coordinated socially, no one can really keep track of the process, let alone take control of it. As a result, we are constantly confronting our own actions and creations as if they were alien powers. Fetishism is simply when this happens to material objects. Like African fetishists, the argument goes, we end up making things and then treating them like gods.

The actual argument in *Capital*, chapter 2, is of course much more complicated. In it, Marx is mainly making a point about value. For Marx, value always comes from labor; or to be more precise, value is the symbolic form through which our labors become meaningful to us by becoming part of some larger social system. Yet, in capitalism, consumers tend to see the value of commodities as somehow inhering in the objects themselves, rather than in the human efforts required to put those qualities in them. We are surrounded by objects designed and produced for our pleasure or convenience. They embody the intentions of people who anticipated our needs and desires and sank their energies into creating objects that would satisfy them; but owing to the workings of the market system, we normally don't have the slightest idea who any of those people are or how they went about it. Therefore, all those intentions end up seeming like they are properties of the object itself. Objects therefore seem to be things we can enter into personal relations with; we become indignant, hit them or kick them when they don't work, and so on. Actually, capitalism seems rife with such subject/object reversals: capital grows, money is always fleeing one market and seeking out another, pork bellies doing this, the annuities market doing that. In every case, what's happening is that we are operating in a system so complicated we couldn't possibly see all of it, so we mistake our own particular perspective on the whole, that little window we have on it, with the nature of the totality itself. Because, from the point of view of the consumer, products might as well have simply jumped out into the market with a personal commitment to play their DVDs or vacuum their apartments; from the perspective of the businessman, money might as well be fleeing some markets, and so on.[23]

This jumbling of agency might seem innocent enough; particularly since, if really challenged on the matter, few would defend the premise that commodities really have minds of their own, or that money really flees markets all of its own accord. For Marx, it becomes dangerous for two reasons. First, because it obscures the process of how value is created. This is of course convenient for those who might wish to extract value they did not play much of a role in creating. Money represents the value of labor, but wage laborers work to get money; it thus becomes a representation that brings into being what it represents. It is thus easy to see it as the source of that value, or *as* value (since again, from the laborer's perspective, it might as well be). In the same way, tokens of honor (rather than honorable actions) can come to seem the source of prestige, tokens of grace (rather than acts of devotion) the source of divine favor, tokens of conviviality the source of fun, and so on. Second, all this makes it much easier to treat the "laws of the market," or tendencies of whatever system it may be, as natural, immutable, and therefore completely outside any possibility of human intervention. This is, of course, exactly what happens in the case of capitalism, even—perhaps especially—when one steps out of one's immediate situated perspective and tries to talk about the system as a whole. Not only are the laws of the market taken to be immutable, the creation of material objects is assumed to be the whole point, the commodities themselves the only human value, so that in Botswana or South Africa, for example, one can witness the bizarre spectacle of government officials and their World Bank advisors declaring that the fact that, in some areas, half of the population is dying of AIDS is a real problem because it's going to have devastating effects on "the economy"—apparently oblivious to the fact that, until fairly recently, "the economy" was universally assumed to be the way we distribute material goods so as to keep people alive.

The emphasis on value theory makes it easier to understand the strange disparity—with which I began—between Marx's view of material production, and the way he talks about what I have been calling social creativity, or revolution. In producing a house or a chair, one first imagines something and then tries to bring it into being. In fomenting revolution, one must never do this.[24] The main reason for the disparity seems to be that, as Hans Joas points out, Marx does seem to reduce human creativity to two modalities: production (which happens all the time), or revolution (which happens only occasionally). Not in principle: in the *German Ideology*, for example, Marx states very clearly that the production of material goods was always, at the same time, the production of people and social relations, and all this was a creative process and therefore in constant transformation. But Joas is right to say that in Marx's concrete analyses of events of his own day, all of this does rather tend to fade away. Social creativity tends to get reduced to political action—even, to dramatic, revolutionary change.

One reason is because, in carrying out this kind of value analysis, one has to assume that the social system surrounding production is pretty much stable.

Let me illustrate. To say that, in fetishizing commodities, or money, one is confusing one's partial perspective on a system with the nature of the system as a whole, does at the very least imply that a whole system exists and that it is possible to know something about it. In the case of a market system, this is a perfectly reasonable claim: all economic study is premised on the assumption that there are things called "markets" and that it is possible to understand something about how they work. Presumably, the knowledge required is not comprehensive: one need not know exactly who designed and produced the pack of cigarettes or Palm Pilot in one's pocket in order to avoid fetishizing it.[25] One simply needs to know how these things generally tend to work, the logic of the system, how human energies are mobilized, organized, and end up embodied in objects. But this, in turn, implies the system tends to work roughly the same way over time. What if it doesn't? What if it's in a process of transformation? What if, to take an extreme example, the system in question does not yet exist, because you are, in fact, trying to bring it into being through that very act of fetishism?

In the case of many of these African fetishes, this was exactly what was happening. Merchants who "drank" or "made fetish" together might not have been creating a vast market system, but usually the point was to create a small one: stipulating terms and rates of exchange, rules of credit and regimes of property that could then be the basis of ongoing transactions. Even when fetishes were not explicitly about establishing contracts of one sort or another, they were almost invariably the basis for creating something new: congregations, new social relations, new communities. Hence any "totality" involved was, at least at first, virtual, imaginary, and prospective. What's more—and this is the really crucial point—it was an imaginary totality that could only come into real existence if everyone acted as if the fetish object actually did have subjective qualities. In the case of contracts, this means: act as if it really will punish you for breaking the rules.

These were, in other words, revolutionary moments. They involved the creation of something new. They might not have been moments of total transformation, but realistically, it's not as if any transformation is ever really total. Every act of social creativity is to some degree revolutionary, unprecedented: from establishing a friendship to nationalizing a banking system. None are completely so. These things are always a matter of degree.[26]

Yet, this is precisely where we find the logic of fetishism cropping up— even the origin of the word "fetish"—and it doesn't seem to be misrepresenting anything. Of course, it would also be going too far to say that the fetishistic view is simply true: Lunkanka can't really tie anyone's intestines into knots; Ravololona can't really prevent hail from falling on anyone's crops. As I have remarked elsewhere (Graeber 2001), ultimately we are probably just dealing here with the paradox of power, something which exists only if other people think it does; a paradox that I've also argued lies also at the core of magic, which always seems to be surrounded by an aura of fraud, showmanship, and chicanery. But one could argue it is not just the paradox of power. It is also the paradox of creativity. This has always been one of the ironies of Marxism. Marx ultimately wanted to liberate human beings from everything that held back or denied them control of their creative capacities, by which he meant first and foremost, all forms of alienation. But what exactly would a free, non-alienated producer look like? It's never clear in Marx's own work. Not exactly like an independent craftsperson, presumably, since the latter are usually caught in the shackles of tradition. Probably more like an artist, or a musician, or a poet, or even an author (like Marx himself). But when artists, musicians, poets, or authors describe their own experience of creativity, they almost invariably begin evoking just the sort of subject/object reversals which Marx saw as typical of fetishism: almost never do they see themselves as anything like an architect rationally calculating dimensions and imposing their will on the world; instead, one almost invariably hears how they feel they are vehicles for some kind of inspiration coming from outside, how they lose themselves, fragment themselves, leave portions of themselves in their products. All the more so with social creativity: it seems no coincidence that Mauss' work on the "origins of the idea of the contract" in *The Gift* led him to meditate endlessly on exactly these kind of subject/object reversals, with gifts and givers becoming hopelessly entangled. Put this way, it might seem to lead to a genuine dilemma. Is non-fetishized consciousness possible? If so, would we even want it?

In fact, the dilemma is illusory. If fetishism is, at root, our tendency to see our own actions and creations as having power over us, how can we treat it as an intellectual mistake? Our actions and creations do have power over us. This is simply true. Even for a painter, every stroke is a sort of commitment. It affects what she can do afterwards. In fact, this becomes all the more true, the less caught in the shackles of tradition one becomes. Even in the freest of societies, we would presumably feel bound by our commitments to others. Even under Castoriadis' ideal of autonomy, where no one would have to operate within institutions whose rules they had not themselves, collectively, created, we are still creating rules and then allowing them to have power over us. If discussion of such matters tends towards metaphoric inversions, it's because it involves a juxtaposition of something that (on some level) everyone understands—that we tend to become the slaves of our own creations—and something no one really understands—how exactly are we able to create new things in the first place?

If so, the real question is how one gets from this perfectly innocuous level to the kind of complete insanity where the best reason one can come up with to regret the death of millions is because of its effects on the economy. The key factor would appear to be, not whether one sees things as a bit topsy-turvy from one's immediate perspective—something like this seems inevitable, both in the realization of value, which always seems to operate through concrete symbolic forms, and especially in moments of transformation or creativity—but rather, whether one has the capacity to at least occasionally step into some overarching perspective from which the machinery is visible, where one can see that all these apparently fixed objects are really part of an ongoing process of construction. Or, at the very least, whether one is not trapped in an overarching perspective that insists they are not. The danger comes when fetishism gives way to theology, the absolute assurance that the gods are real.

Consider again the confrontation between Pietz' European merchant adventurers in the sixteenth and seventeenth centuries, and their West African counterparts—many merchants themselves. I've already argued that while both arrived with a number of broadly shared cosmological assumptions—for instance, that we live in a fallen world, that the human condition is fundamentally one of suffering—there were also a number of profound differences which the Europeans found deeply disturbing (whether their African partners were equally disturbed by the encounter we are not in a position to know). To reduce the matter to something of a caricature: the European merchants were, as Pietz stressed, budding materialists. They were Christians, but for the most part their interest in theological questions seems to have been negligible; the main effect of their faith was to guarantee the absolute assurance that ideas they did not see as Christian were, by definition, wrong. This, in turn, had an effect when they thought about things they really did find interesting: matters of trade, material wealth, and economic value. Confronted with abundant evidence of the arbitrariness of value, they instead fell back on the position that Africans themselves were arbitrary: they were fetishists, willing to ascribe divine status to a completely random collection of material objects.

In the European accounts, social relations tend to disappear. They were simply of no interest. For them, there was therefore virtually nothing in between God and the world of material objects. But the Europeans could at least compliment themselves that, unlike Africans, they managed to keep the two apart. Of course they were wrong. The whole thing was largely a projection. They were, in fact, already well on the way to the kind of fetishism described by Marx where social relations, for the very reason that they are made to disappear, end up getting projected onto objects. All this was in dramatic contradistinction with the Africans, for whom social relations were everything. As Jane Guyer (1993, Guyer & Belinga 1995) has pointed out, conventional economic categories are hard to apply in such contexts, because people (rights in women's fertility, authority over children, the loyalty of followers, disciples, recognition of titles, or status, or accomplishment) were the ultimate form of wealth. Material objects were interesting mainly insofar as they became entangled in social relations, or enabled one to create new ones. Since wealth and power could not, ultimately, be distinguished, there was no way to idealize government (which disturbed Europeans); it also made for an enchanted world—one in which, for that very reason, the mechanics of enchantment were never very far from the surface (which disturbed them even more). It was as if everything existed in that middle zone which the Europeans were trying to evacuate; everything was social, nothing was fixed, therefore everything was both material and spiritual simultaneously.

This is the zone in which we encounter the "fetish." Now, it is probably true that most gods have always been in the process of construction. They exist at some point along the passage from an imaginary level of pure magic—where all powers are human powers, where all the tricks and mirrors are visible—to pure theology, with an absolute commitment to the principle that the constructive apparatus does not exist. But objects like *akombo*, *minkisi, sampy*—or, for that matter, the improvised "fetishes" made of Bibles and bits of wood through which half-Portuguese *tangomaos* negotiated business deals—seem to have existed at a point almost exactly in between. They were both human creations and alien powers at the same time. In Marxist terms, they were fetishes from one perspective, from another, they were not fetishized at all. Both perspectives were simultaneously available. But both perspectives were also mutually dependent. The remarkable thing is how much, even when the actors seemed perfectly aware that they were constructing an illusion, they also seemed aware that the illusion was still required. It rather reminds one of the practice of shadow puppetry in Southeast Asia: the whole point is to create an illusion, the puppets themselves are supposed to be invisible, mere shadows on the screen, but if you observe actual performances, you usually find the audience is ranged around in a big circle so that many of them can only see the puppets and can't actually see the illusion at all. There doesn't seem to be a feeling that they're missing out on much. Nonetheless, it would not be a performance if the illusion did not take place.

This is what one might expect in a world of almost constant social creativity; in which few arrangements were fixed and permanent, and, even more, where was little feeling that they really should be fixed and permanent; in which, in short, people were indeed in a constant process of imagining new social arrangements and then trying to bring them into being. Gods could be created, and discarded or fade away, because social arrangements themselves were never assumed to be immutable.

In this sense, one might even propose that classic African fetishes are almost precisely the opposite of the phenomenon described by Marx, or, for that matter, Freud. The remarkable thing about these sorts of fetish objects, from an ideological point of view, is—as Valerio Valeri (2001), for example, points out—that the fetishist is ostensibly aware he is dealing with an illusion. Freud insisted that his patients were perfectly well aware that a shoe, for example, was not really a sexual object, let alone a maternal penis. It's just that this knowledge did not make any difference to them. One could say exactly the same thing of the businessman reading the *Wall Street Journal* and contemplating the latest adventures of pork bellies, futures funds, or "the market" in general. If one were to point out to such a person that pork bellies do not really "do" anything, he would no doubt groan or throw up his eyes at the painful obviousness of this observation. Of course they don't. It's just a way of speaking. At the same time he acts *as if* that way of speaking were in fact true. Awareness of the illusion makes no difference. In fact, one could go further: this is an illusion that manages to deceive its victims precisely by reassuring them that it is an illusion, that they are not deceived.

African fetishes then could be said to work on the opposite principle. Those who made, drank, hammered, or "repaired" them insisted as loudly as possible that they were, in fact, taken in by the illusion. Yet their actions were otherwise.

What does all this teach us about the grand theoretical issues raised at the beginning? If nothing else, that if one takes seriously the idea of social creativity, one will probably have to abandon some of the dreams of certainty that have so enchanted the partisans both of holistic and individualistic models. No doubt, processes of social creativity are, to some degree, unchartable. This is probably all for the best. There are certain things that ought not to be tabulated. Making it the centerpiece of a social theory, regardless, seems like it would be an increasingly important gesture at a time when the heirs of Pietz's merchants have managed to impose their strange, materialist theology on not just Africans, but almost everyone—to the extent that human life itself can be seen as having no value except as a means to produce fetishized commodities.

Endnotes

1   In the last chapter of *Towards an Anthropological Theory of Value* (Graeber 2001), subtitled "The Problem of the Fetish, IIIb." What follows was, in large part, originally written for that chapter but ended up having to be cut for reasons of space. I was tempted to call it "The Problem of the Fetish IIIc," but decided the joke was too obscure even for my tastes.

2   Especially in Italy. The most familiar representative for most readers in the Anglophone world is Toni Negri, but most of the ideas presented in *Empire* are the products of a long tradition involving many other writers and activists.

3   For Castoriadis, history is no longer a matter of the development or play of productive or class forces, but the work of the "the imaginary, which is creation ex nihilo," such that change is "the positing of a new type of behavior...the institution of a new social rule, ... the invention of a new object or a new form" that is "an emergence or a production which cannot be deduced on the basis of a previous situation" (Castoriadis 1987: 3, 44).

4   The tie to the Autonomist school can be seen by looking at the early work of Toni Negri, on constituent power (1999). Essentially, he's trying to work out exactly the same problems: what is that popular power of creativity that emerges during moments of revolution and how would it possible to institutionalize it?

5   Actually there's no particular reason why gold should be a better medium of exchange than beads. Economists of course might make the argument that the supply of gold in the world is inherently limited, while glass beads can be manufactured in endless number. However, there is no way that European merchants of that day could have had the slightest idea how much of the earth's crust was composed of gold; they saw it as precious because it was got with difficulty from far away, just as Africans did beads.

6   At least, he does not in the first three, best-known articles (1985, 1987, 1988). He does address West African ideas in two later articles concerned with debt and human sacrifice (1995, 1997). These essays, however, are concerned with a later historical period, and somewhat different sorts of questions.

7   This would be one reason why Africans have been, from such an early period, comparatively receptive to religions like Christianity and Islam.

8   Most African cosmologies posit the creator as in one way or another beyond good and evil, as, for instance, an otiose creator who has abandoned the world, or a force of violence beyond all moral accounting whose very arbitrariness demonstrates his local priority to, and hence ability to constitute, any system of human justice.

9   More precisely, symptoms.

10   Bohannan interprets these movements as regular features of Tiv social structure. More recently, Nigerian scholars (Tseayo 1975; Makar 1994) have placed them in the colonial context, as a result of British efforts to force a highly egalitarian group into the framework of a state based on indirect rule. In fact, there's no real way to

know whether such movements did occur earlier, but it seems reasonable to assume some such mechanism existed, at least, for as long as Tiv egalitarianism itself did.

11   MacGaffey (1986) suggests the archetypal BaKongo ritual cycle leads from affliction to sacrifice to retreat to receiving gifts to new status.

12   The text is as in MacGaffey except I have translated *nganga* ("curer, keeper of a nkisi") and its plural (*banganga*) into English.

13   Personal communication, March 2000. Just as in Hobbes, this creates some overarching power of violence which can ensure people fulfill their contractual obligations and respect one another's property rights—which, if we look again at Pietz's material, becomes especially ironic. Here we have European merchant adventurers swearing oaths and making agreements with Africans over objects they called "fetishes," at exactly the same time authors like Hobbes were inventing social contract theory back home. But it was apparently the Africans who saw the act as creating a sort of social contract; the Europeans seem to have had other fish to fry.

      All this obviously raises the question of whether there is any reason to believe that Hobbes, among others, were aware of what was going on in Africa at the time. In Hobbes' case at least, I have managed to find no concrete evidence. While Hobbes grew up in a merchant household, in his entire published corpus his only mentions of Africa, as far as I am aware, are via Classical references.

14   Clearly, what I am suggesting here could be considered a variant of the famous "wealth in people" argument (see for instance Guyer 1993, Guyer & Belinga 1995).

15   Obviously, this is a bit of a simplification.

16   According to Bohannan & Bohannan (1968: 233), having a "strong heart" means you have "both courage and attractiveness."

17   This is by no means unique to Madagascar. In the BaKongo case, too, royal power was seen as created through the same means as fetishes.

18   In fact, the word "fetish" derives from a Portuguese term meaning "something made," or even "artificial." This is why the term was also used for cosmetics ("make-up") (Baudrillard 1972: 91). Baudrillard's conclusion—that fetishes do not make some arbitrary ideology seem natural, but instead inspire a kind of fascination with its very artificiality—while wildly overstated, it seems to me, still has something profoundly insightful about it, and might be compared with my own conclusions at the end of this article.

19   The phrase is adopted from Frederick Jameson. Jameson's notion of "cultural revolution" (1981: 95–97), in turn, goes back to a certain strain of Althusserian Marxism: the idea is that as one ruling class is in the gradual process of replacing another, the conflict between them can become a crisis of meaning, as, radically different "conceptualities, habits and life forms, and value systems" exist alongside one another. The Enlightenment, for example, could be seen as one dramatic moment in a long cultural revolution in which those of the old feudal aristocracy were

"systematically dismantled" and replaced with those of an emerging bourgeoisie. In the case of the West African coast one is, of course, speaking not of one class replacing another but a confrontation of different cultural worlds.

20 Mauss for example advised his students that the term "fetish" was useless as a theoretical term and should be eliminated.

21 This is why, as I've suggested (2001: 239–47), Marxists have such a difficulty figuring out what to think about magic.

22 That is to say there was nothing like the fixed, mythological pantheon one finds among the Greeks, or Babylonians, or Yoruba, where objects of cult could be identified with some enduring figure like Athena, Marduk, or Shango.

23 As Terry Turner and others have argued at some length (see Graeber 2001: 64–66), all this is pretty much exactly what Piaget was talking about when he described childish "egocentrism": the inability to understand that one's own perspective on a situation is not identical to reality itself, but just one of an endless variety of possible perspectives, which in childhood too leads to treating objects as if they had subjective qualities.

24 Even this is somewhat deceptive language because it implies the production of people and social relations is not itself "material." In fact, I've argued elsewhere (see chapter 3) that the very distinction between "material infrastructure" and "ideological superstructure" is itself a form of idealism.

25 In point of fact, if one does, this can lead to fetishism of a different sort, as in the sort one sees in heirloom valuables in many gift systems, which are seen as embodying or including the personalities of certain former owners.

26 From a Marxian perspective it might be rather disturbing to see business deals as a prototype for revolutionary activity; but one must bear in mind it comes with the argument that the prototypical form of contract, even between business partners, is communism.

Bibliography

Abrahamsson, Hans
1952 *The Origin of Death: Studies in African Mythology.* Studia ethnographica Upsaliensia; III. Uppsala : Almquist.

Akiga
1939 *Akiga's story; the Tiv tribe as seen by one of its members.* Translated and annotated by Rupert East. London, New York, Published for the International African Institute by the Oxford University Press.

Akins, David and Joel Robbins
1999 "An Introduction to Melanesian Currencies: Agencies, Identity, and Social Reproduction." In *Money and Modernity: State and Local Currencies in Melanesia* (David Atkins and Joel Robbins, eds.). Pittsburgh: University of Pittsburgh Press.

Apter, Emily and William Pietz, eds.
1993 *Fetishism as Cultural Discourse*. Ithaca: Cornell University, 1990.

Bhaskar, Roy
1979 *The Possibility of Naturalism*. Hempstead: Harvester Wheatshaft. (Second edition 1989).
1993 *Dialectic: The Pulse of Freedom*. London: Verso.
1994 *Plato Etc*. London: Verso.
2001 *Reflections on Meta-Reality: Transcendence, Emancipation, and Everyday Life*. New Delhi and Thousand Oaks, Ca.: Sage Publications.
2002 *From Science to Emancipation: Alienation and the Actuality of Enlightenment*. New Delhi and Thousand Oaks, CA: Sage Publications.

Bohannan, Laura
1952 "A Genealogical Charter." *Africa* 22: 301–15.

Bohannan, Paul
1955 "Some Principles of Exchange and Investment among the Tiv." *American Anthropologist* 57: 60–67.
1957 *Justice and Judgment among the Tiv*. London: Oxford University Press.
1958 "Extra-Processual Events in Tiv Political Institutions." *American Anthropologist* 60: 1–12
1959 "The Impact of Money on an African Subsistence Economy." *Journal of Economic History* 19: 491–503.

Bohannan, Paul and Laura Bohannan
1953 *The Tiv of Central Nigeria*. London: International African Institute.
1968 *Tiv Economy*. Evanston: Northwestern University Press.
1969 *A Source Notebook on Tiv Religion*. 5 volumes. New Haven: Human Relations Area Files.

Bosman, Willem
1705 *A new and accurate description of the coast of Guinea, divided into the Gold, the Slave, and the Ivory Coasts*. London: Knapton (New York: Barnes & Noble, 1967).

Caillé, Alain
2000 *Anthropologie du Don: le Tiers Paradigme*. Paris: Descelée de Brouwer.

Callet, R. P.
1908 *Tantara ny Andriana eto Madagascar*. Tananarive: Académie Malgache.

Castoriadis, Cornelius
1987 *The Imaginary Institution of Society* (Kathleen Blamey, trans.). Cambridge: Polity Press.
1991 *Philosophy, Politics, Autonomy: Essays in Political Philosophy* (David Ames Curtis, ed.). New York: Oxford University Press.
1992 "Philosophie ist eine Ausdrucksform der Autonomie," *Deutsche Zeitschrift für Philosophie* 40 no 5: 464

Ciaramelli, Fabio
1998 "The Circle of the Origin." In *Reinterpreting the Political: Continental Philosophy and Political Theory* (Lenore Langsdorf and Stephen H. Watson with Karen A. Smith, eds.). Albany: State University of New York Press.

Cousins, William E.
1963 *Fomba Gasy*. (H. Randzavola, ed.) Tananarive: Imarivolanitra.

Dant, Tim
1996 "Fetishism and the Social Value of Objects." *Sociological Review* 44: 495–516.

Durkheim, Emile
1901 *Les formes élémentaires de la vie religieuse, le système totémique en Australie.* Paris: Presses Universitaires de France, 1968.

Ekholm, Kajsa
1991 *Catastrophe and Creation: The Transformation of an African Culture.* Philadelphia: Harwood Academic Publishers.

Ellen, Roy
1988 "Fetishism." *Man* (n.s.) 23: 213–35.
1990 "Nuaulu Sacred Shields. The Reproduction of Things or the Reproduction of Images?" *Etnofoor* 3 (1): 5–25.

Ellis, William
1838 *History of Madagascar.* 2 vols. London: Fisher & Son.

Frazer, James
1911–15 *The Golden Bough: A Study in Magic and Religion.* London: Macmillan and Company.

Godbout, Jacques T. and Alain Caillé
1998 *The World of the Gift.* Montréal: McGill-Queen's University Press.

Graeber, David
1996 "Love Magic and Political Morality in Central Madagascar, 1875–1990." *Gender and History* 8(3): 94–117.
1997 "Manners, Deference and Private Property: the Generalization of Avoidance in Early Modern Europe." *Comparative Studies in Society and History* 39(4): 694–728.
2001 *Toward an Anthropological Theory of Value: The False Coin of Our Own Dreams.* New York: Palgrave.
2006 "Turning Modes of Production Inside Out: Or, Why Capitalism is a Transformation of Slavery (short version)," *Critique of Anthropology* Volume 26 no 1 (March 2006), 61–81.
2007 *Lost People: Magic and the Legacy of Slavery in Madagascar.* Bloomington: Indiana University Press.

Guyer, Jane I.
1993 "Wealth in People and Self-Realization in Equatorial Africa." *Man* 28 (2): 243–65.

Guyer, Jane I. and Samuel M. Eno Belinga
1995 "Wealth in People as Wealth in Knowledge: Accumulation and Composition in Equatorial Africa." *Journal of African History* 36: 91–120.

Hobbes, Thomas
1651 *Leviathan, or, The Matter, Form, and Power of a Common-Wealth Ecclesiastical and Civil.* London: Printed for Andrew Crooke, at the Green Dragon in St. Pauls Churchyard.

Joas, Hans
1993 "Institutionalization as a Creative Process: The Sociological Importance of Cornelius Castoriadis' Political Philosophy." In *Pragmatism and Social Theory.* Chicago: University of Chicago Press.
1996 *The Creativity of Action.* Chicago: University of Chicago Press.

2000 *The Genesis of Values.* Cambridge: Polity Press.

Keane, Webb

1997 "From Fetishism to Sincerity: On Agency, the Speaking Subject, and Their Historicity in the Context of Religious Conversion." *Comparative Studies in Society and History* 39: 674–693.

1998 "Calvin in the Tropics: Objects and Subjects at the Religious Frontier." In *Border Fetishisms: Material Objects in Unstable Spaces* (P. Spyer, ed.). New York: Routledge.

MacGaffey, Wyatt

1970 *Custom and Government in the Lower Congo.* Los Angeles: University of California.

1977 "Fetishism Revisited: Kongo nkisi in Sociological Perspective." *Africa* 47 (2): 172–184.

1983 *Modern Kongo Prophets: Religion in a Plural Society.* Bloomington: Indiana University Press.

1986 *Religion and Society in Central Africa.* Chicago: University of Chicago Press.

1987 "Lulendo: The Recovery of a Kongo Nkisi." *Ethnos* 52: 339–49.

1988 "Complexity, Astonishment and Power: The Visual Vocabulary of Kongo Mikisi." *Journal of Southern African Studies* 14 (2): 188–203.

1991 *Art and Healing of the Bakongo Commented by Themselves: Minkisi from the Laman Collection.* Stockholm: Folkens Museum Etnografiska.

1994 "African Objects and the Idea of the Fetish." *RES: Journal of Anthropology and Aesthetics* 25: 123–31.

2000 *Kongo political culture: the conceptual challenge of the particular.* Bloomington: Indiana University Press.

Marx, Karl

1846 *The German Ideology.* New York: International Publishers, 1970.

1858 *The Grundrisse.* New York: Harper and Row, 1973.

1858 *Pre-Capitalist Economic Formations.* (Jack Cohen, trans.). New York: International Publishers, 1965.

1859 *Contribution to the Critique of Political Economy.* New York: International Publishers.

1867 *Capital.* New York: New World Paperbacks, 1967. 3 volumes.

Mauss, Marcel

1925 "Essai sur le don. Forme et raison de l'échange dans les sociétés archaïques." *Annee sociologique,* 1 (series 2): 30–186.

1925a "Socialisme et Bolchévisme." *Le Monde Slave,* Year 2 number 2, 201–22. Translated as "A Sociological Assessment of Bolshevism" by Ben Brewster in *The Radical Sociology of Durkheim and Mauss.* London: Routledge.

1947 *Manuel d'ethnographie.* Paris: Payot.

1965 *The Gift: Forms and Functions of Exchange in Archaic Societies.* (I. Cunnison, trans.). New York: Norton.

1968–69 *Oeuvres.* 3 volumes. Paris: Editions de Minuit.

1997 *Écrits Politiques: Textes réunis et présentés par Marcel Fournier.* Paris: Fayard.

Miklitsch, Robert

1996 "The Commodity-Body-Sign: Toward a General Economy of Commodity Fetishism." *Cultural Critique* 33: 5–70.

Munn, Nancy

1977 "The Spatiotemporal Transformations of Gawan Canoes." *Journal de la Société des Océanistes.* Tome 33 (mars–juin) 54-55: 39–53.

1986   *The Fame of Gawa: A Symbolic Study of Value Transformation in a Massim (Papua New Guinea) Society.* Cambridge, Cambridge University Press.

Myers, Fred

1986   *Pintupi Country, Pintupi Self: Sentiment, Place, and Politics among Western Desert Aborigines.* Washington: Smithsonian Institution Press.

Negri, Antonio

1999   *Insurgencies: Constituent Power and the Modern State.* (Maurizia Boscagli, trans.). Minneapolis : University of Minnesota Press.

Pels, Peter

1998   "The Spirit of Matter: On Fetish, Rarity, Fact, and Fancy." In *Border Fetishisms: Material Objects in Unstable Spaces* (P. Spyer, ed.). New York: Routledge.

Pietz, William

1985   "The Problem of the Fetish I." *RES: Journal of Anthropology and Aesthetics* 9: 5–17.

1987   "The Problem of the Fetish II: The Origin of the Fetish" *RES: Journal of Anthropology and Aesthetics* 13: 23–45.

1988   "The Problem of the Fetish IIIa: Bosman's Guinea and the Enlightenment Theory of Fetishism." *RES: Journal of Anthropology and Aesthetics* 16: 105–23.

1993   "Fetishism and Materialism: The Limits of Theory in Marx." In *Fetishism as Cultural Discourse* (Emily Apter and William Pietz, eds.). Ithaca: Cornell University Press.

1995a   "The Spirit of Civilization: Blood Sacrifice and Monetary Debt" *RES: Journal of Anthropology and Aesthetics* 28: 23–38.

1995b   "Death and the Deodand: Accursed Objects and the Money Value of Human Life." In *(Un)Fixing Representation* (Judith Farquar, Tomoko Masuzawa, and Carol Mavor, eds.). Minneapolis: University of Minnesota Press.

Piot, Charles

1991   "Of Persons and Things: Some Reflections on African Spheres of Exchange." *Man* (n.s.) 26: 405–424.

Pool, Robert

1990   "Fetishism Deconstructed." *Etnofoor* 3 (1): 114–127.

Quiggin, A.H.

1949   *Trade Routes, Trade and Currency in East Africa.* Rhodes-Livingstone Museum: Occasional Papers no.5.

Rospabé, Philippe

1995   *La Dette de Vie: aux origines de la monnaie sauvage.* Paris: Editions la Découverte/ MAUSS.

Sahlins, Marshall

1972   *Stone Age Economics.* Chicago: Aldine.

1976   *Culture and Practical Reason.* Chicago: University of Chicago Press.

1981   *Historical Metaphors and Mythical Realities.* A.S.A.O. Special Publication no. 1. Ann Arbor: University of Michigan Press.

1982   "Individual Experience and Cultural Order." In *The Social Sciences: Their Nature and Uses* (William Kruskal, ed.). Chicago: University of Chicago Press.

1985   *Islands of History.* Chicago: University of Chicago Press.

1988   "Cosmologies of Capitalism." *Proceedings of the British Academy* 74: 1–51.

1991   "The Return of the Event, Again: With Reflections on the Beginnings of the Great Fijian War of 1843 to 1855 Between the Kingdoms of Bau and Rewa." In

Clio in Oceania (Aletta Biersack, ed.). Washington: Smithsonian Press.

1995   *How "Natives" Think: About Captain Cook, For Example.* Chicago: University of Chicago Press.

1996. "The Sadness of Sweetness: or, The Native Anthropology of Western Cosmology?" *Current Anthropology* 37 no. 3: 395–428.

Sibree, James

1875   *Madagascar: the Great African Island.* London: Trübner & Co.

1897   "The Malagasy Custom of 'Brotherhood by Blood.'" *Antananarivo Annual and Malagasy Magazine* 21: 1-6.

Spyer, Patricia

1998   *Border Fetishisms: Material Objects in Unstable Spaces* (P. Spyer, ed.). New York: Routledge, 183–207.

Thornton, John

1987   "The Kingdom of Kongo, ca. 1390–1678: the Development of an African Social Formation." *Cahiers d'Études africaines* 22: 325–42.

Tseayo, Justin Iyorbee

1975   *Conflict and Incorporation in Nigeria: The Integration of the Tiv.* Zaria, Nigeria: Gaskiya.

Turner, Terence

1979   "Anthropology and the Politics of Indigenous Peoples' Struggles." *Cambridge Anthropology* 5: 1–43.

1984   "Value, Production and Exploitation in Non-Capitalist societies." Unpublished essay based on a paper presented at the AAA 82nd Annual Meeting, Denver, Colorado. To appear in *Whose Creative Energy?: Action and Reflection in the Creation of Society (*ed. David Graeber and Setsuko Nakayama, Berghahn Press.)

1987   *The Kayapo of Southeastern Para.* Unpublished monograph prepared for CEDI, Povos Indigenas do Brasil, Vol. VIII, Sul do Para, Part II.

Turner, Victor

1967   *The Forest of Symbols: Aspects of Ndembu Ritual.* Ithaca, N.Y., Cornell University Press.

Valeri, Valerio

2001   "The Fetish" (Sarah Hill, trans.). In *Fragments from Forests and Libraries, A Collection of Essays by Valerio Valeri* (Janet Hoskins, ed.). Durham: Carolina Academic Press.

Van Gennep, Arnold

1960   *The Rites of Passage.* Chicago: University of Chicago Press.

Vansina, Jan

1973   *The Tio Kingdom of the Middle Congo 1880–1892.* Oxford: Oxford University Press.

1990   *Paths in the Rainforests: Toward a History of Political Tradition in Equatorial Africa.* Madison: University of Wisconsin Press.

PART II

PROVISIONAL AUTONOMOUS ZONE: DILEMMAS OF AUTHORITY IN RURAL MADAGASCAR

5

PROVISIONAL AUTONOMOUS ZONE: OR, THE GHOST-STATE IN MADAGASCAR

Shortly before I left for Madagascar I was talking to Henry Wright, an archeologist who had worked there for more than a decade. "You have to be careful," he said, "poking around the countryside." State authority was dissolving. In many parts of the island, he said, it had effectively ceased to exist. Even in the region around the capital there were reports of *fokon'olona*—village assemblies—beginning to carry out executions.

This was one of the many concerns forgotten almost as soon as I actually arrived in Madagascar. In the capital, there was quite obviously a functioning government; almost every educated person seemed to work for it. When I moved to Arivonimamo, a town about an hour to the West, things did not seem particularly different. Certainly, people talked about the government all the time; everybody acted as if there was one. There was an administrative structure, offices where people typed up documents, registered things, kept track of births and deaths and the number of people's cattle. One even had to get permission to carry out the most important rituals. The government ran schools, held national exams; there were gendarmes, a prison, an airfield with military jets.

It was only after I had been in Arivonimamo for some time—and even more, in retrospect, after I'd left—that I began to wonder whether what he told me might actually have been true. Perhaps it was simply my own bias, the fact that I had always lived under an efficient and omnipresent government, that made me read the cues the wrong way. Perhaps there really wasn't a state in Betafo at all; perhaps not even in Arivonimamo—or anyway, not one that behaves in any way like what I or other Westerners have come to assume a state is supposed to behave.

Before I explain what I mean by this, though, perhaps it would help to set the scene.

Arivonimamo and Betafo

I arrived in Madagascar on June 16, 1989. For the first six months, I lived in Antananarivo, the capital, studying the language and doing archival research. The National Archives in Antananarivo are a remarkable resource. In their collection are thousands of documents from the nineteenth century kingdom of Madagascar, most from the highland province of Imerina, which surrounded the capital. Almost all of it was in Malagasy. I went through hundreds of folders, carefully copying out everything concerned with the district of Eastern Imamo, the part of Imerina in which I intended to work. Eastern Imamo seemed, at the time, to have been a rather sleepy place, a rural hinterland far from the tumultuous political struggles of the capital, but at the same time insulated from the unstable fringes of Imerina, half-empty territories full of raiding bandits, industrial projects, and periodic revolts. It was a place where not much ever happened—and, thus, the perfect field on which to study the slow-moving processes of social and cultural change I was interested in.

Once I felt I had a minimal command of Malagasy, I set out for Arivonimamo, the major town of the region. It was not at all difficult to get there: Arivonimamo is only an hour from the capital by car. Before long I had established myself in town, and had begun making regular trips to the surrounding countryside, gathering oral histories, keeping an eye out for a likely place to do more detailed research.

Arivonimamo is a town of some ten thousand people that clusters around a stretch of the main highway leading west from the capital. In the 1960s and 1970s, it had been the home of the national airport, which sat in a broad valley to the south of town; but though the airport brought money and employment, it never seemed to become an integral part of the town's economy. It was largely a thing grafted on. The road from the airport did not pass through Arivonimamo itself; there wasn't even a place for travelers to spend the night there. In 1975, the airport was replaced by another, nearer the capital. The old airport was given to the military, which rarely, however, had the funds to use it. By 1990, all that remained to show that foreigners had once passed through here was the battered plywood shell of an empty restaurant, standing where the airport road merges with the highway just on the outskirts of town.

The current town centers on a taxi station, a wide asphalt expanse flanked by two great churches, Catholic and Protestant. At most hours, it was crowded with vans and station wagons filling up with passengers and bags and crates and heading off the capital, or further west down the highway. On the southern edge of the taxi stand is a wide spreading *amontana* tree, a very ancient sycamore that is considered the symbolic center of the town, the mark that it was once the place of kings. To its north is a marketplace with food stands and red-tiled arcades, which every Friday fills to overflowing with rural people and vendors under white umbrellas. The town itself clings to the road (the only place there is electricity); its houses are mostly two or three stories, with graceful pillars supporting verandahs around the second floor, and high-pitched roofs of tin or tile.

Arivonimamo is the capital of an administrative district of the same name. It contains several government offices and three high schools: one state school (CEG), one Catholic lycée, and one Protestant one. There is a clinic and, on a high bluff somewhat to the west of town, a small prison. Together with a gendarmes' barracks nearer the old airport, a post office, and a bank, these constitute the government presence. There was once a factory nearby but it had been abandoned for years by the time I was there; no one I knew was quite sure what, if anything, had ever been produced there. The town's commercial economy fell almost completely outside the formal (taxed, regulated) sector: there was a pharmacy and two large general stores, but that was about it. Otherwise, the population conformed to the general rule for Malagasy towns: almost everybody grows food; everybody sells something. Streets were fringed with dozens of little booths and stores, all stocked with the same narrow range of products: soap, rum, candles, cooking oil, biscuits, soda, bread. Anyone who had a car was a member of the taxi collective; anyone who had a VCR was a theater operator; anyone who had a sewing machine was a manufacturer of clothing.

The province of Imerina has always centered on the gigantic irrigated plains surrounding the national capital, Antananarivo, which have long had a very dense population and been the center of powerful kingdoms. In the nineteenth century, the Merina kingdom conquered most of Madagascar; since the French conquest of 1895, Antananarivo has remained the center of administration, and the surrounding territory remains the ancestral lands of most of Madagascar's administrators and educated elite. The territory that now makes up the district of Arivonimamo was always somewhat marginal. It was late to be incorporated into the kingdom, and it was never more than weakly integrated into the networks of cash and patronage centered on the capital. So it remains. Now, as then, it is a political and economic margin, a place where not much ever happens.

To the north of Arivonimamo is a rolling country of endless red hills, some covered only with grass, others wooded with eucalyptus trees, stretches of *tapia*—which look like dwarf oaks—and occasional stands of pine. The hills are cut by narrow twisting valleys, each carefully terraced for the cultivation of irrigated rice. Here and there rise granite mountains, supposed to have been the seats of ancient kings.

In this back country, there are no paved roads. People walk—very few can afford bicycles. Goods are transported in ox-carts, along mud paths that are, even in winter, too rutted for any but the toughest automobiles. With the start of the summer rains, they become impassable. It is largely because of the difficulties of communication that there is no large-scale commercial agriculture, despite the proximity of the capital. Farmers do end up carting a fair proportion of their crops to markets in town, and much of this ends up helping to feed the population of Antananarivo, but it's all piecemeal, individual cultivators selling to very small-scale merchants in an endless multitude of tiny transactions, almost as if people were intentionally trying to ensure that the meager profits to be had from buying and selling local products ended up divided between as many hands as possible.

As I have said, my first work was on oral history: I started visiting villages usually accompanied by one or two Malagasy friends from Arivonimamo. I ended up fixing on the village of Betafo in which to carry out my intensive fieldwork: a community that fascinated me, in part, because it was divided almost evenly between *andriana* (usually translated "nobles") and the descendants of their former slaves. Betafo lies along the southern flank of a long mountainous ridge called Ambohidraidimby, most of it only a thirty- to forty-minute walk from the center of Arivonimamo. It is close enough that one can live in town and still cultivate one's fields in Betafo—as many people do—or have a house in both places and move freely back and forth between them.

Most rural communities in Imerina have some economic specialization, which occupies people especially in winter. In one village, the men will all be butchers, in another the women all weave baskets, or make rope; spaces in the marketplace in Arivonimamo are mapped out as much by the origin of the vendors as by the goods they have for sale. The people of Betafo have been traditionally known as blacksmiths. Nowadays, roughly a third of its households still have a smithy out back. Of those who do not, a very large number are involved in supplying smiths with iron ingots, and selling the plows and shovels they produce in markets and fairs in other parts of Imerina. What had started as a local effort had, by the time I was there, expanded dramatically, since in most of the region to the west of the capital, Betafo was mainly known for selling plows, despite the fact that no one in Betafo itself actually produced plows—they were all manufactured in other villages in the vicinity of Arivonimamo, with iron supplied by speculators from Betafo.

The intensification of commerce is one response to the economic crunch that has caused a dramatic fall in standards of living throughout Madagascar since the 1970s. It led to a great increase in side occupations, so that in any one household, one woman might be spending much of her time running a coffee stand in town, or weaving, another making fermented manioc to sell to vendors in the market, one man driving an ox-cart part time and spending several months a year selling pineapples in a different part of Imerina, while yet another might only drop by in the country occasionally, spending most of his days refilling disposable lighters near the taxi-stand in town. All this makes membership in a community like Betafo a bit hard to define. Not that I was trying to gather much in the way of statistics. In fact, one of the peculiar effects of my situation was that I had some fairly detailed bits of information about the demographics and property-holdings of the inhabitants of Betafo in the 1840s and 1920s, culled from the archives, I never managed to get such statistical information for the time I was actually there. This fact is important. I think it reveals something quite profound, actually, about what sort of place I was actually in.

While I was living in Arivonimamo and working in Betafo, I spent a lot of time thinking about the political aspects of conducting research. Almost all anthropologists do. In my case, it was especially hard not to be a little self-conscious in a milieu where urbanites seemed to find a special joy in telling me how terrified country folk were of *Vazaha* (people of European stock, such as myself)—and country folk, in telling me how terrified children were. For most Malagasy, the very word "*Vazaha*" evoked the threat of violence. Fortunately for me, it also had as its primary meaning "Frenchman," and (as I endlessly had to explain) I did not even speak French. Speaking only in Malagasy took a bit of the edge off things. But even more crucial: conducting research itself had associations. On the one hand, Imerina is a highly literate society: no one had any problem understanding what I meant if I said I was an American student carrying out research for his doctorate in anthropology. Nor did anyone seem to doubt that this was a legitimate, even an admirable thing to be doing. But techniques of knowledge were very closely identified with techniques of rule, and I quickly got the impression that there were certain sorts of inquiry people were much more comfortable with than others. Perhaps I was overly sensitive, but as soon as I got the feeling I was moving onto territory someone didn't want me delving into, I desisted. I would rather people talked to me about the things they wanted to talk about. As a result, I know more about the distribution of property in Betafo in 1925—or even 1880—than I do for the time I was there. Property surveys were the sort of the thing governments would carry out, backed by the threat of force, in order to aid in the forcible extraction of labor or taxes. This meant that there were extensive records in the archives; it also meant it was exactly what people wanted to be sure I wasn't ultimately up to. Even the act of systematically going from door to door surveying household size would have been...

well, nothing would have been more guaranteed to get people's backs up. Lack of hard numbers seemed a minor price to pay.

The Very Existence of the State

Let me return, then, to the initial question of the state.

Was there a government in Arivonimamo and the surrounding countryside? On one level, the answer was perfectly obvious. Of course there was. There were government personnel, government offices, and at least in town, government-run schools, banks, and hospitals. Almost all economic transactions—even if they were generally off the books—were carried out using government-issued Malagasy currency. The territory as a whole was claimed under the sovereign authority of a Malagasy state that was recognized by all other states in the world, and no one, in this territory, was openly contesting that state's sovereign authority. Certainly, there was nobody else claiming to represent a different state or claiming to represent a political alternative: there were no insurrectionary communities, no guerilla movements, no political organizations pursuing dual power strategies.

From a different perspective, though, the situation looked quite different. Because the Malagasy state, in this region at least—and this was a region quite close to its center of power in the capital—was either uninterested in, or incapable of, carrying out many of what we consider to be a state's most elementary, definitional functions.

The key issue in most Western definitions of the state is its power to coerce. States employ "force"—a euphemistic term for the threat of violence—to enforce the law. The classic definition here is Weber's: "A compulsory political association with continuous organization will be called a 'state' if and in so far as its administrative staff successfully upholds a claim to the monopoly of the legitimate use of physical force in the enforcement of its order" (1968 I: 54). But Weber's definition was itself really just a matter of repeating the conventional jural wisdom of his day. In fact, he seems to have been drawing directly on the work of an earlier German legal theorist named Rudolph von Ihering, who in 1877 had defined the state this way:

> The State is the only competent as well as the sole owner of social coercive force—the right to coerce forms the *absolute monopoly* of the State. Every association that wishes to realize its claims upon its members by means of mechanical coercion is dependent upon the cooperation of the State, and the State has in its power to fix the conditions under which it will grant such aid (cited in Turner & Factor 1994: 103–104).

A definition like this is mainly a way to focus the mind; it is not of that much use for determining whether or not any particular organization is a state, since for that, everything depends on whether or not one feels a would-be state has been "successful" in claiming its monopoly. Nonetheless, these definitions do capture the implicit common sense behind modern Western institutions of government—one in no way foreign to the Malagasy state, which was organized very much on this same model under the French colonial regime, and whose current form is based largely on colonial institutions. And most Malagasy, I think, would have agreed that the ability to apply force in this way was, essentially, what made a state what it was. This made it all the more striking that, in most of the Malagasy countryside, the state had become almost completely unwilling to do so. Far from maintaining an absolute monopoly of the right to coerce, or to authorize others to do so, the state simply did not exercise what was ostensibly its primary function there at all.

In the capital, there were police. Around Arivonimamo the closest thing to a police force was a unit of gendarmes who had a barracks somewhat to the west of town. Mainly, they patrolled the highway. Occasionally, I was told, they would fight bandits further west; but they did not like to travel off the paved roads, over the rutted dirt tracks that led into the countryside where almost everyone actually lived. In the countryside, gendarmes would never show up unless someone had been murdered. Even then, it would usually require something drastic—like a large number of witnesses appearing at their doorstep demanding they take action, and, usually, having already rounded up the culprit(s) themselves—before they would actually come and take anyone away.

Even in town, they did not act much like police. In Arivonimamo I heard a lot about a bully named Henri, a large and powerfully built man, perhaps insane (some said he was just pretending), who had terrorized its inhabitants for years. Henri used to help himself to merchandise at the local shops, daring anyone to stop him; he was a particular danger to the town's young women, who lived in constant fear of sexual assault. After much discussion, the young men of the town finally decided to join together and kill him. This took some time to arrange because, in fact, there was an informal tradition in that part of the highlands that if one wishes to lynch someone, one has to get their parent's permission first. Normally this is just an effective way to reinforce parental authority, a kind of ultimate sanction—or, a way of allowing someone's mother or father to inform them that it's really time one should be getting out of town—but in this case, after many vain efforts to apprise his son of the seriousness of the matter, Henri's father threw up his hands and allowed things to take their course. The next time he provoked a fight, a crowd immediately appeared armed with knives and agricultural implements. As it turned out, they didn't quite succeed in killing him: badly wounded, Henri managed to take refuge in the Catholic church and demanded sanctuary, claiming persecution due to mental illness. There, no one was willing to follow him. The Italian priest hid him in the back of a van and smuggled him out to an insane asylum. He was soon discharged (he beat the other patients), but didn't dare show his face again in Arivonimamo for many years to come. The first time I heard the story I was mainly interested in the details of parental permission. Only later did it occur to me that this event took place in a town with an actual police station. How could Henri have managed to terrorize the town for years without anything being done about him? "Why hadn't the gendarmes done anything," I asked? "Haven't you seen Henri," people would reply. "He's enormous!"

"But the gendarmes had guns!"

"Yes, but even so."

Events like this were in every way exceptional. The most significant thing about violence around Arivonimamo was that there was very little of it. Murders were shocking, isolated events; there were very few Henris. Nonetheless, rural assemblies had to develop all sorts of creative strategies to overcome the reluctance of the forces of order to enforce the laws. Towards the end of my stay, there was a *fokon'olona* meeting in Betafo—a village assembly—to deal with an instance of violence. A man named Benja, notorious for his fiery temper, had a quarrel with his sister over some mutual business arrangement, and, the story went, had beaten her to within an inch of her life. Actually, stories varied considerably about how badly she was really beaten, but the matter was considered a very serious affair requiring immediate attention. After much deliberation, the *fokon'olona* ordered Benja to write an undated letter confessing to having murdered his sister, and then, brought the confession down to be lodged at the local gendarme station in town. That way, if his sister was ever to be found the victim of foul play, he would already have confessed and could simply be delivered to the authorities. The message was that his sister's safety and well-being were to be his personal responsibility from then on. In this case, the state was being used as a kind of ghost-image of authority, a principle but not a threat, since if his sister was found dead, the *fokon'olona* themselves would have to be the ones to arrest him and carry him down to the gendarmes' office; the papers would merely make it much more likely that he would then have to spend some time in jail. In other cases, the state authorities were bypassed entirely. The 1980s, for example, began to see the revival of collective ordeals. In a case of theft—for instance, in Betafo, after someone had made off with the entire contents of a rice storage pit belonging to a prominent elder—elders would gather a whole community together, and each would drink from a specially prepared bowl or eat a piece of a specially prepared liver, and call on their ancestors to strike them down if they were guilty. The next person who died a sudden death was thus presumed to be a victim of ancestral vengeance. Two such collective ordeals had been held in Betafo alone in the decade before I came there. There were even rumors, further out in the countryside, of the revival of actual poison ordeals. Everywhere, one began to hear about invisible powers enforcing justice—buried charms, standing stones, ancient places of sacrifice newly charged with the power to detect and punish evil-doers. Almost anyone of any wealth or political prominence started to begin hinting that they might have access to dangerous magical powers: hail or lightning charms, vindictive ghosts, access to the protection of ancient kings. Anyone who intended to amass—or maintain—a great deal of wealth had almost by definition to be able to at least create the suspicion in others' minds that they might have access to dangerous hidden powers of some sort or another. But it was a very delicate game: since anyone who boasted openly of such powers was assumed almost by definition not to really have them, and anyone who employed dangerous magic against their fellow villagers was by definition a witch. I even heard rumors of wealthy men deep in the countryside who so infuriated their neighbors by dark hints of magical powers that those neighbors eventually sought counter-medicine, disguised themselves as bandits, and attacked and ransacked their possessions.

The State as Guarantor of Property Relations

Theories of social class almost always assume that a key role of the state—perhaps, its most important role—is to underpin property relations. For a Marxist, certainly, this is a state's primary reason for being. Contractual, market relations can only exist because their basic ground, the basic rules of the game, are enshrined in law; those laws in turn are effective only in so far as everyone knows they will be backed up—in the last instance—by clubs and guns and prisons. And, of course, if the ultimate guarantor of property relations is state violence, then the same is true of social classes as well.

But, in the countryside around Arivonimamo, the state simply did not play this role. I cannot imagine a situation under which it would dispatch armed men to uphold one person's right to exclude another from their land—let alone to enforce a contract or investigate a robbery. This, too, was something whose full significance dawned on me only afterwards, because everyone acted as if the government did play a crucial role in such matters. The government kept track of who owned each piece of land: whenever someone died, the division of their fields and other property was meticulously recorded at the appropriate offices. Registering property, along with births and deaths, was one of the main things such offices did. There were all sorts of laws concerning land, and no one openly contested them, just as when talking in the abstract, they always spoke as if they felt land registration did give an accurate picture of who had ultimate rights to what. In practice, however, legal principles were usually only one, relatively minor, consideration. If there was a dispute, legalities had to be weighed against a welter of "traditional" principles (which usually provided more than one possible solution to any given problem), the intentions of former owners, and not least, by people's broader sense of justice—the feeling, for instance, that no accepted member of the community should be completely deprived of the means of making a living. Certainly no one would think of taking the matter to court—except in a few rare cases where one of the disputants was an outsider. Even then, the court served mainly as a neutral mediator; everyone knew no police or any other armed official would enforce a court decision.[1]

In Arivonimamo, in fact, there was one man with a gendarme's uniform who would occasionally rent himself out to money-lenders or merchants to intimidate people into paying debts or surrendering collateral. An acquaintance of mine from Betafo was terrified one day when he showed up in the company of a notorious loan-shark—even after his neighbors explained to him that the man could hardly be a real policeman, because, even if you could find an officer willing to trudge out into the country on such a trivial matter, lending money at interest was against the law for private individuals and a real gendarme would have had just as much cause to arrest his creditor as he. This struck me as a particularly telling case, because it underlined just how little the forces of order cared about economic affairs. Normally, there is nothing more guaranteed to infuriate police than the knowledge that someone is going around impersonating an officer. Doing so strikes at the very essence of their authority. If this particular impostor got away with it—as he apparently did—it appeared to be because he confined his activities to a domain in which the gendarmes had no interest. After all, the gendarmes never did anything to protect shopkeepers from Henri, either—and that was in town; the counterfeit officer seems to have confined his activities almost exclusively to the countryside.

There are various ways one might chose to assess this situation. One would be to conclude that people of rural Imerina, or in Madagascar in general, had a different conception of the state than Marxists and Weberians are used to. Maybe the protection of property is simply not one of the functions anyone expects a government to fulfill. To the extent people seemed to say otherwise, they might just be paying lip service to alien principles imposed by the French colonial regime. But, in fact, the pre-colonial Merina state was veritably obsessed with protecting property. King Andrianampoinimerina, its founder, emphasized this role constantly in his speeches (Larson 2000: 192). Law codes, beginning with his own, always made the regulation of inheritance, rules about buying and renting, and the like, one of their most important areas of concern. Even the registration of lands predates the colonial period; records began to be kept in 1878, seventeen years before the French invasion.

On the other hand, existing evidence gives us no reason to believe that people then paid much more attention to this elaborate legal structure than they do today—although neither is there any record of anyone openly challenging it. Legal systems have always been accepted in principle, and appealed to only very selectively in practice. Mostly, people go about their business much as they had done before. It is this phenomenon, I think, which gives the best hint as to what's really going on.

Let me make a broad generalization. Confronted with someone bent on imposing unwanted authority, a typical Malagasy response will be to agree heartily with whatever demands that person makes, and then, as soon as they are gone, to try to go on living one's life as if the incident had never happened. One might even say this was the archetypically Malagasy way of dealing with authority: one's first line of defense is simply to deny that the event in question (a government official coming to count cattle and announce the required tax payments, or negotiate the requisitioning of laborers to replant trees or build a road) ever occurred. Admittedly, it is hardly a strategy limited to Madagascar. Something along these lines is often considered a typically "peasant" strategy: it is an obvious course to take when one is in no way economically dependent on those trying to tell one what to do. But there are many other routes to take, all sorts of possible combinations of confrontation, negotiation, subversion, acquiescence. In Madagascar, where there is often a strong distaste for open confrontation in daily life in general, the preferred approach has always been to do whatever it takes to make the annoying outsider happy until he goes away; then, insist that he had never been there to begin with, or if that doesn't work, to simply ignore whatever one has agreed with and see what the consequences might be. It even takes on a cosmological dimension. Malagasy myths on the origins of death claim that life itself was won from God in a deal that humans never really intended to keep (hence, it is said, God kills us). Here is one, drawn early in the century from the Betsimisaraka of the east coast. There are endless variations, most obviously tongue-in-cheek, with the Creator often bearing an uncanny resemblance to the sort of passing colonial official who would periodically show up in villages, with armed retainers, demanding the payment of taxes:

Once upon a time, a Vazimba [aboriginal] couple were the only two occupants of the earth. They were sad because they had no children, so one day they found some clay and gave it human form. They made two figures, one a little boy, the other a little girl. The woman blew in their noses to animate them but she wasn't able to give them life. Then, one day, she happened to meet a god who was traveling on the earth. The woman asked him to give life to the two statues and promised him, if he succeeded, two cows and a sum of money. So he did so.

When the children grew up, the parents married them to one another. Then the god returned to claim his payment.

"We have no money," the parents said, "because we're old, but in twelve years our children will pay you."

"Because you have tricked me," replied the god, "I will kill you." And he did.

After twelve years the god returned to again ask the children for his payment.

"You've killed our parents," said the couple, "so the money we've gathered up to pay you has all been spent. We have to ask you for ten more years to acquit our debt."

Ten years later, the god returned and the couple had three children but no money.

"I will kill you," said the god, "you and your descendants, whether you be old or young."

Since that day, humans have been mortal, and when one quits life, Malagasy people say, "they are taken by the god that made them." (Renel 1910 III: 17–18; my translation from the French).

The mythological point is, to say the least, suggestive. One might well argue that this whole attitude is ultimately one with the logic of sacrifice, which at least in Madagascar is often explicitly phrased as a way of fobbing off the Divine Powers with a portion of what is rightfully theirs, so as to win the rest for living people. The life of the animal, it is often said, goes to God; hence (implicitly), we get to keep our own. Consider, then, the curious fact that all over Madagascar, sacrificial rituals—or their functional equivalents, such as the *famadihana* (reburial) rituals of Imerina—always seem to require government permits. The fact that this permit has been received, that the paperwork has been properly done, is often made much of during the ceremony itself. Here is a fragment of a Betsimisaraka speech, spoken over the body of a sacrificial ox:

> For this ox is not the kind of ox that lazes in its pen or shits anywhere on entering the village. Its body is here with us, but its life is with you, the government. You, the government, are like a great beast lying on its back: he who turns it over sees its huge jaws; so we, comrades, cannot turn that beast over! It is this official permit that is the knife that dares to cut its hide, the ax that dares to break its bones, which comes from you who hold political authority (Aly 1984: 59–60).

Not only is the state figured simultaneously as a potential force of violence and its victim; the act of acquiring a permit becomes equated with the act of sacrifice itself. The main point I am trying to make here is about autonomy. Filling out forms, registering land, even paying taxes, might be considered the equivalents of sacrifice: little ritualized actions of propitiation by which one wins the autonomy to continue with one's life.

This theme of autonomy crops up in any number of other studies of colonial and postcolonial Madagascar—notably, those of Gerald Althabe (1969, 2000), about these same Betsimisaraka, and Gillian Feeley-Harnik (1982, 1984, 1991) on the Sakalava of the northwest coast. But in these authors it takes on a sort of added twist, since both suggest that, in Madagascar, the most common way to achieve autonomy is by creating a false image of domination. The logic seems to be this: a community of equals can only be created by common subordination to some overarching force. Typically, it is conceived as arbitrary and potentially violent in much the same way as the traditional Malagasy God. But it can also be equally far from everyday human concerns. One of the most dramatic responses to colonial rule, among both peoples, was the massive diffusion of spirit possession; in every community, women began to be possessed by the souls of ancient kings, whose will was considered (at least in theory) to have all the authority it would have, had they been alive. By relegating ultimate social authority to entranced women speaking with the voices of dead kings, the power to constitute communities is displaced to a zone where French officials and police would have no way to openly confront it. In either case, there was the same kind of move: one manages to create a space for free action, in which to live one's life out of the grip of power, only by creating the image of absolute domination—but one which is ultimately only that, an image, a phantasm, completely manipulable by those it ostensibly subjects.

To put the matter crudely, one might say that the people I knew were engaged in a kind of scam. Their image of government had, at least since the colonial period, been one of something essentially alien, predatory, coercive. The principal emotion it inspired was fear. Under the French, the government apparatus was primarily an engine for extracting money and forced labor from its subjects; it provided relatively little in way of social benefits for the rural population (certainly, from the point of view of the rural population it didn't). In so far as it did concern itself with its subjects' daily needs, it was with the conscious intention of creating new ones, of transforming their desires so as to create a more deeply rooted dependence. Nor did matters change much after independence in 1960, since the first Malagasy regime made very few changes in its policy or mode of operation. For the vast majority of the population, the common-sense attitude was that the state was something to be propitiated, then avoided, in so far as it was in any way possible to do so.

It was only after the revolution of 1972 that things really began to change.

An anti-colonial revolt in its origins, the 1972 events introduced a succession of state-capitalist, military-based regimes—from 1975 until 1991, dominated by the figure of President Didier Ratsiraka. Ratsiraka found his political inspiration in Kim Il Sung of North Korea. In theory, his regime was dedicated to a very centralized version of socialist development and mobilization. From the beginning, though, he was uninterested in what he considered a stagnant, traditional peasant sector with little revolutionary potential. In agriculture as in industry, his government concentrated its efforts on a series of colossal development schemes, often heroic in scale, involving massive investment, funded by foreign loans. Loans were easy enough to get in the 1970s. By 1981, the government was insolvent. Ever since, Malagasy economic history has mainly been the story of negotiations with the IMF.

There is no room here to enter into details on the effects of IMF-ordered austerity plans. Suffice it to say their immediate result was a catastrophic fall in living standards, across the board. Hardest hit were the civil service and other government employees (who made up the bulk of the middle class) but—aside from a narrow elite surrounding the President himself, who stole liberally—pauperization has been well-nigh universal. Madagascar is now one of the poorest countries on earth.

For Ratsiraka's "peasant sector"—rural areas not producing key commodities—this whole period was marked by the gradual withdrawal of the state. The most onerous taxes from the French period—the head tax, cattle tax, house tax—intended to force farmers to sell their products and thus to goad them into the cash economy, were abolished immediately after the revolution. Ratsiraka's regime first ignored rural administration; after 1981, it increasingly became the object of triage. The state, its resources ever more limited as budgets were endlessly slashed, was reduced to administering and providing minimal social services to those towns and territories its rulers found economically important: mainly, those which generated some kind of foreign exchange. Places like Arivonimamo, where almost all production and distribution was carried out outside the formal sector anyway, were of no interest to them. Indeed, it is hard to imagine anything that could happen there—short of the area becoming the base for armed guerrillas (hardly a possibility)—that would seriously threaten the interests of the men who really ran the country.[2]

Resources for rural areas dried up. By the time I was in Arivonimamo, the only sector of administration that was receiving any significant funding was the education system. Even here the sums were paltry: the main government role was to post the teachers (who were sometimes paid, at least in part, by parents' associations), provide curricula, and administer the tests. The latter, particularly the baccalaureate examination, were of particular concern to the center because they were the gateway into the formal, state sector: those who passed their baccalaureate were obliged to undergo several weeks of military training and then carry out a year's "National Service," though—as I've pointed out—this mainly consisted of lounging around in meaningless make-work jobs. But National Service was, I think, important. It was a way of marking passage into a domain where effective authority really did exist, where orders had to be obeyed. For those not ensconced in the educational system, the government provided nothing, but it also had almost no immediate power over their lives. [3]

Still, even in the countryside, government offices continued to exist. The typewriters were often crumbling, functionaries were often reduced to buying their own paper, since they could no longer requisition any, but people dutifully continued to fill out forms, requesting permission before uprooting trees or exhuming the dead, reporting births and deaths, and registering the number of their cattle. They must have realized that, had they refused, nothing would have happened. So: why did they play along?

One might, I suppose, call it inertia, sheer force of habit: people were still running the same scam, propitiating the state without having noticed its huge jaws were toothless. Certainly, memories of colonial violence were still vivid. I was told many times of the early days of mass executions, or of how terrified rural people used to be when they had to enter a government office, of the endless pressure of taxation. But I think the real answer is more subtle.

Memories of violence were mainly important because they defined what people imagined a state to be about. I found little notion that the state (for all its socialist pretensions) existed to provide services; at least, no one much complained about the lack of them. People seemed to accept that a government was essentially an arbitrary, predatory, coercive power. But the one theme of official ideology everyone did seem to take seriously was the idea of Malagasy unity. In the highlands, at least, people saw themselves as "Malagasy"; they hardly ever referred to themselves as "Merina." Malagasy unity was a constant theme in rhetoric; it was the real meaning, I think, of the Malagasy flags that inevitably accompanied any major ritual (whose official meaning was to mark that the forms had been filled out, the event approved). It seems to me that it was the very emptiness of the state which made it acceptable as a unifying force. When it was powerful, the state in Imerina was essentially seen as something French—this remained true even in the early years of independence. The 1972 revolution was first and foremost an effort to achieve genuine independence, to make the state truly Malagasy. For the highland population, I would say, this effort was largely successful—if only because, at the same time, the state was stripped of almost all effective power. In other words, the government became something along the same lines as the ancient kings discussed by Althabe and Feeley-Harnik: absolute, arbitrary powers that constitute those they subjugate as a community by virtue of their common subjugation, while at the same time, extremely convenient powers to be ruled by, because, in any immediate practical sense, they do not exist.

Provisional Autonomous Zone

In contemporary anarchist circles it has become common to talk of the "TAZ," or "temporary autonomous zones" (Bey 1991). The idea is that, while there may no longer be any place on earth entirely uncolonized by State and Capital, power is not completely monolithic: there are always temporary cracks and fissures, ephemeral spaces in which self-organized communities can and do continually emerge like eruptions, covert uprisings. Free spaces flicker into existence and then pass away. If nothing else, they provide constant testimony to the fact that alternatives are still conceivable, that human possibilities are never fixed.

In rural Imerina, it might be better to talk about a "provisional autonomous zone," rather than a "temporary" one: in part, to emphasize that it does not stand quite so defiantly outside power as the image of a TAZ implies; but also, because there is no reason to necessarily assume its independence is all that temporary. Betafo, even to a large extent Arivonimamo, stood outside the direct control of the state apparatus: even if the people who live there passed back and forth between them and zones, such as the capital, which are very much under the domination of the state. Their autonomy was tentative, uncertain. It might be largely swept away the moment a new infusion of guns and money restores the apparatus; but then again, it might not. Some might consider the current situation scandalous. Myself, I consider it a remarkable accomplishment. After all, austerity plans have been imposed on nations all over the world; few governments have reacted by abandoning the bulk of the population to govern themselves; nor would many populations have been so well prepared to do so.

Why were they able to do so? I would guess there are various reasons. One is the maintenance of active traditions of self-governance, and what would, if it were observed in, say, European or Latin American social movements, undoubtedly be called a culture of direct democracy. The art of coming to decisions by consensus was something everyone simply learned as part of growing up. It was so much a part of everyday common sense that it was difficult, at first, for an outsider to even notice it. For instance, there was a general principle that no course of action that might have negative consequences on others should legitimately be carried out without those others' prior consent; the resultant meetings were called "*fokon'olona*" meetings— meaning, basically, "everybody"—but despite the consistent misunderstanding of colonial ethnography, "the" *fokon'olona* was not a formal institution, but a flexible principle of deliberation by groups that could vary from five to a thousand, depending on the dimensions of the problem they were collectively trying to solve. Within those meetings, however, anyone, male or female, old or young, formally had equal right to speak: the only criteria was to be old enough to be able to formulate an intelligent opinion.[4] What's more, anyone engaged in an ongoing project had the power to engage in what would in contemporary consensus process be referred to as a "block": one could simply declare "I am no longer in agreement" (*tsy manaiky aho*) with the general direction of things, and it would cause a general crisis until one's concerns had been publicly addressed. Suffice it to say, then, that even during the colonial period, when all political gatherings were technically illegal, ordinary people had maintained institutional structures and political habits that allowed them to govern their own affairs with minimal appeal to outside force. They had also managed to develop forms of resistance sufficiently subtle that, when the state was emptied of its substance, they were able to allow it to effectively collapse with minimal loss of face.

I don't mean to romanticize the situation. What autonomy rural communities have has been won at the cost of grinding poverty; it is hard to enjoy one's freedom if one is in a constant scramble to have enough to eat. Institutions of rule—most obviously schools and Christian churches—still functioned, and in the same hierarchical way as ever, even if they did now largely lacked the power to back up their efforts with the threat of physical force. There were certainly profound social inequalities within many of these rural communities, not to mention in town: both differences of wealth (perhaps minor by world standards, but nonetheless real), and even more, divisions between what were called "white" and "black" people, descendants of nobles or commoners in the ancient kingdom, and their former slaves. In order to understand what places like Betafo were like, then, one must first understand that it was a place that stood outside state power; then, that it did not stand entirely outside it. For all the efforts to maintain zones of autonomy, the reality of coercion has by now reshaped the terms by which people deal with each other; in certain ways, it has become embedded in the very structure of experience.

In Imerina, just about everyone considers themselves a Christian (about two thirds of the population is Protestant, one third Catholic). Many regularly attend church. The government may no longer have the means to compel children to attend school, but attendance is still close to universal, at least on the primary level. At the same time, however, there is a certain ambivalence about both these institutions, particularly the schools. As I already remarked when speaking of the politics of research, the educational system in Imerina has always been seen as a tool of power, and always, too, identified with Vazaha. The present educational system took form under the French colonial regime. It is important to bear in mind that this was not a regime that could ever make the most remotest claim to being the expression of popular will. It was a regime imposed by conquest, maintained only by the constant threat of force.

It is worth considering for a moment what maintaining a credible threat of force actually requires. It is not merely a matter of having an adequate number of men willing to use violence; not even a matter of arming and training them. Mostly, it is a matter of coordination. The crucial thing is to be able to ensure that a sufficient number of such violent men will always be able to show up, whenever and wherever there is an open challenge to one's authority—and that everyone knows that they will indeed do so. But this, in turn, requires a great deal. It requires an extensive cadre of trained functionaries capable of processing information, not to mention an infrastructure of roads, telephones, typewriters, barracks, repair shops, petroleum depots—and the staff to maintain them. Once built, such an infrastructure can and doubtless will serve other purposes as well. Roads built to transport soldiers will also end up carrying chickens to market and people to visit their ailing relatives. But, if it wasn't for the soldiers, the roads would never have been there, and at least in Madagascar, people seemed perfectly well aware of that.

Most of the people who work in a state bureaucracy—pretty much any state bureaucracy, anywhere—are, on a day to day level, much more concerned with processing information than with breaking people's skulls. But the same is true of soldiers and police. Rather than see this fact as proof that violence plays a minor role in the operation of a state, it might be better to ask oneself how much these technologies of information are themselves part of the apparatus of violence, essential elements in ensuring that small handful of people willing and able to break skulls will always be able to show up at the right place at the right time. Surveillance, after all, is a technique of war, and Foucault's Panopticon was a prison, with armed guards.

Viewed from Madagascar, the essentially violent nature of the state is much harder to deny. This was not only because of its colonial history. It was also because most Malagasy—at least the ones I knew—were accustomed to different standards of perception. The best way to put it is that, unlike most Americans, they did not see anything particularly shameful about fear. This was one of the things it took me longest to get used to there: seeing grown men, for instance, gazing into the street and casually remarking "scary cars," "I'm scared of those oxen." For someone brought up as I had been it was very disconcerting. I may not come from a particularly macho background, by American standards, but I had been brought up to assume confessions of fear, at least fear of being physically harmed by others, were at least a little bit embarrassing. Most Malagasy seemed to find the subject pleasant and amusing; they took a veritable delight in telling me how afraid some people were of *Vazaha*, sometimes, even, how much they themselves were. That governments work largely through inspiring fear in their subjects was simply obvious to them. It seems to me that, in so far as Western social science has a tendency to downplay the importance of coercion, it is partly because of a hidden embarrassment; we find it shameful to admit the degree to which our own daily lives are framed by the fear of physical force.[5]

Schools, anyway, are ultimately a part of this apparatus of violence.

In Malagasy, one does not speak of education as conveying facts and information so much as skills: the word used, *fahaizana*, means "skills, knowhow, practical knowledge." The kind of *fahaizana* one acquires at school however was seen as an essentially foreign one, a *fahaizana Vazaha*, opposed, as such, to Malagasy forms of know-how. The techniques taught in school were seen as, essentially, techniques of rule. In part this is because the school system was itself part of the infrastructure of violence: it was designed primarily to train functionaries; secondarily, technicians. The style of teaching was entirely authoritarian, with a heavy emphasis on rote memorization, and the skills that were taught were taught with the expectation they were to be employed in offices, workshops, or classrooms organized around certain forms of social relation—what might be referred to as relations of command. The assumption was always that some people would be giving orders, others were there to obey. In other words, not only was this system designed to produce the competences required to maintain an infrastructure of violence, it was premised on social relations completely unlike those current in other aspects of daily life, ones that could only be maintained by a constant threat of physical harm.

The ambivalence towards research and book learning, then, was based on a perfectly sensible appreciation of the situation. Everyone considered knowledge in itself a valuable, even a pleasant, thing. Everyone recognized that the skills one learned in school opened spheres of experience that would not otherwise be available, to types of information and networks of communication that spanned the globe. But these skills were also techniques of repression. By training people in certain methods of organization and not others (how to keep lists and inventories, how to conduct a meeting...), the system ensured that no matter what their purposes, any large-scale network they put together capable of coordinating anything—whether it be an historical preservation society, or a revolutionary party—will almost inevitably end up operating somewhat like a coercive bureaucracy. Certainly, one can, and many did, try to rework these devices to operate in a more consensual, democratic manner. It can be done, but it is extremely difficult; and the tendency, the drift, is for any system created by people trained in these competencies, no matter how revolutionary their intentions, to end up looking at least a little like the French colonial regime. Hardly surprising then that most people wrote these techniques off as inherently foreign, and tried as much as they could to isolate them from "Malagasy" contexts.

But, at the same time, there was another, perhaps more subtle effect of the existence of these hierarchical institutions. They allowed people to make clear distinctions between everything that was "*gasy*"—Malagasy—and everything that was considered "*Vazaha*," alien, authoritarian, repressive, French. They guaranteed that everyone had at least some experience of the latter, that zone where the state was "the only competent as well as the sole owner of social coercive force": even if it was simply a matter of being forced to stand in uncomfortable lines as a child, jump at orders in gym class, and dutifully copy and memorize boring and apparently pointless lessons. The experience of state-like discipline became a way of constantly reminding oneself what was, in contrast, considered "Malagasy"—the habits of consensus decision-making, for example, the reluctance to give orders to fellow adults, the general suspicion of anything that smacked of confrontation or even charismatic leadership (compare Bloch 1971). It is fairly clear that many of these traits had not always been considered quintessentially Malagasy, much though I suspect that Malagasy had, from the very beginning of their settlement of the island, always tended to define themselves against foreigners of some kind or another.[6] In this way, paradoxically enough, the provisional nature of local autonomy actually becomes, in a sense, self-sustaining. We all live in a larger world of gross inequalities of wealth and power. Malagasy rice farmers and blacksmiths and seamstresses and video operators were all well aware of that. But precisely through such constant reminders, people managed, to a large degree, to insulate themselves as well.

A Final Question

I doubt that the hinterland of Arivonimamo is an isolated case. As Henry Wright had pointed out to me, similar things were happening all over Madagascar: in fact, probably they had been for much longer and in more profound ways in many other parts of the island, since Arivonimamo was, after all, with its military airport and gendarmes and prison, an hour away from the capital, one of the last places one would expect the state authority to disappear. In Madagascar itself, state authority appears to have ebbed and flowed, sometimes asserting itself, sometimes retreating, in the intervening years; but in much of the country—particularly areas that, like Arivonimamo, do not contain vanilla plantations, bauxite mines, or nature preserves—the situation has remained essentially unchanged. One wonders if there might not be hundreds, even thousands, of similar communities in other parts of the world—communities that have withdrawn from or drifted away from the effective control of national governments and become to all intents and purposes self-governing, but whose members are still performing the external form and tokens of obeisance in order to disguise that fact.

It is a question we might well ponder when reading the contemporary literature on "failed states" and particular, the crisis of state authority in Africa. As James Ferguson has recently noted (2006), in many parts of Africa, about the only significant meaning of "state sovereignty" left is international recognition of a government's legal right to represent its citizens in international arenas, and particularly, to guarantee contracts concerning access to resources within its territory, for those from other states. Few even pretend to maintain a monopoly of violence in the manner described by Rudolph von Ihering or Max Weber. The withdrawal of resources, the abandonment of any sense that the government can or would even wish to provide equally for the basic needs of all its citizens, has had devastating effects on health, education, and livelihood. But at the same time, even IMF-imposed austerity plans have been known to have their curious unintended side-effects.

It is, in fact, something of an irony that it is only when "anarchy," in the sense of the breakdown of state power, results in chaos, violence, and destruction—as in the case of say, Somalia in the 1990s, or many parts of southern and central Africa today—that non-Africans are likely to hear about it. What I observed in Madagascar suggests that for every such case, there might well be dozens, even hundreds that outsiders simply do not know about, precisely because local people managed to make the transition peacefully. Like Malagasy villagers, they avoided confrontation, ensured that state representatives never had to feel publicly humiliated or to lose face, but at the same time, made it as difficult as possible for them to govern, and easy as possible to simply play along with the façade. Neither is this strategy, or the existence of newly autonomous communities, likely to be limited to Africa. There are many parts of the world—in southeast Asia, Oceania, most notably, but even, say, parts of Latin America—where the presence of the state has always been a somewhat sporadic phenomenon. Its visits have, perhaps, always borne less resemblance to the forms of constant monitoring and surveillance we are familiar with in both totalitarian states or industrial democracies, and more the occasional, if often disastrous, appearance of a vindictive Malagasy god. So, often, with the world-system as a whole. Such gods can rarely be eliminated entirely, any more than the monsoons or earthquakes that they are often seen to resemble. But their visitations can be rendered equally occasional.

Of course, the institutional structure did remain: there were schools, banks, hospitals. They ensured that the "state form", as Mario Tronti for instance calls it, was always present: everyone had some idea what it was like to live inside institutions that were premised on coercion, even if for the most part these were ghostly shadows of real state institutions, since the actual violence had been stripped away. Or perhaps one should be more precise here. The violence was still there. It had simply retreated. There were certainly still police in the city, or anywhere where there was, say, a bauxite mine, or other resource that generated significant foreign exchange. Even more, the global allocation of resources—what medicines and equipment actually appeared in the local hospital, for example—was maintained by the systematic threat of violence to enforce property arrangements. In a place like Arivonimamo, however, one could only deal with its distant effects, and strange, hollow institutions that largely served to remind local people of precisely how they were not supposed to ordinarily behave.

Endnotes

1   One might contrast the situation here with what obtains in, say, much of rural Brazil, where the situation is quite the opposite, since police, effectively, are only interested in enforcing property rights, and can be expected to ignore mere cases of murder—unless, that is, the victim is a member of the property-owning elite.

2   The gendarmes' occasional zeal in pursuing bandits probably did have something
    to do with a perception that they were the only organized, armed group that had
    the capacity to form the nucleus of a rebellion—unlikely though that might have
    been. There had been times, mainly in the nineteenth century, when bandits actu-
    ally had turned into rebels. But I suspect the concern was rooted in deeper under-
    standings about what a state was all about: under the Merina Kingdom, bandits
    (referred to in official documents simply as *fahavalo*, "the enemy") were, along
    with witches, the archetypal anti-state, that which legitimate royal authority de-
    fined itself against. The connection with witches also helps explain the otherwise
    puzzling fact that, much though they were unconcerned with Henri's depreda-
    tions, Arivonimamo's gendarmes did leap into action to arrest and interrogate a
    teenage girl suspected of being behind an outbreak of *Ambalavelona*, or posesssion
    by evil ghosts, which affected a whole dormful of students at the state high school
    in 1979.

3   Medical services for instance were in theory provided free, but had been effectively
    privatized by corruption, which, in turn, became universal once government sala-
    ries declined to next to nothing.

4   As Jacques Dez (1975: 54–57) notes in a generally excellent summary; though in
    the end, he reproduces colonial assumptions by concluding that "the" *fokon'olona*
    was "invented" by the late-eighteenth century king Andrianampoinimerina. On
    the underlying ethos of consensus decision-making see Andriamanjato (1957).

5   In Europe or North America, this is more true of men than women; in Madagascar
    it was, if anything, the other way around.

6   Contemporary archeologists now believe that significant human settlement in
    Madagascar was surprisingly late: perhaps from the eighth century CE, and at first
    seem to have consisted of heterogeneous populations probably of very different ori-
    gins, Austronesian, African, and perhaps others. During this early period there was
    even a small Islamic city, Mahilaka, almost certainly Swahili-speaking, engaged
    in lively trade with East Africa and the Arabian peninsula. Early Malagasy thus
    had experience of states and world religions from the very beginning; and the mo-
    ment of "synthesis," when contemporary Malagasy culture appears to have born,
    seems to have occurred around the time of the height or perhaps even downfall
    of Mahilaka. After this, however, it proved surprisingly persistent throughout the
    island and capable of resisting frequent Islamic attempts to convert and incorpo-
    rate the island's population. I strongly suspect that insofar as Malagasy culture
    emerged as a coherent entity, it was in conscious contrast to everything that was
    considered "*Silamo*"—Swahili, Islamic—just as it is maintained in conscious con-
    trast to everything that is "*Vazaha*" today.

Bibliography

Althabe, Gérard
1969 *Oppression et Libération dans l'Imaginaire: les communautés villageoises de la côte orientale de Madagascar.* Paris: Maspero.
2000 *Anthropologie politique d'une decolonization.* Paris: L'Harmattan.

Aly, Jacques
1984 "Le Discours Rituel chez les Betsimisaraka de la Côte Est de Madagascar." *Presénce Africaine* 132: 54–61.

Andriamanjato, Richard
1957 *Le Tsiny et le Tody dans la pensée Malgache.* Paris: Presénce Africaine.

Bey, Hakim
1991 *T.A.Z: The Temporary Autonomous Zone, Ontological Anarchy, Poetic Terrorism.* New York: Autonomedia.

Bloch, Maurice
1971 "Decision-making in Councils Among the Merina" In *Councils in action* (Audrey Richards and Adam Kuper, eds.). Cambridge Papers in Social Anthropology. Cambridge: Cambridge University Press.

Dez, Jacques
1975 "Premiére structure d'encadrement rural: le Fokonolona." *Asie du Sud Est et Monde Insulindien* 6: 31–69.

Feeley-Harnik, Gillian
1982 "The King's Men in Madagascar: Slavery, Citizenship and Sakalava Monarchy." *Africa* 52: 31–50.
1984 "The Political Economy of Death: Communication and Change in Malagasy Colonial History." *American Ethnologist* 8: 231–254.
1991 *A Green Estate: Restoring Independence in Madagascar.* Washington: Smithsonian

Ferguson, James
2006 *Global Shadows: Africa in the Neoliberal World Order.* Durham: Duke University Press.

Larson, Pier
2000 *History and Memory in the Age of Enslavement: Becoming Merina in Highland Madagascar, 1770–1822* (Social History of Africa). Portsmouth: Heinemann.

Renel, Charles
1910 *Contes de Madagascar* (3 volumes). Paris: Ernest Leroux.

Turner, Stephen, and Regis Factor
1994 *Max Weber: The Lawyer as Social Thinker.* London: Routledge.

Weber, Max
1968 *Economy and Society: An Outline of Interpretive Sociology.* 2 vols. (Guenther Roth and Claus Wittich, eds.; Ephraim Fischoff, trans.). New York: Bedminster Press.

6

DANCING WITH CORPSES RECONSIDERED: AN INTERPRETATION OF *FAMADIHANA* (IN ARIVONIMAMO, MADAGASCAR)

In September of 1990, I was talking with a woman named Irina about something an ancestor of hers had done some sixty years before. Like all of the *andriana* or nobles of Betafo (a community to the north of the town of Arivonimamo, in Imerina, Madagascar) she was descended from a certain Andrianambololona, whose body, together with that of his wife and daughter and those of three of his retainers, was buried in a large white tomb in the center of the village of Betafo, a five-minute walk across the rice fields from her house.

This particular ancestor, she was telling me, has long had the custom of appearing to his descendants in dreams to announce when the occupants of the tomb felt cold, and needed to have a *famadihana* performed: that is, to be taken out and wrapped in new silk shrouds. When this happened in 1931, his descendants quickly got together and organized the ritual; but, in their hurry perhaps, forgot to exhume the bodies of his three retainers, who were buried at the foot of the tomb somewhat apart from the rest. "The afternoon after they'd finished," she said, "the town suddenly caught fire and burned to the ground. And the next morning he came once more to the person"—the one who had originally had the dream—"and said: 'if you don't wrap us all, next time I'll kill you outright...' So they got the tombs ready again and rewrapped them."[1]

This story is a good place to begin an essay about the Merina practice of *famadihana*, if for no other reason because it shows how high the stakes involved can be. Admittedly, this was the worst disaster of its kind I heard about. Irina was doubtless justified in concluding that her ancestor was unusually "arrogant and cruel." But stories like this were in no way unusual. Rural communities in Imerina were, I found, largely organized around the memory of ancestors whose presence in the lives of their descendants made itself felt largely in terms of the constraint and violence they were capable of inflicting on them. The dangers surrounding *famadihana*—and these were said to be great—really only marked them as the culminating moment in an ongoing relationship between memory and violence that was implicit in the organization of everyday life, but was here played out over the actual bodies of the ancestral dead.

The theme of ancestral violence was not one that everyone in Betafo was entirely comfortable with. Older men usually did their best to avoid speaking about such matters at all, at least with me, and instead echoed the themes of formal rhetoric, where ancestors were represented as the benevolent guardians of the moral unity of the community of their descendants. Several people besides Irina told me much the same story about the fire of 1931 as she did. The few older men I asked denied anything of the sort had ever happened.[2]

Generally speaking, points of view like Irina's have not found their way into the ethnographic literature on Madagascar (there are exceptions: cf. Astuti 1995), so, in part, this essay is meant to fill a gap. More importantly, it's meant to address the question of why such radically different perspectives should exist within the same community to begin with.

Some Background

The classic interpretation of *famadihana* is that of Maurice Bloch (1971, 1982), who has argued that, through such rituals, participants create the image of a timeless, idealized ancestral order identified with death and the past; one explicitly set apart from life, fertility, and the mundane contingencies of everyday existence. Most people's fundamental sense of social identity, he says, is based on membership in descent groups that are still identified with territories from which their families have long since moved away. Hence, groups which no longer exist on the level of daily life have to be reconstituted in death, by reassembling and reordering the bodies of the dead.

My intention in this essay is not so much to take issue with this argument, but to take off from a different point Bloch made in his early writings on famadihana—that these are rituals more than anything else about the connection between memory and violence (1971: 168–169). Bloch's analysis is based on fieldwork in a part of Imerina that had experienced unusually high levels of out-migration; it also reflects an ongoing theoretical interest in questions of ideology—particularly, in how ritual acts legitimate relations of authority. My own fieldwork was in an area where local descent groups still provided the basic framework of local politics, and I am more interested in immediate questions of action: just what are the dead supposed to do to the living, just what are do the living do to the dead?

Let me begin, however, by explaining precisely what *famadihana* are, and what they are like.

A century ago, the word *famadihana* was used to refer any ritual which involved transferring a body from one place of burial to another.[3] According to contemporary accounts (Callet 1908: 272–3; Cousins 1963 [1876]: 79–81; Haile 1891), there were several reasons why this might be done. In dedicating a new tomb, for instance, it was (as it still is) the custom to remove the bodies of one's immediate ancestors from wherever they had been buried and place them in positions of honor within it. *Famadihana* might also be held to return the body of someone who had been buried temporarily in some other part of the country. Finally, if for some reason it was considered dangerous or inauspicious to open a person's ancestral tomb at the time they happened to die, that person would often be buried in a shallow grave at the tomb's foot, and left there for months or even years, until such time as the astrologer determined it was safe to let them enter. Transferring such bodies was also considered a form of *famadihana*.

Now, it had long been the Merina custom to wrap dead bodies before burial in one or more *lambamena*, mantles made of colorfully dyed Malagasy silk. It had also been a common practice, when tombs were opened during funerals or *famadihana*, to replace the worn-out *lamba* of those ancestors already in the tomb with new ones. At some point around the end of the nineteenth century, doing so sometimes became an end in itself, and people began to perform *famadihana* simply for the purpose of renewing their ancestors' shrouds.[4] And, it would seem, this aspect became more and more important as time went on, to the point that, while the older forms are certainly still practiced, everyone I talked to between 1989 and 1991 from the region of Arivonimamo and, for that matter, elsewhere took it for granted that the rewrapping of ancestral bodies was what *famadihana* were basically about.

Usually, I was told this should be done once every six or seven years—the exact number is often said to vary from tomb to tomb. Often, also, *famadihana* are said to be held because some ancestor demanded it, appeared like Andrianambololona appearing in a dream or vision to complain of being cold.

The overwhelming majority of *famadihana* about which I have information fell into one of two categories. The first were "return *famadihana*" (Bloch's phrase: 1971: 146), their sponsors almost always families no longer living in the region who still periodically disinterred their dead for reburial there. When they did so they would almost always take advantage of the occasion to rewrap other ancestors in the same tomb. While some return *famadihana* were quite elaborate, the most celebrated and important *famadihana* of any given year were almost always of the second kind: dedicated to one particular ancestor who, dead usually some five to ten years, had never been the object of a *famadihana* before.[5] Four or five different tombs might be opened at a *famadihana* of this kind, since it was considered important to honor, as well, each of the ancestor's own immediate ascendants (mother, father's mother, mother's father, and so on), and often these more distant ancestors were buried in different tombs. But the focus was always on the final tomb, from which the ancestor around whom the ceremony was organized was always the very last to emerge.

A Capsule Description

No matter what sort of *famadihana*, or how many tombs were involved, the sequence of events at each tomb was always more or less the same. It's fairly easy, then, to construct a generic description. What follows is an outline of this basic sequence of events, roughly modeled on the sort of accounts participants would give me when speaking of such things in the abstract, but mainly drawing on my own observations from the eight or nine *famadihana* I attended between June 1989 and January 1990, all in the region of Arivonimamo and all but two in Betafo.[6] Most of what I say could be a description of any one of these.

Having decided to hold a *famadihana*, the sponsors would first consult an astrologer to find the appropriate date and time for the opening of the tombs. Next, they had to inform the local government offices—an old colonial law stipulates that no tomb can be opened without the names of the ancestors to be exhumed being registered and a tax paid for each tomb to be opened. During the two or three months which usually intervene before the ceremony, everyone affiliated with the tomb had to be informed, and money raised to pay for the feast, musicians, and the *lambamena* themselves. In Arivonimamo some families weave their own *lambamena* (which are very expensive); if so, work had to begin at least a month or two in advance.

The night before the tomb was to be opened, the sponsor and a few companions mounted the tomb and call out the names of the ancestors to be rewrapped, asking them all to return if they happen to have strayed. This stage is always important in accounts of *famadihana*, but it's conducted largely outside the public gaze by a few close kin.

The *famadihana* proper began the next day with a procession from the sponsor's home town or village to the tomb. Between the *zana-drazana*—the "children of the ancestors"—and their guests there were usually at least several hundred people in attendance, dressed in what's called "Malagasy" style: this, in effect, means that rural people wore their best attire short of formal Sunday clothes, while city people dressed down in something approximating rural dress. This is important because any such gathering will necessarily involve a certain amount of tension between the members of a group who still live on the ancestral lands, called the *valala mpiandry fasana* or "crickets minding the tombs," and the *zanaka ampielezana* or "children spread out," who are only really connected with their place of origin through their tombs. The emphasis is self-consciously egalitarian and often whole households will make a point of all wearing shirts and dresses made from the same cloth.[7]

The astrologer always led the procession, often accompanied by people carrying photographs of the most important ancestors, and always by a man carrying the Malagasy flag (whose presence confirmed the ceremony's legal authorization). There were always musicians, and usually women carrying rolled-up papyrus mats close behind.

On arrival, the flag was planted on the roof of the tomb, and men took shovels and began removing the earth that covered its buried stone door. Only the *valala mpiandry fasana* have the right to dig open the doorway, and, if the sponsor was a *zanaka ampielezina*, there was often a squabble here, the diggers demanding rum before they'd work. Once the digging began, the atmosphere was festive and informal, though with a certain feeling of anticipation: there was music, and some people danced, others carried shovels and other tools back and forth, took breaks from work, and returned.

Once the door was fully uncovered, some of the diggers splashed it with rum and began to move it aside, as others readied candles or lamps, and then began to descend the stairs leading to the inner vault. As they disappeared inside, the female *zanadrazana* (their numbers sometimes augmented by some young men or boys) arranged themselves in rows, sitting with legs extended on level ground near the tomb. Usually the men splashed a bit of rum over each of the bodies in the tomb and made a brief invocation asking for its blessing before rolling it from its place onto a papyrus mat. Once they had, three or four of them would carry it up the stairs and, as they emerged, shout out the ancestor's name as the crowd whooped and shouted its enthusiasm. The music picked up at this point; often other men would join in to help carry the body around the tomb three times, and their abrupt stops and starts would lead to its being twisted and crushed inside the mats.[8]

After being taken around the tomb three times, the ancestors were placed on the laps of the women (who were arranged in hierarchical order from east to west or north to south) and the next phase of the *famadihana* began. Men and women produced bottles, some full of honey and rum, others cow fat or, occasionally, cologne. There were plastic bags full of honeycombs or pastel-colored "Malagasy" candies, pieces of ginger, and coins. Some moved from body to body, pouring rum and honey over each; others handed the bottles to the seated women, often after taking a sip or swig themselves. Sometimes, a woman would produce a stick of tobacco, put half in her mouth, and the rest inside the tatters of a dead husband's *lamba*. Others broke off pieces of honeycomb to place inside the folds of cloth around where the ancestor's head or chest would be. The same was done with the coins, ginger, and pieces of candy. I've been told that some people leave small bottles of rum in the wrappings during one *famadihana* and drink them during the next, and often I heard about people who take dust from inside the wrappings and smear it on their faces or gums as tooth medicine (though I must say I never saw it done myself), or take a handful of beads from the ancient cloth to preserve for the same reason.

This sequence of giving, taking, and sharing was always referred to as a *fangatahana tsodrano* or "request for the blessing" of the ancestors—though *famadihana* as a whole could also be spoken of in this same way. The gifts were called *fangataka*, "tokens of request," and participants occasionally called out to the ancestors, beseeching them to give their blessing. It was also always a moment of great emotional intensity. Women, particularly if they had the remains of a close relative on their lap, clearly found what they are doing frightening, sad, and disturbing. Many appeared in something close to a state of shock, barely managing to hold back tears, and in every *famadihana* I myself attended at least one such woman did break down and cry—others quickly crowded around to do their best to reassure, comfort, or distract her, always reminding her that "this is an act of celebration, not of mourning."

Next, men divided into teams around each ancestor to begin the actual wrapping. The old *lamba* were never removed but left in place; nor were the bodies allowed to touch the ground—in fact, the initial stages are done while the body was still on the women's laps—since it was very important to ensure that at no time will an ancestor touch the earth. Generally, they were rolled first into white sheets, and then one by one into the thicker and more durable *lamba*. There were almost always at least two layers of cloth all told: mainly silk *lambamena* for the more important ancestors, polyester for the rest. While women looked on and often gave advice, the actual process of wrapping the bodies, and then tying the resulting bundle together with cords or strips of cloth (there should ideally be seven of these) was always performed by men—who spared no efforts to roll and bind the ancestral bundles as tightly as they could.

This being done, the music picks up once again in volume and tempo and the final, joyous part of the ceremony begins. Mixed groups of men and women carry the bodies, once again carried in their mats, one by one around the tomb, this time stopping and starting and dancing even more vigorously and even violently than they had in the beginning, with all sorts of rough-house, shouting, whoops, and cries, people generally throwing themselves about in a sort of delirious abandon.[9] The *razana* are once more twisted and crunched about a great deal over the course of the dancing, which may last around fifteen minutes, until finally being returned to their places inside.

With this, the business is basically finished. If there are more tombs to be opened, a procession will form behind the astrologer once again. If this was the last, the sponsor and some local elders or politicians will mount the head of the tomb to make brief formal speeches summarizing the days events and their significance, and thanking everyone who came. After this the crowd begins to drift off, and a group of men take shovels and begin to pile back the dirt removed from the door to the vault. In theory, it should be the oldest man among the local *zanadrazana* who removes the first shovelful of earth from the doorway at the beginning of the ceremony; the first returned at the end should, I was told, be done by a young man whose father and mother are both still living.

Later still, often around nightfall when everyone else has long since left, the astrologer and a few assistants will come back to the door of the tomb to make a *fanidi-pasana*—a "lock to the tomb"—by burying a few magical objects in or around the doorway. These, if placed correctly, should ensure that the ghosts of those "turned over" remain in the tomb and cannot emerge again to trouble the living.[10]

Descent Groups

Merina society is divided up into a number of cognatic descent groups, which in the literature are usually referred to as *foko*.[11] Bloch calls them "demes" because they tend towards endogamy and are closely identified with ancestral territories. About a third of them claim *andriana*, or "noble" rank; the rest are *hova* or "commoner" demes. There's also a significant portion of the population made up of people descended from nineteenth-century slaves. These *mainty*, or "black people," are not organized into demes and don't usually intermarry with the *fotsy* or "whites," though in other respects they share the same social organization.

Each deme has its history, usually beginning with an account of the origins of its founding ancestor, how he came to the territory on which his descendants now reside, how by his various movements he defined its boundaries, created its villages, named various prominent aspects of its landscape, and so on. In most cases, the stories go on to how he subdivided the territory by giving each of his children (or sometimes, each of his wives) their own village or territory: that of the eldest furthest to the east, with the others ranging westward in order of seniority (cf. Condominas 1960: 199–203; Rasamimanana & Razafindrazaka 1957 [1909]: 9–13, etc.).

If most people could tell you from which of these branches they consider themselves to descend, it's not because they could trace any genealogical link to the founder. Genealogical memory was extremely shallow: I met very few people who could remember further back than to their grandparent's generation or, at any rate, to people they personally remembered from their childhood. Nor are deme divisions in most cases any longer identified with clearly bounded territories (if they ever really were). What's significant is not where one lives, but the location and history of one's tomb.

Merina villages are surrounded by tombs—usually there's literally no place one can stand outside without being in sight of one. Ancient tombs, by now little more than grassy mounds of earth, sit next to white-washed stone and cement ones topped with wreathes and stone crosses, and—now and then, if there's a particularly wealthy family in the neighborhood—brightly painted palatial structures on wide platforms, their doorways shielded by metal lattice gates. Whatever their size though, their granite solidity is meant to contrast with houses, which are never built of stone but usually of mud brick. Clearly, tombs were meant to be symbols of permanence; constant reminders of the enduring presence of the ancestors.

They are also organized into a hierarchy: and it's this hierarchy of tombs which forms the real physical framework of the deme, and provides the terms of reference by which people can place themselves within it. Most people I knew had only the haziest idea of their deme's history, but anyone could point out their own tomb, and explain how it fits in.

Andrianambololona, for example, was as I've mentioned buried with his wife and daughter in an impressive stone tomb to the east of the village of Betafo.[12] In the western part of the same village were four tombs, each said to hold the bodies one of his five eldest sons, and half an hour's walk further to the west was a fifth, that of his youngest son who had had a falling out with his seniors and moved away.[13] Each of the deme's divisions were said to descend from one of these brothers—whose relative rank is remembered even if their names have long since been forgotten. And, while only a handful of the present-day inhabitants actually expected to be buried in one of these ancient tombs, each new tomb that was created was linked to one of them by the affiliation of its founder. In other words, what really knits a deme together is not a human genealogy but a genealogy of tombs. Older tombs are seen as generating younger ones, and the organization as a whole inscribes a pattern of historical memory in the landscape, in a form that makes it seem indelible and permanent.

"Playing with Corpses"

This is not to say that this framework is any sense really permanent and unchanging. In fact it is continually being transformed and redefined through human action. New tombs are constantly being built, old ones emptied and abandoned. Bodies are transferred back and forth; they are broken apart and combined with one another. And in a purely practical sense, it's this which *famadihana* can be said to *do*.

Whatever their outer appearance, Merina tombs are always much the same inside. The doorway always faces west; the door itself is a huge buried slab of stone. Moving it aside, one descends a stair to enter a single large chamber from whose northern, western, and southern walls emerge stone "beds" (*farafara*) or shelves, set one above the other. Typically there are three shelves on each wall, making nine in all, but people are rarely willing to place bodies on the bottom shelves, so that in most tombs the number available is, effectively, six.

In principle, everyone who has the right to be buried in a given tomb is descended from a single individual, who is referred to as the *razambe* or "great ancestor" of that tomb. The *razambe*'s body is always placed either on the highest shelf to the north, or the highest to the east, usually together with his (or her) eldest child. Each of the other children is allotted a different shelf on which they become, as it were, minor *razambe*, and on which only their descendants have the right to be buried.[14] Sometimes, individual shelves are further subdivided along the same lines. Shelves and spaces on the shelves thus become a form of property: I have even heard of a case of a man in extreme financial trouble who tried to sell his space in a prestigious tomb, though I'm not sure anyone would have dared to buy it from him and eventually his relatives talked him out of the idea.

In practice, however, it's not only lineal descendants who have access; one can draw on a variety of other connections (marriage, fosterage, blood brotherhood, and so forth), so that most men and almost all women have a fair degree of choice over what tomb they intend to be buried in.[15] However, it was often stressed to me that each tomb has its own regulations concerning who can and cannot be buried in it, and on which shelves. In one, children linked through women are not allowed on the upper shelves. In another, only actual descendants of the *razambe* are allowed in, not their husbands or wives. These regulations can take many forms but they are always negative in their phrasing—in fact, they are usually referred to as the tomb's *fady* or "taboos," and not distinguished from taboos against, for instance, wearing clothes with buttons that apply inside some tombs, or against the giving of tobacco or participation of slaves during *famadihana* in others.

The first few times I actually went inside one of these tombs, I was surprised by how few bodies they seemed to contain. Even in very ancient tombs, only two or three of the shelves might hold bodies and, even when there were more, there were frequently only three or four bodies lying on any given one of them—remarkably few, considering some of these tombs had been in continual use for over a hundred years. There were, I found, a number of reasons for this. For one thing, new tombs are constantly being built. On completing a new tomb, it's customary to take at least one ancestor from one's former tomb (typically the founder's grandfather or great-grand-father) to be the new *razambe*. If one can get all the owners' permission, a whole shelf's worth of ancestors might be cleared out, and divided up among those of the new tomb.[16] And since the division of shelves in the old one is considered to have been fixed by ancestral decree—which makes people very reluctant to rearrange the bodies—whole walls of shelves may end up lying empty as a result. For the same reason, demographic vagaries can lead to empty or nearly empty shelves as some branches die out without their space being reapportioned.

A more important reason, however, is that the number of bodies is kept limited by the habit of consolidating them.

Here the reader should understand that these bodies—the Malagasy term *razana* which is used to refer to them actually means at the same time both "ancestor" and "corpse"—are not really "bodies" at all in any sense suggested by the English word.[17] Certainly they didn't look anything like human bodies. Mainly they looked like wrapped bundles of red earth.

On death, corpses are always wrapped in one or more *lambamena*— cloth made of a material that (like the polyester now sometimes used to sub-stitute for it) is valued for its hardness and durability—before being placed in the tomb. New *razana* have to be left there, undisturbed, for several years until they are considered to be "dry," by which time little but dust and bones are likely to remain. During a *famadihana* the bodies are usually subjected to a great deal or rough handling: they're danced with, pulled and tugged at, wrapped and bound with extreme force, and then danced with again in an even more tumultuous manner before being returned to their shelves. After twenty years and several *famadihana*, they have been quite literally pulver-ized: even the skeletons have largely crumbled away, and there's very little left to serve as a reminder that the thing had once had human form.[18] People say they've turned into "dust" (*vovoka*), and in fact it's basically impossible to tell what was once body from what was once cloth, both having turned the same brick red color—which, incidentally, is the same as that of the lateritic Malagasy soil.

Bodies can only be combined after their first *famadihana*—that is to say, after they have been already largely reduced to dust. It's a relatively simple matter to rewrap two such bodies in the same cloth. In fact, if one doesn't, ancestors—unless they're famous ancestors, regularly rewrapped in large numbers of shrouds—tend to become thinner and thinner as time goes on, until in the end they look like mere tubes of cloth that bulge in the middle, the whole bundle the thickness, say, of a person's arm or leg. On the other hand, *razana ikambanana* or "combined ancestors," which for all anyone knows may be made up of the remains of a dozen different individuals, along with all of their old *lamba*, can often attain a very large size, two or three times that of a living human being.

The most frequent practice was to wrap children in one *lamba* together with their parents, and husbands together with their wives. I was frequently told that two siblings could never be combined. Apart from this, it's difficult to generalize, since, as in so many things, different families and tombs have different customs; but almost always, the ancestors combined together are those on the verge of being forgotten—that is, contemporaries of the parents or grandparents of the tomb's oldest living descendants. Usually, children who died at an early age are the first to be so treated (these are incorporated in their parents); next, adults who died childless, or anyway who no longer have living descendants, and thus no one to provide them with *lambamena* during future *famadihana*.[19] These are incorporated with ancestors that do. The names of such minor *razana* are for the most part quickly forgotten; the same is usually true of wives wrapped together with their husbands, or the occasional husband buried in his wife's family tomb who's been combined with her. But in the end, unless the tomb's owners make a point of marking certain *razana* with written labels or keep family notebooks—which few do—all but two or three of the most famous older names will inevitably pass from memory. Most older tombs end up containing at least one and often several large bundles referred to only as a *razambe ikambanana*, or "combined great ancestors," since none of the current owners have the slightest idea what the name of any of its component ancestors might be.

Since none of these *razambe*—named or nameless—can ever be removed to another tomb, no tomb, however old, can ever be entirely stripped of bodies. But, as some of the branches of descendants die out and others build new tombs and remove their own immediate ancestors, many tombs reach the point where they are no longer used for burial.[20] Most such tombs will still be opened now and then during elaborate *famadihana*, and one or two bodies rewrapped. But, at least in my experience, this is usually the occasion of a good deal of confusion, as the *zanadrazana* inspect the half-dozen or so ancestral bundles left in the tomb, trying to identify their own.

And even these connections are not remembered forever. Hillsides are dotted everywhere with the remains of ancient tombs, which often look like nothing more than low mounds with a few worked stones here and there visible through the grass, whose remaining occupants have long since been forgotten. In fact, it might well be that the most prestigious ancient tombs—which are seen as key nodes in the hierarchical framework of the deme—are really just the oldest ones that have managed to avoid being forgotten.

The whole process of pulverizing and then consolidating bodies in *famadihana* can be seen as the concrete or tangible aspect of a process of genealogical amnesia. The bodies of the ancestors are gradually dissolved away at the same time as their identities are gradually forgotten. In the end, both are destined to be absorbed into that of some more famous *razambe*. Something of this sort occurs wherever genealogies are important, but, in the Merina case, the whole issue of remembering and forgetting is much more of a tangible problem than it usually tends to be—if only because ancestors are much more tangible objects. If relations with ancestors have to be worked out in so absolutely material a medium, the process of forgetting itself has to be made an active one, rather than something that just happens.

Similarly, while ancestral names played an important role in *famadihana*—they were called out from the tomb the night before, called out again as the bodies emerge, and usually, listed a fourth time in the speeches which close the ceremony—next to no one made the slightest effort to preserve these names permanently in writing.[21] There's no reason they couldn't be: Merina society is a highly literate one. *Famadihana* are referred to as "memorials" (*fahatsiarovana*) for the dead, but one of their central ironies is that what they actually accomplish is to make descendants actively complicit in forgetting them.

Cursing and Taboo

Outside of purely ritual contexts like *famadihana* however, the main way that ancestors manifest themselves in the lives of their descendants is through the imposition of *fady* or taboos—which, unlike the practices surrounding tombs, have a constant and immediate impact on people's practical affairs.

A great deal has already been written about Malagasy *fady* (Standing 1883; Van Gennep 1904; Ruud 1960; Lambek 1992) but rather than review the literature, I'll limit myself to a few critical points. The first is that the logic of *fady* is not really the same as, say, that of Polynesian taboo. *Fady* are not a mark of the sacred or, for that matter, usually of pollution; they are not about the state of persons or things at all so much as about actions which one cannot do. A *fady* takes the form of a simple statement: "do not do X"; "it is *fady* to do Y." It's the action, not the object or actor which is "tabooed."[22] To be able to impose such a restriction on others is one of the most basic ways of demonstrating authority over them; to share such a restriction with others is one of the most basic ways of demonstrating solidarity.[23]

There are various sorts of *fady*. Some are rules of conduct that apply to anyone (or to anyone in a given situation: e.g., "it is *fady* for a pregnant woman to sit in a doorway"), others apply only to people using or being protected by certain forms of magic, others are imposed by some ancestor and shared by all of his or her descendants. It's with the latter sort that I'm concerned right now.

The older men who were considered the ultimate authorities on matters of local history and custom almost always described these restrictions to me in moralistic terms: they were the means whereby ancestors maintained the harmony and integrity of the deme. The examples they'd choose were almost always the same: *fady* against stealing from one's kindred, against selling deme land to outsiders, or against intermarrying with inferior groups (especially the descendants of slaves). Though always attributed to the local ancestors, the list stayed pretty much the same from group to group. But there were other taboos that really did set one deme apart from another: usually there were certain other demes or divisions of demes of equal status into which its members could not marry; always, a range of animals and plants which they couldn't raise, or grow, or eat.[24] Tombs often had, as I've mentioned, their own sets of *fady*, usually attributed to their respective *razambe*; and even living parents had the power to "curse" their descendants never to eat pork, or own white cattle with black markings, or whatever else—thereby creating a taboo.

Many demes had stories about how their most important *fady* had originally come about. People were in fact much more likely to know these than the more formal deme histories—if only because they were usually much more entertaining as stories. Many were explicitly comic and clearly meant to poke fun at their ancestral protagonists. A Betafo ancestor for instance was supposed to have so gorged himself on pork and garlic that he burst apart and died (whereupon his survivors imposed a taboo on their descendants to prevent them from doing the same). The ancestor of the neighboring Andriamasoandro similarly stuffed himself with the caterpillars he discovered crawling out of trees during a brush fire—but, in some versions, he came to his senses before it was too late and, realizing what a stupid thing he'd been doing, cursed his descendants never to eat caterpillars again.[25]

One might argue that the absurdity is meant to underline the perceived arbitrariness of so many ancestral restrictions. But these were not the only genre of stories concerning *fady*; there was another which tended to be even more universally known, and for the most immediate practical reasons. These concerned the consequences of their transgression.

The consequences were, with few exceptions, devastating. A rich *andriana* who married a woman descended from slaves suddenly lost everything he had: now he is a pauper. Someone grew garlic where he shouldn't have; his crops were destroyed by hail. Someone else tried to remove a body from a tomb in violation of its regulations; he was blasted by lightning and died. There's no one, young or old, male or female, who could not easily recount a dozen such stories or more. They play an important role in local politics, since there was always a great deal of subtle maneuvering around who can convince others to accept their version of the local taboos. Moreover, it's almost exclusively these stories that described how the *hasina* or invisible power of the ancestors actually manifested itself to living people—or, to put this another way, how ancestors continued to act and to play a direct role in their descendant's daily lives. What's surprising is that, when they did, it was almost always by attacking them—in fact, by actions which would, had they been carried out by a living person, be instantly condemned as the most reprehensible kind of witchcraft.

No one would openly suggest that ancestors were anything like witches: as I've mentioned, elders in particular tended to picture them as the benevolent guarantors of the unity and moral integrity of the group. On the other hand, many of these old men grew distinctly uncomfortable whenever anything touching on the question of ancestral retribution was brought up—just as they would if any mention was made of witchcraft. Within a community, it seems it's mainly women who pass these stories on. And most of the women I spoke to didn't hesitate to express their own opinions about the ancestors' behavior—in fact, the word that came up most often in talking about them, *masiaka*, means "savage," "violent," or "cruel."[26] Part of the older men's reluctance to talk about ancestral violence probably had to do with the fact that they were very close to being ancestors themselves and simply as figures of authority, tended to identify with their position. They themselves wielded the power of *ozona*, or "cursing," over their own children. And, insofar as it could be used as a weapon to punish offspring who had proved utterly resistant to advice or admonition, it was the ultimate bastion of parental authority.

I only heard of two or three instances involving people I knew where someone really was cursed, but the possibility of doing so was always being alluded to. By all accounts, such curses always took a negative form: "you will never have any children," "you will never find prosperity in your life," or "you will never enter the family tomb." In other words, whatever the content of a curse, or the means of its enforcement, it never took the form of a direct assault (e.g., inflicting a disease on someone, or causing them to lose all the wealth they did have) but, instead, specified something the victim will never be able to do.

One might say that, while the stories of distant ancestors separate the imposition of restrictions and punishment for their transgression, here the two are merged in a single gesture.[27] But this only underlines what I think is a general principle: that the power to impose restrictions is ultimately continuous with the violence through which those restrictions are enforced.

An Initial Synthesis

One reason that Merina ancestors were felt to be a constraint on the actions of their descendants is that the ultimate aspiration, at least of any man, was to become a prominent ancestor himself. To do so however, he must manage both to overshadow the memory of his own ancestors, and constrain his children—particularly his sons—from either moving away, or overshadowing him in turn.

Ancestors, while they were still alive, were simply people; people who were born, had children, built tombs, and died. This is something which emerges very clearly in deme histories, in which ancestors were never represented as having had powers of action and creativity different from those available to people now.[28] Even when magical powers enter in to these stories (and they only rarely do), they are never magical powers one couldn't come by in the present day, if one had the skill or was willing to pay for them.

This is very different than a situation in which social divisions are said to have been instituted by, say, divine beings or totemic animals in the mythological past. People still have children and build tombs, and in principle, there's no reason why they shouldn't be able to become famous *razambe* themselves, even—and I met plenty of people willing to entertain this possibility—a *razambe* on the order of the founder of a deme. This obviously opens up at least the possibility of a rivalry between the living and the dead, since, from any individual point of view, the only reason one can't achieve such a status is because someone else already has. One might even see the stories about the origins of *fady* as being statements about the essence of this relationship: because our ancestor took this action (e.g., ate caterpillars), therefore we, his descendants, are never allowed to take that action again. At any rate, the fact that the presence of the ancestors is generally felt through a series of constraints on human action becomes much easier to understand.

In this light, consider the kinship relations which dominate people's daily lives. Madagascar has been one of those places anthropologists have found troubling in the past owing to the lack of "structure" or rules (Wilson 1977, 1991). Many authors have stressed the degree to which even links of descent are seen as created rather than received ("achieved" rather than "ascribed" is Southall's usage [1971, 1986]), and underlined the importance of links like fosterage, adoption, blood brotherhood, or other sorts of "friendship" in creating links between people (Vogel 1982; Kottak 1986; Feeley-Harnik 1991, etc.). In Imerina, for instance, property and rights of group membership are conveyed as easily through men and through women, marital residence is flexible and marriage easy to dissolve. Most people have a very wide range of options about how and with whom to live their lives.

At the same time tremendous emphasis is placed on parental authority and the role of elders—of which *ozona* is only the highest form. In other words, people's freedom of action is not seen to be much limited or constrained by explicit rules, but very much seen to be constrained by other people, especially those who stand over them in positions of authority. As a result, the social groups which, unlike those organized around tombs, do provide a context for people's daily affairs and are the stuff of local politics are, in most cases, very much the result of some one ambitious man or woman's personal project.

A Politics of Movement

Not everyone's personal project was the same, but there was, I found, a clear idea of what constituted a truly successful career (at least for males), the contours of which can already be made out in folktales written down over a century ago (cf. Dahle 1984 [1878]). The story is always roughly this: the hero leaves home as a teenager or young man to seek his fortune. He succeeds, becoming rich in money, cattle, or slaves. At this point he may return home again, or he might also establish himself somewhere new, but in either case he will acquire land, marry, and sire numerous progeny. His ultimate aim however is not simply this, but, first, to build himself a large and impressive tomb, and second, to prevent his own children from acting as he did. That is to say, he has to provide them with enough land and wealth that at least the larger part of them, along with their own descendants will be content to stay, to keep up the tomb in which he will be remembered as *razambe*.

It was certainly exceptional for someone to achieve the rank of *razambe* of an entire deme, but by no means inconceivable.[29] And the deme histories themselves almost always describe the founders as people who had abandoned their ancestral territories in the east to "find themselves a better living" (*mitady ravinahitra*)—which is exactly the same phrase used to describe what

young men do today when they go off to the city, or to Tsiroanomandidy, a
former frontier region seventy or eighty kilometers to the west which is still
considered a kind of land of opportunity, abounding in cattle and cheap
land, in the hopes of striking it rich.

Generational politics, then, comes down largely to a politics of movement, with fathers striving to keep their descendants from leaving, and sons
at least dreaming of being able to break away.

I've already remarked that, in present-day Imerina, much though a kinship group like a deme is identified with a certain *tanindrazana*, or ancestral territory, most of its members are likely to live elsewhere. People have
been following the same pattern—migrating but keeping their links with the
tanindrazana—for well over a century, and it's fair to say that the majority
of the "owners" of any given tomb in, say, Betafo no longer live there. Many
reside in the capital, which is only an hour away by van, but there are people
living in almost every part of Madagascar as teachers, officials, traders, and
the like. In addition, little colonies of people from the Arivonimamo area are
scattered throughout Tsiroanomandidy. Since almost all of the men (and a
fair number of the women) spend a good deal of their time away from their
villages engaged in petty commerce of one sort or another or otherwise looking for money, even those who have relatively little education have access to
a larger world.

What this means in the end is that it's only the wealthiest or most successful farmers who have the means to keep any large proportion of their
children around them. The less fortunate see them disappear one by one.
Daughters marry away; sons may well do the same, or they may follow their
mothers, be adopted by wealthier relatives, or simply head out west or to the
capital—intending to stay only long enough to make a little money, really
never to return. The result, when combined with that of demographic vagaries, can be quite dramatic: in the space of one or two generations whole
villages can disappear; once large and prosperous families can be left with no
living descendants in the area at all. On the other hand, the most successful
can not only keep most or all of their own sons and even daughters at home,
but attach to him- (or occasionally her-) self a whole range of dependents or
semi-dependents: poorer brothers or sisters and their children, affines (en-
dogamous marriage is often used to cement such ties), kin through adoption
or blood brotherhood, the occasional unrelated servant such as a cattle-herd,
and so on. To do so required land, and it is largely to keep their children and
dependents around them that most parents divide the lion's share of their
rice fields among their inheritors around the time the latter get married,
keeping only a modest portion for themselves.

Local Families and Their Tombs

It was these groups, named after and organized around one prominent individual (again following Bloch [1971: 81–86], I'll call them "local families"), that provided the real framework for everyday existence.[30] At any given time, a community was basically seen as an agglomeration of such local families, which often held together under a nominal head for a decade or more after the original founder had died. The largest quarter of Betafo, for instance, was made up of three of them: in only one of which was the founder still alive. Between them, they accounted for fifteen of the quarter's twenty households. The remaining five households were all, in some sense, marginal or fragmentary—most were composed of a single elderly man or woman living with an unmarried adult child, or else, with a small number of younger children or grandchildren. Such families were typically quite poor, and made no particular claim to a public voice.

Local families had a strong tendency to become small social universes unto themselves, working their fields cooperatively even after the patrimony had already been divided, fostering each other's children, sharing meals freely, and generally allowing people and things to circulate in a far more intimate manner than they would with other neighbors, who were always potential sorcerers. Often, their founders would break away from larger settlements entirely and build little hamlets of their own on a stretch of hillside overlooking their paddy fields.

While different members would have different options, most of the members of any local family would normally expect to be buried in its founder's tomb. Often, this was one he himself had created; if not, it was usually because he had already succeeded in establishing himself as the exclusive effective owner of one of the most famous ancient tombs—with whose *razambe* he might ultimately, in the eyes of the neighborhood, be substantially confused.[31]

Now, in either case, this might seem to contradict the notion that the head of the family aspired to be remembered after his death as a local *razambe*, since in founding a new tomb he would have had to bring in the body of one of his own ancestors to be its *razambe*, and in the case of the ancient tomb, one is often dealing with an ancestor so famous (one of the children of the deme's founder for instance) that the identity of the owner could hardly help but be overshadowed. But, in practice, there are a number of different ways things could work themselves out. Even a *razambe* can be forgotten, or can end up absorbed into some more famous successor (with whom he is often physically merged). I frequently discovered, on inspection of old documents, that the ancestor generally assumed to be the *razambe* of some tomb was in fact not its oldest ancestor at all, but rather the man who built it. There was a complex politics going on here; one whose very existence was never openly admitted. Everyone spoke of the need to remember and honor their parents after they were dead, but they also knew that the ultimate fame of a father almost necessarily meant the eventual oblivion of his sons (and vice versa). At the same time, much of the daily authority living people had, in their own communities, was derived from that of a more venerable ancestor—most often, in fact, a father—who was no longer alive.

It's true that in any community there were some people who really didn't seem to be promoting their own immortality so much as seeking it vicariously through others. But this, according to my own experience, was a strategy mainly adopted by prominent women, and rarely, if ever, by men. Many widows promoted the prestige and memory of a late husband (as daughters often would for their fathers) as *razambe* of a tomb, thinking little of their own name and reputation in comparison. But women had a very different position in the politics of local families than men, and the relation between fathers and daughters was not at all like the difficult and contradictory relation between fathers and sons. It was, in fact, held to be a particularly close one. I often heard people explain preferences for cousin marriage or other forms of endogamy, for instance, as the result of paternal sentimentality: fathers just weren't willing to see their daughters move away. A women who has moved always knows that her father would be happy, if he were at all able, to welcome her back should she wish to leave her current husband—all the more so if she has children to bring with her, who will add to the number of his local descendants. To most women, then, a father's house was a potential refuge; and this was doubtless one factor contributing to the universal assertion that girls naturally form their closest emotional attachments with their fathers, just as boys always tend to remain primarily loyal to their mothers, in childhood as well as later on in life.[32]

The Adults Are All Dead

When I first arrived in Arivonimamo in 1990, I began making the rounds of nearby villages to gather local histories. That each deme should have a history worthy of being told was taken for granted by everyone I talked to. Often, however, it was very difficult to find any one person considered worthy of telling it. Recounting oral histories—at least to outsiders—was felt to be the role of the *Ray aman-dReny*, or elders of the community; but next to no one, whatever their age, would be so presumptuous as to lay claim to this status themselves. So, if I asked a small group of people if there was anyone who might be able to tell me something about local history, the usual response was to start naming people that were dead. "Well, you could talk to Ingahibe Raoely...except he died six years ago. Then there was Ramatoa Rasoa, but she died just last summer." In the end, someone would usually come up with the name of a living person, but only after repeating the same stock phrases: "the grown-ups here are all dead; all that's left are we children who've succeeded them."[33]

This was, I think, more than just a colorful figure of speech. In many ways, the course of a man or woman's life really is defined in such a way that no one was considered to be unequivocally an adult until they are quite well along in years.

It is reflected, for one thing, by the age categories people used to refer to one another in common speech. While there were a great number of terms for infants and children, there were next to none which formally discriminated between the stages of life that come afterwards. If speaking about someone in a more or less respectful fashion, one normally used titles which were to some extent based on age: a young married woman for instance may be referred to as a *Madama*, one in her forties or fifties as a *Ramatoa*, an elder as *Ramatoa be* (men however have only a much less systematic and less formal set of titles).[34] If speaking of someone younger than oneself—even if it be a fifty-year-old discussing a forty-year-old—or, if speaking in informal or slightly disparaging terms of someone of about one's own age, one generally employed terms that would best be translated into English as "that kid," "that boy," or "that girl" (*zaza, ankizy, ankizilahy, bandy, baoikely, ankizivavy, sipa, ikala, ikalakely, idala*, etc.). Anyone whose parents were still alive was talked about in such terms constantly, and there was a general feeling that one had not really reached full social maturity until one was at least a grandparent.

Considering that the position of *Ray aman-dReny* is even more exalted, it should hardly be surprising that there were very few of them around. The simple fact was that anyone fortunate enough to attain such eminence was not likely to enjoy it very long.

What's more, one effect of the organization described above was to eliminate the vast majority even of the old people in a given community from consideration as elders. The heads of fragmentary families, like the dependent elders within local families, might have been respected for their age, but were never really considered proper *Ray aman-dReny* whatever their years. Women could in principle be elders, but in practice they were almost never considered so. Other men were disqualified by questions of character. Of the roughly 118 people who lived in Betafo, for instance, there was, in the end, only one man who everyone agreed could be considered an elder—and this was hardly unusual. If anything, Betafo was slightly unusual for having one elder whose status was absolutely uncontested.

On the other hand, anyone who did reach this status attained a social significance so great that it lingered on for many years after they died. Their names were always cropping up in conversation. Time after time, I would note people speaking of Rakoto's field or Rabe's house, only later to find out that the Rakoto or Rabe in question had been dead for over a decade. Often, it turned out that the groups these men had founded still existed, perhaps headed now by the man's widow, or an elder son of less intrinsic authority. As I've mentioned, a large share of the local families that exist in any community were of this sort—often, the final division of rights in land and houses among its members had not yet been made. In other cases, the local family had largely broken up, only a few former members were still scattered about the area, and the speaker either was not quite sure who owned the land now, or considered the owner insignificant.

It's hard to escape the conclusion that the people I talked to about gathering oral histories were really not too far off the mark. The socially determined life-course was so protracted it outruns most biological life spans entirely, and as a result, the *Ray aman-dReny* of most Merina communities were largely made up of people who were dead.

Gender and the Politics of Memory

Now, I mentioned at the beginning of the essay that the most prominent *famadihana* of any year were generally dedicated to a single person who had died some four or five years before. In my experience, this person was always the head of a local family whose memory still dominated the lives of his descendants in the way I've been describing.

During the winter of 1990, there were four *famadihana* in Betafo: two return *famadihana* sponsored by people from Tsiroanomandidy, and two dedicated to important elders. The first was dedicated to a remarkably successful man. A local official under the colonial regime, he had managed to keep all thirteen of his children from leaving his village of Ambaribe. The *famadihana*, sponsored by his elder sons in conjunction with his widow, involved four tombs and perhaps a thousand celebrants.

The second *famadihana*, sponsored by the widow and seven surviving children of a man named Rakotondrazaka, also involved four tombs and almost as many participants. It might be useful to go into this example in some more detail to get some idea of what a "famous" *famadihana* might actually involve. Rakotondrazaka had died in 1982 at the age of sixty-six, two years after having finished a tomb of his own. He also had managed to keep almost all of his descendants around him.

The first tomb to be opened was really not a tomb at all, but a grave containing a single nameless skeleton. The occupant was presumed to be a man killed by the poison ordeal in precolonial times and, for that reason, denied entrance to his family tomb as a witch. He had, however, appeared in a dream to Rakotondrazaka's eldest son many years before and had ever since been included in the family's *famadihana*. The second tomb was that of Rakotondrazaka's father. Rakotondrazaka had, in fact, removed his father's body from it when he dedicated his own tomb in 1980, but four of his father's ancestors remained there. They were rewrapped, and some unrelated people took advantage of the occasion to move in two bodies that had been buried in temporary graves nearby. The third was his mother's tomb. Here, there were a large number of bodies to be wrapped—most of them not directly related to his mother at all, but the ancestors of a rich but childless woman who had passed on her land to him on condition that he take care of them. The final tomb was Rakotondrazaka's own, where all of the five *razana* were taken out, the honoree himself, again, the last of all.

Even at the first and most ancient tombs, there was always a certain feeling of fear and anxiety as the ancestors first emerged, a certain air of triumph and rejoicing as they were returned. But the bodies themselves no longer revealed even the suggestion of a human form, and were not considered particularly pitiful or frightening. Nor were they the bodies of people any of the participants had actually known: in fact, the vast majority knew nothing about them, not even their names.

By the time the last tomb had been opened, and the final ancestor was about to emerge, on the other hand, the tension had built up to the point where it many of the *zanadrazana* clearly found it almost unbearable. Some of the young men carrying out the bodies appeared—despite the rum they'd been drinking all day to build up their courage—so overwhelmed by what they were doing that their faces were those of people in physical pain, as they forced themselves to carry out their parts in the ritual. Others seemed in to have fallen into an almost trancelike state, stumblingly oblivious to what was going on around them. When the final ancestor did emerge—immediately to be surrounded by a press of descendants who flooded him with rum and other offerings—the emotional pitch reached a climax; few were the women who didn't at least choke back sobs when the ancestors were first placed on their laps, and one or two would always dramatically break down and cry.

As the process of giving gifts and wrapping the ancestors continued, people gradually regained their composure and, by the end, more or less everyone took part in a mood of celebration. But, after the ceremony, women always tended to remark on who had cried—particularly if they had. "It's because you still remember the person so vividly," I was told on several occasions, always in more or less the same words, "and then you see just how little is still left."

I once asked one of these women why, if *famadihana* were supposed to be such a happy occasion, there was always someone who burst into tears. She looked at me a bit quizzically, and, observing that these were often people who had often just had their father's corpse placed across their laps, asked "well, how would you feel?" Not wanting to give anyone the idea that we foreigners were lacking in normal human sentiments, I hurriedly assured her that just about anyone in the world would probably have much the same reaction, were they to find themselves in a similar situation. Only later did it occur to me that I could have added that that is precisely the reason the rest of us never put people's dead fathers on their laps in the first place. If they do in Imerina, it can only be because the memory of the living individual—or at least of some of them—remains so powerful and so persuasive a presence in the minds of their descendants that only a confrontation as dramatic as this can really bring home to them the fact that he's dead.

That *famadihana* are largely concerned with transforming the memories of the living is a point that's already been made by Maurice Bloch (1971: 168–169). This, he adds, makes them quite different from the secondary burials made famous by Robert Hertz (1907), which are primarily concerned with freeing the souls of the dead person from its lingering existence halfway between this world and the next. But, in a way, the two are not so very different: here too the dead could be said linger on in a kind of suspended half-life in the memories of their contemporaries.

In the ritual, it was women's memories that were most prominently brought into play, while the ancestors who are the real emotional focus of the ritual were almost always male.[35] This was quite in keeping with the emotional bonds that were felt to—and often clearly did—exist between fathers and daughters (as also between mothers and sons). In fact, these attachments colored both women's and men's attitudes towards ancestors more generally. One older woman from Betafo told me, for instance, that if she dreamed of her mother, it was always to warn of ill news, while if some particularly fortunate event was about to occur, her grandfather would appear instead. The same pattern—female ancestors boding ill, and males boding well—appeared constantly in accounts of women's dreams. In one of the more dramatic ones I heard, a woman said to have been neglecting her children saw her mother's sisters appear to her inside the tomb to say that, if she didn't change her ways, they would soon be taking her to join them. On the other hand, Rakotondrazaka's daughter Irina—the woman who had broken down in tears over his body during the *famadihana* described above—later told me that her father regularly appeared in her dreams as a kind of guardian spirit, protecting her from danger and giving her advice.

This latter was unusual. While astrologers or magicians almost always claimed to have some "ancestral" advisor who appeared to them in dreams or visions, it was rarely said to be their own ancestor—and, even in those few cases where it was, never someone they had known personally. Irina was not an astrologer or magician of any sort, but she had been very close to her father while he was alive. Her father's favorite child, and only daughter, she had never married or left the village in which she was born, and had seven children (all by different men) that her father had helped her take care of. And, while I know a good deal less about men's dreams than about women's—since men were less inclined to tell me about such things—my impression is that the terms were typically reversed. Fathers appeared mainly to chide their sons when they'd been quarreling with each other or had otherwise strayed. This was certainly true of Rakotondrazaka, anyway: Irina told me that aside from being her personal guardian, her father had also made a deathbed promise to his six sons that he would continue, even after his death, to counsel and admonish them when there was a quarrel in the family.

A remarkable feature of dreams about people recently dead was the way that images of real living people become mixed up with images of death. This was true whatever the reason for their appearance. Frequently, as in the following dream, one reported to me by Irina, they appeared in or near their tombs; or the images recounted—particularly when they were chiding the living—shifted back and forth between those of living human beings and those of frightening corpses.

> I dreamed that I saw my father in 1989 (this was when he was already dead) to the north of Ambodivona. There were some trees and we were talking among them [and I asked myself] "is this daddy here, not yet dead?"
>
> Then, "give me your blessing," I said (because I wasn't well)... So we were talking, when he said "you shouldn't do such things, Irina," and, right there, he plunged back into being dead and bound. Later, I went up to the village where my older brother was; and he too just took off out of the village, and plunged into death like that. It was, like, disgusting—and frightening![36]

On first seeing her father, she wonders whether he isn't really alive. She asks for his blessing—but then he suddenly chides her, and turns into a corpse. The image changes from that of a living person to an ancestor, bound head and foot by the ropes used to fasten on his shrouds. What happens in Irina's dream—she confronts a vivid memory of an ancestor, asks for his blessing, and then suddenly sees him transformed into a dead, bound corpse—is just what happens to women in *famadihana*: except that in *famadihana*, of course, it's living men who bring about the confrontation by calling out the names of the dead, and thus evoking memories of living persons, before placing those persons' decomposed bodies on the women's laps.[37]

The memories evoked by names are tied to physical objects—objects which, as I've already described, are then gradually dissolved at the same time as the names themselves are gradually forgotten. The process as a whole can be thought of as one of effacing the individual identities of the dead—or, of all but the very small number who are or will become a tomb's *razambe*.

I've already described this process as a kind of active form of genealogical amnesia, in which the living begin to combine the remains of ancestors about to pass from memory with others whose names thought more likely to endure. But few endure for long. In examining the names that were actually called out during *famadihana* at particular tombs, I found that, aside from one or two *razambe*, almost all of them were those of people who had died within the last ten or fifteen years. In other words, most names continued to be memorialized only so long as memories of the bearers themselves were likely to remain vivid in the minds of any number of the living; or, perhaps more to the point, as long as the social relations to which those memories relate still have some reality in people's daily lives.

Names like that of Rakotondrazaka however remain enormously important—so much so that local society can be said to be largely organized around them. Local families continued to be referred to by the names of their founders as long as they hold together and, as I've said, these same names were regularly invoked when talking about the ownership of houses, rice fields, and tombs long after their bearers had died. The expression most often used to refer to ancestors on one's father's side literally means "name of the father" (*anaran-dray*). It was also used to refer to what might be called "ancestral property": houses, tombs and rice fields passed on through the male line (as was *anaran-dreny*, or "name of the mother" for the female line). A number of scholars have remarked on the oddness of this expression, since Malagasy society does not use patronymics or, for that matter, matronymics of any kind (Razafintsalama 1981; Gueunier 1982: 237n2). Why then should the most important elements of one's inheritance be identified with one of the few aspects of a father or mother's social identity that was *not* inherited?

It seems to me that, by using this expression, one underlines the fact that such property does not entirely belong to the person holding it. Sometimes, this is quite literally true: if a group of brothers and sisters postpone the formal division of their parents' property, land and houses can remain for years legally registered in the dead ancestor's name. In fact, I was told that one reason why children might decide to hold a *famadihana* in honor of the founder of their local family was to ask for their "blessing"—or *tsodrano*—before dividing up such a joint estate. Even when descendants do hold legal title, possession is not without its obligations, because if one holds a rice field inherited from a given ancestor, then one is responsible for providing *lambamena* and otherwise contributing to the expenses whenever that ancestor is involved in *famadihana*—an obligation which endures as long as does the memory of the ancestor.[38] But, here again, the logic of the ritual leads back to the theme of the dissolution of identity: several people told me that the reason why it was necessary to combine *razana* together was to keep such expenses down.

I certainly never heard anyone put it to me quite this way, but one might think of *famadihana* as a process of transferring ancestral names from an attachment to property to an attachment to stones. Standing stones have always been the archetypal form of memorial in Malagasy culture.[39] In a sense, tombs were themselves memorial stones; in former times they were always crowned by a stela which was said to stand directly over the head of the *razambe* (then called the *tompon'ny fasana* or "owner of the tomb" [Jully 1896]) and which received any sacrifices offered to him. In contemporary tombs, the stelae have become crosses, but the implication and positioning remain the same. The stone, in effect, represents the tombs as a whole, and both are ultimately to be identified with a single ancestor, whose name in turn would be attached only to it, and not to any property shared by living people.

Famadihana as Reversal

The difference between men's and women's attitudes, at any rate, would explain the very different roles they're given in the ritual—particularly at the critical moment when the confrontation between ancestral bodies and human memories takes place. Women carry ancestors on their laps. The expression used for this is *miampofo*, which literally means "to nurse a child sitting on one's lap," and the candy, honey, trifling sums of money, and so on are just the sort of thing one gives as treats to small children. Even the fact that the *zanadrazana* clothe the ancestors, and carry them rolled like infants in a blanket-like *lamba*, could be seen in a way treating them like children—which, assuming the ancestors are here being thought of as symbolically male, reverses the relation between fathers and daughters, turning it into a relationship between mothers and sons.[40]

The men's part, on the other hand, is to carry the ancestors, to wrap them, to bind them, and to lead the dancing with which they are returned to the tomb at the end of the ceremony. In effect, what this means is that it's the male role to destroy them, since it's the combination these actions—none of which are carried out at all gingerly—which result in the dry body being broken apart and turned to dust. One woman told me this was the reason it was men who have to bind the ancestors: the binding has to be done with such "outrageous" (*mahatsiravana*) force that only men are strong enough to do it.

The word usually used for "wrapping the ancestors," *mamono razana*, sounds suspiciously like the phrase for "attacking" or "killing" them.[41] The word *famadihana* itself, for that matter, can also mean both "reversal" and "betrayal." Admittedly, I never heard any participant remark on the parallel. But it could certainly be argued that the male role in the ceremonies involves a reversal of roles which goes even beyond that of the living attacking the dead. What is being inflicted on the ancestors is precisely what the ancestors inflict on the living: a form of constraint continuous with a form of violence. This is perfectly summed up in the act of binding the bodies—each cord is yanked so forcefully that the very bones are crushed. There's also a particular emphasis on the politics of movement. Just as any father or grandfather would strive to keep his male descendants from moving away, so the process of the *famadihana* is largely one of containing the dead ancestors in space: after being called to return from their wanderings to the tomb, at the start of the ritual, they're removed, bound tightly with ropes, and locked back into the tomb with magic charms.

Ancestral Blessings

I have been arguing so far that rural society in Imerina was largely organized around the identities of a handful of prominent elders who had succeeded in assembling descendants around them, or at least in keeping them from moving away. The memory of such elders tends to retain enormous social force long after they themselves have died—so much so that to overcome it requires a ritual of profound trauma and violence, in which the relation between ancestors and descendants is turned completely on its head. By transforming their dead ancestors into children, the living can turn back on them the very forms of constraint and violence that constitute ancestral authority and, in doing so set off a process by which the memory of the ancestors themselves will be largely effaced.

This is not an interpretation a participant would be likely to offer, or even to agree with. When discussing *famadihana* in the abstract, almost everyone tended to avoid references to violence, and instead lay great stress on the *tsodrano*, or blessing that ancestors convey to their descendants. Usually, they would echo the themes of *famadihana* orations: that the living wish to honor the dead and so secure their blessing—a blessing which will ensure the continued health, prosperity, and fertility of themselves and their families. While older men and figures of authority were particularly inclined to emphasize these themes, this was a notion familiar to everyone: the formal expression meaning "to ask for a *tsodrano*" (*mangataka tsodrano sy ranombavaka*) was the one piece of ritual language even the most ignorant person was guaranteed to know, and the term was constantly invoked in ritual contexts, or in any other context in which a certain formality of speech was felt appropriate.

The notion that the ancestors remembered in *famadihana* provide positive benefits for their descendants appears, on the face of it, to be in complete contradiction with my own interpretation. But, on closer examination, one finds these positive benefits are very hard to pin down. The "health, prosperity, and fertility" provided by the ancestors is only of the most abstract and unspecific kind. Nobody ever sponsored a *famadihana* in order to cure someone who was ill, to bring success to some financial project, or cause someone infertile to conceive. In any of these situations, one might make a vow at the tomb of an ancient king or *Vazimba* spirit, or one might consult a magical specialist of one kind or another—and I don't think there was anyone I knew in Madagascar who hadn't done at least one of these things at some time or another—but no one would consider appealing to their own ancestors. Unless, perhaps they thought that their ancestors had been responsible for causing the problem to begin with.

It's true that some people would occasionally "ask for a *tsodrano*" from their ancestors by placing small offerings of rum, candies, or honey on the roof of their tomb, accompanying the gesture with a prayer (the offerings are mainly the same as the "tokens of request for *tsodrano*" given ancestors at *famadihana*). This appears to have been a common practice: at least, there are almost always one or two empty bottles or the remains of other offerings to be seen on the tombs of deme founders; and occasionally similar offerings on less prominent tombs as well. But it's hard to say exactly who did this and why, since with one exception, I never found anyone willing to admit to ever having done it themselves. This was in itself unusual: I rarely ran into anyone reluctant to talk about, say, offerings she had made at the shrine of some ancient king, or the rituals performed in consulting an astrologer or spirit medium.

The one man who did admit to having made one was something of a social pariah, notorious for having offended his *razambe* by violating a number
of ancestral taboos. He was said to have fallen into abject poverty and debt
as a result. One night, while drunkenly celebrating an unexpected windfall,
he declared to his neighbors that he had appealed to this same *razambe* for
relief from his debts, and that his prayers had been answered. It was clear to
everyone that his real motive was to broadcast as far as possible that the ancestor had forgiven him. They were not convinced. I strongly suspect that, in
most, if not all, cases where people left offerings on the tops of tombs "to ask
for their ancestor's *tsodrano*," what they were really doing was appealing to
them for relief from some punishment which those ancestors had themselves
inflicted. At any rate this would explain their reluctance to admit having
done so.[42]

The word *tsodrano* literally means "to blow water." At its simplest it refers to a domestic ritual in which a child or younger person requests his
elder's blessing, and the latter responds by sprinkling him with water, usually
adding a few words of benediction, which, using a relatively conventional-
ized language, wish good health, prosperity, and many descendants on the
person being blessed.

There are two very important points to be made here. The first is that elders never give such blessings on their own initiative. A *tsodrano* must always
be requested. In the past, I was told, children had to "buy" their parents'
blessing by presenting a coin or small piece of money to them as a token of
request. The giving of small change and other gifts to ancestors as "tokens of
request" would seem to echo this same ritual logic.[43]

The second point is that the effect a blessing has on its recipient is the
precise opposite of that of cursing or *ozona*. By cursing, parents impose taboos and restrictions on their descendants. By "blessing" they remove them.
In one village, for instance, I heard that the local elders gave such a blessing
after a number of teenagers who were studying in Antananarivo approached
them complaining it was impossible to maintain their deme's *fady* on pork
while living in the city. The elders blew water over them, so freeing the whole
deme from the taboo. In fact, in almost every context in which I heard of
someone asking for a *tsodrano*, giving it could be construed as releasing the
recipient from some constraint or restriction to which the giver would otherwise have had the right to hold them. The archetypical example was that of
a young man leaving home, whether to pursue his education or simply "look
for money." Such a person, I was told, will always go to his parents and ask
for their blessing, particularly if he is leaving the country or going very far
away. In common speech, one can say that two lovers have "blown water over
one another" (*mifampitsodrano*) if, on parting temporarily, they agree that

each is free to see other people until they are reunited. Shortly before leaving Madagascar in December 1990, just as the war in Kuwait was heating up, I heard on the radio news that "the American Congress has given President Bush their *tsodrano* to use force in the Persian Gulf."

More elaborate rituals were often organized in terms of requests for *tsodrano*. This was true especially of the rhetorical contests which surrounded the payment of the vody ondry (a kind of symbolic bridewealth—cf. Bloch 1971: 175–205, 1978; Keenan 1973). In all the examples I myself witnessed, the speechmakers treated the entire affair as a request, by the boy's family, for the girl's family's *tsodrano*. The theme was repeated over and over in their speeches. Even the money which the suitors present was referred to as a token of respect, given in way of requesting a *tsodrano*. In fact, the payment itself is often divided into a large number of small payments, each named after some task that a woman would normally be expected to perform in her parents' household—*maka kitay* (gathering firewood), *tsaka rano* (fetching water), *alam-bolofotsy* (plucking out her mother's white hairs), and so on—all of which clearly imply that the money is at least symbolic compensation for the services the daughter would have provided her aged parents were she to have remained at home. After the money has finally been accepted and the woman's parents have formally agreed to the match, the latter actually did blow water over the couple, adding some conventional words of advice and wishing them seven male and seven female children. It seems clear to me that it was this act of *tsodrano* which really effected the change of status of the woman: by giving it, her parents release their rights in her, or more precisely the constraints their authority as parents allows them to place on her freedom of action and of movement. In effect, it parallels the *tsodrano* a boy's parents give him before he leaves home to seek his fortune: both are a release from the obligations and constraints of parental authority.[44]

The only other occasion I know of, aside from *famadihana* and the tomb ritual, when anyone was said to request a *tsodrano* from the dead was a ritual said to be performed privately by a widow who wishes to remarry. She has to "ask for her husband's *tsodrano*" before being free to do so. This she does by approaching his tomb carrying two stones. One, a piece of quartz, is called "stone of the living"; the other, granite, is called the "stone of the dead." The ceremony itself is simple—she throws the dead stone at the tomb, and carries the living one home—but one can see it too as a capsule *famadihana*, at least in so far as it involves the same combination of violence and request for release.

A War Against Death?

What I am arguing then is that, since there is no clear line between positive benefits and the benefits of simply being left alone, the notion of *tsodrano* can be used as a kind of euphemism. This became particularly clear when, instead of asking what you accomplished by performing *famadihana*, I asked what would happen if you didn't perform them at all. While answers to the first question was usually preceded by a good deal of reflection and casting about for the right words, the second response was instantaneous: your children will die. Or you will fall desperately ill. Or you and your family will fall deeper and deeper into poverty. The catalogue of misfortunes could, admittedly, be seen as simply a negative image of the fertility, health, and prosperity *tsodrano* was said to bring; but since people were always much more concrete and specific in speaking of the misfortunes than they were of the benefits, it would make better sense, I think, to look at it the other way around.

The danger of ancestors coming to kill a family's infant children was, in fact, a constant concern. Ghosts (*lolo, angatra, matoatoa*) were said to linger around tombs and anyone unwise enough to come in too close contact with a tomb in ordinary circumstances should light a small fire in the doorway of their house and enter by stepping over it lest a ghost follow them inside. The same thing is done after attending funerals. There are any number of customs having to do with placement and maintenance of tombs which are explicitly concerned with keeping the dead from having access to the living—and the sure way of knowing that one has failed to maintain the separation is that the young children in one's family begin to die. Most of the people I knew could tell stories about waking in the middle of the night because they (or someone in the same room) were in the middle of being strangled by some malevolent ghost—which, when they appear in one's sleep, are typically characterized by their naked, black forms and huge size—and any marketplace would be sure to contain two or three vendors selling charms aimed at keeping ghosts away or getting rid of them.[45] These ghosts were anonymous, generic beings and contrasted in this with individualized, "good" ancestors who, when they appeared in dreams and visions, were usually robed in white. But even such relatively benevolent ancestors were, to say the least, troublesome: one of the most frequent reasons for their appearance was to complain of being cold and demand that their descendants perform *famadihana*—and I've already mentioned what is considered likely to occur if they are not satisfied with the results. When asked about the origins of the dark, murderous specters that disturbed children's sleep or otherwise plagued the living, most people immediately suggested they were ancestors whose descendants no longer "took care of them."

Since some would say that it was most often the recently dead who demanded *famadihana*, one might be tempted to look to Hertz's secondary burials once again for a parallel. In the societies he discussed, the vindictive ghosts of the recently dead were believed to linger near their old habitations; and the ritual served to release them into another world where they would be harmless to the living. *Famadihana* could be thought of as doing something similar: dissolving away the identities of the dangerous, recent dead, so they could ultimately be absorbed into that of a relatively benevolent *razambe*. But, as the example which began this essay makes abundantly clear, *razambe* are not necessarily all that benevolent.

One married couple from Betafo—who had, in fact, just earlier told me their own version of the story about the fire in 1931—mentioned that, after the most recent *famadihana* for Andrianambololona's someone broke into his tomb and stole several expensive *lambamena* that, having been bought for the ceremony but never used, had been left behind inside it. "That's odd," I said. "You'd think a thief would be afraid to enter such a tomb." "Well this one must not have been." "But he's supposed to be so powerful and fearsome! Isn't this the same one who burned down the town?" "Well," they both replied, more or less at once, "he wasn't cold any more, was he? If he starts appearing to you, it can only be because he's cold." But, in this case, there had just been a *famadihana*. He'd just been wrapped; he wasn't cold at all, and unless he was, the husband added, "he's really nothing but a pile of dust."

Heat did play an important role in the symbolism of *famadihana*. Honey, rum, cow fat, ginger, and even candies, all of which are prominent among the "tokens of requests for *tsodrano*" given to the ancestors, are also things one eats when one has a cold—precisely because they are considered food with heating properties, that can relieve the coldness in one's head or chest responsible for coughing or congestion. In fact, these gifts were supposed to be placed roughly where the ancestor's head and chest ought to have been.

Fire too had a complexly ambiguous relation with the dead. Ghosts were frightened by it. Everyone knew that, if in danger of being accosted by a ghost, the best thing to do was to light a match: a flashlight I was told wouldn't do, because it isn't light ghosts fear, but actual flames. I've already mentioned that stepping over a candle or other flame when entering a house prevents ghosts from following one in. Charms to drive away ghosts almost always involve heat and flames: most involved incense. But, at the same time, I heard people insist that one had to carry a candle or lantern—again, a flashlight would not do—when descending into a tomb to fetch the dead during a *famadihana*; and it was common practice to burn candles at the tombs of ancient kings or other benevolent spirits, or while invoking them elsewhere.

A friend of mine called Ramose Parson, a biology teacher at the Catholic secondary school in Arivonimamo, told me that he always thought of the practice of *famadihana* as being basically the same as cremation, except carried out over a much longer period of time. Cremated bodies are reduced to dust through the application of heat; afterwards, the dust is encased in an urn which ensures it never mixes with the surrounding earth. All of which, he pointed out, is also the case in Malagasy mortuary ritual—the place of the urn here being taken by the *lambamena*, which is valued for its hardness and durability, and by the care people take to ensure the ancestral bundles never come in contact with the earth. This is of course one man's theory, and a rather eccentric one at that, but, if nothing else, it would make the story with which I began this essay all the more poetically appropriate: by forgetting to carry out the *famadihana* in its entirety, the hapless descendants of Andrianambololona ended up bringing the destructive fire on themselves instead.

Some Conclusions

It can also be interpreted to mean that remembering and forgetting are equally matters of violence; that it is only the direction of the violence that varies between the two. This is, of course, the argument I have tried to develop over the course of this essay. The ancestors whose enduring memories give shape to social groups—whether these be recent *Ray aman-dReny* or ancient *razambe* like Andrianambololona—do so in practical terms mainly by their power to constrain and punish their descendants, by ancestral violence; while *famadihana*, seen as the highest expression of group unity, were occasions on which descendants could turn a form of violence precisely modeled on that of their ancestors against them, and by doing so gradually blot those memories away.

In Imerina, the rather commonplace dynamics by which genealogies are made and transformed—ones which, it has been clear since Evans-Pritchard's work on the Nuer, require a continual process of forgetting people's names—are transformed into a veritable struggle for existence between the living and the dead. This was true in the most literal sense. The dead, as a Malagasy proverb puts it "wish to become more numerous"—by murdering the living; the living respond by crushing and consolidating the bodies of the dead so as to keep their numbers low.

This is not to say that *famadihana* were not also memorials to the dead, just as participants said they were. The memory of ancestors was in its essence double edged: particularly so from the point of view of the most important men in rural society, who wield an authority and fame largely borrowed from ancestors who are ultimately their rivals—as well as being people they knew and cared for while they were alive. As I've said, the contradictions of their position often seem to put such men in a position of wanting to deny the existence of such violence altogether. For all that, in describing the moral unity of the community that ancestors create they are in effect speaking of the effects of that violence itself. Women, whose position in relation to ancestors is very different, though equally complex, feel much more comfortable talking about such matters, but even they did not really know how to reconcile the "cruelty" of which ancestors were capable when enforcing moral principles and the sheer egotistical violence of ancestors who simply wanted to be remembered for their own sake. It was presumably this latter dilemma—itself a transformation of the same central contradiction—which caused images of the dead, in effect, to split in two: between the one idea of benevolent elders who bring their descendants together in a moral community, and the other of rapacious ghosts who carry their descendants' children off to join them in the tomb.

Endnotes

1   *Dia vita ohatran'ny androany antoandro izao ny fonosan-damba, dia injany fa nirehitra ny tanana... Dia may izany. Dia maraina dia iny niavy tamin'ny olona indray hoe ho taperiko mihitsy aza ny ainareo raha ohatra ka tsy mamono lamba fa avelao izahy fonosona... Dia novonona indray ireo fasana ireo dia fonosina indray.*

2   Though it's only fair to point out the fact that all of these men had been alive at the time, or at least had first heard the story from eyewitnesses. All described the fire in naturalistic terms and denied a *famadihana* had anything to do with it.

3   *Mamadika* is a verb meaning "to turn over," "to reverse," or "to betray"; *famadihana* its nominalization.

4   For most of the nineteenth century, it was apparently the actual construction of new tombs which was the real focus of mortuary ritual, as it still is in Betsileo according to Kottack (1980: 229). A complete history has not yet been written, but at least in western Imerina, the modern pattern began to take form around the mid-1880s.

5   Bloch found this to be true as well (1971: 157–8). My sources, by the way, are not only based on direct observation of the ritual season of 1990, but on documents preserved in the offices of the firaisam-pokontany (former canton) covering the years 1985–90, checked against people's recollections. This latter proved a

good way of determining which *famadihana* people really considered significant or memorable.

Some *famadihana* did concentrate on a particular tomb rather than on a particular individual, especially if a number of important people belonging to one tomb had recently died. But these were much less common than those dedicated to individuals. The transfer of bodies from temporary graves was, in my own experience, never celebrated as an event in itself; it was mainly children who were buried this way, and their parents generally moved them when their tomb was opened for someone else's *famadihana*.

6   This account is in a number of ways different from Bloch's (1971: 145–161), which is based on what he observed in the Avaradrano region in the late-1960s. This may be partly due to regional variation, partly a reflection of historical change. Most of these differences however are relatively minor.

7   On the other hand, in the funerals I attended, people dressed in their most formal and expensive church clothes. The contrast, when a rich *zanaka ampielezina* is buried in the countryside was in fact quite striking: the village is suddenly full of expensive cars, men in black suits and ties, women in white dresses and gold jewelry carrying elegant parasols. The resentment of the country folk was often palpable.

8   Everyone agreed the body should properly be carried around seven times, but that this is no longer done. All such details depend on the astrologer's decision. He may forgo the rounding of the tomb completely and have the bodies carried out directly to the laps of the women.

9   *Famadihana* around Arivonimamo, on the other hand, appear relatively staid: I never saw anyone tossing skulls in the air, snatching skeletons from each other, and so on, as others have reported (eg, Ruud 1960: 169).

10   The next day was one of feasting: pigs slaughtered the day before were cooked in huge vats and ladled out to all; there was music and dancing and almost inevitably, drunken quarrels between rural and urban kin, which could, if the sponsors did not effectively intervene, degenerate into brawls. But the celebrations were only considered part of the *famadihana* in the broadest sense.

11   My own experience indicates this is something of a misnomer. Rural people did not even recognize this usage. In fact, there was there was no generic term for "deme" in common use at all. In the nineteenth-century demes were most often referred to as *firenena*, which is now the term for "nation."

12   The *andriana* of Betafo are descended from military colonists placed there after the Merina kingdom's conquest of Imamo around 1800. The colonists were from a famous *andriana* group called the *Zanak'* ("children of") *Andrianamboninolona*. Not only do Betafo nobles regularly refer to themselves as children of Andrianamboninolona, most think it is he who is buried in the *razambe*'s tomb.

13   The descendants of this younger son still predominate in that portion of the deme's
      territory. The people of this division, who became Catholics when their eastern kin
      converted to Protestantism in the last century, remember the deme history quite
      differently. Many claim at least half of the *razambe*'s sons for their own division,
      identifying them with each of the division's oldest tombs. This kind of contesta-
      tion is more the rule than the exception, though.

14   Hence, the internal structure of a tomb is much like that of a deme: there is a single
      razambe embodying the unity of the group, with a set of ranked children who, in
      so far as they are remembered, can be appealed to make distinctions between seg-
      ments.

15   Women tend to have more options because they can always choose to be buried in
      their husband's tombs (or often one of several husbands' tombs), while only oc-
      casionally are husbands buried in their wives' family tombs. For statistics on actual
      choices see Bloch 1971: 115; Razafintsalama 1981: 190–200; Vogel 1982: 162).

16   All the shelves of a new tomb should properly hold at least one body, since, if one
      is left empty, the spirits of the dead were likely to carry off a child or other family
      member in order to fill it. So if human bodies were not available, the trunk of a ba-
      nana tree was usually placed on the empty shelf to substitute for a human being.

17   Nor were they necessarily ancestors, in the technical sense. All of the bodies in a
      tomb were *razana*, whether they had descendants or not.

18   No *famadihana* seems complete without at least one argument between the men
      removing the bodies—who are supposed to carry it out head first—over which end
      of the *razana* is its head. Admittedly the bearers are never completely sober (if they
      had been, they would probably have remembered the way it was facing when the
      first picked it up) but rarely were there any physical clues to help them.

19   Some even argue that bodies are combined because it would be too expensive after
      a while to wrap all of them (and it would be shameful to open a tomb and leave
      some of them unwrapped). True, infertile *razana* are rarely given silk but usually
      polyester; but, if combined with the body of an ancestor who does have descen-
      dants, there's no expense at all.

20   Such tombs are said to be "full," though in fact they're more likely to be largely
      empty.

21   Examination, however, usually revealed that these lists represented only a tiny
      proportion even of those ancestors involved in the ceremony—for each tomb, just
      one or two *razambe* and those who had died in the last decade.

22   A Maori chief, for example, could be said to be intrinsically *tapu*, meaning sacred
      in the sense of set apart from the rest of the world. The word *fady* however is never
      applied to persons in this way. It is applied primarily to actions. Even when one
      speaks of, say, a "onion *fady*" this is usually shorthand for some specific rule of ac-
      tion, like eating or growing one.

23 I think this is one reason why I found it impossible to come up with anything remotely resembling a coherent list of local *fady* for the community of Betafo. Everyone agreed that such a list could be written, but no two gave anything like the same account, and many indignantly denied what their neighbors had told me. Spheres of influence were constantly being marked out by who could convince others to accept their view of the local *fady*, and, Betafo being a place in which authority and group solidarity were in a constant state of flux, opinions about *fady* tended to being equally shifting and chaotic.

24 They most often involved pigs and different kinds of onions—particularly garlic, which is called *tongolo gasy* or "Malagasy onion." Some of the more erudite held that pigs and onions, being "dirty," negated the power of magical charms and annoyed the spirits of the dead, and were, for this reason, a frequent subject of *fady* for users of magic and those who enter sacred places. But it was very rare for taboos to involve such an explicit notion of pollution. I note in passing that typically, restrictions on pork or onions applied only to specific situations—only once or twice did I run into someone never allowed to eat pork or garlic at all. They are, after all, probably the most popular foodstuffs in Imerina, and this would appear to be one of the reasons they were so often the focus of taboo.

25 Actually, he cursed them not to eat *bokana*, a variety of caterpillar used in local silk production as well as occasionally as food. Be this as it may, everyone I talked to found the restriction highly amusing and rarely avoided an opportunity to remark on it. The death by gluttony motif is in fact probably the most popular story used to explain group *fady* (and was a theme most found intrinsically funny in any context). Stories about the origins of marriage restrictions usually traced them back to some incident where the ancestors gambled, cheated, and got mad at each other—as with the gluttony stories, most of the people who told them to me made it clear that, as far as they were concerned, the ancestors were acting like fools.

26 A few very old and venerable women would try to put a moral slant on this: e.g., the ancestors are merciless in the punishing of evil-doers; most did not.

27 Parental *ozona* and ancestral *ozona* were seen by at least some to depend on one another: one woman told me you should be careful to observe all the ancestral *fady* lest you lose the ability to curse your own children.

28 In Imerina, in fact, I could find no popular interest in a cosmological time of origins at all; *tany gasy*, or "Malagasy times," which is the time of historical origins in which the ancestors lived and demes were founded, is seen as differing from the present mainly in a political sense.

29 While most of the demes and deme-territories in the area around Arivonimamo do not seem to have changed in any dramatic way since the last century, archival documents reveal the existence, in Ambohibe (a town near Ambohibeloma, seven or eight kilometers north of Arivonimamo) of an enormously rich man with the appropriate name of Andriampenovola—"lord full of money"—who, throughout

the 1880s and 1890s seems to have gone about accumulating descendants through adoptions: each adoptee was guaranteed a portion of his land, slaves, and other property as long as he or she remain on the ancestral territory. When I passed through Ambohibe in 1990 no one remembered the name of the 19th century deme (the Zanak'Andriandoria) but instead gave Andriampenovola as the name of the local *razambe*.

30 While there is again no generic term in Malagasy for such groups, people usually would refer to particular local families after their founders; as, e.g., "the offspring of Ranaivo" (*ny terad-Ranaivo*). Vogel (1982) for this reason calls such groups *teraka*, or "offsprings," but the term would never be so used by a native speaker.

31 By this I mean that, while there may be other descendants still using the tomb, there are none that live nearby. Often, though, the head would feel responsible for the upkeep of a whole set of tombs he had links to, if no other descendants were to be found who were capable of keeping them up in a respectable fashion.

Otherwise, it was largely left to the heads of the fragmentary families I've described to keep up local relations to the less famous tombs in any given area that were still in use. This gave them much of their local social importance, since the other owners tended to be city people, migrants, or children of migrants who depended on them to mediate in dealings with the tomb.

32 When women talked about leaving their husband they always, I noticed, spoke of "going home to father" and never "to mother."

33 *Efa maty daholo ny efa lehibe, fa izahay zaza mpandimby fotsiny no sisa.*

34 For example Ramose, technically the male equivalent of *Madama*, was in practice only used for men of that age who are also schoolteachers; *Rangahy*, the male parallel for both *Ramatoa* and *Ramatoabe*, is much more informal and in practice used much like the English word "guy"; finally, the term *Ingahibe* is a term of great respect applied only to the one or two oldest men in a given community. In all of this, by the way, I am only speaking of the vernacular Merina I am familiar with from Arivonimamo: I can't say for sure how far these generalizations hold beyond it.

35 I only saw women crying and male ancestors being cried over, but I only witnessed four or five incidents first-hand.

36 *Izaho izao ohatra tamin'ny 1989, nanofy izany izaho eto hoe hitako i dadanay—izy izany efa maty io—ary Avaratr'Ambodivona ary—fa misy hazo eo, dia niresaka aminy izahay fa ity dada ity ve mbola tsy maty hoy izy izany; mbola miseho eto indray. Dia omeo tsodrano aho hoy aho fa izaho tsy salama... Dia niresaka eo izahay mianaka: tsy fanao izay Irina hoy izy, dia iny izy dia nidaboka maty tamin'izy nafatotra iny. Dia izaho niakatra tamin'ny tanana misy an'ilay zokinay lahimatoa hafareny tery. Dia izy koa mba nikisaka niala an-tanana izy izany nidaboka an'iny fahafatesan'iny, Ohatran'ny hoe: mahatsiravana mampahatahotra.*

37   Her dream is somewhat complicated, though, by the fact that she had it at a time
      when her siblings were all quarreling—which probably explains his sudden trans-
      formation from benevolent to stern and authoritarian. It's unclear whether Irina
      meant to imply her illness was caused by her father's disapproval or not.

38   In Betafo, for instance, I heard of the case of several absentee owners living in the
      capital who, on converting to an Evangelical sect that did not allow them to par-
      ticipate in *famadihana*, immediately sold off their rice fields in Betafo.

39   No post-independence Malagasy government has to my knowledge ever erected a
      statue in the European sense—that is, one bearing some kind of likeness. Public
      monuments always take the form of standing stones.

40   About clothing: one elderly man made a great point of this, in speaking of his
      father, who he resented for not having taken care of him as a child. "He never so
      much as clothed me, but even so, I clothe him now" (meaning at *famadihana*).
      About the *lamba*: as Gillian Feeley-Harnik reminds us (1989) these are feminine
      products; ideally, they should be the handiwork of the participants themselves.

41   Though, admittedly, it's really just a homonym, and only works in the active voice
      (*mamono*), since the two verbs actually come from different roots (*fono* for wrap-
      ping, *vono* for beating/killing).

42   Irina's request for a *tsodrano* in the dream cited above might be an example of the
      same thing; it's unclear from the context whether her father's annoyance with his
      squabbling children was the cause of her illness or not.

43   Generally speaking, every ritual gesture which involved giving something to the
      ancestors—i.e., pouring rum over the door of the tomb or over the bodies inside,
      giving gifts when the ancestors are placed on women's laps, and so on, are all
      referred to as "requests for *tsodrano*." Likewise, anything taken away by the *zanad-
      razana*, such as the pieces of mats which are said to bring fertility to women and
      the tooth medicine mentioned above, can be called "*tsodrano*."

44   Also—though this was a matter of some debate among my own acquaintances—
      tsodrano could be given to relieve the consequences of *tsiny*, which is the guilt or
      blame a person may have due to the detrimental effects their actions have had on
      others (Andriamanjato 1957). Parents, for instance, might give an errant child
      who has returned such a *tsodrano*. This is, of course, in keeping with what I've
      said about people who leave bottles of honey and so forth on top of tombs. It also
      may relate to the notion that *famadihana* are meant to counteract *tsiny*, which was
      very important to Bloch's informants though I never heard much about it where I
      worked.

45   There's no room here to enter into *ambalavelona*, which involves a sorcerer's ma-
      nipulation of material from tombs to cause an enemy to become possessed by such
      an evil ghost, typically driving the victim mad. Similar charms are used to cure
      ambalavelona, and to drive off *Vazimba* spirits, which are considered by some to

be the final malevolent form which ancestors take when their descendants do not "take care of" them.

Bibliography

Astuti, Rita
1995 *People of the Sea: Identity and Descent Among the Vezo of Madagascar.* Cambridge: Cambridge University Press.

Bloch, Maurice
1971 *Placing the Dead: Tombs, Ancestral Villages, and Kinship Organization in Madagascar.* London: Seminar Press.
1982 "Death, Women and Power." In *Death and the Regeneration of Life* (M. Bloch and J. Parry eds.). Cambridge: Cambridge University Press, 211–230.
1985 "Almost Eating the Ancestors." *Man* (n.s.) 20: 631–646.
1986 *From Blessing to Violence: History and Ideology in the Circumcision Ritual of the Merina of Madagascar.* Cambridge: Cambridge University Press.

Callet, R. P.
1908 *Tantara ny Andriana eto Madagascar.* Tananarive: Académie Malgache.

Condominas, Gerard
1960 *Fokonolona et Collectivités Rurales en Imerina.* Paris: Berger-Levrault.

Cousins, William E.
1963 *Fomba Gasy.* (H. Randzavola, ed.) Tananarive: Imarivolanitra.

Dahle, Lars
1984 *Anganon'ny Ntaolo, Tantara Mampiseho ny Fombandrazana sy ny Finoana Sasany Nanganany.* (L. Sims, ed., original edition 1878). Antananarivo: Trano Printy Loterana.

Evans-Pritchard, Edward E.
1940 *The Nuer: A Description of the Modes of Livelihood and Political Institutions of a Nilotic People.* Oxford: Oxford University Press.

Feeley-Harnik, Gillian
1989 "Cloth and the Creation of Ancestors in Madagascar." In *Cloth and Human Experience* (J. Schneider and A. B.Weiner, eds). Washington, DC: Smithsonian Institution Press.
1991 *A Green Estate: Restoring Independence in Madagascar.* Washington, DC: Smithsonian Institution Press.

Gueunier, Noël Jacques
1982 "Review of *Le Tsimahafotsy d'Ambohimanga*, by Adolphe Razafintsalama." *Asie du Sud Est et Monde Insulindien* 13: 235–241.

Haile, John
1891 "*Famadihana*, a Malagasy burial custom." *Antananarivo Annual and Malagasy Magazine* 16: 406–416.

Hertz, Robert
1907 "Contribution à une étude sur la représentation de la mort." *L'Année Sociologique* 10: 48–137.

Jully, Antoine
1894 "Funerailles, tombeaux et honneurs rendus aux morts à Madagascar." *Anthropologie* 5: 385–401.

Kottak, Conrad Phillip
1986 "Kinship Modeling: Adaptation, Fosterage, and Fictive Kinship among the Betsileo." In *Madagascar: Society and History* (C. P. Kottack, J.-A. Rakotoarisoa, A. Southall and P. Vérin, eds). Durham: Carolina Academic Press.

Lambek, Michael
1992 "Taboo as Cultural Practice among Malagasy Speakers." *Man* 27: 245–266.

Raison-Jourde, Françoise
1991 *Bible et pouvoir à Madagascar au XIXe siècle.* Paris: Karthala.

Rasamimanana, Joseph and Louis Razafindrazaka
1957 *Contribution a l'histoire des Malgaches: Ny Andriantompokoindrindra.* Tananarive: Volamahitsy.

Razafindratovo, Janine
1980 "Noms Passés, Noms Presents chez les Merina." *Asie du Sud Est et Monde Insulindien* 11: 169–182.

Razafintsalama, Adolphe
1981 *Les Tsimahafotsy d'Ambohimanga. Organisation familiale et sociale en Imerina (Madagascar).* Paris: SELAF.

Ruud, Jørgen
1960 *Taboo: A Study of Malagasy Beliefs and Customs.* New York: Humanities Press.

Southall, Aidan
1971 "Ideology and Group Composition in Madagascar." *American Anthropologist* 73: 144–164.
1986 "Common Themes in Malagasy Culture. In *Madagascar: Society and History* (C. P. Kottak, J.-A. Rakotoarisoa, A. Southall and P. Vérin, eds.) Durham: Carolina Academic Press.

Standing, Henry L.
1883 "Malagasy 'Fady.'" *Antananarivo Annual and Malagasy Magazine* 8: 253–265.

Van Gennep, Arnold
1904 *Tabou et Totemism à Madagascar.* Paris: Ernest Leroux.

Vogel, Claude
1982 *Les quatres-méres d'Ambohibao: étude d'une population régionale d'Imerina (Madagascar).* Paris: SELAF.

Wilson, Peter
1977 "The Problem with Primitive Folk." *Natural History* 81: 26–35.
1991 *Freedom by a Hair's Breadth: Tsimihety in Madagascar.* Ann Arbor: University of Michigan Press.

LOVE MAGIC AND POLITICAL MORALITY IN CENTRAL MADAGASCAR, 1875–1990

This essay sets out from a simple question. Why is it that at the end of the last century, people in Imerina in central Madagascar seem to have universally assumed that it was men who used *ody fitia*, or "love medicine"— while, when I was living there between 1989 and 1991, absolutely everyone I spoke to took it for granted that it was women who did so? This question is linked to another. In both periods, love medicine was clearly the stuff of scandal. But over the last hundred years, what is scandalous about it appears to have changed. Nineteenth-century texts invariably emphasized that what were called love medicines were really forms of violence: not only did they humiliate their victims, often in spectacular ways, they also could do very real physical harm. The people I knew were just as disapproving. But what they disapproved of in love medicine was something very different: the fact that people under its influence would do whatever their enchanter told them, that they were, in effect, enslaved.

The change is all the more dramatic because if one looks at most of what was written about medicine in the nineteenth century—what we would ordinarily call "magic"—it's almost exactly the same as what people say about medicine in the present day. You see the same lists of charms and spells, the same sorts ceremonies and ingredients: bits of wood, metal ornaments, the same colors and varieties of magical beads. What people say about the sorts of medicine used in protecting crops or helping one in lawsuits or business deals has hardly changed at all. What people say about love medicine on the other hand seemed to have transformed completely. Why? What had happened in the meantime?[1]

The Argument

For an anthropologist, one of the more unusual things about Madagascar is that it seems to lack any sense of a bygone mythical age. Most societies have a fairly clear sense of a time of origins, a time when, say, the distinctions between animals and humans and gods were not yet established, when creatures far more powerful than exist nowadays were able to create rivers and mountains and institutions like marriage, or even life itself. Often this is followed by a heroic age, in which humans, while no longer capable of such cosmic acts of creativity, were still able to wield powers that no longer exist in these current, fallen, times. In Madagascar this sort of view of history was strikingly absent. Founding ancestors, for example, were almost never represented as being in any way superhuman: they were simply men and women who traveled, farmed, and raised families just as men and women do today.

This is not to say, however, that amazing powers were not available in the past. Folktales often feature mythic heroes who, by dint of their magic charms, or *ody*, are able to fly through the air, turn invisible, become impervious to their enemies, or even to blast them with lightning. The point is that none of these powers are seen as limited to mythic times. Any *ody* mentioned in stories are assumed to still exist and to be available to anyone sufficiently determined to obtain them. Some, perhaps, were more arcane, more difficult to come by. Love medicine, by contrast, was assumed to be readily available just about anywhere. Pretty much anyone could, if they had the money or connections, get hold of the knowledge and ingredients. Most were probably available at local markets. Insofar as mythic times existed, then, people were still potentially in them; and this made the social universe unusually dangerous. The danger that someone you knew might use *ody fitia* was something any reasonable person had to take account of. To talk of love medicine, then, is to talk about fears: about the dangerous powers people saw lurking in their social environment, and about how those fears found shape in startling images that, in the nineteenth century, centered on women driven mad by sorcery, ripping off their clothes to run through the streets, and, in the twentieth century, on men ridden like horses by naked witches in the night. This is my central thesis: that such fantasies are ultimately fantasies about power, and the only way to understand them is by casting them in a broader political context.

Between the end of the last century, when Imerina was the center of an independent kingdom, and the time when I lived there, lie sixty-five years of French colonial occupation. The experience of colonial rule had a profound impact on popular conceptions of power and authority—by which I mean, the ways in which it was considered possible, and legitimate, to influence others. Now, the authority of ancestors and elders in highland Madagascar had long been conceived in basically negative terms: authority was seen most of all as matter of forbidding, of binding, of restraining others from acting rather than causing others to act. True, it was not the only kind of authority people recognized; the power of kings, for instance, was conceived quite differently. One effect of colonial rule, though, was that this kind of authority—I will call it "negative authority"—came to be seen as the only traditional "Malagasy" one and, as such, explicitly counterposed to relations of command, which were identified with an alien, military, government. It was the only kind of authority that was considered entirely legitimate. Nor was this simply a matter of abstract ideology. This shift appears to have entailed a genuine change in attitudes, and especially, in the standards by which people judged each other's actions. It was this new social world which created the fears that found shape in the new images of witchcraft and love medicine.

Such an argument is a little unconventional. Feminist scholarship has long contended that traditional distinctions between "public" and "private" domains are profoundly deceptive, and that the forms of power and authority assumed to be characteristic of each are entirely interdependent. Still, there is a tendency to assume that if, say, sexual politics, or the fears and fantasies surrounding imagined dangers in domestic life have any relation to national politics, it will be as a kind of infrastructure. It is easy to imagine how the appeal of a fascist regime or nationalist movement might ultimately be based in male anxieties about a threatened loss of power in the home; much more difficult to imagine how affairs of state might have an effect on people's most intimate anxieties. But this is precisely what I am arguing here.

Of course, it is easier to see how things might work this way in Madagascar, under a colonial regime imposed by foreign conquest and maintained by force, which did not have to maintain even the fiction of the consent of the governed. But, as an approach to colonial history, this is a bit unusual as well. First of all, I am not primarily interested in colonial policy, with what the French regime in Madagascar thought it was doing. Nor am I dealing with questions of hegemony and resistance, with the degree to which colonial institutions like schools and churches could impose their definitions of reality on the colonized, or the degree to which the colonized were able to develop their own counterposed ideologies.[2] Or not exactly. Certainly I do recognize that this happened: that people in highland Madagascar came to redefine their entire sense of what it meant to be Malagasy in opposition to what they saw as the logic of the colonial regime. But I also want to emphasize that this did not occur in a vacuum. By focusing on the question of authority, I am starting from an existing moral order with its own characteristic tensions and dilemmas, its own ways of arguing about right and wrong. Doing so casts the problem not so much as how people dealt with their conquerors—most, in fact tried as far as possible to avoid having to deal with them at all—but on how, as a result, they ended up having to reconsider their relations with each other.

On the Ethics of Magical Practice

Malagasy *fanafody*, or "medicine" consists mainly of objects called *ody*, a word usually translated "charms." Most *ody* consist of bits of rare wood, often along with other ingredients, preserved in an ox-horn, wooden box, or similar receptacle. Different ingredients can act on the world in different ways, but the power that lies behind them is not seen to come from any intrinsic property of the ingredients but from the conscious agency of an invisible spirit, which the user has to invoke with prayers each time the charm is used. In ordinary conversation, though (and this is as true then as now), people do not tend to speak of *ody* either as objects or as spirits. They speak of them as a form of knowledge. One never says, for instance, that one suspects some person "has an" *ody fitia*, one says that one suspects they "know how to use" *ody fitia*. In common conception, *ody* become a kind of knowledge that extends their owner's powers to act on the world.[3] This latter is crucial. Charms are almost never said to act *on* the users, but always on someone, or something, else. Love medicine, for example, is never said to make its user more attractive or desirable but always to inspire desire directly in another. On the other hand, *ody* are more than mere extensions of their owners; *ody*, or at least the more important ones, have their own will and intelligence, and their owners have to appeal to them, sacrifice to them, and generally treat them as hierarchical superiors.

Just about everyone I talked to, and every source I consulted, agreed on one thing. Medicine is governed by one absolute moral principle: to use it to harm other people is always wrong. Such behavior can never be justified. It is witchcraft, and witches (*mpamosavy*) are the very definition of evil. If medicine has always had a somewhat morally dubious cast to it, then it is because it has such a tremendous potential to cause harm. Only *fiarovana*, or medicine used for protection from harm, is entirely above suspicion. As a result, people will always try to represent their medicine as a form of protection if it is at all possible to do so.

Early sources speak of *ody* that can protect their owners from hail, crocodiles, guns, thieves, witches, knives, locusts, fire, and an endless assortment of other dangers. I heard practically identical lists myself. But, then as now, the protection such charms afforded took a distinctly active form. Rather than fortifying the user or her possessions against harm, they were almost always said to intervene to prevent or disrupt the harmful actions of others, though never in such a way that they could be said to be actually attacking them. An *ody* that provided protection against bullets, for instance, did not make the bearers' skin invulnerable: it made those shooting at them miss, or turned their bullets into water. Charms employed in lawsuits never made the bearer's own words more persuasive, but always prevented his antagonist from arguing effectively, or at all.

There is a very famous book called *Le Tsiny et le Tody dans la pensée Malgache* [*Blame and Retribution in Malagasy Thought*], written in 1957 by Richard Andriamanjato, then a young Protestant pastor (he has since become a major figure in national politics). In it Andriamanjato argued that since traditional Malagasy thought assumes that anything one might do will inevitably bring at least indirect harm to someone else, all action is intrinsically problematic. One can easily imagine the ethics of protection as a kind of corollary: if acting is so problematic, then at least in areas in which one is wielding extraordinary powers—for instance, the invisible powers of medicine—actions could only be entirely above question if meant to prevent the even more harmful actions of someone else. The same logic applied to the more public powers involved in communal authority as well. In my experience, the role of elders was never represented as a matter of initiating or even coordinating communal projects, but of imposing prohibitions, and stepping in to prevent younger people from taking actions likely to shatter the solidarity of the community. Ancestors are seen as acting in much the same way, imposing taboos or rules of conduct that were always stated in the negative. This is a point which will become very important as the argument develops; for now, suffice it to say that this meant love medicine, which could hardly be represented as a form of protection, was seen as lying at least on the borders of morality.

On the Inducement of States of "Amorous Madness"

"The love charm," one missionary wrote, "gives the wearer control over the affections of any person he desires, and is chiefly in requisition by unfortunate ill-looking youths in search of a wife, or by profligate characters seeking to seduce their prey" (Haile 1893: 12–13). The assumption here, as in all the nineteenth-century sources, is that it was typically men who made use of *ody fitia*, even if some added that women could do so on occasion.

The reigning assumption a hundred years later, when I was living in the town of Arivonimamo in western Imerina in 1990–91, was precisely the opposite. Several women, in fact, made a great point of this to me, suggesting it provided a profound insight into the difference between male and female psychology. If a girl, they said, is attracted to a boy but finds he has no interest in her, her instinct will be to try to make him change his mind; if she appeals to medicine, she'll try to find something that will make him love her as much as he possibly can. If a boy is turned down by a girl, he's much more likely to get angry and look for medicine that will enable him to take revenge, say, by blasting her with lightning or driving her insane. While everyone conceded that men had been known to use love medicine, this was considered an exception. On the other hand, *ambalavelona*, a form of sorcery which caused its victim to be possessed by an evil ghost and thus driven insane, was often said to be employed by men against women who had rejected their sexual advances.[4]

This is useful to bear in mind while considering nineteenth-century accounts, because the *ody fitia* described in them can be seen as a combination of the two: that is, they punished women by driving them insane at the same time they were said to evoke love and desire.

The greatest source on nineteenth-century Merina medicine is a book by a Norwegian Lutheran missionary named Lars Vig, who lived in the far south of Imerina between 1875 and 1902. It was common practice for new converts to turn in their *ody* to the local missionaries, but Vig seems to have become an enthusiastic collector, quizzing their former owners on their ingredients and manner of use, and later publishing his notes. Of the 130 charms or elements of charms Vig lists, twenty-four are described as love charms. Some of these were meant to strengthen, or disrupt, existing relationships; but the majority—and these were the archetypical ones—were meant to arouse passion in a woman[5] who had proved resistant to the user's advances.

The implicit scenario seems to have been roughly similar to the one assumed by the people I talked to in Arivonimamo: a man makes advances, the woman is "proud" (in other words she is not interested), he resorts to medicine. The charm Imahaka, for example,

> helped to overcome the resistance of a "proud" woman... [It] was supposed to have the power to render women mad, of provoking amorous madness. This is the prayer one makes to it: "Listen o Imahaka. There's a woman who is proud towards me: render her mad, demented like a rabid dog... Make it so that her heart moves, bubbles, boils, so that she can no longer be kept back by her father, by her mother, by her kin" (Vig 1969: 30–31).[6]

The woman would thus be compelled to the caster's bed. This sort of "amorous madness" was said to be a feature of almost all such charms, but the descriptions often suggest, not a person caught up by a frenzy of desire, but one simply torn away against her will. Often, it seems as if the enchanter is acting out of a vindictive desire to humble and humiliate the woman who had rejected him. Consider, for instance, the prayer to another charm:

"...even when the woman is before the eyes of her brother,[7] or in public, may you render her so mad as to throw off her clothing to run to me. Even if the rivers are deep and the current strong, even if the day is dark and the place she lives very distant, may she be obliged to come. Even if she is hidden away and a thousand men let forth a cry of war to retain her, make it so they can do nothing"

The poor enchanted woman would be like a rabid dog, like a mad thing; "the foam would keep coming from her mouth like a rabid dog, and like a rabid dog she would fling herself about, run and run without aim or reason, and all the while raving like a lunatic. This state would continue until she came to the man who had enchanted her using the charm" (1969: 87–88).

If held back or confined in her house, the woman would be overwhelmed by fits of trembling and breathlessness; she would weep uncontrollably; she would be ravaged by fevers of malarial intensity, unable to move from her bed but hearing her enchanter's voice in every rooster's crow outside; or else, she might suddenly become so overpoweringly strong that it was impossible to hold her back from running off to him (1969: 84–97).

Vig himself tended to downplay the punitive, sadistic overtones in these descriptions. Noting that for a woman to be too consistently "proud" was considered an affront to sociability, he suggests that those spurned could represent themselves as acting within their rights.[8] Perhaps so: but there is little reason to think that anyone else would have taken such claims seriously. Elsewhere, Vig himself admits that love medicine was always considered to be very close to simple vindictive witchcraft, and reports that Queen Ranavalona I (1828–1861) was said to have taken such umbrage against the idea that men were driving women mad with love medicine that she sent emissaries around the country to have every known practitioner rounded up and killed.

A Professional Perspective

The one Malagasy source we have from this period, an account of the diviner's art preserved in a collection of documents called the *Tantara ny Andriana*, is quite different in its tone—far less sensationalistic—though this is hardly surprising, since it appears to have been written by a *mpisikidy*, a diviner and specialist in the arts of medicine. Actually, says the author, there are two very different sorts of *ody fitia*. One is indeed a form of sorcery. Inspired by the desire for revenge, it drives its victims insane and, unless treated by a skilled diviner, will ultimately kill them. But there is also a second kind that does not cause amorous madness but instead inspires enduring mutual love. This, the diviner himself can provide: as he might, for instance, when a boy wishes to marry a girl against the wishes of her parents (Callet 1908: 106–107).

This model would seem to leave little place for most of the *ody* Vig collected from his parishioners, all which were apparently thought to cause only temporary madness and were certainly never fatal. But as a diviner—and potential victim of one of Ranavalona's purges—he would hardly have wanted to leave open the possibility that the sort of love medicine he himself could provide could possibly harm anyone. Thus his separation of love and vengeance, which he takes so far as to make it impossible to tell what his evil "love medicine" has to do with love at all. What Vig's material suggests is that, for most people, things were not nearly so clear-cut; most believed that even medicine used to inspire desire in others could have violent, punitive effects to the precise measure that the user's desires were mixed with wounded pride and desire for revenge.

The diviner's text fleshes out certain other details left ambiguous in Vig: for example, concerning the psychic mechanisms that were seen as lying behind the *ody's* power. In nineteenth-century Imerina each person was (at least according to professional curers) said to have an *ambiroa* or *avelo*—a "double" or "reflection"—a kind of active, detachable soul that wandered in dreams and at times could wander off entirely. Soul-loss led to dizziness, erratic, confused behavior and eventually to illness and death. One of the most common ways sorcerers had of killing their victims was to separate them from their *ambiroa*, and one of the most common tasks for curers of the time was to retrieve them. There were a wide variety of rituals used to accomplish this, but the most common ended with the patient contemplating his own reflection in a bowl of water—a bowl that was then suddenly slapped by the curer, causing the reflection to vanish and—ideally—the soul to leap back into the startled patient's body (Vig 1969: 92–3).[9] According to the author of the passage in the *Tantara* (Callet 1908: 106; cf. Vig 1969: 84, 86, 89), the ritual a *mpisikidy* would perform to cure a woman smitten by love medicine worked by the exactly same principle. It was necessary to call the woman's spirit back again from where it had been taken by her seducer, and it otherwise took exactly the same form. In other words, the symptoms of "amorous madness" Vig describes were actually provoked by drawing the victim's soul to the man working the charm, thus causing the victim herself first of all to be in a state of soul-loss (hence dizziness and confusion), and as a result, to be seized by a frantic desire to unite with her enchanter—ultimately, as a way of restoring the disrupted unity of her own self.[10]

This same diviner provides closest one can find to a nineteenth-century reference to women using *ody fitia* in a rather unusual moral tirade about young men from the highlands who leave their wives and families to engage in petty commerce on the coast, take local mistresses to help them with their business, and then ultimately abandon them. Often, he says, these coastal women know how to place *ody* on their lovers which will only begin to work once the men have returned to their wives and children in the highlands. When they do, the effects are spectacular. The victim loses all sensation in the lower half of his body, he becomes incontinent, he is impotent, he soils the floor and the bed. Eventually, he dies.[11] While the author never actually refers to these charms as *ody fitia*, they are treated as part of the same broad category, and he represents the women as acting out of exactly the same motives of jealous spite and desire for retribution. In fact, the words he puts in their mouth, "if he won't be mine, he won't be anybody else's" (*tsy ho ahy, tsy ho an'olona*), are the exact words he places in the mouths of users of vindictive *ody fitia* (Callet 1908: 106,108). And as in the case of *ody fitia*, retribution takes the most visceral, tangible, and humiliating form.

Varieties of *Ody Fitia* Today: or, The Borders of Morality Revisited

In the nineteenth century, then, love medicine lay on the borders of witchcraft for the simple reason that it was most often employed when sexual desire was mixed with desire for revenge. Even when the ostensible purpose was winning a woman's affections, there was likely to be a very strong current of retributive violence in its effects. After all, there would be little reason to suspect anyone had actually used *ody fitia* in the first place unless someone—typically a young woman—began to suffer from suggestive symptoms; in which case, her family's first reaction would presumably be to ask if there were any men whose advances she had recently turned down.

When I was living in Arivonimamo, on the other hand, if a woman developed similar symptoms, the assumption would have been that someone was trying to drive her insane by means of a malevolent ghost.[12] The term *ody fitia* was normally confined to charms meant to inspire love, either as a means of seduction or as a way to inspire selfless devotion in one's current spouse or lover. In practice, it was undue devotion that people mainly tended to remark upon. If a man suddenly became infatuated, it might never occur to anyone to wonder if medicine was involved. But if he was seen to be slavishly indulgent of his wife or lover, and most of all, if she could be said to be enriching herself or otherwise exploiting him as a result, then rumors of *ody fitia* would inevitably begin to circulate. This was the reason people I talked to about the matter, men as well as women, would often point out that the motivations of women who used this kind of medicine often had less to do with love than with a desire for wealth and power.

In one village I knew well, there was a woman in her forties who had married into the community some eight or nine years before; both she and her husband had children from previous marriages. After several years, the man—who, had according to his neighbors, all this time grown increasingly moody and contentious—abruptly disinherited his own children by his former marriage and adopted hers. Whatever his wife tells him, they said, he does without question. This alone was evidence enough to compel several women to make me promise never, if I visited their home, to accept any food or drink she might offer me. After all, they pointed out, she still had several unmarried daughters, and she obviously knew how to use *ody fitia*.

An even more dramatic case had occurred a few years earlier. One of the wealthiest men in the village, a man of very modest origins who had raised himself to prominence by marrying a local heiress, had suddenly decided at the age of fifty to divorce his wife and marry a much younger woman he had met while off on business in the nearby town of Analavory. No sooner had the woman moved in with him than she began selling off his property—houses, fields, cattle, everything she could lay her hands on—as he dutifully signed the papers, refusing to discuss the matter with other members of his family. When after a few years there was nothing left to sell, she left him for an itinerant Tandroy cattle merchant, and eventually moved back to her old home in Analavory. At this point the man had nothing left to his name except for three cows. One by one, I was told, he sold them, each time using the money to fund a trip to Analavory to beg his wife to return to him. Each time she sent him away. The third time, he collapsed in exhaustion on the road back to Arivonimamo, had to be carried home to his village, and died there the next day. Almost everyone concluded she had not only used love medicine, but finally placed some kind of charm on him that would kill him as soon as he got home.

Other *ody* were referred to as "kinds of *ody fitia*": the two most famous were *fanainga lavitra* ("fetching from afar") and *tsy mihoabonga* ("does not pass beyond the mountain"). The first was used to summon a person to the caster; once they fall under its effects, I was told, wherever they were or whatever they might be doing, they would fall into a trance, drop everything, and immediately travel to the caster by the quickest possible means available, not regaining consciousness until they arrived. *Tsimihoa-bonga* on the other hand acts to confine its victim within a certain perimeter. If the victim tried to walk out of a village they were confined to, they would suddenly find themselves turning back again without being aware of doing so; if forcibly removed, they would grow seriously ill or even die. While the archetypical users of *fanainga lavitra* were woman trying to force lovers to return to them, and I heard several reports of rural women who were supposed to have used *tsimihoa-bonga* to keep government functionaries posted to their villages from returning to their wives, these forms of medicine were often used in contexts which had nothing to do with "love."[13]

As these examples would suggest, love medicine was typically the stuff of scandal. Most considered *fanainga lavitra* to be witchcraft pure and simple, no matter what the pretext for its use.[14] But if the moral standing of *ody fitia* had not much changed since Vig's time, the issues involved seem to be entirely different. No one even suggested that *fanainga lavitra* was wrong because of the harm it could bring to its victims; in fact, it often did no immediate harm to them at all. What they stressed was that such medicine causes its victims to lose their autonomy, to act like slaves, to be completely at the will and bidding of another. And this is precisely what they stressed about more conventional forms of *ody fitia* as well. "If a man always does whatever his wife tells him," one woman told me, "especially if she has him constantly out working, looking for new ways to get her money—that's how you can tell she probably knows how to use *ody fitia*."

Bear in mind that most Malagasy medicine is not said to make its victims *do* anything. Legitimate medicine prevents others from acting; witchcraft attacks them. In fact, almost all forms of medicine which *are* said to have a direct effect their victims' behavior are considered varieties of *ody fitia*. And the one or two exceptions that do exist are looked on with much the same attitude of suspicion. A good case in point are *ody* used to protect crops from theft. Now, this is a purpose which would seem on the face of it about as intrinsically legitimate as one could get. Almost all farmers in Imerina use some variety of medicine to protect their crops, and most fields are decorated with *kiady*, flags of brightly colored strips of cloth and plastic or poles topped with bundled straw. These usually contain medicine said to guard against birds or animals, and perhaps also to prevent thieves from entering the field or alert the owner if they do. Some downplayed the importance of the medicine in *kiady* altogether, saying they were mainly just marks of ownership. Almost everyone stressed that any medicine they did contain was likely to be very mild in its effects. The really potent medicine, called *kalo*, tended to be buried in the ground rather than placed around the field on poles. Some *kalo* made thieves sick: if anyone ate food taken from the field protected by such a *kalo*, I was told, their feet or stomach would swell up to twice their normal size. Often they would die as a result. Almost everyone I talked to considered this simple witchcraft, not a legitimate way to protect one's crops. A more acceptable form of *kalo* trapped intruders: having entered the field, a would-be thief would find himself unable to leave it until the owner returned to release him. This most considered inoffensive; but it was only one step from here to the most notorious variety of all, called *kalo mampiasa* or "*kalo* which make one work." A proprietor could leave a shovel or basket out on his property before heading home; if anyone entered the field intending to make off with them, or with the crops, he would find himself compelled to grab the tools and start working there, digging the owner's ditches or carrying his fertilizer for as long as it took him to return. These were clearly witchcraft, almost as reprehensible as poisoning one's victims outright, and most of the people I knew cast quite a jaundiced eye on anyone rumored to have anything to do with them.

Background: Royal Service and Slavery

I have suggested that these new concerns were the result of a general re-evaluation of modes of power and authority which followed the French conquest of Madagascar. Perhaps the easiest way to understand what happened is to follow the changing meaning of the term *fanompoana*, usually translated "service," which is used throughout Madagascar to describe the obligations of subjects to their rulers and, secondarily, slaves to their masters. In early Imerina, as in most Malagasy kingdoms, obligations to rulers centered on certain ceremonial tasks, particularly the building and rebuilding of royal houses and tombs. But, in principle, such obligations were unlimited; and under the Merina government that ruled most of Madagascar during the nineteenth century, *fanompoana* was used to justify any number of newly created obligations, including a program of forced labor applied on a massive scale both in the provinces and in Imerina. After the French conquest, colonial authorities continued the use of forced labor, which they too referred to as *fanompoana*.

In most of Madagascar, the French usage was not taken very seriously. Gillian Feeley-Harnik reports that the Sakalava people of western Madagascar never referred to colonial corvée labor as *fanompoana*, reserving the term instead for the ritual labor they continued to perform on royal tombs and dwellings. By continuing to carry out these rituals under French rule, she suggests, they were in effect making covert assertions about what they considered legitimate authority to be (Feeley-Harnik 1991: 349).[15] In Imerina, what happened was entirely different. There, the meaning of *fanompoana* had already been broadened before the French arrived to include most of the institutions—church, school, and government—that were soon to become the basis of colonial rule. Most Merina, therefore, seem to have accepted that what the French imposed on them was, indeed, a kind of *fanompoana*. Certainly, unlike Feeley-Harnik's Sakalava, they still refer to it as such today. The result was that the concept of *fanompoana* itself was thoroughly discredited. It came to be thought of not as service but as servitude, as something tantamount to slavery.

This change of meanings had profound consequences, in part because *fanompoana* had provided perhaps the only context in which it was considered appropriate for adults to give direct orders to each other. Within local communities and among kin, authority had long been seen most of all as a matter of imposing taboos or otherwise preventing others from acting, rather than telling people what to do.[16] Before the nineteenth century, the distinction between the two ways of exercising authority might have been little noticed; but after the French conquest, once *fanompoana* had become inextricably caught up in notions of servitude and foreign domination, it began to take on a broader political meaning. Traditional, ancestral authority—what I have called negative authority—became the only kind which people accepted as fully legitimate. It has come to be seen as the "Malagasy" way of doing things, and explicitly opposed to relations of command, which are seen as typical of foreigners and the French.

In other words, where other Malagasy have used relations of domination and control (and to be possessed by a spirit is to be under the control of another in about as total a form as is imaginable) to define a sort of autonomous "Malagasy" sphere for themselves in opposition to the colonizer, "Malagasy" identity in Imerina has instead come to be based on the very rejection of such relations.

It is worth pointing out again that all this was not simply ideology, a utopian image of a Malagasy identity which could be counterposed to the French regime (or, later, to the national government that replaced it.) In fact, it was not really a self-consciously formulated ideology at all. It has always remained somewhat implicit, immanent in the moral standards by which people judge each other's actions, the traits they single out for criticism in others. I never heard anyone say "we Malagasy do not give each other orders" (such a statement would have been obviously untrue); but the whole issue of giving orders had clearly become a tremendous problem, and this in turn has had all sorts of effects on domestic and political relations. These were the issues and anxieties that took shape in fears of *ody fitia*.

Forms of Labor

These issues and anxieties also had their roots in Imerina's historical experience. King Andrianampoinimerina (1789–1810) had already invoked the principle of *fanompoana* to draft his subjects into vast irrigation projects around the capital; but the reign of his son Radama (1810–1828) marks the real break with past traditions. After the British governor of Mauritius agreed to provide him with military trainers, missionary teachers, and artisans, Radama used the principle of *fanompoana* as the basis for recruiting young men for a standing army, industrial projects, and mission schools. The army allowed Radama to expand Merina rule across most of Madagascar and, over the next several decades, to bring home a steady supply of captives to be sold as slaves. The influx of slaves, in turn, was to permanently transform the demography of Imerina. Property censuses carried out in the early 1840s indicate that slaves already made up about 40% of the Merina population, and ownership was remarkably widespread.[17] Greater access to slave labor allowed the state, in turn, to make ever-greater demands on the free population. From the time of Radama I, adult males not serving in the military were organized into brigades that were called up regularly for months of *fanompoana*. After Queen Ranavalona II converted to Protestant Christianity in 1869, the scope of *fanompoana* expanded even further to include compulsory education in mission schools, building of and attendance in local churches, and a host of new labor obligations. Most of these appear to have been widely resented, even while most Merina continued to accept the underlying principle of personal service to the Sovereign.

The immediate effect on daily life was undoubtedly a vast growth in the scope of relations characterized by the direct giving and taking of orders. It is important to remember that the nineteenth-century Merina government was essentially a military government. Almost all important officials, even in the civil administration, held military rank, and civilian *fanompoana* brigades were organized in exactly the same way as military units. Even the schools—primary education became compulsory by the late 1870s—acted mainly as recruiting centers for the military. From the beginning, there is evidence that these principles of organization and conduct were considered profoundly alien from those which applied in everyday affairs, where authority was still imagined to be mainly a matter of preventing harmful actions. The Malagasy language did not even have a word for "order" or "command," and the term coined, *baiko*, had the additional meaning of "foreign speech."

But, even within households, this was a time when more and more of the daily interaction was taking place between masters and slaves.

In the early years, the slave population was made up overwhelmingly of women and children, who were generally under the direct authority of their owners. But as the flow of slaves into Imerina tapered off in the 1850s and the proportion of slaves born to their condition increased, so too did the proportion of adult males. Apparently, owners found it extremely difficult to keep grown men under their systematic control. While the matter needs much further research, most male and a substantial proportion of female

slaves appear to have won a large measure of autonomy, becoming a floating stratum of itinerant craftsmen, porters, laborers, and petty traders, only
occasionally under the direction of their masters.[18] In addition, it appears
that slaves were almost the only people willing to work as wage laborers. For
instance, in the 1880s, when abolitionists in England were scandalized to
discover that Protestant missionaries were regularly being carried around by
slaves and employing slaves as domestic servants, the missionaries insisted
that despite their best efforts they had found it impossible to find anyone else
willing to work for wages.[19]

In 1895, a French expeditionary force seized the Merina capital,
Antananarivo. Within a year, Madagascar's new rulers had issued a series of
edicts which abolished virtually all the institutions that had been the basis of
the Merina state: the monarchy, aristocratic privileges, and finally and most
dramatically, the institution of slavery itself. *Fanompoana*, in fact, was about
the only major institution left in place. If anything, forced labor probably
intensified in the first years of colonial rule, with the mass levying of men for
such projects as the building of roads and bridges. Of course, under the colonial regime, labor obligations applied equally to every inhabitant of Imerina,
regardless of their former status; for masters and slaves to have to work side
by side under foreign oversight must have made an enormous impression as
a tangible expression of their newfound equality in common subjugation to
the French.[20] In theory, *fanompoana* was only maintained for a few years. In
reality, forced labor continued in one form or another until the late 1940s,
maintained by an ever-changing series of laws and legal subterfuges. And,
since colonists found it extremely difficult to find anyone willing to sign
labor contracts, additional laws were issued exempting those holding such
contracts from corvée. This allowed employers to set pretty much whatever
terms they cared to, and made wage-labor appear, from the Malagasy point
of view, a mere extension of forced labor, which in effect it was (Fremigacci
1975, 1978; Raison 1984: 180–84).

During the first generation of colonial rule, the old rural elite largely
abandoned the countryside, finding themselves places in the administration,
commerce, or liberal professions and leaving their rice fields to be share-
cropped by former slaves. Those who remained quickly fell into a fairly uniform poverty. Partible inheritance and constant migration to new lands may
have prevented any extreme disparities of wealth from reemerging, but the
steady increase of population also ensured that most families did not have
access to enough land to support themselves. This process only intensified
with independence, by which time almost everyone in Imerina was forced to
combine farming with crafts, petty commerce, wage-labor, or some combination of the three.

Wage-labor is by far the least popular alternative. Most descendants of free people will only fall back on agricultural day-labor when there is absolutely no alternative, and even then, prefer to work for kin on a temporary basis. In the countryside and small towns where the vast majority of Merina live, long-term relations of wage-labor between adults basically do not exist. Even in the city they are rare, outside of the very limited formal sector, which consists mainly of the government itself, and other colonial institutions. The only stratum of the population who does not share this aversion to wage-labor is composed of the descendants of slaves; still a third of the population, and still considered a caste apart, who do not, generally speaking, intermarry with the descendants of former slave-owners. With little access to land or other resources, they follow much the same occupations they did at the end of the nineteenth century. They remain the only people who are normally willing to work for wages.

Fanompoana as Slavery

Two years after the emancipation of 1896, a colonial official wrote that:

> Questioned on this occasion, a woman of the highest caste of nobility, rich, the owner of numerous slaves, responded with melancholy: "What does it matter if our slaves have been freed? Haven't all Malagasy, beginning with the Queen, now become slaves of the French?" (Carol 1898: 38–39)

If this was a mere figure of speech, it has proved a remarkably enduring one. Even when talking with very well-educated people I would often hear comments like "the French you know treated their slaves much better than the British"—referring by this to policies of colonial rule. Discussions of chattel slavery would slip seamlessly into discussions of colonialism and back. In fact, almost all political relationships, including those identified with the Merina kingdom itself, appear to have been re-evaluated and largely reshaped in the popular imagination through assimilation with slavery. In modern Malagasy, the meaning of the word *fanompoana* is closer to the English term "servitude" than it is to "service"; it implies work carried out under threat of coercion, and is most often used as a euphemism for slavery.[21] There were any number of such euphemisms. One of the more striking was "soldier." It took me some time to figure out that when someone recounting oral traditions referred to a lord's "soldiers," they usually meant his slaves. In fact, the terms "soldier" and "slave" were often used interchangeably—a startling identification, since in the nineteenth century, slaves would have been the last people ever allowed to carry guns. The connection seemed to be simply that both were people who obey orders. In oral traditions, historical relations of command always tended to be treated as so many refractions of slavery, and therefore as essentially unjust.

If slavery had the importance it did in setting the measure of all other relations, this did not mean it was a subject anyone enjoyed discussing. It was more the sort of issue that no one wanted to talk about but everyone always seemed to end up talking about anyway, if only in hushed tones and euphemistic language, whenever they talked about the past. It was as if the continuing presence of a population of ex-slaves, living in close, if often uncomfortable, proximity with the descendants of their former masters, had made the whole issue so troubling that it had to be continually hidden, until, in the end, it began to be seen as the hidden reality behind everything.[22]

This attitude was almost certainly the legacy of the early years of colonial occupation. By the time the French appeared on the scene, the meaning of *fanompoana* had already been broadened to include obligations to pay taxes, perform military service, attend state schools and even churches—all the institutions that were soon to become the bulwarks of the colonial state. The organization of such institutions was already seen as essentially military, based on relations in which some were giving orders and others were expected to obey without question, and therefore, as standing at a certain remove from daily life. After the French conquest, this remove became a chasm. Colonial phrase books, for instance, leave one with the impression that French officials and colonists hardly spoke to their subjects in anything but the imperative voice. In literary Malagasy, French is still known as *ny teny baiko*: "the language of command." One is also reminded of the proverb *aza manao Vazaha fito antrano*. A Malagasy version of "too many cooks spoil the broth," it literally means "don't act like seven French people all in the same house"—the idea being that, if this were to happen, everyone would just sit around giving everyone else orders and nothing would get done. At the same time, in the small towns and rural villages where most of the population lived, people appear to have become increasingly averse to using imperative forms at all. When Elinor Ochs carried out a sociolinguistic study in a Merina village in the late 1960s, her informants insisted that giving direct orders to another person was not a "Malagasy" way to behave, explicitly contrasting it with the manners of the city, and the French (Ochs 1974: 131–134; 1975).

I should point out here that, while I have been following conventional usage and calling these people Merina, I never heard anyone there spontaneously refer to themselves as such. They always spoke of themselves as

"Malagasy"; just as they spoke of "Malagasy" customs, "Malagasy" beliefs, and "Malagasy" forms of knowledge, all of which they defined in contrast to those they considered foreign, European or French. After the French conquest, then, all these institutions (forced labor, wage-labor, military, schools) came to be seen as so many tokens of foreign domination, analogous with slavery, and people's identity as Malagasy became in large part defined in opposition to them. One reason the constant reminders of slavery in daily life became so embarrassing, then, was that they made clear that Merina had once treated their fellow Malagasy in the same way that foreigners were now treating them. It had become an acute contradiction within their sense of national identity.

This political identity became embedded in daily life and standards of moral judgment. The reluctance to command others openly is part of a more general aversion to any relationship in which one party is seen as directing the actions of another. I think this aversion is the real explanation for the reluctance to engage in wage-labor. Most rural people nowadays will occasionally hire themselves out as day laborers; but, when they do, they work in teams that operate autonomously. Often I found myself watching workers hired to replant or harvest someone else's rice fields animatedly discussing how best to proceed, while their employer watched silently from a few yards away, not presuming to tell them how to go about their task. Even fathers would avoid openly directing their adult children; in fact, of all the inhabitants of a rural community, the older men who were its primary figures of authority were also the least likely to be seen giving orders in public. Their quintessential role was seen to lie in preventing any action that might prove disruptive to solidarity: breaking up fights or "admonishing" the young when their individualistic projects seem likely to lead to conflict.

Perhaps if one had shown up in a Merina village two hundred years ago, things would have not looked very different. But once the principle of *fanompoana* began to be identified with foreign domination, this sort of negative authority became the only kind people took to be wholly legitimate. To be Malagasy came to mean rejecting entanglement in relations of command as far as it was practical to do so.

Madagascar, of course, is no longer a French colony, but these attitudes have by no means disappeared. The rural population (and for that matter the bulk of the urban poor) still tend to see the government and governing class as existing at a certain fundamental remove from "Malagasy" life. As one might expect, the educated, urban elite, who live their lives in a context of cash employment, have a much more accepting attitude towards relations of command.[23] Even in the country, though, relations of command have not been by any means eliminated. They continue to exist, if often in rather euphemistic forms, in any number of different aspects of daily life. Teachers and bureaucrats have affected a more consensual, "Malagasy" style since independence, but the schools and offices are basically the same. Malagasy do hire one another, if rarely for very long; elders do direct other people's actions, if usually indirectly or under a consensual veneer. Like memories of slavery, relations of command in everyday life tend to be suppressed and hidden and, as such, they become social issues much more important than they would otherwise have been.

Witches Who Go Out at Night

From here, it's easy to see how the pieces fall together. While something like an ethic of negative authority had long existed in Imerina, during the twentieth century it came to be explicitly framed as the true "Malagasy" ethic and opposed to relations of command, which were increasingly conceived as intrinsically foreign, military, oppressive, and unjust. However, such a position was full of obvious contradictions. First of all, everyone was perfectly well aware that Malagasy people did used to treat each other this way: there were once kings, and slaves, and both still had descendants whose typical occupations were not so very different from their ancestors'. More immediately: there is a reason why all languages have imperative forms. It is absurd to imagine a society in which no one ever told anyone else what to do.

Not only was the ideal of negative authority practically impossible; it also created a social world rife with hidden purposes, in which everyone—elders most of all, perhaps—were trying to influence others to do things without being able to fully acknowledge they were doing it. It was in this social environment that people in towns and villages across Imerina began to grow increasingly concerned with the prospect of women enslaving men by means of medicine; with images of people seized by *fanainga lavitra*, compelled to travel to their summoners; with thieves forced to spend the night carrying baskets of manure for their intended victims. Not all of these dangers were identified with women, but many were. Perhaps the most dramatic change, in fact, involved images of witches, which during the colonial period became increasingly interwoven with ideas about *ody fitia*.

I should explain here that the term *mpamosavy*, which I have rendered "witch" or "sorcerer," has always had two somewhat different meanings. On the one hand, it can refer to anyone—archetypically, men—driven by envy, spite, and resentment to harm others by means of medicine. But there are also "witches who go out at night," creatures of absolute depravity who prowled the surroundings of Merina villages after dusk. These were the ultimate image of moral evil. Even in the nineteenth century, they were also seen as predominantly women:

> No village is free from supposed witches, who are said to take their walks abroad at midnight to visit the tombs, on top of which they dance and revile the dead. They are said to be mainly elderly females of sinister aspect, joined by young women of bad character, with occasional male associates... At the dead of night they knock at the doors of neighbors they wish to injure, and should there be anyone sick, they howl most dismally around the house (Haile 1893: 11).[24]

Witches were said to gather together to plan and carry out their more elaborate acts of sorcery, or terrorize those keeping vigil over the dead, accompanied by wild cats and owls. They went about naked, their clothing bundled on their heads and their fingers tipped with poisons. They had tremendous, uncanny strength, could span great distances almost instantly, dive into moats or out of windows and land unscathed.

As for how these women became witches, only one source—Vig again—suggests an explanation. "According to Malagasy ideas, whoever lends himself to the adoration of a charm is drawn irresistibly to do whatever that charm's task may be." The power of *ody*, the reader will recall, was seen as coming from an invisible spirit, which gave it a consciousness and agency of its own. Witches, then, were people taken over by their own evil medicine; people who were driven by spite and resentment to harm others until finally the power of their *ody* drove them to band together with others of the same kind and work evil for its own sake. Indeed, most nineteenth-century descriptions of witches focus on the elaborate ceremonies bands of witches would undertake at night, including elaborate mock funerals, to make new victims waste away and die.

Many of these details still appear in descriptions of modern-day Merina witches; witches still dance on tombs, for instance, and they still have the same extraordinary physical powers. But the emphasis on malicious sorcery, mock funerals, and the like has very much faded into the background. Instead, almost everyone insisted to me that, if women ended up prowling the outskirts of villages at night, it was not because of the abuse of malicious medicine but because of the abuse of *ody fitia*.

The way it was commonly expressed was this: if a woman uses too much love medicine or gets love medicine that's "too powerful" she may in the end be overwhelmed by the power of her own medicine.[25] When night falls, the *ody*'s spirit will take possession of its owner in much the same way an evil ghost possesses a victim of *ambalavelona*, or the soul of an ancient king possesses a medium. Such witches are no longer in control of their own actions: by some accounts they are not even conscious of them. "Carried" by the power of their *ody*, they strip off their clothes and abandon their houses to find and meet with other witches and work evil.[26] Women would usually insist that the typical witch was an old women; but I suspect this mainly reflects the fact that older women, particularly those who head households or are otherwise independent, were the most likely to be suspected by their neighbors of "going out at night." Just about everyone I talked to who claimed to have themselves had run-ins with witches were men, and they always seemed to have a more sexualized image of a younger woman in mind.

As for what happens to a man unfortunate enough to meet up with a witch at night: here, accounts were pretty much unanimous. If you see the witch before she sees you, then, generally speaking, you'll be able to get away. But if she sees you first, she will immediately make use of her *ody* and you will suddenly find yourself unable to move, or even to cry out. Once captured, the helpless victim may be tormented by the witch—or more likely by a group of them—in various (usually vaguely specified) ways. But what witches are really famous for is riding men like horses. (This is always something women do to men—people would laugh when I so much as suggested other possibilities). They mount their victims' backs and drive them along until dawn, they make them eat dirt or abase themselves in ways too horrible to even mention, and finally abandon them, filthy and exhausted, on their doorsteps before dawn. Often, the victim awakes with only distant memories of his ordeal; sometimes he is mute for days afterwards and cannot speak of it; in extreme cases, his strength never returns to him and he dies.

In the last century, witchcraft was a nightmare image of human malevolence carried to its ultimate extremes. In the twentieth century, it has become an extension of love medicine. And if stories about love medicine told nowadays can be said to reflect a deep-seated suspicion of any sort of any relationship in which one person gains complete control of the actions of another, the image of a woman "carried" by her medicine riding a man who is "carried by" her, of a man possessed by a woman who is herself possessed by a charm, is one of control stripped of any rationale or even of any agent. An *ody*, after all, has no identity apart from its purpose, so that a witch's *ody* is really a pure abstraction, the sheer desire to dominate others and nothing else. Stories about women who try to win over men through medicine, but who end up riding men at night, are fantasies about the principle of control bursting all possible boundaries—stories which, however, through an elaborate series of reversals and displacements, end up in a rather similar place to those about nineteenth-century *ody fitia*: in a highly sexualized image of degradation and cruelty.

So: Why Women?

Why, finally, should it be women in particular who are seen as embodying the frightening power of command—a power which, after all, is otherwise located mainly in images of slave-owning lords and French colonial officials? This is a subtle question, and no doubt there are many reasons, but one is obvious: Merina women tend to use the imperative form much more than men.

Ochs makes a great point of this in her analysis of speech patterns. Avoiding giving others orders in public, she said, was part of a broader feeling that one should never place others in a situation which might prove publicly embarrassing. But it was men in particular, and most of all, older men in positions of authority, who were expected to behave this way. Men were assumed to be by nature more discrete, shy, and less competitive than women, whose behavior even in public was more assertive and direct. This was even more true within the household, where women are very much in charge. Older women especially spend much of their time issuing orders and coordinating tasks, casually dispatching siblings and children off on errands. Rarely if ever did I see a man giving a direct order to a woman; but I very often saw women using the imperative form when speaking with men. Having read Ochs' work before I arrived in Madagascar, I was rather surprised to discover how often the imperative form actually was used in such contexts. When I asked women why men were so much more reserved in public and women so forthright, they would almost invariably reply that women were responsible for running households and had to be assertive in order to do so.

But as Maurice Bloch has pointed out, it is precisely through such mild postures that older men assert their authority: by acting this way, they are seen as embodying in their own comportment the solidarity and moral unity of the community as a whole. [27] In public fora, it is women's very direct manners, their greater propensity, if not to issue commands, then at least to make direct demands on others, to propose schemes of action, which ensures they will not be seen as real figures of authority. There are few formal barriers to women becoming elders, but in fact they only rarely do. This is not only because of styles of action. It is also because it is precisely those women who are the most obvious candidates for an independent political role, especially, the venerable women heads of large families or other older, independent women, who are most likely to be accused of "knowing *ody fitia*" or even "going out at night," sufficient tarnish on anyone's character to ensure they can never be taken seriously as public figures. For most women the only safe way to achieve a position of public influence is indirect, as the wife, mother, or daughter of some significant man. The end result of course is that Merina women (like any group with little or no access to the formal mechanisms of power) tend to acquire a reputation as manipulators, which, in turn, ends up reinforcing the impression that they are more likely than men to have access to mysterious powers to influence others through invisible means.

We are left with an image of three social levels, each with its own archetypal figure of authority. On the level of the household, this was the woman giving orders, directly overseeing household tasks; on the communal level, most closely identified with "Malagasy" tradition, the mild and self-effacing male elder, ready to step in to break up disputes and impose restrictions but otherwise a passive embodiment of solidarity; on the level of the overarching state, a whole plethora of images—the colonial official barking orders; the military officer, or gendarme; or ancient king with his retinue of "soldiers"— in every case, of figures who operate within formal hierarchies of command. If nothing else, this makes it easier to understand the political color that talk of *ody fitia* always seemed to take. A woman who used love medicine in fact was often said to "rule" over her husband (the same word used for kings or governments) or even to "enslave" him.[28] Even in its most fantastic forms, where it detached itself from any human purposes and became a sheer force of domination that turned its owners into night-riding witches, it was still basically a political image, of a certain type of power distilled to its purest form and, in so far as it was also an image of utter evil, perhaps the single most dramatic statement of the ethos of negative authority. It was as if the moment a woman was in a position to exert any real authority or even influence on the communal level, she was likely to be accused of secretly drawing on arcane powers to exert a shadowy version of the very kind of foreign authority against which the communal sphere defined itself.

All this, of course, is something of an abstraction; political reality is much more complicated. For one thing, it is overwhelmingly women who actually tell these stories. On the one hand, this seems to make the narrators prime agents in their own political suppression, but since women by such means control much of the moral discourse about public affairs, it is also one of the main ways in which women do exert political influence. While there is hardly room here to go into the subtleties of practice, it might help to end with an illustration. A friend of mine from Arivonimamo told me that, when she was eight or nine, her father, then a wealthy and respected teacher, became obsessed with another woman. Before long he had moved in with her, and began running through his savings to shower her with gifts, all the time sending his wife and numerous small children back empty-handed whenever they would come begging for support. What she particularly remembers about those trips, she said, was that at dinner, the woman would be openly scraping bits of wood into his food. The psychology was no doubt complex, but at the very least, by doing so she provided him with a ready-made alibi to excuse his behavior in the eyes of his family.

Not that it was completely successful. He came back to his family a year or two later, but his daughter has barely spoken to him since.

Conclusions

In the beginning of this essay, I suggested that the fantasies surrounding *ody fitia* have always been fantasies about power. Stories about medicine were perhaps the closest thing there was to an abstract idiom in which the nature of power itself could be defined. In both periods, images of power in the raw were almost always images of women: if that is how one can interpret the nineteenth-century image of the woman invested with sudden and overwhelming strength, tearing herself from the arms of her family (from their entirely vain effort, one might say, to exert negative authority), or of night witches, with their uncanny speed and physical strength. These stories were not just a medium through which people could think about the nature of power: even more, they were a medium through which they could argue about its rights and wrongs. It was through endless arguments about hidden powers and hidden motives—about envy, sexual desire, pride, greed, resentment—that people worked out their common understandings of how it was legitimate for human beings to influence each other. In this light, it is not surprising that the basic logic of what I have been calling negative authority was first made explicit in the ethic of protection, that is, in ways of talking about the morality of medicine, long before it emerged as a way of imagining a traditional Malagasy way of exercising power over others. This also makes it easier to understand how intimate anxieties and domestic politics could have been transformed as a result. After all, these might have been ways of imagining power and authority, but they were not abstractions: they were the kind of representations, one might say, that helped to bring into being the things they represented. Political reality—and here I am referring to every sort of politics, domestic or communal, national or sexual—can never, really, be distinguished from its representations, if only because politics itself is largely a matter of manipulating and arguing about representations, of circulating stories and trying to control how those stories are interpreted.

This was a game in which Merina women were certainly as much players as were men. Yet at the same time, they labored under a peculiar disadvantage. Often, in fact, women seemed to act as agents of their own ultimate repression: circulating stories that served as profound meditations on the nature of desire and human decency, but which, at the same time, had the ultimate effect of reflecting and reinforcing men's fears of women, and radically circumscribing the ability of women—any women—to become respected figures of authority. It was almost as if they were, somehow, the victims of their own psychological insight. Certainly, just as most of the best story-tellers I knew in Arivonimamo were women, so were most of the most acute social psychologists and social theorists. To some degree, of course, their sensitivity to their surroundings was itself an effect of their relative lack of social power: a large part of privilege, anywhere, is the luxury of being able to remain oblivious to much of what goes on around one. The most troubling questions, it seems to me, are two-fold. The first is how that greater perceptiveness and sensitivity to one's social environment itself seems to contribute to women's ultimate subordination. The second is how this still seems to happen where women's moral reflections are one of the principal media for social changes that in almost every other way dramatically anti-authoritarian. What has happened in rural Imerina over the last century could even, by certain definitions, be described as a revolution. The trauma of colonial rule sparked a profound reassessment of the very nature of power and authority. That reassessment was couched in the terms already familiar to rural people—such as the logic of protection—but as a result, rural people's relations with one another genuinely changed. All this ensured that when the power of colonial (and colonial-inspired) regimes went into retreat, in part in the face of persistent passive resistance, political life itself had changed as well. It had become in most ways far more egalitarian than it appears to have been in, say, in the nineteenth century. Women played a crucial role in all of this; yet at the same time, they did so in ways that ended up guaranteeing that gender relations remain among the least affected by the change.

Endnotes

1   I would like to thank Jennifer Cole, Jean Comaroff, Gillian Feeley-Harnik, Michael Lambek, Pier Larson, Nhu Thi Le, Stuart Rockefeller, Marshall Sahlins, Johanna Schoss, and Raymond T. Smith for all sorts of useful comments and suggestions. My fieldwork in Madagascar was funded by a Fullbright/IEE. I should note also that the language and people of Madagascar are referred to as Malagasy, the inhabitants of Imerina are called Merina, and that *ody fitia* is pronounced OOD fee-TEE.

2   A Foucauldian approach, for instance, might emphasize how imported disciplines of education or hygiene transformed domestic relations; but this is not my project either. At least among the majority of people in Imerina, colonial disciplines really did not have that direct an impact on the kind of issues I am dealing with here.

3   The richest source on nineteenth century *ody* is a catalogue assembled by the
     Norwegian Lutheran missionary, Lars Vig, between 1875 and 1902 (Vig 1969),
     but there is a fairly abundant literature, including material by Malagasy authors
     (R.P. Callet 1908: 82–103) and European ones (Dahle 1886–88; Edmunds 1897;
     Renel 1915), as well as some material extending to the middle of the present cen-
     tury (Bernard-Thierry 1959; Ruud 1969). I have discussed the relation between
     spirit and object in much greater detail in an earlier work (Graeber 1996).

4   My information is drawn mainly (though not exclusively) from women—where
     the nineteenth-century material was presumably drawn almost entirely from
     men—and this may be the cause of some distortion. But I did talk to dozens of
     men as well, and never found their basic understanding of *ody fitia* to be signifi-
     cantly different. If anything, women were more likely to point out that men could,
     occasionally, employ such medicine—if only because for them the fact was more a
     matter of immediate practical concern.

5   Since all the accounts I draw on assume a female victim, when speaking in the
     abstract, it seems best to follow their usage. Still, the reader should note that Vig
     at least occasionally indicates that any of these charms could be used by women
     against men, and cites two charms said to have been used primarily by women.
     (Vig 1969: 94–97).

6   Here, as elsewhere, my translation from the French.

7   A shocking breach of decorum: adult brothers and sisters were never supposed to
     see each other naked.

8   "The man could tell her 'why are you proud towards me?... The custom of our an-
     cestors applies to us all.'" "During the persecution of Christians under Ranavalona
     I," he adds, "one accusation made against the Christians was that their wives were
     chaste..." (Vig 1969: 20). On the other hand, on the subject of sexual relations, Vig
     was apparently willing to believe almost any scandalous story his more whimsical
     parishioners could tell him. He interrupts descriptions of charms on two different
     occasions to relate that in previous times, old men would regularly gather at the
     village gates to watch young men fight battles over women, with the women going
     to those who prevailed; adding that in these times men were afraid even to bring
     their daughters with them to the weekly markets because "if she gave preference to
     only one, nine or ten rejected suitors would join forces and attack the father's house
     the next night" (1969: 26, 88). All of this had of course completely disappeared, he
     added, with the advent of Christianity some twenty or thirty years before.

9   Vig actually describes this ceremony as a cure for a condition known as *kasoa*, the
     one form of "amorous madness" whose effects he says can indeed lead to perma-
     nent insanity. People still talk about *kasoa*, but nowadays it is classed with *ambala-
     velona* as a form of aggressive witchcraft—both are ways of driving a victim insane
     by causing them to be possessed by an evil ghost.

10   I might note that this is, in fact, the premise used in the Malay love magic from
      around the same period described by Skeat (1900: 566–580), which was also con-
      sidered to be similar to sorcery for this very reason.

11   The rhetoric here is particularly colorful:

      Manara-mody, rao-dia, fehitratra: these are diseases that come with you
      when arrive here in town. That's why so many young men die on return-
      ing home from traveling. And that's why people say "life is the slave of
      wealth": people know that the distant land is dangerous; but they have
      to get what others have got, though the pursuit of wealth has to be dif-
      ficult. "If my eight bones aren't broken! a road others have gone down,
      yet I can't go? Other people's children have all got rich, I perhaps am the
      child of an idiot? Do other people's children know how to do something
      I don't know how to do?" So he gets the money on loan, and when he
      goes trading, he's bewitched; and when he arrives back, he dies; and his
      wife and children are enslaved because of the debt he owed to the people
      here in town (Callet 1908: 106).

12   The condition, called *ambalavelona*, was often said to have been used by rejected
      suitors out of spite. It involved many of the symptoms Vig described—the great
      strength of the woman, the raving, the fits, the throwing off of clothes in public—
      but it was never thought of as inspiring love. It was merely a means of revenge.

13   Other medicines referred to as "kinds of *ody fitia*" included *tsy tia mainty* ("to de-
      spise," or literally "hate blackly"), which causes enmity to rise up between lovers or
      spouses, and *manara-mody* ("follows one home"), the *ody* used by coastal women
      to kill their Merina lovers and which apparently killed the man with three cows.
      Manara mody most considered a form of witchcraft pure and simple, and some de-
      nied it was a kind of *ody fitia* at all. In every story of its use I heard about, though,
      it was used in conjunction with other forms of *ody fitia*.

14   Even women whose lovers abandoned them on learning they were pregnant would
      not publicly admit to having used *fanainga lavitra* to bring them back. The only
      people I found willing to (quietly) admit they had employed it was a married cou-
      ple who had used it to recover a teenage daughter who had run away from home.

15   Something along these lines appears to have happened throughout most of
      Madagascar during the colonial period; *tromba* cults, in which the spirits of an-
      cient kings began to possess the living and demand ritual propitiation, brought
      royal service even to parts of the island which had never been ruled by kings at
      all. See Althabe (1969). Here too, *fanompoana* rendered to ancient kings became
      a principle by which people could assert their cultural autonomy in the face of
      colonial rule.

16   I have written of the importance of taboo in my piece on *famadihana* (Graeber
      1995), and in more detail about negative authority in chapter 3 of *Lost People*
      (2007).

17   While the class of truly large-scale slave holders was always relatively small, perhaps only the poorest fifth of Merina households had no access to slave labor whatever. Most of the figures that follow are derived from documents preserved in the
     IIICC and EE sections of the Malagasy National Archives.

18   Owners would usually accept a portion of their earnings and expect their attendance at certain critical moments, such as harvest, when labor was in particular
     demand. But it was often difficult to enforce even these requirements, and some
     masters appear to have been forced to pay wages to their own slaves. The situation was further complicated by the fact that by the end of the century partible
     inheritance had ensured that many slaves, perhaps most, had several different masters. For some contemporary accounts, see Sewell (1876), Cousins (1896), Piolet
     (1896).

19   See the debate in the *Anti-Slavery Reporter*, February–March 1883.

20   The transformation affected women as well as men; some observers note that many
     wealthy women had to learn to do manual labor for the first time in their lives after
     the liberation of their slaves (Pearse 1899: 263–64).

21   I do not believe that, in all the time I was in Imerina, I ever heard the term used
     with anything but negative connotations. Apart from its political meaning, the
     only other phrase in which I heard it employed was the expression *fanompoana
     sampy* ("serving the idols"), adopted by the missionaries to translate the English
     "heathenism." The expression is only used as a term of denigration; no one, no
     matter how nominal their Christianity, would ever apply it to themselves.

22   This was, I should remark, much less true of the educated, urban elite than it was
     with rural people, white or black. Members of the former class would often speak
     quite casually about their "ancestors' slaves" (*andevon-drazana*), clearly seeing
     their existence as a token of their former glory. Rural people, on the other hand,
     when they did discuss the matter openly, made it equally clear that they saw it as
     evidence of their ancestors' misdeeds. Quite a number who claimed noble descent
     confided in me that they believed their own present-day poverty was a judgment
     rendered on their ancestors for having kept other Malagasy as slaves (Graeber
     2007).

23   Interestingly, so do the descendants of their former slaves, who were also considered more loyal to the colonial regime, and more amenable than other Merina not
     only to wage-labor, but to taking part in the hierarchically organized institutions
     identified with it. For instance, "black people" served in greatly disproportionate numbers in the military and police, as well as converting in large numbers to
     Catholicism. Significantly, too, I found them to be much more accepting of the use
     of *kalo* and even certain varieties of *ody fitia* than other Merina.

24   Other sources on nineteenth-century witches include James Sibree (1880: 202),
     Bessie Graham (1883: 62–3), and, again, Vig (1969: 112–24).

25 "So the brigands and thieves who present themselves to me to be catechized throw away their charms, being persuaded that they will lead them back to their careers as brigands without their being able to resist" Vig (1969: 123–24).

26 *Tsy mahazaka an'ilay herin'ilay fanafody.* Unfortunately there is very little literature on witchcraft from the colonial period itself. The one main exception I know of is Mary Danielli's "The Witches of Madagascar" (1947). Danielli's information comes from exactly half way between my two periods, and offers what seems a unique synthesis between the two sets of ideas: there are *ody fitia* which simply cause love and devotion, Danielli's informants told her, and these women do not become witches; but some love medicine has punitive effects, driving its victims mad or making them violently ill, and it is women who acquire this type of medicine who end up becoming possessed and "going out at night." This seems to be a transitional moment. I never heard anyone say anything of the sort in 1989–1991.

27 Maurice Bloch (1982, 1986). In addition to Elinor Ochs' work, Pier Larson (1995) has contributed important insights into differences in male and female speech.

28 *Manjaka* ("to rule," nominalized as *fanjakana*, "government") is in fact the reciprocal of *manompo* (to serve, nominalized as *fanompoana*). "To enslave" is *manandevo.*

Bibliography

Althabe, Gerard
1969 *Oppression et libération dans l'imaginaire: les communautés villageoises de la côte orientale de Madagascar.* Paris: Maspero.

Andriamanjato, Richard
1957 *Le Tsiny et le Tody dans la pensée Malgache.* Paris: Presénce Africaine.

Bernard-Thierry, S.
1959 "Perles magiques à Madagascar" in *Journal des Africanistes,* 29: 33–90.

Bloch, Maurice
1971 *Placing the Dead: Tombs, Ancestral Villages, and Kinship Organization in Madagascar.* London: Seminar Press.
1982 "Death, Women and Power." In *Death and the Regeneration of Life* (M. Bloch and J. Parry, eds.). Cambridge: Cambridge University Press.
1986 *From Blessing to Violence: History and Ideology in the Circumcision Ritual of the Merina of Madagascar.* Cambridge: Cambridge University Press.
1989 "The Ritual of the Royal Bath in Madagascar: The Dissolution of Death, Birth, and Fertility into Authority." In *Ritual, History and Power: Selected Papers in Anthropology.* London: Athlone Press.

Callet, R.P.
1908 *Tantara ny Andriana Eto Madagasikara.* Tananarive: Academie Malgache.

Carol, Jean
1898 *Chez les Hova (au pays rouge).* Paris: Pavanne.

Cousins, William
1896 "The Abolition of Slavery in Madagascar: with Some Remarks on Malagasy Slavery Generally" *Antananarivo Annual and Malagasy Magazine* 21: 446–50.

Dahle, Lars
1886–88 "Sikidy and Vintana: Half-Hours with Malagasy Diviners" *Antananarivo Annual and Malagasy Magazine,* 11 (1886): 218–34; 12 (1887): 315–24; 13 (1888): 457–67.

Danielli, Mary
1947 "The Witches of Madagascar," *Folklore* 58: 261–76.

Edmunds, William
1897 "Charms and Superstitions in Southeast Imerina." *Antananarivo Annual and Malagasy Magazine,* 22: 61–67.

Feeley-Harnik, Gillian
1991 *A Green Estate: Restoring Independence in Madagascar.* Washington, DC: Smithsonian.

Fremigacci, Jean
1975 "Mise en valeur coloniale et travail forcé: la construction du chemin de fer Tananarive-Antsirabe (1911–1923)" *Omaly sy Anio,* 1–2: 75–137.
1978 "L'administration coloniale: les aspects oppressifs" *Omaly sy Anio* 7–8: 209–237.

Graham, Bessie
1883 "Notes." Report of the Medical Mission for 1882, *Friends' Foreign Missionary Society Annual Report*: 62–3.

Graeber, David
1995 "Dancing with Corpses Reconsidered: an Interpretation of Famadihana in Arivonimamo, (Madagascar)" *American Ethnologist* 22: 258–278.
1996 "Beads and Money: Notes Toward a Theory of Wealth and Power." *American Ethnologist,* 23: 1–36.
2007 *Lost People: Magic and the Legacy of Slavery in Madagascar.* Bloomington: University of Indiana Press.

Haile, John
1893 "Malagasy Village Life: Pen and Ink Sketches of the People of Western Imerina." *Antananarivo Annual and Malagasy Magazine* 18: 1–20.

Larsen, Pier
1995 "Multiple Narratives, Gendered Voices: Remembering the Past in Highland Central Madagascar," *The International Journal of African Historical Studies,* 28: 295–325.

Ochs (Keenan), Elinor
1974 "Norm-makers, Norm-breakers: Uses of Speech by Men and Women in a Malagasy Community." In *Explorations in the Ethnography of Speaking* (Robert Bauman and John Sherzer, eds). Cambridge: Cambridge University Press.
1975 "A Sliding Sense of Obligatoriness: the Polystructure of Malagasy Oratory," *Language in Society* 2: 225–43.

Pearse, John
1899 "Women in Madagascar: Their Social Position, Employments and Influence," *Antananarivo Annual and Malagasy Magazine,* 23: 263–64.

Piolet, J.B.
1896 "De l'Esclavage à Madagascar." *Le Correspondant (Paris)*, 10 February 1896: 447–80.

Raison, Jean-Pierre
1984 *Les Hautes Terres de Madagascar et leurs Confins Occidentaux: enracinement et mobilité des sociétés rurales.* Paris: Karthala.

Renel, Charles
1915 "Les amulettes malgaches, Ody et Sampy." In *Bulletin de la Academie Malgache* (n.s) 2: 29–281.

Ruud, Jørgen
1960 *Taboo: A Study of Malagasy Beliefs and Customs.* New York: Humanities Press.

Sewel, Joseph
1976 *Remarks on Slavery in Madagascar.* London: Elliot Stock.

Sibree, James
1880 *Madagascar: the Great African Island.* London: Trübner & Co.

Skeat, Walter
1900 *Malay Magic: Being an Introduction to the Folklore and Popular Religion of the Malay Peninsula.* London: Macmillan and Co.

Vig, Lars
1969 *Charmes: Spécimens de Magie Malgache.* Oslo: Universitetsforlagets Trykningssentral.

8

OPPRESSION

In Malagasy there is a word, *tsindriana*, that means "oppressed." The literal definition is "to be pressed down, crushed by a heavy weight." Used in a political context, it means to suffer under some kind of unjust power or authority.

Malagasy is hardly alone in having such a word. Actually, most languages do. The English sentence "the people are oppressed" (or the Malagasy equivalent, *tsindriana ny vahoaka*) could be translated directly into the languages spoken by a majority of human beings, using the same metaphor, with no need for exegesis or elaboration. Even in those languages that do not have an explicit term for "oppression," I would hazard to say that if a competent speaker were to improvise such a metaphor, no one would find it in any way difficult to understand what he was talking about.[1]

It's easy to see why the metaphor might seem obvious. Power is almost invariably figured as something placed over people: what better way to express abusive power than by something above you pressing down? Here, though, I want to ask: What would an anthropologist have to say about this? Because, if one is speaking of most contemporary anthropologists, it's pretty obvious the answer would have to be: nothing. Presented with such a generalization, the first reaction of most anthropologists would be to try to show it isn't true. If this proved impossible, they would try to dismiss its significance.

It seems to me, though, that such connections are potentially extremely significant: mainly, because they point a way out of certain political dilemmas born of cultural relativism. Let me state the dilemma as simply as I can.

Most anthropological fieldwork has been conducted among subsistence farmers, slum dwellers, or indigenous peoples, the vast majority of them marginal even within the relatively poor countries in which they live. Most have been, at one time or another, victims of conquest, exploitation, state terror, or outright genocide. In other words, anthropology, more than any other discipline, has tended to focus on people who might by most definitions—including their own—be considered oppressed. Politically, we anthropologists tend to identify quite strongly with those we study. Often, we act as advocates. Yet, unlike activists involved in radical social movements, anthropologists almost never speak of such people as being "oppressed."

Why? Mainly because anthropologists tend to be keenly aware that one can only create the machinery of oppression once one has first dehumanized or infantilized one's victims, which in practice means, first and foremost, delegitimizing their point of view. What's more, that dehumanization, and its attendant humiliation, is one of the most damaging forms that oppression itself tends to take. Hence, we tend to be very suspicious of any sort of argument that assumes that certain people's perspectives are more legitimate than others, let alone, universally true. The obvious problem with this position is that, if you take it to its logical conclusion, it would mean there would be no basis on which to claim anyone was being oppressed (or even treated unfairly) to begin with. No one really wants to argue that a rapist's perspective is just as legitimate as his victim's, or a master's just as legitimate as his slave's. So the usual solution is to appeal to some notion of cultural relativism: yes, we have a category "rape" or "slavery" by which we can make moral judgments, the argument goes; the Nuer, or Nambikwara, have different ones. They live in a different moral and conceptual universe, and who are we to say ours is more intrinsically legitimate? Politically, this generally leads to a kind of uncomfortable compromise: while few anthropologists would deny that phenomena we would normally describe as "rape" or "slavery" are indeed evils, wherever they are practiced, they also tend to insist that imposing our own definitions in another cultural context is an even greater evil, especially if our judgments are backed up (as so often ultimately comes to be the case) by force of arms.[2]

In practice, this seems reasonable. Since at least the nineteenth century, with the British abolition of the slave trade, colonial empires have largely been justified by what we'd now call "humanitarian intervention." This is, of course, if anything even more true today. Still, adopting such a position leads to one significant, if largely unnoticed, conceptual problem. In order to say that "the Nuer" live in their own moral and conceptual universe, we are necessarily assuming that "the Nuer" actually exist: that is, that there is a relatively coherent set of ideas and principles that can be identified and described as belonging to the Nuer, and systematically compared with our own.[3] This implies bounded entities, which is a problem, but even more, it means even once you have decided who the Nuer are, you are not treating all Nuer perspectives as equally legitimate, since, after all, it will be nearly impossible to find any statement that every single person you have identified as "Nuer" will agree with. As a result, the entire project of cultural relativism depends on being able to identify structures of authority, and thus certain individuals who, more than others, can legitimately speak for the Nuer as a whole. But here is the logical dilemma. By what criteria are these authorities to be identified? One cannot employ "Nuer conceptions" of authority, because, until one has identified who those authorities are, there is no way to know what those "Nuer conceptions" are. Like it or not, the relativist has to use some sort of external criteria. The paradoxical result is that, if one is to take a consistent position of cultural relativism, authority is the one thing that *cannot* be treated relativistically.[4] The classic relativist has to assume that all cultures or societies do have structures of authority similar enough that they can be identified by an outside observer, and, furthermore, that these structures are intrinsically legitimate. The political implications are, to say the least, disturbing.

We seem to be caught, then, between three almost equally bad choices. Either we relegate to ourselves the authority to determine what's right and wrong everywhere in the world, or we relegate to ourselves the authority to determine who holds legitimate authority everywhere in the world, or we give up on making moral judgments entirely.

Could things really be so bleak? It seems to me there is a way out. It starts with the recognition that there are two problems here—a conceptual problem and a political problem—that we would do well not to conflate. After all, there's nothing intrinsically oppressive about universalism. If a Tibetan Buddhist like the Dalai Lama claims the right to make judgments about America based on privileged access to universal spiritual truths, Americans rarely feel they are thus the victims of a terrible injustice. Some might find it inspiring, others might find it ridiculous: but no one is likely to feel particularly oppressed. This is because the Dalai Lama holds no power over them. The real problem, it seems to me, is not with the mere fact of universalistic judgments, but with the existence of a global apparatus of bureaucratic control, backed up by a whole panoply of forms of physical and economic violence, that can enforce those judgments: whether by imposing itself directly, or by reserving to itself the power to recognize what are legitimate groups and who are their legitimate representatives, anywhere in the world. If one accepts that some such apparatus is inevitable, then, yes, we have little choice but to agonize over the moral quandaries it creates. But there is an alternative: we can ask what it would take to eliminate such coercive structures entirely. To do so would mean asking a very different set of questions. First and foremost, on what basis can one hold these structures to be intrinsically illegitimate? It is here that the existence of terms like *tsindriana* becomes so important, because they demonstrate not only that the authority is always contested, everywhere—but even more, because they suggest that the ways in which it is contested, even down to popular metaphors and images, are often surprisingly similar. They hold out the possibility that even if no consensus on such questions exists now—there's probably nothing everyone on earth currently agrees on—there is at least the *possibility* for such an agreement in the future. After all, what is most essential about human beings is not what they are at any given moment, but what they have the capacity to become.

At this point we can come back, I think, to the conceptual problem: except now I think it looks quite different. Once we allow that structures of authority are everywhere contested, and that the terms of contestation are at least close enough that we can all begin talking to each other, what do we do with the fact that, in most ways, a Malagasy term like "*tsindriana*" and an English term like "oppression" are extremely different? Like similar terms elsewhere, they draw on certain apparently universal—or universally comprehensible—metaphors: the sense of being stifled, crushed, ground down, overburdened, struggling under a heavy weight. But they speak so powerfully because they also draw on images that are extraordinarily specific. For the typical American, "oppression" might evoke images from movies about Medieval serfs or the building of Egyptian pyramids, personal memories of bad jobs, gym teachers, tax auditors, strident and rather foolish radical rhetoric, or stiflingly hot summer nights. These images, in turn, tend to open on a whole series of assumptions about the nature of freedom, autonomy, justice, and the individual, each with endless concrete associations of their own. A Malagasy using the term *tsindriana* would be evoking an entirely different fan of historical and personal associations. It is the vividness of such associations that gives these words their almost visceral power; but, at the same time, their specificity that makes it seem slightly absurd to even consider using them as terms of social analysis.

What I want to do in this essay is to begin to begin to ponder how to think our way out of this problem by looking more carefully at the Malagasy term *tsindriana*—not to reject any notion of relativism, incidentally, but rather, in order to think about how we might go about developing one without the same authoritarian implications. This means unpacking some of the dense constellation of ideas, images, and moral practices surrounding the bearing of burdens, the experience of being crushed by heavy weights, and how they are seen to bear on the legitimacy of different forms of authority. I think Madagascar is a particularly appropriate place to start because the non-Malagasy reader is likely to find so much of the larger cultural context profoundly alien and exotic. We will be looking at very different assumptions about the nature of the family, government, and spiritual practices that are, in these respects in particular, most likely very different from our own. But this, of course, is in keeping with one of the founding assumptions of anthropology: that if one is to try to understand what all human beings have in common, it behooves us to start with the cases that seem maximally unfamiliar.

I will be using material mainly drawn from the province of Antananarivo in the Malagasy highlands, an area historically referred to as Imerina. Most of it comes from a region of Arivonimamo where I lived and worked between 1990 and 1991. This was not, at the time, a place where there was a whole lot of oppression going on. The people there were, certainly, very poor. But almost no adults of either sex spent any prolonged period of their lives working under the direction of anyone else, and state control was practically nonexistent. On the other hand, it had not always been this way and people were keenly aware of that. The nineteenth-century state had been based on a combination of forced corvée labor and slavery that most people now saw as the very definition of oppression; tokens of this state were present everywhere. The same was true of the French colonial regime which most saw as having been even worse. Everyone saw themselves surrounded everywhere by the traces of oppressive regimes, and living in a landscape that had been largely created by them. As a result, as in so much of Madagascar, some forms of authority were seen as inevitable, but all forms of authority were seen as inherently problematic.

The body of the essay falls into three parts: the first concerning the family, the second concerning the nineteenth-century kingdom, the third about idioms of pressing and carrying in spirit possession today. Only then will I return to the problem of relativism.

PART I
BEARING BURDENS WITHIN THE HOUSEHOLD

In Malagasy one can refer to a sibling in one of two ways. One can refer to their gender (my brother, my sister...) or to their order of birth: "my senior," or *zoky*, "my junior," or *zandry*. One almost never refers to both at the same time. In part, this is because when it comes to matters of seniority within the household, or at least among siblings, gender should not, in principle, make a difference. If parents are away, for example, the oldest child is considered to be in charge of the household. Whether that child is a boy or a girl should be irrelevant.

In Madagascar, relation of older and younger, *zoky* and *zandry*, is a relation of simple hierarchy. It is perhaps the most elementary form of hierarchical relation. It is also often described as a based on a principle of mutual responsibility: it is the responsibility of older siblings to speak for their younger brothers and sisters in any situation which requires a degree of tact, or delicacy. It is the responsibility of younger siblings to carry their elders' things. Hence the well known proverb, *Manan-jandry, dia afak'olan'entina; manan-joky, dia afak'olan-teny*: "If you have a younger sibling, then you'll have no problems with carrying, if you have an older one, then you'll have no problems with speech" (Houlder 1915: #1901; Cousins 1963: 37; Camboué 1909: 385).

Around the turn of the century, a Catholic missionary posted to the area north of Arivonimamo observed that this principle was taken so seriously it often led to scenes that seemed, to the European eye, quite unreasonable. "By the age of about ten," he wrote, "children begin to help in the gardens and rice-fields by carrying burdens and packages. What is remarkable about the practice is that: it is to the youngest that the heaviest parts usually fall" (Camboué 1909: 385). Almost a century later, I observed much the same thing: one might often spot a sixteen-year-old girl strolling up the hill after a morning of weeding in the rice fields, with her ten-year-old sister struggling with a basket behind her, or a healthy middle-aged man coming back for lunch followed by a twelve-year-old son carrying his spade. Indeed, some have been known to go so far as to say that it is taboo for an elder to carry such tools if a younger family member physically capable of carrying it is anywhere around (so Ruud 1960: 25)—just as it would be inappropriate for a young man to speak in a village assembly or court case if he had a father or elder brother available to state his case for him. No one I knew in Arivonimamo would go that far. Most, even in the countryside, insisted such hard-and-fast rules were largely things of the past; though neither did they deny that, in practice, younger members of the family generally did end up doing a lot of the carrying, and that if one really needed a spokesman, and asked one's father or elder brother, they would normally feel they needed a very good excuse to refuse.[5]

One can think of *zoky/zandry* relations as an "atom of hierarchy" in two senses, actually. First of all, because talking about how older and younger siblings should relate to one another has always been one of the main ways to talk about relations of superiority and inferiority in general; second of all, because it was by growing up within families organized along these lines that people in Imerina have, over the last several hundred years or so, developed their most elementary, deeply embedded, experiences of what being inside hierarchical relations is like.

Let me give an example of each.

Whenever people talk about how *zoky* and *zandry* should behave towards one another, they tend to produce idealized statements, almost invariably prefaced by some statement to the effect of "of course, the kids nowadays no longer really do this, but in ancestral times, it was like this..." Apparently, this has always been the case. The very first account of household etiquette we have, written in the 1860s by a Merina Christian and assembled by a British missionary named Cousins in a book called *Fomba Gasy* or "Malagasy Customs" (Cousins 1963: 124–127), begins exactly the same way: "there's nothing older people complain about so much as the lack of respect for etiquette among the young people nowadays." The author then launches into a detailed account of how *zoky* and *zandry* should properly behave in each others' presence (leaving it a bit ambiguous whether he is talking just about siblings, or older and younger people in general). The account that follows revolves around three central principles, that can be summarized as follows:

1) Height.
Zandry should never place themselves physically higher than *zoky*, particularly during meals or other formal occasions; neither may their beds be placed higher than their elders'.
2) Priority.
At meals, the eldest must eat first. Neither can *zandry* take the lead when walking on a path, but they must follow their *zoky*.
3) Fetching and carrying.

The most extreme taboo (*fady*), the author notes, is to send one's *zoky* to fetch something. Great apologies are in order if one is to so much as ask them to pass something at table. If at all possible, the younger person should make sure their *zoky* do not have to carry any burdens at all. Should one, say, run into one's elder brother or sister carrying something on the road, one ought to immediately offer to take it. (This was an obligation, notes the author. A parent or elder sibling's responsibility to speak for their junior, "if there's something that needs to be explained to someone" is different; since the *zoky* need only do it if the *zandry* specifically asks.)

The theme of bearing burdens, however, resonates throughout. This is from the original text:

> It was the custom of the ancients, too, for brothers, or sisters, etc., to eat from the same plate. Once the *zoky* had eaten the larger part, he would leave the rest to his *zandry*, and when the *zandry* deferred, saying "eat

on," his *zoky* would reply, "no, you eat, because it is you who will be carrying the baskets" (Cousins 1960: 124).

Now, as I say, all this is rather an idealization. In practice, such rules always tend to apply to certain contexts, and certain people, more than others. It's hard to imagine that even the strictest family would have kept a constant eye on a five-year-old child to ensure she never sat with her head at a higher elevation than her ten-year-old sister. In fact, if Malagasy in 1860 were anything like the ones I knew, under ordinary circumstances, no one paid much attention to where five-year-olds sat at all. Rules of seniority were observed mainly on more or less formal occasions—in fact, one might say this is what a "formal" occasion was: one in which rules of seniority were strictly observed. And this was still true among the people I knew. Principles of height and priority were almost entirely ignored in everyday practice, but were carefully observed at ritual moments. On mildly formal occasions, they tended to be observed in abbreviated, allusive form: for instance, in the way that, when guests were in the house, anyone getting up to leave the room would always stoop down slightly when walking past those still seated, to indicate they knew they really shouldn't be allowing their heads to be in a position higher than those of anyone older or more exalted than themselves.

Still, these principles did have an effect on early family experience. The issue of fetching and carrying, for example, remained extremely important, even among the relatively educated and not especially traditionally-minded families I knew best in Arivonimamo, and certainly among farmers in the countryside. Children's lives, one might say, went through three broad stages. During the first, before they could walk, children were usually carried on their mother's backs, or on that of some other female relative. As soon as they could get about themselves, however, they were left largely to their own devices. We can call this the stage of autonomy. When not at school, they were expected to spend their time with other children, who formed a sort of autonomous community of the young, roving about in bands, reappearing only occasionally, mainly at mealtimes. During this period—which lasts till eight or ten—boys and girls were both treated very indulgently, and not expected to do much of anything around the house. But as soon as a child could walk, their elder sisters and other women of the household would also begin playing at sending them off to fetch small items—often to much amusement if the child wandered off or refused. As time went on, tasks grew more serious: it was common in town to send even children of six or seven to buy things at the store, and the child would often return triumphantly to great adulation if he or she had completely the mission successfully. The term used for such fetching, *maniraka*, literally means to send someone as an envoy, agent, or representative (*iraka*), and is the same verb that's used for more serious household chores, such as sending girls to fetch water, or spell their mothers or sisters from carrying babies, sending boys to carry their parent's tools or packages, all of which also begin around the ages eight to ten.[6]

It was at this third stage, when a child started having to carry burdens, that he or she first became integrated into the adult world, with its endless distinctions of seniority. One became part of the adult world, then, not only by sitting lower or following behind, but especially by following behind carrying heavy things on one's head or in one's arms. It happened in a way that often seemed seamless, even natural; play tasks turned into real duties, just as the inevitable way parents or older siblings would speak for children began to take on a new, more formal, significance as young people slowly became more capable of speaking for themselves. In the end, even outside the household, carrying burdens could be seen by obvious common sense as an emblem of subordination; and something quite naturally opposed to the power of speech.

Of course, real households have always been more complicated than these idealized accounts suggest. One has to take account of gender and generation as well as birth order; and on top of that was the fact that during, say, the 1860s, when *Fomba Gasy* was written, the majority of Merina households owned slaves. After several decades of predatory warfare, the Merina kingdom had become the center of a state that, in theory at least, controlled the whole of Madagascar. About a third of the population came to be made up of slaves captured in these wars, and ownership of slaves was so widespread that probably only one out of every three families had no access to slave labor. This began to happen at the same time that mission schools were introduced, part of a larger government plan to build the foundations of a modern, bureaucratic state.

The largest slaveholding families made up the state apparatus itself: most of the men in such households were officers in the Merina army, or government officials (who themselves held military rank)—and became stalwarts in the Protestant church. Their wives and children formed a leisured class, who, unless they became involved in the schools or government, usually did nothing at all. "They have all their needs attended to by slaves," remarked one Quaker missionary, "their beds made, clothes washed, food cooked and even cut up for them, so there is nothing much to do but eat food and sit about talking scandal" (in Ratrimoharinosy 1986: 202). This was the stratum European missionaries were most familiar with, from which the author almost certainly derived our earlier passage on etiquette.

These were the most enthusiastic supporters of the missionaries, but the latter found many of their habits disconcerting. Many remarked on the way that members of this class would never appear in public bearing anything remotely resembling a burden. James Sibree of the LMS wrote:

> It appears strange to the Malagasy to see us Europeans walking out for short distances unaccompanied by a servant or some attendant; for no free Malagasy, male or female, would think of going abroad without at least one follower at his or her heels... So again, no respectable Malagasy would carry with him any small article, such as a Bible or hymn-book; that must be taken by a slave boy or girl following them: and they wonder to see us carrying a map or roll of drawings as we go to our schools or Bible-classes (Sibree 1880: 183).

Joseph Sewell of the Society of Friends similarly remarked how "ludicrous" it was, to foreign observers, to see "ladies followed in the street by a slave holding some trifling thing like an umbrella or a bible... Even schoolchildren will have a little slave to carry their books and slates" (1867: 11).

Now, as I say, these authors are describing a particular social milieu.[7] Churches and schools were (then as now) places for the well off to make a show of affluence. But I suspect there is more going on in these descriptions than mere conspicuous display. Note the nature of things being carried: Bibles, hymn books, maps and rolls of drawings, school books and slates. They were all objects which embodied, in one sense or another, the power of words.[8] The Malagasy government saw missions and mission schools mainly as the means to acquire technologies of bureaucratic rule: the lists and ledgers, registries and correspondence that would enable them to make their kingdom an effective, "modern" state. Objects of verbal learning had a particular place as emblems of power. One rather suspects the Reverend Sibree's parishioners would not have been so quick to remark on the impropriety of carrying, say, a shaving brush, a hammer, or a ukulele.

Once again, then, we have an explicit opposition between bearing burdens and the power of speech.

Since most men in this period spent the bulk of their time performing government service (or trying to avoid it), the presence or absence of slaves mainly affected the workloads of women and children, who did the bulk of domestic and agricultural work. In contrast with the pampered Christian ladies who did not deign to carry their own parasols, another missionary complains that, "in heathen households" (a word often used as a synonym for "poor"), a wife is often "regarded by her husband in the light of a superior slave" and terribly overburdened (Haile 1893: 8). After the abolition of slavery in 1895, much of the emphasis once put on children's responsibility to carry burdens seems to have been refocused on women: when townspeople nowadays think of backwards country folk, one of the stereotypical images is that of the dutiful wife following behind her unburdened husband with a basket on her head. I did, occasionally, witness such scenes in rural Imerina—in fact, even some of my more educated female friends from town would, occasionally, offer to carry my bags for me, insisting that it was properly women's work (they never insisted very hard)—but, in fact, there are so many principles at play that in practice, there is a great deal of room for adjustment and negotiation. Would an older sister ever carry her brother's things? Certainly not; he should carry hers—that is, if it's the sort of thing it would be appropriate for a male to be carrying. What if the wife is older than the husband? Well, she shouldn't be older than her husband. But it happens sometimes: what if she is? That would depend on the family...

PART II
EMBLEMATIC LABOR AND THE NINETEENTH-CENTURY KINGDOM

The state, as has often been noted, tends to construct its own legitimacy by drawing on the idiom of the family, appropriating bits and pieces of family ritual or symbolism. The Merina state was no exception (Bloch 1989). If one looks at the structure of traditional kingdoms in the highlands, and particularly the organization of public works, one discovers a meticulous attention to what sort of people have to carry what sorts of objects—though, as we'll see, on this level the bearing of burdens was contrasted as often with powers of speech as with powers of material creation.

Kingdoms were organized around a figure called the *Andriana*, which means sovereign or king. Roughly a third of the free population were also considered *andriana*, either because they could claim descent from the royal line, or because their ancestors had been raised to *andriana* status because of some heroic act of devotion or self-sacrifice on behalf of royalty. In the nineteenth century, there were seven orders of *andriana*, with the sovereign's immediate family at the top; at the bottom were local descent groups hardly distinguishable from their *hova*, or "commoner" equivalents. Maurice Bloch refers to all these groups as "demes"; each occupied their own valley and network of terraced rice fields amidst the vast rolling country of Madagascar's central plateau. *Hova* were defined as people who owed some form of work—*fanompoana*, or "service"—to the king. There were other groups, such as the Mainty Enin-Dreny, who were specialized royal warriors. Finally, slaves did not have descent groups of their own and did not perform *fanompoana* for the king (in fact, anyone who could prove they had performed royal service

was automatically manumitted), but, rather, did the bidding of their owners.

The whole system was constructed around service. The status of any
given deme was largely determined by what particular type of service it performed for the royal family. This was particularly true before British missionaries and military advisors arrived in the 1820s and King Radama I
began using the principle of *fanompoana* as the basis for creating a modern-
izing state. Since our historical sources also begin around this time, it is a
little difficult to reconstruct exactly what "royal service" really meant in the
eighteenth century, when Imerina was still broken into dozens of warring
principalities. While, in theory, a local king could demand most anything
from his subjects, it seems that a ruler's ability to extract goods and services
from groups who did not happen to live in the immediate vicinity of a royal
residence was quite limited. Those services they did receive revolved largely
around what we consider ceremonial tasks, such as building and rebuilding
royal palaces and tombs, or participating in the annual New Year's ritual.
During such events, each deme was usually assigned some very specific set
of tasks, which marked their status, as forming part of a more generic labor
pool. It's important to bear in mind that, except for a handful of the very
most exalted *andriana*, almost all of these groups were, in terms of how they
earned their livelihoods, remarkably similar: all devoted most of their energies to farming in the summer, and to handicrafts or petty trading in the
agricultural off-season. It was what one did for that king that determined
one's status in the kingdom as a whole and, therefore, such tasks could be
referred to as "emblematic labor," which defined the nature of each group,
what kind of people they really were.[9]

Andriana were not entirely exempt from royal service; but their services tended to focus on a few, relatively privileged tasks. Take, for example, the building and repair of royal tombs, a task so exalted only *andriana*
and certain very high-ranking *hova* groups had the privilege of taking part.
Malagasy accounts (once again, written in the 1860s: Callet 1908: 260–2,
267, 1213–14) broke down the tasks into two broad categories. The first were
acts of production: the actual fashioning of the tomb and manufacture of the
objects that would be placed inside. These tasks were monopolized by *andriana*. The orders of the Andriamasinavalona and Andriantompokoindrindra,
for example, provided the stone-masons and carpenters who built the tomb
itself; the Andrianandranado provided the smiths who made the huge silver
coffin in which kings were buried, and later, who made the tomb's tin roof;
women of the Andriamasinavalona and Zazamarolahy orders wove the mats
that would be hung on the walls inside; three other groups were expected
to provide the silk shrouds used for wrapping the dead (Callet, Ibid.). The

second set of tasks were always phrased as matters of "carrying" things; especially, carrying off the tattered mats and other rubbish from inside a tomb when it was opened or repaired, and gathering and conveying baskets full of the red clay that was used to seal it afterwards (Callet 1908: 164, 307, 490, 534–5, 812–3). These tasks were never assigned to *andriana* but always to *hova*.[10]

This distinction carries through all sorts of other tasks as well. In such ritual moments, *andriana* were defined as the kind of people who produce things; commoners, as those who fetch and carry them. At times, these emblematic tasks leaked over into broader contexts. The Andrianandranado, for instance, the order of *andriana* who provided the smiths for royal rituals, also produced all the gold and silver objects used at court. As a result, they eventually managed to win a formal monopoly on gold- and silver-working within the Merina kingdom as a whole. During the nineteenth century, other branches of this same order provided also almost all the tin smiths and a large number of the skilled iron-workers in the capital.[11] Other groups were famous for other specialties. As a rule, *andriana* were seen as producers, makers; it was their basic identity in the structure of the kingdom, a fact which was perhaps most clearly revealed when, in 1817, British envoys asked King Radama I chose a handful of boys from his kingdom to study artisanal trades in England. Every young man the king chose were *andriana*.

I am not sure if any foreign scholar has ever drawn attention to the connection between *andriana* and industrial and craft production before, probably because it seems so odd to see "nobles" as industrial producers.[12] Though perhaps it is easier to conceive if one sees the privileged stratum as monopolizing the powers of creativity. Nobles spoke first at council and were seen as being the masters of oratory and poetic speech (Domenichini Ramiaramanana 1983). They also created the most beautiful objects.

King Andrianampoinimerina, who unified the country at the end of the eighteenth century, used his right to demand *fanompoana* to marshal the manpower to reclaim thousands of hectares from swamps. King Radama and his successors in the nineteenth century expanded it to include such things as military service, school attendance, and participation in all sorts of industrial projects. The vast majority of these new tasks fell to commoners. Still, certain tasks remained emblematic, in the sense that they were seen as defining the essence of the relation between subjects (*Hova*) and the Sovereign (*Andriana*). Sources speaking of *fanompoana* in the abstract in the nineteenth century tended to produce a remarkably standardized list of emblematic tasks—and the same list reappears as those tasks from which andriana demes were specifically exempt. These lists always emphasized four, typically in the following order:

1) *Manao Hazolava*, or "dragging trees." Since Imerina proper was largely devoid of timber, it was necessary to form crews of workmen to drag
the vast trunks needed for royal houses and palisades from the edge of
eastern forests up to the center of the country. The right to set up the
central poles of royal houses was, again, a highly esteemed privilege.

2) *Mihady Tany*, or "digging earth." This mainly refers to leveling and
the making of embankments for royal building projects.[13]

3) *Manao Ari-Mainty*, or "making charcoal." In practice, this mainly involved transporting baskets of charcoal produced in the eastern forests
to the royal court in the capital, Antananarivo.

4) *Mitondra Entan'Andriana*, or "carrying royal baggage." Most often
this involved transporting imports bound for the court from the port of
Tamatave, but it could include any number of other transport duties.[14]

The reader will no doubt have noted that in every case, these were tasks
which, once again, centered on dragging or carrying heavy things—usually,
in baskets on one's head. (#2 might seem a partial exception, but anyone who
has ever taken part in a large scale digging project knows the lion's share of
the labor, and usually the most onerous part, involves hoisting and carrying
containers of displaced earth.)

The emphasis on bearing burdens, of course, did have something to do
with existing physical conditions. Imerina in the nineteenth century lacked
beasts of burden or wheeled vehicles. It was also notoriously lacking in decent
roads. As a result, just about everything had to be moved by human beings,
and often with great difficulty. But choosing these tasks as paradigms of *fanompoana* also clearly drew on a broader sense that, in the kingdom as in the
household, carrying things for someone was emblematic of subordination.
Indeed, in the case of royalty the principle was taken even further, because
royals and officers of state did not walk for long distances at all. Like foreign
visitors, they were carried everywhere on palanquins borne on the shoulders
of trained bearers. The royal bearers were a class of relatively esteemed spe-
cialists, in their own right, of a status similar to royal warriors.[15] Important
court figures, or local grandees, tended to keep specially trained bearers of
their own, who usually formed an elite corps amongst their slaves. Actually,
there was something of an irony in their position: since free people were
defined as those who served (i.e., carried things) for the king, and slaves, as
those who did so for private citizens, European merchants found it almost
impossible to recruit free-born Malagasy as bearers, either for palanquins, or,
more importantly, to carry goods along the difficult roads that lead from the
capital to the seaports of the coast. Only slaves were willing to do such work.
As a result, many slaves ended up in a surprisingly advantageous economic

position, working independently of their owners (to whom they were usually obliged to turn over only a certain portion of their earnings), forming semi-corporate guilds that ended up dominating the overland carrying trade in much of Madagascar and securing very high wages as a result (Campbell 1981). This pattern of turning extreme subordination into practical power is one we will be seeing again and again.

The Ambivalence of "Carrying"

So far, the picture I have been presenting has been fairly simple. Merina children learn about the nature of hierarchy in large part through the experience of carrying heavy burdens—being literally "oppressed," pressed down by the weight of objects balanced on their heads, or backs, or shoulders—objects which, significantly belonged to someone else.[16] Within the structure of the kingdom as a whole, such tasks became emblematic of subordination. In either case, the experience of physical compression could be posed against ways in which one might be said to expand, or extend oneself into the world: by producing words (if one was a *zoky*), or objects (if one was an *andriana*) which can then be detached from their creator and influence others.

Probably, the difference is mainly one of emphasis. In households, when a man is working a forge or a woman weaving, it is generally the most senior person who actually fashions the object, while younger people scurry back and forth carrying supplies. And when kings assembled their people to pass down rulings or ask their permission to begin some project (for example, dragging trees to make a new palace) it was the Andriamasinavalona and Andriantompokoindrindra—the same orders who had the privilege of actually building royal tombs—who had the privilege of being the first to respond to the royal words. In doing so, they were seen as acting as spokesmen for the kingdom as a whole, in much the same way as a *zoky* can speak for his *zandry* (Callet 1908: 288). And of course, as we have already seen, whether or not the identification of elite status with the control of words was salient in the formal organization of the kingdom, it certainly emerged with the spread of Christianity and mission schools later in the century.

What's more, the image of bearing burdens carried with it a certain ambivalence. In ordinary usage, for example, "carrying" by no means always means subordination. Sometimes it means exactly the opposite. The word *mitondra* means not only "to bring" or "to carry"; but also "to lead." One can say a person arrived "carrying a shovel" or "leading a detachment of a hundred soldiers"—it's exactly the same word. Authority itself is often spoken of as a burden, so that one "carries" a certain responsibility, even a certain office. Active governance is a matter of "carrying the people" (*mi-*

tondra vahoaka) and the most common word for governance is in fact an abstract noun, *fitondrana*, which might best be translated as "the manner of carrying."

Such idioms might not mean much in themselves, but they seem to draw on a much broader sense of reciprocal obligation which again, seems to be rooted in relations of hierarchy in the family, which ultimately became central to the way people imagined their relations to the state.

In the household, the duties one owes to one's elders are often framed in terms of a kind of reciprocity. In speaking of child-raising, the image of a woman carrying a baby on her back became itself an emblematic form of work, an image that summed up all the work of caring for, feeding, clothing, cleaning, teaching, and attending to a child's needs, which parents—and, of course, particularly mothers—provide. Obligations of support which adult children later owe to their parents and ancestors, in turn, could be collectively referred to as *valim-babena*: "the answer for having been carried on the back." Alternately, they can be called *loloha* or *lolohavina*, "things carried on one's head." The term was used as way of referring to any responsibility to support others, but particularly, the obligation to provide dead ancestors with cloth and other gifts when their bodies are taken out of the tomb to be rewrapped at periodic *famadihana* ceremonies, and to build and repair their tombs.[17]

So far, then, we have a reciprocity of carrying: the labor of child-rearing is pictured as a matter of carrying on one's back, it is repaid by maintaining the parents themselves when they are old, and their tombs and bodies after they have died—that maintenance, then, becoming a figurative burden borne on their descendants heads (see Lambek 2002; Cole 2000: 319–20).[18]

Not surprisingly, some nineteenth-century documents actually use the term *filolohavina*, "things carried on the head," to refer both to one's responsibilities to one's ancestors, and one's responsibilities to provide taxes and labor to the state. What is particularly interesting here is that, as a result, relations between the people and ruler were often represented as nurturing ones. Perhaps the one term most constantly invoked in discussions of the people's relation to their ruler is *mitaiza*, which literally means to breast-feed, to take care of a child not yet capable of taking care of its own needs (Rajemisa-Raolison 1985: 909). Used in a broader sense, it can mean to nurture, care for, as well as to foster a child not one's own. In the nineteenth-century literature, the people, or their representatives, are always being represented as nurturing the king. This is another aspect of Merina royal symbolism which has been largely ignored in the historical and ethnographic literature, apparently because it seems so odd. Seeing a king as a small child being nursed by his subjects so flies in the face of our own accustomed image of a ruler as the patriarchal "father of his people" that, in its way, it jangles even more oddly than the idea of "nobles" as industrial producers.[19]

Commoners who served as royal advisors, like those who, beginning in the reign of Queen Ranavalona I, took effective control of the kingdom in the role of royal "ministers," were always referred to in Malagasy texts as *"mpitaiza andriana,"* "the king's nursemaids" as well. Among the most desirable ritual services owed to royalty, many specifically involved the caring for royal children: for example, the Antehiroka, commoners considered the real autochthonous population of the plain of Antananarivo, had the privilege of blessing young princes during their circumcision ceremonies, and the Manendy, one of the specialized warrior clans, were also the privileged playmates of young Merina princesses (Domenichini-Ramiaramanana & Domenichini 1980).[20] All this was, in part, simply the recognition of a certain dependency: a person who is carried by someone else is obviously dependent on them. Kings who are fed by the people are also, in a sense, infantilized.

One may ask how much of this was simply rhetoric, and how much it had any effect on practice. The answer is, probably, that this varied. In royal service, for example, the tasks that were considered particularly legitimate focused on the needs of the royal household itself. This was true even—indeed, particularly—of such spectacular tasks as dragging tree-trunks across miles of countryside, which were always seen as part of building or rebuilding royal residences. Other tasks, such as working on national industrial projects or serving in the army, were not seen as legitimate in anything like the same way, and were widely resisted. Different people managed to make more or less effective claims on royalty on the basis of their role as "nourishing" and "caring for" the king or queen. For instance, the (mainly commoner) guardians of the royal *sampy*, or national "palladia," who formed as close as the Merina kingdom had to a priestly class, also regularly represented themselves as *mpitaiza andriana* (see e.g., Jully 1899: 325; Domenichini 1977). So did the families of commoner politicians and generals who, after the reign of Radama, became the effective rulers of the state. When they tried to use *fanompoana* to extract labor for their own personal projects however, this was treated as profoundly illegitimate by those summoned to tend their cattle or carry their commercial wares to port.

Popular factions could try to play the *mpitaiza andriana* card as well. One of the earliest visitors to Imerina, a French slave trader named Nicholas Mayeur, noted in 1777 how representatives of a kingdom's women would periodically assemble to scold the same monarch—Andrianamboatsimarofy—rather as one would a disorderly child, ordering him, for instance, to stop drinking rum and lower taxes. When King Radama I instituted a permanent standing army in 1822, and declared that half the kingdom's young men were to be military recruits and have their hair cropped short as indication of status, a large number of women, claiming to be "nursemaids" of the king (Ellis 1838; Larson 2000: 240–253), attempted a similar protest. But things didn't go so well. Radama was notorious for his contempt for traditional institutions, and reliance on brute force. He had soldiers pen them up for two days without food and the leaders thrashed before sending them all home.

However, exactly the same imagery appeared in what was certainly the most dramatic protest of the nineteenth century—in fact, one might think of it as a kind of uprising—the outbreak of the *Ramanenjana*, the "dancing mania" of 1863 (Davidson 1889; Raison 1976).

I should explain here that one of the most dramatic images of royal power—one which appears to have made a profound impact on the popular imagination—was the rounding up of people to carry royal baggage during court outings. This was apparently particularly disastrous during the reign of Queen Ranavalona I (1828–1861). Whenever the Queen traveled abroad, she brought her entire court and enormous quantities of furniture and provisions, so that she had to be preceeded by agents summoning almost the entire population of surrounding villages for forced labor. This was a very ambivalent demand, since on the one hand carrying royal baggage was indeed personal service to the crown and hence seen as inherently legitimate; however, the results were usually catastrophic. Since the workers were not fed, and the Queen's party tended to absorb all available supplies, hundreds if not thousands would perish of a combination of exhaustion, starvation, and disease. "Never," wrote the Queen's secretary Raombana, after one royal expedition to Manerinerina in 1845, "was an excursion of pleasure more productive of famine and death" (488).

Ranavalona was Radama I's wife and, later, successor on the throne, established there by several prominent commoner generals. She is famous for expelling missionaries and other foreigners from the country, restoring the *sampy*, but at the same time, maintaining the army and bureaucratic apparatus created by Radama. Her reign was considered the most oppressive in popular memory, between the endless demand of *fanompoana* and the systematic use of the poison ordeal to root out rebels and enemies, real and imagined.

When she finally died in 1861 and her son, Radama II, came to power, he immediately attempted to reverse almost all of her policies, abandoning most court ritual and allowing foreign missionaries and economic adventurers of every stripe to flood back into the country. Within a year or so, churches and plantations were being set up all around the capital, and the resulting popular suspicions, apparently, sparked one of the most famous moments of popular resistance in Malagasy history. Thousands of people all over Imerina—the vast majority women, many slaves—began to be affected by what foreign observers described as a "dancing mania," a "disease" referred to as the Ramanenjana. It was, in fact, a form of spirit possession and, since it was widely held that the only way to cure such a condition was to allow the spirit to emerge, to dance itself out, musicians quickly appeared to help victims—who soon began gathering together into bands and then descending on the capital. Those affected claimed to be bearing the luggage of the late Queen, who, they said was returning to the capital in order to chasten her son for abandoning her policies, opening up the country to outsiders, and especially for reintroducing Christianity.[21] It was in its way quite similar to the revolt of 1822, but it also came in a form that the government found almost impossible to suppress. Faced with an army of entranced women surrounding the royal palace, swirling about and making periodic forays into its precincts, Radama II was paralyzed with confusion. He kept asking his Christian advisors if he was witnessing the apocalypse. In the end, military officers took the occasion to assassinate him and ordered his most objectionable policies—particularly, granting foreigners the right to buy land and other economic assets in Madagascar—reversed.

In each case, note the specifically maternal relation between representatives of the people and the (male) king; maternal authority, which, at least towards male children, is always thought to be a particularly close and affectionate kind, was the proper medium for reversing power relations. In the second case, those possessed even represented themselves as bearing the burdens of the Queen: in classical possession fashion, taking an image of total subordination and, by a kind of dialectical jujitsu, turning it into a way of yielding power. But this in turn adds yet another wrinkle to an already complicated set of principles and images surrounding authority in Merina culture. Let me turn, then, in the next section, to look at the phenomenon of spirit possession and mediumship as I encountered it in twentieth-century Imerina to see how all these principles continue to work themselves out in the way people imagine the nature of political power.

PART III
ARIVONIMAMO AND ITS SPIRIT MEDIUMS

The town of Arivonimamo hugs the highway that runs west from the capital. Most of it lies on an extremely gentle slope. As a result, the town's porters have developed a unique system for transporting goods. Anyone hanging around the taxi station near the market, or just gazing from the verandah of one of the houses that line the highway, is likely to see a wagon—or maybe it would be better described as a very large dolly—rolling down the hill every ten minutes or so. Almost always, these dollies are crowded with bags and boxes and packages of commodities of one sort or another, with two or three young men at the helm—one steering, others simply there to enjoy the ride and to help with loading when they arrive. When I was there between 1989 and 1991, these porters were almost invariably "black people" (*olona main-ty*)—descendants of nineteenth-century slaves—except for a smattering of men of slightly higher birth who are, largely for that reason, considered even more the detritus of society: drunks, ne'er-do-wells, losers unfit for any decent occupation. For all that, these are also the only people one can regularly see having fun in public: rolling down the hill is a very pleasant job, even if the same people do have to drag the dollies back up afterwards. It's not really all that onerous: as I say, it's a very gentle slope.

The taxi stand centers on a little booth near the marketplace, very much the fulcrum of the town, always full of vans and station-wagons loading and unloading. This work was hardly limited to descendants of slaves. Almost anyone could be a member of the taxi cooperative. It was the more simple, physically taxing business of actually carrying things around—since the men who worked the dollies, I soon found, were also readily available to strenuously carry burdens by hand over side roads and difficult rural paths—which was a class apart. The prejudice against carrying things for a living, then, remained very much alive.

It was next to this same taxi-stand, in a line of tiny restaurants that was part of Arivonimamo's market, that, during one of my first visits to the town, I met a very peculiar person who I shall call Ramose. The very first time I met him, I was not sure if he was entirely sane. He was a pale, middle-aged man who wore a patchwork outfit rather reminiscent of a European court jester, but with a loud and very self-confident voice. Born to an illustrious family (his father had been the Malagasy ambassador to the U.N. under an earlier regime), Ramose was a notorious eccentric, having frittered away his share of the family fortune on an endless series of wives and adventures, eventually even abandoning his job as a teacher of French and Malagasy in the local public high school (CEG) to take up work as an astrologer and part-time curer with a specialty in locating stolen goods. He first discovered his true talents, I was told, when he proved the only person capable of curing an outbreak of *ambalavelona*, a form of spirit possession, at the CEG. While talking about the incident with him and his daughter, Chantal, I first became aware of how important, and strangely entangled, idioms of oppression and carrying things were in discussions of such phenomena.

Spirit Possession

There are two terms in the colloquial Malagasy spoken in Arivonimamo one might use to translate the English "possessed by spirits." One is *tsindrin-javatra*, which literally means "pressed down by something." The other, is *entin-javatra*, which means "carried by something." In general, "pressed down" implies a somewhat milder state, in which a person enters into some relation with a spirit. It is used, say, of the experience of being addressed by a spirit in dreams, or falling into a trance in which a spirit seems to be whispering in one's ear or otherwise speaking to one, but such phenomena also seem to shade into more extreme forms of trance, in which the personality of the medium begins to be effaced. *Entin-javatra* is usually only used for the most extreme forms, in which the possessed person has lost all consciousness of their own identity, but simply acted as an extension of the spirit's will. [22] Almost always, someone "carried along" by a spirit would be said to have no memory of how she behaved during the incident.[23]

However, the confusing thing is the way that, when people tried to explain exactly what happened during possession—that is, those few who felt they could even make the attempt, since most insisted they had no idea—their descriptions slipped back and forth between the two: between representing people as interacting with external forces, and being entirely effaced by them. This is what became clear when I first talked to Ramose because he was probably the one person best able to talk about such issues—he was not only educated in Malagasy studies, but was an experienced lecturer—and even his account was remarkably confused.

The *ambalavelona* outbreak in which he became famous occurred in 1977. An entire dorm of teenage girls at the local CEG fell prey to a condition rather like *Ramanenjana*, usually caused by an evil-doer who exposes his victims to the influence of hostile ghosts. I heard many accounts of the spectacular results. The victims first began to be seized by sudden panics which lead them to suddenly bolt from the classroom; matters soon escalated to the point where some began tearing off their clothes and running naked across campus, others ripping their clothes to shreds as they lay writhing and screaming on the ground. There were stories of possessed girls jumping out of second- or third-story windows and landing unharmed, suddenly developing such enormous strength it was impossible to subdue them. How? Here is Ramose's description of what happens when one is afflicted by *ambalavelona*:

> *Ramose*: The first thing that happens is that the person develops a sudden headache, then eventually, their minds become lost. They start

speaking in words that make no sense, and it's like there's a second person inside them.

There's something frightening the sick person. It chokes them. It torments them. It feels like they're struggling with a snake, or some fierce beast (depending on how the evil spirit (*fanahy ratsy*) manifests itself).

That's why one says: there's a "second person" that comes over them.

Chantal: So they can see this second person?

Ramose: They can see it. The person can see it—see the snake which is hurting them and choking them—and tries to fight it.[24]

At one point, he was called in to question a girl who had been afflicted but had temporarily come to her senses. She told him she had been attacked by an invisible beast—but all she could see of it was its hands, grabbing at her. That was the reason she tore off her clothes, she said, because it seemed as if the beast had attached itself to them. That was why she seemed to be writhing and screaming for no reason. She was struggling to shake it off.

But then in summing up, he asserted the exact opposite. Actually, it was the ghost itself—the "second person"—that was screaming and struggling:

Ramose: The first person no longer has any control of herself: it's the second person who rules over her.

David: So it's the second person who...

Ramose: It's the second who's acting strangely, who's speaking without making any sense, who's ripping their clothes off...

David: But is this really a second *person*, or is it...?

Ramose: It's an evil spirit. The soul of someone who has died, which frightens them. It appears as a snake, as a ferocious human, as a hostile ghost...

Chantal: And is that what makes them so strong?

Ramose: And that's what makes them so strong—because a girl with *ambalavelona* has the strength of five men. Her strength is truly remarkable.[25]

I was completely confused. At first I assumed it must be a language problem. I must have been missing something. It was only the next day, after having transcribed the tape and satisfied myself that what he was saying was really as contradictory as it sounded, that I brought up the matter again. It's confusing, I said. Sometimes, it sounds as if these victims were conscious, struggling with the ghost. At others, it's as if their minds were entirely effaced and it was the ghost itself speaking or acting, making them speak non-sense, or giving them enormous strength, and not the victims at all.

He reflected for a moment. Well, yes, he replied. Sometimes they were more possessed than others. At those times, their own personalities would be entirely effaced, and it was the spirit that was acting through them. Later they would begin to regain consciousness (to "remember themselves"), and then it would seem the spirit was outside, struggling with them. They would shift, in other words, from being "carried" to being "pressed down."

Zanadrano

Mass outbreaks of *ambalavelona* are rare. But professional spirit mediums, called Zanadrano, are everywhere—in every town and most villages in rural Imerina—and séances occur on a daily basis. Everyone has been to such a séance at some time or other and most people attend whenever they are seriously ill, even if they normally seek the services of the local clinic or hospital as well. Like the porters, Zanadrano consist overwhelmingly of the descendants of slaves. One of the defining features of a slave is that they are people "lost" to their own ancestors, particularly to their ancestral territories. To this day, descendants of slaves don't really have their own ancestral territories in the same sense that other Merina do. Zanadrano, however, created a different way of linking up to the ancestral landscape because they rely on a pantheon of "*Andriana*," the souls of ancient kings, whose mountaintop tombs have become places of pilgrimage. Most visit these compounds periodically, to renew contact with the spirits, and sometimes in difficult cases they bring their patients to such compounds for curing rituals.[26]

Now, there are a lot of things one can say about rituals of curing and the work of Zanadrano more generally, but what I really want to emphasize here is the division of labor between spirits in their practice. Most compounds contain several tombs and, generally, each royal spirit is accompanied by at least one other spirit—often buried just outside the compound proper—who is often referred to as his "soldier" or "worker," or sometimes, less euphemistically, as his "servant" or his "slave." Both the royal spirits and the spirits of the slaves possess people and take part in curing ceremonies, but they play radically different roles. The role of the first centers on speaking; the second, on fetching and carrying.

What mediums basically do is treat people who have been victims of one or another kind of magical attack (or witchcraft; while there were many different kinds, most Zanadrano I talked to insisted that their single most common task was to cure cases of *ambalavelona*). As such, mediums can be referred to generically as *mpitaiza olona*, "nurturers" of those they cured and otherwise took care of. Almost always, a family will come to a Zanadrano complaining of some malady. The first stage of treatment is dedicated to finding out who was responsible, their motives, and how they went about working their witchcraft. Music is played, the medium will enter into a trance; often they will call on a number of different "*andriana*"—here meaning, royal spirits—for advice, each of whom is often said to have their own specialty: for instance, Andriantsihanika is noted for his ability to diagnose and cure cases of *ambalavelona*, Rafaramahery is an expert in problematic pregnancies and women's ailments, and so on. Often the medium will brandish a mirror, in which he or she is said to be able to see the culprit or the place in which they have hidden *ody*—that is, "charms," horns, sacks, or boxes containing dangerous medicine—which almost always turn out to have been planted around the victim's house or property, and which are the prime cause of their affliction.[27]

This first stage, diagnosis, typically consists of a kind of multi-sided dialogue involving the medium, various spirits, the patient, and various members of the patients' family. In a sense, the medium is seen as merely conveying the spirits' words, constantly interspersing his words with "he says," to mark it as reported speech. However, the medium says nothing of his own, and there is a certain ambiguity in his state—he is almost always considered in a state of what we would call trance, and, while one or two mediums claimed they were simply conveying words they heard whispered in their ears, the majority insisted that, even at this stage, they no longer "remembered themselves," that they remembered nothing of the experience afterwards, or if they did, that it was only in isolated snatches and fragments that melted away soon afterwards, rather as in waking from a dream.[28]

Once the problem has been identified the most dramatic stage comes: extracting the *ody* from their hiding places. While the spirits who diagnosed the problem were always referred to as *andriana*, often as "holy spirits" (*fanahy masina*), the extraction was always performed by another class, by the agents of the royal spirits, slave spirits, who were not so much "holy" (*masina*) as "powerful" (*mahery*).[29] Where spirits of the first type are sometimes referred to as *mpanazava*, "explainers," the latter are called *mpaka ody*, or "*ody* takers."

This stage is usually referred to as "drawing forth" (*misintona*) the evil medicine. The idea is that the royal spirits dispatch (*maniraka*) one or more powerful spirits to remove the various ody hidden on the victim's property, and whisk them away invisibly through the air, until they arrive at the ceremony. This phase is, as one might suspect, the climax of the curing drama, and often involves intense participation by all concerned—the curers and their family, the family and friends of the victim, other attendees—as the music picks up to a fever pitch, all clap, until the medium rises, possessed by the spirits of the *mpaka ody* themselves.

Here there is a great deal of room for variation in techniques. One Zanadrano I knew would stay seated until at the very end of the ritual, then rise from his seat to begin dancing in a deep state of trance, with a horn full of powerful wood in one hand and a wand in the other, with which to guide the *ody* in the last stages of its flight into the antechamber of the house—where it would descend, invisible to the gathered multitude, into a bucket of water treated with medicines meant to break its power. One of his daughters or other assistants would then rush in to bind it with vines. Another Zanadrano would hold two mirrors, each treated with significant marks of white clay, and struggle with the invisible forces protecting the charm until it finally comes flying through the window into the room where the session is taking place (usually breaking one of the mirrors in the process), whereupon he too would plunge the object into a basin of treated water. In all cases, though, the struggle is conducted silently; the *mpaka ody* never speak.

After the *ody* has been removed, the royal spirits normally return and prescribe various medicines, perhaps remove *sisika* (small objects that a witch places under the victim's skin), or paint daubs of earth and water collected near the tombs of different royal spirits on the patient's body, to protect her from further attacks.[30] But, by this time, the real crisis has clearly passed.

Once again, the same pattern: *andriana* who speak, and underlings who serve by silently carrying. But in this case, too, the opposition becomes mapped on the distinction between two types or perhaps levels or intensities of engagement with a spirit: the ancestral, benevolent spirit who "presses down" on one, with whom one can at least potentially enter dialogue, and the dangerous unruly spirit which can only "carry one away," entirely displacing one's mind or subjectivity.[31]

There is, of course, a very complex play of displacements going on here. Royal spirits send off their "soldiers" or "slaves" to do the actual work of taking the evil medicine—according to some mediums this involves actually having to do battle with the spirits the witch has left to protect it. They are sent to fetch and retrieve things, like children sent on errands, or teams of commoners sent to drag trees for royal building projects. At the same time, the role of the medium themselves in some senses reproduces that of the *mpaka ody*—they also call themselves the royal spirits' "soldiers" and, of course, in effect are conveying or following their orders, but from another perspective, they are somewhat in the position of older brothers, who speak for the royal spirits—since they speak not in the voice of the spirit but in their own, merely conveying the royal words. [32]

The ambiguity emphasizes how much one is witnessing precisely the kind of complex play of oppressions within oppressions that marked the "dancing mania" which overthrew King Radama II a century and a half before. Because, as noted earlier, the sort of people who become Zanadrano are also overwhelmingly descendants of slaves. They are people whose very presence in Arivonimamo is a testimony to past acts of injustice and oppression,[33] and who remain an oppressed minority—mostly poor, mostly landless, mostly without social networks connecting them with government officials or members of other powerful institutions—but whose (universally acknowledged) talent for mediumship itself is largely about making effective theatrical displays of oppression that can often win social prominence and (see Graeber 2007) even, when things go very well, a certain degree of political power.

PART IV:
CONCLUSIONS

On the Morality of Hierarchy

We are left with a picture which is admittedly pretty confusing.

When one wishes to say that someone is "oppressed" in Malagasy, one uses the word *tsindriana*, which literally means "pressed down" as by a heavy weight. The term is used much as it is in English: it implies having one's subjectivity squashed, not being able to act for oneself because one is forced to do onerous tasks for others. Or it can simply mean that one is part of a class of people treated badly by their superiors. Given the evident importance of carrying weights as one's first experience of hierarchy, the usage might not seem particularly surprising. But in another way it is. After all, it is not as if, even now, one can find many people in Madagascar who would say that hierarchy itself is wrong. To the contrary, just about everyone assumes as a matter of course that there must always be *zoky* and *zandry*, elders and juniors. They note that it is ancestral custom that dictates that younger brothers should carry the older one's baskets or tools. Ancestral custom is never seen as immoral or unfair. Rather, it is usually treated as the very definition of morality. The same could be said of *fanompoana* in the late nineteenth century: one examines the sources in vain for any suggestion that commoners felt that it was in principle wrong that they should have to carry things for the Queen. In the Malagasy literature that has come down to us, whether government documents, historical accounts, or texts like *Fomba Gasy*, such responsibilities are simply assumed. As in so many monarchies,

one does find complaints about "evil councilors," a tendency among the oppressed to interpret any particularly oppressive royal decision as the product
of some coterie of selfish politicians who don't really reflect the royal will.
But, as foreign observers invariably noted, loyalty to the sovereign herself
was unquestioned.[34] Presumably, this was true even when Ranavalona I was
sweeping up thousands of bearers for her pleasure tours and leaving a trail of
corpses behind her. When common people did try to make claims against
royal power, they did so using a language that assumed its legitimacy: for
example, by representing themselves as "nursemaids of the king."[35] Or, like
the Ramanenjana (or contemporary spirit mediums), they wielded images of
absolute subservience to make covert claims to higher authority.

If one were to base oneself exclusively on nineteenth-century sources,
it would be hard to escape the conclusion that hierarchy was universally
assumed to be a natural and inevitable principle of all human life, deeply
embedded in the family, the basis of all social life in the kingdom, and that
it would never have occurred to anyone to challenge this.[36] But, if so, we
are left with something of an historical puzzle. Because all of this changed
remarkably quickly following the French conquest in 1895, and the abolition of slavery and dismantling of the monarchy in 1896. Almost immediately, one begins to see signs the kind of moral discourse so prevalent across
rural Imerina today: one in which kings and queens are almost invariably
represented as oppressors who treated their subjects like slaves and whose
descendants have since been punished by sterility and death (Graeber 2007).
Where did this sort of rhetoric come from if such ideas had been literally
unthinkable a mere generation before? One could argue, of course, that they
were introduced by the French themselves: point to the newfound importance of Christianity as a focus of nationalist resistance, or of Western egalitarian ideals picked up from the French educational system. But this would
be a very difficult case to make. First of all, one would have to explain how
a set of alien concepts managed to so completely supplant traditional ideas
that no one now even remembers what those traditional ideas were. Even
more puzzlingly, one would have to explain why it is that the well-educated,
devoutly Christian, Francophile elites of the capital and larger towns remain
to this day the only significant group of people in Imerina who do *not* subscribe to this new, egalitarian view, but instead tend to insist that ancient
Malagasy kings and queens were noble and just, and ancient Malagasy forms
of hierarchy, intrinsically legitimate. Meanwhile, the descendants of the oppressed, with the least access to foreign Enlightenment ideas, have come to
see that very elite as the heirs of their former royal oppressors.

Now, there is one obvious explanation. Perhaps our sources—which
after all mostly consist of missionary reports, government documents, and

official rhetoric of one sort or another—are not giving us the full picture. James Scott (1992) has argued that, at least in cases of very clear-cut oppression—slaves, untouchables, serfs, that sort of thing—this will always, necessarily, be the case. Part of what it means to have a situation of extreme inequality, he argues, is that there will always be an official ideology which claims that this situation is just and reasonable—an ideology that no one really believes, neither those on top nor those on the bottom, but that everyone feels obliged to go along with in public. Plantation slaves do not really feel that their masters take a paternal interest in their well-being (any more than masters really do); rather, it is part of the nature of any masters' power—its first line of defense, one might even say—to insist that slaves play along with the pretense in their masters' presence. The result is that, in such situations, people act almost exactly as they would if they were conspiring to falsify the record for future historians, since it is, of course, the official events and opinions, and not what people are saying offstage (what Scott calls the "hidden transcript") that makes it into the kind of documents likely to come down to historians.

Scott is writing primarily about situations where the hierarchical lines are clearly drawn: where there are two clearly defined groups, one obviously on top and the other clearly subordinate. Still, he also suggests that, even in more complicated situations, where the lines are blurrier, something like this will tend to occur. This is precisely what appears to have happened in Imerina. Hence, Pier Larson, an historian who has done a thorough survey of sources on popular attitudes in eighteenth- and early-nineteenth-century Imerina, reports to have found no evidence for explicitly egalitarian sentiments in existing texts. "Social equality was neither a reality nor a cultural ideal in central Madagascar," he concludes, "hierarchy was a fundamental principle of human interaction," never questioned in itself (2000: 89).[37] In fact, Scott would argue this is precisely what one would normally expect.

On the other hand, it does seems rather unsatisfying just to insist that people must have been whispering egalitarian sentiments to one another, because people always do. It seems reasonable to assume that if egalitarian principles were present, they must have manifested themselves in some way that left traces of some sort or another. In fact, if one examines the record carefully, I think principles of equality can be detected—often, perhaps especially, inside some of the most ardent assertions of hierarchy themselves. At times, it is true, Merina kings emphasized that they were guardians of property and maintained the ranks and divisions of the kingdom; at others, though, they emphasized that, as Andrianampoinimerina is said to have put it, "you should all be equal because you are all equally my subjects." The absolute gulf between ruler and ruled made internal distinctions between subjects irrelevant in comparison, even perhaps a bit subversive. Similarly, in royal labor projects: here one can turn for evidence to some of the very texts in which foreign observers emphasize absolute loyalty of subjects to the Queen. Where many early Malagasy sources emphasized how ranks and divisions are worked out through the allocation of different sorts of royal labor, foreign observers were often struck by how, when actually performing personal service to the Queen, all such status distinctions would simply be thrown aside:

> When there happens to be special work requiring to be done in connec-
> tion with the royal courtyards, such as rebuilding or extending the lofty
> retaining walls, all ranks of the people, from the highest to the lowest,
> take a pride in doing with their hands some of the actual labour. Under
> the eye of their Queen, who sits on a raised seat looking on, the highest
> officers are seen with their *lambas* [mantles] girded round their loins,
> working harder than their slaves, carrying stone, digging or ramming
> earth, and doing whatever manual labour may be required. Much of
> the same kind of feeling exists in clearing the ground for the erection of
> their chapels, when every one—male and female, *Andrians* and slaves,
> officers and soldiers—will all labour with the greatest zeal; some dig-
> ging, others bringing stone, others laying bricks, while their wives will
> mix the mortar and fetch the water required for the work (Sibree 1880:
> 189–90).

One needs to be careful with texts like this. It's hard to know how much the author really understood of what was going on. For instance, the text implies (but doesn't quite say) that free people and slaves worked together on royal projects. This could not have been true. Slaves were strictly forbidden to work on royal projects, and any slave who could prove in court that he had could win his freedom. But the rest seems accurate enough. And masters and slaves did indeed work side by side in building Protestant churches; a perfect example of how the logic of existing practices made ordinary Merina disposed to be receptive to the Christian message that at least in religious contexts (and by implication, potentially, other ones) everyone was equal before the Lord.[38]

One can see this as an example of a something inherent in the nature of hierarchy, whose logic always seems to create images of equality as a kind of side-effect (Graeber 1997). Or one can see it as an example of a particularly Malagasy variation on this logic, whereby one creates freedom and equality by effecting common subordination to some distant, absolute Power which, in any practical sense, does not really exist (Althabe 1969; Graeber 2007).[39]

Both would, I think, be true. What I want to draw attention to here, though, is the way that principles like hierarchy and equality are always available to people as ideas because they are always immanent in forms of practice. They tend to become thoroughly entangled in one another as a result. It is only right and according to ancestral custom that a ten-year-old girl should carry her fourteen-year-old sister's basket; but obviously, only within reason. No one would want a child to be so burdened as to experience real pain, risk serious injury, or, for that matter, to stumble along with such difficulty that it takes everyone forever to get home. At some point, the hierarchical principle will always come up against others: that adults are responsible for the welfare of children, or that, among people performing a common task, each can only be expected to contribute according to their capacity to contribute, and each ought to be given the resources which make it easiest for them to do so. At least, within the work process itself, people practice a form of unreflective, pragmatic communism—"from each according to their abilities, to each according to their needs." As the quote above indicates, even *fanompoana* seems to have had a tendency to slip into this sort of equalizing logic outside of certain highly ritualized contexts (foundations, royal funerals) where there were particular issues of status to be worked out (who gets to put up the central pillar? who gets to provide the mats?). There was a common task to perform, it was in the interest of all to perform it well, therefore, each took on tasks according to their abilities. All forms of hierarchy, I would venture, rest on egalitarian, even communistic, practices whose logic can always be invoked to subvert them, since it is the basis of so much everyday morality. This is, I suspect, the reason for the strange ambivalence of the proverb with which we began: "If you have a younger sibling, then you'll have no problems with carrying, if you have an older one, then you'll have no problems with speech." Even the most basic atom of hierarchy has to be represented as somehow equal and reciprocal, in order to seem fair.[40]

Terms of Conversation

So what is oppression, then? In the Malagasy context, it appears to be the point where an experience of subordination (which here, as elsewhere, tends to be expressed by being set underneath something or someone) clashes against a broad and not even necessarily all that clearly articulated sense of fairness, equality, and justice. For each individual, this probably calls up all sorts of deeply internalized childhood memories—for instance, the indignation which any child would feel upon discovering that, where once it seemed to amuse adults when they refused to perform ordinary tasks, and they would be treated as conquering heroes when they did deign to do them,

suddenly they were being handed the most onerous tasks and actually being expected to do them, not because their youth made them particularly
special, but, rather, because it suddenly made them the bottom of the heap.
Such indignant memories would, for any Malagasy adult, be inextricably
bound up with memories of carrying heavy burdens on one's shoulders or
one's head. The underlying structure of ideas about speaking and carrying
might have been so deeply embedded that it tended to shape even dream-
like, unconscious states (as we've seen in the case of mediums above). For
any individual, oppression was a potentially universal abstract principle, a
particularly Malagasy set of cultural practices, and a unique collection of
very personal memories—all at the same time.

The interesting thing is that this richness of sensuous experience does
not make such concepts incommunicable across cultures—any more than
the fact that any two Malagasy are drawing on a different set of personal
experiences when they talk about oppression makes it impossible for them
to really understand each other. If anything, I am convinced the opposite is
the case. This very richness is a source of endless creativity that ultimately
is an essential part of what makes it possible for us to speak across apparent
cultural boundaries to begin with.

Perhaps the original inspiration for this paper was a conversation I had,
in English, with a university student from Antananarivo, quite soon after
I'd arrived. I was still living in the capital, learning the language, beginning to get a sense of what was in the archives. I spent a lot of time sitting
in cafés and restaurants, thinking about posture, gesture, the movement of
bodies in space. Most anthropologists spend a lot of time thinking about
such matters, in that very early stage, when they can't really talk to anyone
and most of time have no idea what the people around them actually think
is going on. Most also know it's a good idea to jot down the thoughts one
has at that early stage because one is likely to notice things that effectively
vanish from consciousness soon after. I became obsessed with the politics of
the gaze: specifically, at who dares to look freely about in public places. On a
couple occasions, when I myself felt entirely constrained and inhibited by the
surety of challenging counter-gazes, I remember reflecting that this must be
something like what most of the planet's women live with constantly in public, and that the effect it produces—of constant contraction inwards, never
knowing quite where to fix your eyes, or searching for safe empty places
nearby, living in a claustrophobic bottle of oneself—could only have a devastating effect on one's sense of investment in one's surroundings, one's way
of occupying space. I had recently been reading Elaine Scarry's book *The
Body in Pain* (1985), so I began reflecting on the analogy between this and
pain and physical discomfort which Scarry describes as a process of destroy-

ing worlds, as something that collapses that very sense of investment in the surrounding world with its networks of meaning and objects, that sucks the meaning away, compressing it into the minimal, circumscribed space of the hurting body. My notebooks were full of speculation about how the play of surrounding eyes, feelings of pain or painlessness, objective potentials for action or the threat of violence, all contribute to (and also flow out of) one's immediate physical bearing, carriage, gestures, how one holds one's arms and legs, tendencies to curl up or splay oneself out, speaking loudly or not at all, and so on.

The problem was that I soon realized this had almost nothing to do with how Malagasy women normally lived or behaved. This became apparent the moment one moved, as I soon did, away from institutions dominated by foreigners. If anything, the situation seemed the reverse of what I was used to. Before long, I was remarking to a friend—a woman named Lala who was a student at the university at Ankatso—how remarkable it was that in terms of ordinary body language, it was often women who seemed more apt to make the bold, expansive gesture, who strode with greater confidence in public. Men, even many young men, more often seemed to contract in on themselves in public, to often seem shy and self-contained. Why was that? (I was expressing myself here as much by imitating postures as by actual words.)

"Well," Lala said, "that's because they are pressed down by their culture," accompanying the words by a gesture: her hand pressing steadily downward, as if on something invisible in front of her. The interesting thing is: idioms of oppression were not, generally speaking, used when speaking about gender, and certainly not about men. But, even between two people who were just learning to speak to each other, playing around with such imagery in original ways seemed the obvious way to begin a conversation.

Over time, with much more observation after many more conversations, my thoughts on gender in the Malagasy highlands evolved and crystallized. Eventually they turned into an essay (Graeber 1996). As it turned out, Lala's comment didn't prove all that relevant. Still, the gesture stuck with me. It seemed somehow important. This was probably the reason I paid attention later when I started hearing different uses of the term *tsindriana*.

One might call that first, basic level—before words—the level of phenomenology. Often, the most profound cultural insights are achieved by intentionally bringing things down to this sort of degree zero, and then working back up again. This was in fact precisely what Scarry was trying to do in *The Body in Pain*, a book which draws richly not just on the phenomenological tradition but on the half-forgotten insights of Existentialism. As such, it did prove useful after all. Scarry begins by proposing an opposition between pain and language. Physical pain, if sufficiently intense, destroys the very possibility of language; language being the most important way in which the self embeds and invests itself in the surrounding world. Hence suffering makes one collapse into oneself. In this sense, having another person bearing your burdens, then capturing their right to speech, could indeed be seen as the most obvious way to expand into larger worlds at their expense. But I ended up using Scarry's work not just to understand Malagasy concepts, but to bounce off them—in fact, to bounce each off the other in a kind of conceptual dialogue. The second half of the book (1985: 159–326) is specifically concerned with production, or as she puts it, "material making," as a kind of meeting point between language and pain.[41] Labor she argues is not experienced as inherently painful, as a form of oppression, unless it's divorced from a sense of agency, of making something. This is true, but the three-part division between words, making, and carrying—the latter emblematic of all sorts of other forms of support and maintenance work, classic forms of women's or menial work—seemed a useful corrective. It reminds us how much our habits of thought have, at least since the time of Marx, made the work of the craftsman or factory worker emblematic of labor in general; and how that focus itself tends to relegate most forms of real work to the shadows.

In fact, none of the Malagasy conceptions I've discussed, however apparently exotic, emerge from an entirely alien conceptual universe. This is why they have the potential to tell us something. To describe kings as children seems bizarre, but only until one really thinks about it. Heads of state in general do tend to be self-important, petulant beings, surrounded at every moment by people taking care of their physical necessities and reminding them how to act. We consider Hegel a great philosopher in part for having made a point that, for most Malagasy, seems to be a matter of simple common sense.

A Plea for Dialogic Relativism

One could even argue that comparisons like this have always been what anthropology is really all about. Or should be: at its best, anthropology is the beginning of a conversation. It is premised on the assumption such a conversation is possible, even if it is difficult to know precisely why. Even if, in fact, when anthropologists wax theoretical, they often seem determined to deny it is possible.

Here, I can finally return to question of relativism. The reason why anthropologists are often so reluctant to make cross-cultural generalizations, it seems to me, is because, when they do look for common terms, they tend to look on precisely the wrong level.[42] They invariably look for forms of constituted authority. If looking for some sort of moral universal, they assume this would mean principles present in all known legal systems; if they are asked to search for aesthetic universals, they look for any quality that might be seen as present in every object formally recognized as "art" (or whatever they decide is the closest local equivalent). The inevitable conclusion, then, is that such universals do not exist.[43] What I am suggesting instead is that it would be better in such cases to look at common ways of arguing about morality, or common ways of thinking and talking about aesthetic pleasure, which seem far more similar cross-culturally than any particular conclusions that such conversations may come to (let alone conclusions that are then given some kind of authoritative stamp). This would be the way to try to get a sense of the common underlying tendencies and capacities—the generative mechanisms if you will. These become easiest to see, perhaps, precisely when someone is challenging what is locally considered received authority or received wisdom.

My main point here is perfectly obvious, even if it is a point to which classical relativists have seemed oddly blind. Questions of cultural difference only become relevant when there's already some sort of conversation going on. There is no reason to ask oneself how and whether one is to sit in judgment on another person's cultural universe unless you have some idea what that universe is; and that means people are, to some degree at least, already communicating.

The fact that people are communicating, in turn, presumes two things. First of all it presumes that there is some ground of similarity between them that makes communication possible. All human languages, for example, seem to have the equivalent of nouns and verbs, subjects and objects, and so on. This is why any Quechua-speaker is capable, if she really puts her mind to it, of learning Swedish and any Swedish-speaker can learn Quechua, but no one, even experts armed with powerful computers, have figured out how to communicate with dolphins or killer whales. This is why some (e.g., Sperber 1985) have remarked that anthropology, in embracing extreme forms of relativism—i.e., trying to deny that all human languages really do have meaningful common features—sometimes seems as if it wishes to deny the possibility of its own existence.

The second point is that the conversation has to take place within some larger social and political context, that this context is not simply a product of the conversation, but, rather, plays a substantial role in shaping what people feel they have to talk about. Cultural relativism in the form we're most familiar—what I've been calling "classical relativism"—took shape within a very particular political context. Its heyday was the mid-twentieth century, a time when anthropology was considered politically relevant largely insofar as it could contribute to describing structures of legitimate authority within

Indian reservations, colonial systems of indirect rule, or newly independent nations within an inter-state system still firmly controlled by the former colonial powers. In other words it was all about helping bureaucrats identify legitimate authorities. "Just talk to the chief," one old teacher of mine reports he was told by his advisor in the 1950s, "he's the only one who really knows anything anyway." It is not surprising, then, that it took the form that it did: even if it was a form that, if taken to its logical extreme, could only lead to a logic of apartheid.

Things have changed, but they probably haven't changed as much as we like to think. An anthropologist in 1925, consulting with the British government to help clarify tribal divisions in the Anglo-Egyptian Sudan, was not doing anything so very different from an anthropologist today, consulting with the United Nations or the World Bank to determine which Nepali ethnic groups should be granted "indigenous" status. Both face very similar moral conundrums. There is no reason to believe this will entirely change any time soon. As long as there are powerful international bureaucracies, they will be asking anthropologists to help them identify who to recognize as legitimate local authorities, at least in those areas they find the most marginal and confusing. Still, there were always other conversations going on and, today, it is at least possible to suggest that these are no longer the most important ones. Increases in mobility and indications of the possible beginning of a major breakdown of traditional power relations (East-West, North-South) make it possible to conceive an anthropology that would be, first and foremost, a mutual conversation—between everyone, equally—about the nature of authority itself.[44] If anthropology is to emerge as a political force of liberation, rather than simply damage control, this is what it must, ultimately, become.

This is not to argue that all forms of authority are illegitimate. If that were so, there would be nothing to discuss. By the same token, neither would such a broader conversation mean a general effacing of boundaries and eradication of difference. Mutual relations—even the most intimate—always involve the recognition of boundaries and acknowledgement of difference: this is, for example, what we are generally referring to when we speak of "dignity" or "respect." Far from suggesting we abandon relativism, then, I am saying that we need to expand our notion of what relativism is, to see it as an aspect of any fundamentally healthy human relationship, whether individual or collective, whether distant or close. At its most minimal, the practice of relativism is just a matter of mutual respect.

One might refer to this as "dialogic relativism"—a mutual recognition of, and respect for, difference founded on the recognition of an even more fundamental similarity (hence, equality) that makes such recognition possible. It could only rest on a commitment to carry on the conversation in a way that never pushes aside uncomfortable questions—such as, for instance, who gets to speak, and who has to do the heavy lifting?—but that also proceeds on the assumption that no single tradition has a monopoly on insight on such issues. If our exploration of the term "oppression" shows anything, I think, it is how rich, and how heterogeneous, the material from which we could thus patch together a shared sense of humanity really is.

Endnotes

1   Pretty much all major European languages have a term paralleling the English "to oppress." A fairly superficial examination of dictionaries, and consultations with a few fluent or native speakers, and leaving out those languages using characters or diacritics too difficult to reproduce (such as say Thai or Arabic), adds Albanian (*studjoj rëndshëm, shtyp*), Basque (*zapalketa*), Biblical Hebrew (*tahan*, lit. "to grind down, to oppress"), Chinese (*yà min*), Coptic (*tmtm, xa0x0*), Finnish (*ahdistaa*), Ganda (*zitoowererwa*), Gurarani (*jopy*), Hawaiian (*kaumaha, koikoi*), Hittite (*siyyaizzi, siyezzi, siyait*), Japanese (*osaetsukeru, yokuatsu-sur*), Malay-Indonesian (*tekan, mameras, tindas, tindih*), Mongolian (*darulal(ta)/daruldug-a*), Nepali (*thichnu*), Nuer (*mieet*), Paiwan (*q/m/ezetj*), Persian (*sarkoob*, lit. "head pressed down"), Quechua (*ñitiy*), Sanskrit (*avapídita*), Shona (*udzvinyiriri*), Somali (*cadaadid*), Tamil (*nerukku/nerukkam*, and other constructions from the root *neri*, also Dravidian *arepuni, arepini, areyuni, arevun*, "to grind down or oppress"), Tswana (*patikèga*), Turkish (*baski, ezmek*), Tuscarora (*turiye*), Vietnamese (*dé nãng, su dàn áp*), and Zulu (*cindezela*). The apparent exceptions are interesting in themselves: Native North American and Australian languages, for example, do not seem generally to have terms glossed "oppression" of any sort. Nor do most spoken by traditionally stateless peoples. African languages are a mix: in Africa words translated "oppression" in dictionaries appear about equally likely to come from terms for injustice or humiliation than "pressure downwards."

2   I am, of course, hardly the first to discuss these dilemmas. For some analogous reflections from a feminist perspective, see Hodgson 1999 and Jackson 1995. Others have made similar points regarding postmodern forms of relativism: so, Maschia-Lees, Sharpe, and Cohen (1989: 27) cite Nancy Cott's remark that a feminist approach, motivated by a political project to oppose the oppression of women, is difficult to maintain if one deconstructs the very category of "oppression"—or even "women."

3   This also raises the perhaps even more thorny problem of who "we" are, but I will leave this to be addressed, at least briefly, in the essay "There Never Was a West," below.

4   It follows that it might be possible to argue the Nuer lack any equivalent to our institutions of religion or the family, but it would not be possible to say they lack any institutional conception of authority, because otherwise, "the Nuer" would not exist.

5   I note the role of gender in all this is ambiguous: while, as I say, in most matters of seniority between siblings, gender should not really weigh in at all, in reality it almost always does. In this case, elder sisters may well have their younger brothers carry things for them, but in formal occasions at least they would be unlikely to speak for them, at least unless they happened to be very good speakers, or very assertive, and no senior male were available.

6   It's a term, then, that could be used either for sending someone to be one's spokesman, or to send someone to carry one's things. In the nineteenth century, for instance, royal representatives were always referred to as the King's *iraka*, here meaning "spokesmen," who carried their words. Sometimes these were literally messengers, but the same term was used for those delegated to make decisions in the King's name.

     It was also the only real way in the language of the time in which people freely talked about relations of command, of ordering people around. The word *baiko*, which literally means "command," existed at the time but mainly referred to military commands; since the latter were largely given in foreign languages, it meant "foreign words" by extension.

7   As if to underline the point, Sibree continues the above-quoted passage by adding: "There is a great respect paid to seniority among the Malagasy; so that if two slaves who are brothers are going on a journey, any burden must be carried by the younger one, so far at least as his strength will allow" (ibid., 183). The obvious assumption is that, if two brothers who are *not* slaves go on a journey, there would be no question of either having to carry anything.

8   An umbrella: an imported luxury, identified with Western styles of comportment, is the only exception.

9   The notion of "emblematic labor" might be compared to Barth's idea of ethnic "diacritics" (1969), where one or two apparently minor features can become the reference to distinguish otherwise overlapping or similar social groups. The situation in eighteenth-century Imerina rather recalls Hocart's definition of caste (1968, 1970: 102–127; Quigley 1993), where each caste's nature is determined by the labor they do for the king. The Merina system is sometimes described in fact as a "caste" system (see Bloch 1977).

10   One group of former *andriana*, of somewhat ambiguous status, did have the special privilege of providing one silk shroud on such occasions. Another group of similar ambiguous status had the privilege of actually "carrying" the royal body to be placed in the tomb—the most exalted form of carrying, but still one not

relegated to a group considered royal kin. These are the closest one has to exceptions.

11   Oral traditions I gathered around Arivonimamo insisted the Andrianamboninolona, the *andriana* order ranked immediately above them, were famous as blacksmiths.

12   One might hazard the following formulation: the production of objects and words are the domain of *andriana*; carrying and construction that of the *hova*; to the *Mainty Enin-Dreny,* in their capacity as royal warriors, is relegated the sphere of destruction.

13   Sources sometimes substitute "digging red earth" (*mihady tanimena*), in an obvious allusion to the task of "digging red earth" for royal tombs, mentioned above.

14   This follows the same order as the list given by Standing (1887: 358), though I left out Standing's fifth category (building and maintaining roads and bridges) since it does not appear in any Malagasy-language account. For evocations of the standard list in nineteenth-century legal cases, see National Archives IIICC 365 f3: 111–112; IIICC37 f2 (Ambohitrimanjaka 1893). For standard lists of exemptions in the *Tantara ny Andriana*, a collection of Malagasy histories, see Callet 1908: 411 (Andriamamilaza), and 545 (Antehiroka). See also, entries in the *Firaketana* (an early twentieth-century Malagasy encyclopedia—Ravelojaona, Randzavola, Rajaona 1937) for Ambohibato, Ambohimalaza, Ambohimirimo, Andriana, and Antsahadinta.

15   They were referred to in royal documents as *alinjinera*, or "engineers."

16   Traditionally these things are gendered: women carry objects on the head or hips; men on the back or shoulders.

17   In fact, as I have argued at length elsewhere (Graeber 1995), these ceremonies ultimately have the effect of infantilizing the ancestors and treating them, in turn, like small children. I should also note that my discussion of mutual obligations of "carrying" owe most of their insight to discussions of the subject with Jennifer Cole, whose work with the Betsimisaraka people of Ambodiharina brought out these issues much more clearly than my own.

18   Lambek's book *The Weight of the Past* (2002) contains a detailed analysis of parallel idioms in a rather different social and political context among the Sakalava of Madagascar's west coast.

19   Not that the more familiar sort of symbolism was entirely absent (see Bloch 1986). A common expression was "the king is father to the people but the people are both father and mother to the king."

20   Domenichini argues that such groups had a *ziva* or "joking relation" with the crown. See Hebert 1958.

21   In the royal case, even baggage being carried for the Queen in a sense participated in the Queen's presence or anyway esteem. Royal carriers, even those carrying jars of water to the palace, were proceeded by a man bearing a spear warning all on the

roads before it to make way, step to the side, and remove their hats as a gesture of respect just as they would if the Queen herself were passing.

22 Literally they did not "remember themselves" (*tsy mahatsiaro tena*).

23 This was true whether one was "carried" by dead kings, evil ghosts, or the power of one's own magic—as were many women who became possessed by their love magic and ended up running around as witches during the night. Generally speaking, the term *tsindriana* was applied to forces that were essentially benevolent or at least neutral in nature; *entina* was used almost exclusively for forces that were intrinsically dangerous or malevolent in nature

The reluctance to speak of being "carried" by, say, ancestors or royal spirits seems to derive from a feeling (which I have described at length elsewhere) that to entirely efface or overwhelm the agency of another person, to replace it with one's own, is a morally dubious way of exercising power.

24 R: *Dia avy hatrany, dia marary andoha tampoka ilay olona, dia very saina avy eo izy. Dia miteniteny foana, toa sahala amin'ny misy olona faharoa ao aminy.*
Ka misy zavatra mampahatahotra ny marary. Voa manakenda azy. Voa mampijaly azy. Sahala amin'ny miady ambiby masiaka iray izy, sahala amin'ny bibilava iray. Arakaraky ny fiseho ilay fanahy ratsy, izay atao hoe, olona faharoa ao aminy.
C: *Hitan'ny maso ve izany?*
R: *Hitan'ny masony izany. Hitan'ilay olona. Nohitany ilay bibilava. Niady amin'ireo heny, izay manimba azy, manakenda azy.*

25 R: *Tsy ny tompon'ny tena intsony ilay olona voalohany, fa ny olona faharoa no manjaka.*
DG: *Fa ny olona faharoa dia...*
R: *Io no adaladala, io no miteniteny foana, io no mandrovitra akanjo...*
DG: *Fa tena misy olona faharoa sa misy, misy...*
R: *Fanahy ratsy.*
DG: *Fanahin'ny olona maty ve?*
R: *Fanahin'ny maty io, ka mampahatahotra azy. Miseho toy bibilava, miseho toy olona masiaka, miseho toy ny angatra...*
C: *Izay no mampatanjaka azy io?*
R: *Izay no mampatanjaka azy io—fa ankizivavy iray voan'ny Ambalavelona no manana ny herin'ny lehilahy dimy. Manana hery manokana.*

26 There is surprisingly little written about Zanadrano in the contemporary ethnographic literature on the highlands: nothing really in English, very little in French, and that largely about shrines and pilgrimage sites rather than ordinary curing practice: e.g., Cabanes 1972; Radimilahy, Andriamampianina, Blanchy, Rakotoarisoa & Razafimahazo 2006.

27 Often there is a whole network of *ody* to be dealt with: the "mother *ody*" may be buried in the fields or yard, with various "children" planted around the house itself.

And, often, also *sisika*—little bits of wood, bone, tooth, or what-have-you—buried in the patient herself, underneath the skin.

28 One medium for instance would pray, gazing into a mirror placed beside a book and candle in his cabinet, waiting for the spirit to come over him. His wife explained that, as he stared, the face of the *andriana* would gradually replace his own. When his own features had been entirely effaced, he would be entirely possessed (*tsindriana*) and begin to speak. Similarly, in *ambalavelona*, victims often were terrified of mirrors, seeing monsters and snakes in them instead of their own image.

Several mediums were eager to hear my tape-recordings of their sessions, claiming they had never had an opportunity to hear what their spirits sounded like.

29 Actually "holy" is not a very good translation for *masina* in most contexts but it will serve for present purposes. For the distinction of *masina* and *mahery*, see Bloch 1986a.

30 Often, too, there is a final ceremony called the *famoizina* or *faditra*, in which some object representing the condition is finally cast away or buried, so that it cannot return.

31 Actually, mediums tend to be reluctant to actually apply the term *entina*, "carried," to any basically benevolent spirit; but the description is otherwise the same.

32 And this is rather unlike better known forms of possession practiced elsewhere in Madagascar, such as *tromba*.

33 And are in fact seen as such by the descendants of their former owners: see Graeber 2007.

34 At least in public. Of course Raombana, the Queen's personal secretary, expressed nothing but hatred for her in his elaborate history from which the earlier quote about the Ranavalona's pleasure expeditions was actually taken. But his history was written in English so no one at court could read it. So it's not as if such a position was unimaginable.

35 Though here it is useful to consult Scott's *Domination and the Arts of Resistance* (1992) on how often the cult of the king and denunciation of "evil councilors" is simply the most obvious practical strategy for peasant farmers to take, and may bear no real relation to what people were likely to say to, for instance, their drinking friends.

36 Even at the birth of twins, it must be noted who emerged from the womb first to establish who is *zoky* and who is *zandry*. For there not to be rank between siblings is inconceivable.

37 Larson not only finds no evidence for a "hidden transcript" that flat out rejected the basic terms of royal ideology (2000: 256–57), he insists no such hidden transcript existed. With all due respect for Larson's exemplary scholarship, I don't understand on what basis anyone could claim to know for certain what Malagasy peasants were *not* saying behind closed doors.

38 There is a similar egalitarian message in mortuary ritual. At *famadihana*, every-one is supposed to dress equally modestly, and if possible, more or less the same. Distinctions are to be effaced in order to emphasize equality in common descent. During the nineteenth century, mortuary ritual focused on the collective dragging of granite stones, much like the dragging of trees for royal houses, to construct tombs.

39 One must bear in mind that, during most of this period, the Queen was in fact a figurehead.

40 For a somewhat analogous argument, see Bloch's excellent "Hierarchy and Equality in Merina Kinship" (1986b).

41 Or to be more accurate, between pain and the imagination. Pain, she argues, is sensation without an object; imagination, object without sensation.

42 Or really, to own up to doing so. After all, no one developing a theory of ritual writes as if ritual is a phenomenon that exists only in Africa and parts of Eurasia, but not in, say, South America. Analytical terms are always universal. As anthro-pologists discovered in the 1970s when they began deconstructing away every fa-miliar term from "marriage" to "religion," once you have done so, you have very little left to talk about, except perhaps some abstract theories of structures of the mind—which then turned out to be ridiculously simplistic.

43 I have been referring to "cultural relativism" in a broad sense. In fact, there are various kinds and degrees of such relativism. Mark Whitaker (1996) distinguishes three: (1) conventional cultural relativism, which holds that any human action can only be understood in its cultural context; (2) epistemological (or cognitive) relativism, which holds that different systems of knowledge are fundamentally in-commensurable; and (3) ethical relativism, which insists that cross-cultural judg-ments are therefore impossible. Each clearly builds on the others. When I speak of "classical relativism" I am really speaking of the rather haphazard mix of the three that seems to emerge when anthropologists find themselves arguing with those they consider universalists.

44 Since scholars have a tendency to read sentences like that in strangely reductionist ways, allow me underline: I said "first and foremost" about authority. Not "only." Obviously it should be about everything else as well.

Bibliography

Althabe, Gerard
1969 *Oppression et libération dans l'imaginaire: les communautés villageoises de la côte orientale de Madagascar.* Paris: Maspero.

Barth, Frederick
1969 *Ethnic Groups and Boundaries: The Social Organization of Culture Difference.* Bergen: Universitetsforlaget.

Berg, Gerald
1979 "Royal Authority and the Protector System in Nineteenth Century Imerina." In *Madagascar in History: Essays from the 1970s* (R. Kent, ed.) Albany: The Foundation for Malagasy Studies.

Bloch, Maurice
1971 *Placing the Dead: Tombs, Ancestral Villages, and Kinship Organization in Madagascar.* London: Seminar Press.
1977 "The Disconnection between Power and Rank as a Process: An Outline of the Development of Kingdoms in Central Madagascar." *European Journal of Sociology* vol. 18: 303–330.
1986a *From Blessing to Violence: History and Ideology in the Circumcision Ritual of the Merina of Madagascar.* Cambridge: Cambridge University Press.
1986b "Hierarchy and Equality in Merina Kinship." In *Madagascar: Society and History* (C.P. Kottak, J.-A. Rakotoarisoa, A. Southall and P. Vérin, eds.) Durham: Carolina Academic Press.
1989 "The Ritual of the Royal Bath in Madagascar: The Dissolution of Death, Birth, and Fertility into Authority." In *Ritual, History and Power: Selected Papers in Anthropology.* London: Athlone Press.

Cabanes, Robert
1972 "Cultes des possession dans la plaine de Tananarive." *Cahiers du Centre d'Étude des Coutumes* 9: 33–66.

Callet, R.P.
1908 *Tantara ny Andriana eto Madagascar.* 2 vols. Tananarive: Académie Malgache.

Camboué, R.P.
1909 "Les Dix Premiers Ans de l'enfance chez le Malgaches. Circoncision, nom, éducation." *Anthropos* IV: 375–386.

Clark, Henry
1896 "The Zanak'Antitra Tribe: Its Origins and Peculiarities." *Antananarivo Annual and Malagasy Magazine* 16: 450–456.

Cole, Jennifer
2001 *Forget Colonialism? Sacrifice and the Art of Memory in Madagascar.* Berkeley: University of California Press.

Cousins, William E.
1963 *Fomba Gasy.* (H. Randzavola, ed.). Tananarive: Imarivolanitra.

Davidson, A.
1889 "The Ramanenjana or Dancing Mania of Madagascar." *The Antananarivo Annual and Madagascar Magazine* 13 (1889); Reprint vol. IV/1: 19–27.

Dominichini, Jean-Pierre
1977 *Les Dieux au Service des Rois: Histoire des Palladium d'Emyrne.* Paris: Karthala.

Domenichini, Jean-Pierre, and Bakoly Domenichini-Ramiaramanana
1980 "Regards croisés sur les grands Sycomores, ou l'armée noire des anciens princes d'Imerina." *Asie du Sud Est et Monde Insulindien* XI (1–4): 55–95.
1982 "Aspects de l'esclavage sous la monarchie merina." *Omaly sy Anio* 15: 53–98.

Domenichini-Ramiaramanana, Bakoly
1983 *Du ohabolana au hainteny: langue, littérature et politique à Madagascar.* Paris: Karthala.

Ellis, William
1838   *History of Madagascar*. 2 vols. London: Fisher & Son.

Firaketana, see Ravelojaona, Randzavola, Rajaona

Graeber, David
1995   "Dancing with Corpses Reconsidered: an Interpretation of Famadihana in Arivonimamo, (Madagascar)." *American Ethnologist* 22 (2): 258–278.
1996   "Love Magic and Political Morality in Central Madagascar, 1875–1990." *Gender and History* 8 (3): 416–439.
1997   "Manners, Deference and Private Property." *Comparative Studies in Society and History* 39 (4): 694–728.
2007   *Lost People: Magic and the Legacy of Slavery in Madagascar*. Bloomington: Indiana University Press.

Haile, John
1893   "Malagasy Village Life: Pen and Ink Sketches of the People of Western Imerina." *Antananarivo Annual and Malagasy Magazine* 18: 1–20.

Hébert, Jean-Claude
1958   "La parenté à plaisanterie à Madagascar." *Bulletin de l'Académie Malgache*, mars 1958 (142): 175–217; avril 1958 (143): 267–303.

Hocart, A. M.
1968   *Caste, a Comparative Study*. New York: Russell & Russell.
1970   *Kings and Councillors: An Essay in the Comparative Anatomy of Human Society*. Chicago: University of Chicago Press.

Hodgson, Dorothy
1999   "Critical Interventions." *Identities* 6 (2–3): 201–224.

Houlder, J.A.
1915   *Ohabolana, or, Malagasy proverbs: illustrating the wit and wisdom of the Hova of Madagascar*. Faravohitra: Friends' Foreign Missionary Association.

Jackson, Jean
1995   "Culture, Genuine and Spurious: The Politics of Indianness in Vaupes, Columbia." *American Anthropologist* 22(1): 3–27.

Jully, Antony
1899   "Croyances et pratiques superstitieuses chez les Merinas ou Hoves" *Revue de Madagascar* tome 1 (October 1899): 311–328.

Lambek, Michael
2002   *The Weight of the Past: Living with History in Mahajanga, Madagascar*. New York: Palgrave Macmillan.

Larson, Pier
2000   *History and Memory in the Age of Enslavement: Becoming Merina in Highland Madagascar, 1770–1822* (Social History of Africa). Portsmouth: Heinemann.

Maschia-Lees, Frances, Patricia Sharpe, Colleen Ballerino Cohen
1989   "The Postmodernist Turn in Anthropology: Cautions from a Feminist Perspective." *Signs* 15 (1): 7–33.

Mayeur, Nicolas
1913   "Voyage au pays d'Ancove, outremente dite des hovas (1777)." *Bulletin de la Academie Malgache* 12 (1): 139–176.

Quigley, Declan
1993   *The Interpretation of Caste*. Oxford: Clarendon Press.

Radimilahy, C., S. Andriamampianina, S. Blanchy, J.-A. Rakotoarisoa, and S. Razafimahazo
2006   "Lieux de culte autochtone à Antananarivo." In *Le dieux au service du peuple* (Sophie Blanchy, Jean-Aimé Rakotoarisoa, Philippe Beaujard, and Chantal Radimilahy, eds.). Paris: Karthala.

Raison, Françoise
1976   "Les Ramanenjana: une mise en cause populaire du christianisme en Imerina, 1863." *Asie du sud-est et le monde insulindien* VII (ii–iii): 271–93.

Raombana
n.d.   *Annales*. Manuscript preserved in the archives of the Academie Malgache, Antananarivo.

Rajemisa-Raolison, Régis
1985   *Rakibolana Malagasy*. Fianarantsoa: Ambozatany.

Ravelojaona, Randzavola, Rajaona,
1937   *Firaketana ny fiteny sy zavatra Malagasy*. Tananarive: Imprimerie Industrielle.

Ratrimoharinosy, Hélène
1986   "La Societé Malgache vers 1800." In *Madagascar: Society and History* (C. P. Kottak, J.-A. Rakotoarisoa, A. Southall, and P. Vérin, eds.). Durham: Carolina Academic Press.

Ruud, Jørgen
1960   *Taboo: A Study of Malagasy Beliefs and Customs*. New York: Humanities Press.

Scarry, Elaine
1985   *The Body in Pain: The Making and Unmaking of the World*. Oxford: Oxford University Press.

Scott, James
1992   *Domination and the Arts of Resistance*. Chicago: University of Chicago Press.

Sewell, Joseph
1876   *Remarks on Slavery in Madagascar*. London: Elliot Stock.

Sibree, James
1880   *Madagascar: the Great African Island*. London: Trübner & Co.
1896   *Madagascar Before the Conquest: The Island, the Country, and the People*. London: T. Fisher Unwin.

Sperber, Dan
1985   *On Anthropological Knowledge: Three Essays*. New York: Cambridge University Press.

Standing, Herbert F.
1887   "The Tribal Divisions of the Hova Malagasy." *Antananarivo Annual and Malagasy Magazine* IX: 354–358.

Toulmin, Stephen
1992   *Cosmopolis: The Hidden Agenda of Modernity*. Chicago: University of Chicago Press.
2001   *Return to Reason*. Cambridge, MA.: Harvard University Press.

Whitaker, Mark P.
1996   "Relativism." In *Encyclopedia of Social and Cultural Anthropology* (Alan Barnard & Jonathan Spencer eds.). London: Routledge.

PART III

DIRECT ACTION, DIRECT DEMOCRACY, AND SOCIAL THEORY

9

THE TWILIGHT OF VANGUARDISM

Revolutionary thinkers have been declaring the age of vanguardism over for most of a century now. Outside a handful of tiny sectarian groups, it's almost impossible to find radical intellectuals who seriously believe that their role should be to determine the correct historical analysis of the world situation, so as to lead the masses along in the one true revolutionary direction. But (rather like the idea of progress itself, to which it's obviously connected), it seems much easier to renounce the principle than to shake the accompanying habits of thought. Vanguardist, even sectarian, attitudes have become so deeply ingrained in academic radicalism it's hard to say what it would mean to think outside them.

The depth of the problem really struck me when I first became acquainted with the consensus modes of decision-making employed in North American anarchist and anarchist-inspired political movements. These, in turn, bore a lot of similarities to the style of political decision-making in rural Madagascar, where I had done my anthropological fieldwork. There's enormous variation among different styles and forms of consensus, but one thing almost all the North American variants have in common is that they are organized in conscious opposition to the style of organization and, especially, debate typical of the classical sectarian Marxist group. Where the latter are invariably organized around some Master Theoretician—who offers a comprehensive analysis of the world situation, and often of human history as a whole, but very little theoretical reflection on more immediate questions of organization and practice—anarchist-inspired groups tend to operate on the assumption that no one could, or probably should, ever convert another person completely to one's own point of view, that decision-making structures are ways of managing diversity, and, therefore, that one should concentrate instead on maintaining egalitarian process and on considering immediate questions of action in the present. A fundamental principle of political debate, for instance, is that one is obliged to give other participants the benefit of the doubt for honesty and good intentions, whatever else one might think of their arguments. In part, this emerges from the style of debate consensus decision-making encourages: where voting encourages one to reduce one's opponents' positions to a hostile caricature, or whatever it takes to defeat them, a consensus process is built on a principle of compromise and creativity, where one is constantly changing proposals around until one can come up with something everyone can at least live with. Therefore, the incentive is always to put the best possible construction on others' arguments.

All this struck a chord with me because it brought home just how much ordinary intellectual practice—the kind of thing I was trained to do at the University of Chicago, for example—really does resemble sectarian modes of debate. One of the things that had most disturbed me about my training there was precisely the way we were encouraged to read other theorists' arguments: if there were two ways to read a sentence, one of which assumed the author had at least a smidgen of common sense and the other that he was a complete idiot, the tendency was always to choose the latter. I had sometimes wondered how this could be reconciled with an idea that intellectual practice was, on some ultimate level, a common enterprise in pursuit of truth. The same goes for other intellectual habits: for example, carefully assembling lists of different "ways to be wrong" (usually ending in "ism" —subjectivism, empiricism—all much like their sectarian parallels: reformism, left deviationism, hegemonism) and being willing to listen to points of view differing from one's own only so long as it took to figure out which variety of wrongness to plug them into. Combine this with the tendency to treat (often minor) intellectual differences not only as tokens of belonging to some imagined "ism" but as profound moral flaws, on the same level as racism or imperialism (and often, in fact, partaking of them), and one has an almost exact reproduction of the style of intellectual debate typical of the most ridiculous vanguardist sects.

I still believe that the growing prevalence of new, and to my mind far healthier, modes of discourse among activists will have its effects on the academy, but it's hard to deny that, so far, the change has been very slow in coming.

Why So Few Anarchists in the Academy?

One might argue this is because anarchism itself has made such small inroads into the academy. As a political philosophy, anarchism is going through a veritable explosion in recent years. Anarchist or anarchist-inspired movements are growing everywhere; anarchist principles—autonomy, voluntary association, self-organization, mutual aid, direct democracy—have become the basis for organizing within the globalization movement and beyond. As Barbara Epstein has recently pointed out (2001), at least in Europe and the Americas, they have by now largely taken the place Marxism had in the social movements of the 1960s. They comprise the core revolutionary ideology, the source of ideas and inspiration: even those who do not consider themselves anarchists feel they have to define themselves in relation to them. Yet this has found almost no reflection in academic discourse. Most academics seem to have only the vaguest idea what anarchism is even about; or dismiss it with the crudest stereotypes ("Anarchist organization! But isn't that a contradiction in terms?"). In the United States—and I don't think it's all that different elsewhere—there are thousands of academic Marxists of one sort or another, but hardly anyone who is willing to openly call herself an anarchist.

I don't think this is just because the academy is behind the times. Marxism has always had an affinity with the academy that anarchism never will. It was, after all was invented by a Ph.D; and there's always been something about its spirit which fits that of the academy. Anarchism, on the other hand, was never really invented by anyone. True, historians usually treat it as if it were, constructing the history of anarchism as if it's basically a creature identical in its nature to Marxism. It was, they say, created by specific nineteenth-century thinkers, perhaps Godwin or Stirner, but definitely Proudhon, Bakunin, and Kropotkin. It inspired working-class organizations and became enmeshed in political struggles. But, in fact, the analogy is rather strained. First of all, the nineteenth-century thinkers generally credited with inventing anarchism didn't think of themselves as having invented anything particularly new. The basic principles of anarchism—self-organization, voluntary association, mutual aid—are as old as humanity. Similarly, the rejection of the state and of all forms of structural violence, inequality, or domination (anarchism literally means "without rulers"), even the assumption that all these forms are somehow related and reinforce each other, was hardly some startlingly new nineteenth-century doctrine. One can find evidence of people making similar arguments throughout history, despite the fact there is every reason to believe that such opinions were the ones least likely to be written down. We are talking less about a body of theory than about an attitude, or perhaps a faith: a rejection of certain types of social relation, a confidence that certain others are a much better ones on which to build a decent or humane society, a faith that it would be possible to do so.

One need only compare the historical schools of Marxism, and anarchism, then, to see we are dealing with fundamentally different things. Marxist schools have founders. Just as Marxism sprang from the mind of

Marx, so we have Leninists, Maoists, Trotskyites, Gramscians, Althusserians. Note how the list starts with heads of state and grades almost seamlessly into French professors. Pierre Bourdieu once noted that, if the academic field is a game in which scholars strive for dominance, then you know you have won when other scholars start wondering how to make an adjective out of your name. It is, presumably, to preserve the possibility of winning the game that intellectuals insist, when discussing each other, on continuing to employ just the sort of Great Man theories of history they would scoff at when discussing just about anything else. Foucault's ideas, like Trotsky's, are never treated as primarily the products of a certain intellectual milieu, as something emerging from endless conversations and arguments in cafés, classrooms, bedrooms, and barber shops, involving thousands of people inside and outside the academy (or Party), but always as if they emerged from a single man's genius. It's not quite either that Marxist politics organized itself like an academic discipline or became a model for how radical intellectuals or, increasingly, all intellectuals, treated one another; rather, the two developed somewhat in tandem.

Schools of anarchism, in contrast, emerge from some kind of organizational principle or form of practice: Anarcho-Syndicalists and Anarcho-Communists, Insurrectionists and Platformists, Cooperativists, Individualists, and so on. Significantly, those few Marxist tendencies that are not named after individuals, like Autonomism or Council Communism, are themselves the closest to anarchism. Anarchists are distinguished by what they do, and how they organize themselves to go about doing it. Indeed, this has always been what anarchists have spent most of their time thinking and arguing about. They have never been much interested in the kinds of broad strategic or philosophical questions that preoccupy Marxists such as, "are the peasants a potentially revolutionary class?" (anarchists consider this something for the peasants to decide) or "what is the nature of the commodity form?" Rather, they tend to argue about what is the truly democratic way to hold a meeting: at what point does organization stop being empowering and start squelching individual freedom? Is "leadership" necessarily a bad thing? Or, alternately, they discuss the ethics of opposing power: What is direct action? Should one condemn someone who assassinates a head of state? When is it okay to break a window?

One might sum it up like this:

1) Marxism has tended to be a theoretical or analytical discourse about revolutionary strategy.
2) Anarchism has tended to be an ethical discourse about revolutionary practice.

Now, this does imply there's a lot of potential complementary between the two—and indeed there has been: even Mikhail Bakunin, for all his endless battles with Marx over practical questions, also personally translated Marx's *Capital* into Russian. One could easily imagine a systematic division of labor in which Marxists critique the political economy, but stay out of organizing, and anarchists handle the day-to-day organizing, but defer to Marxists on questions of abstract theory; i.e., in which the Marxists explain why the economic crash in Argentina occurred and the anarchists deal with what to do about it.[1] But such imaginary divisions of labor also make it easier to understand why there are so few anarchists in the academy. It's not just that anarchism does not lend itself to high theory. It's that it is primarily an ethics of practice. It insists, before anything else, that one's means must be consonant with one's ends; that one cannot create freedom through authoritarian means; that, as much as possible, one must embody the society one wishes to create. This does not square very well with operating within universities that still have an essentially Medieval social structure, presenting papers at conferences in expensive hotels, and doing intellectual battle in language no one who hasn't spent at least two or three years in grad school would ever hope to be able to understand. At the very least, then, anarchism would tend to get one in trouble.

All this does not, of course, mean that anarchist *theory* is impossible—though it does suggest that a single Anarchist High Theory in the style typical of university radicalism might be rather a contradiction in terms. One could imagine a body of theory that presumes, and indeed values, a diversity of sometimes incommensurable perspectives in much the same way that anarchist decision-making process does, but which nonetheless organizes them around a presumption of shared commitments. Clearly, it would also have to self-consciously reject any trace of vanguardism. This, then, leads to an important question: if the role of revolutionary intellectuals is *not* to form an elite that can arrive at the correct strategic analyses and then lead the masses, what precisely is it? This is an area where I think anthropology is particularly well-positioned to help. Not only because most actual, self-governing communities, non-market economies, and other radical alternatives have been mainly studied by anthropologists, but also because the practice of ethnography provides something of a model, an incipient model, of how non-vanguardist revolutionary intellectual practice might work. Ethnography is about teasing out the hidden symbolic, moral, or pragmatic logics that underlie certain types of social action; how people's habits and actions make sense in ways that they are not themselves completely aware of. One obvious role for a radical intellectual is precisely that: looking first at those who are creating viable alternatives on the ground, and then trying to figure out what the larger implications of what they are (already) doing might be.

A Very Brief History of the Idea of Vanguardism

Untwining social theory from vanguardist habits might seem a particularly difficult task because, historically, modern social theory and the idea of the vanguard were born more or less together. On the other hand, so was the idea of an artistic avant-garde ("avant-garde" is, in fact, simply the French word for vanguard), and the relation between the three might itself suggest some unexpected possibilities.

The term "avant-garde" was actually coined by Henri de Saint-Simon, a French aristocrat, political visionary, pamphleteer, and activist writing in the early nineteenth century. It was actually one of his last ideas, the product of a series of essays he wrote at the very end of his life. Like his one-time secretary and disciple (and later bitter rival) Auguste Comte, Saint-Simon was writing in the wake of the French Revolution and, essentially, was asking what had gone wrong: why the transition from a Medieval, feudal Catholic society to a modern, industrial democratic one seemed to be creating such enormous violence and social dislocation. How can we do it right? At the time, Catholic and Royalist thinkers like Bonald (1864) and de Maistre (1822) were arguing that the Revolution had descended into the Terror because it had destroyed the principles of order and hierarchy of which the King had been merely the embodiment. The social system, they argued, had been since the Middle Ages upheld above all by the Church, which gave everyone the sense of having a meaningful place in a single coherent social order. Saint-Simon and Comte rejected their reactionary conclusions—they didn't feel it would be possible to simply place the Medieval Church back in power. What was needed was to invent a new institution that would play the same role in the world created by the industrial revolution. Towards the end of their lives, each actually ended up creating his own religion: Saint-Simon called his the "New Christianity" (1825), Comte named his the "New Catholicism" (1852). In the first, artists were to play the role of the ultimate spiritual leaders. In an imaginary dialogue with a scientist, Saint-Simon has an artist explaining that, in their role of imagining possible futures and inspiring the public, they can play the role of an "avant-garde," a "truly priestly function" as he puts it. In his ideal future, artists would hatch the ideas which they would then pass on to the scientists and industrialists to put into effect. Saint-Simon was also perhaps the first to conceive the notion of the withering away of the state: once it had become clear that the authorities were operating for the good of the public, one would no more need force to compel the public to heed their advice than one needed it to compel patients to take the advice of their doctors. Government would pass away into, at most, some minor police functions.

Comte, of course, is most famous as the founder of sociology; he invented the term to describe what he saw as the master-discipline which could both understand and direct society. He ended up taking a different, far more authoritarian approach: ultimately proposing the regulation and control of almost all aspects of human life according to scientific principles, with the role of high priests (effectively, the vanguard, though he did not actually call them this) in his New Catholicism being played by the sociologists themselves.

It's a particularly fascinating opposition because, in the early twentieth century, the positions were effectively reversed. Instead of the left-wing Saint-Simonians looking to artists for leadership, while the right-wing Comtians fancied themselves scientists, we had the fascist leaders like Hitler and Mussolini who imagined themselves as great artists inspiring the masses, and sculpting society according to their grandiose imaginings, and the Marxist vanguard which claimed the role of scientists.

At any rate, the Saint-Simonians actively sought to recruit artists for their various ventures, salons, and utopian communities: though they quickly ran into difficulties because so many within "avant-garde" artistic circles preferred the more anarchistic Fourierists and, later, one or another branch of outright anarchists. Actually, the number of nineteenth-century artists with anarchist sympathies is quite staggering, ranging from Pissarro to Tolstoy and Oscar Wilde, not to mention almost all early-twentieth-century artists who later became Communists, from Malevich to Picasso. Rather than a political vanguard leading the way to a future society, radical artists almost invariably saw themselves as exploring new and less alienated modes of life. The really significant development in the nineteenth century was less the idea of a vanguard than that of bohemia (a term first coined by Balzac in 1838): marginal communities living in more or less voluntary poverty, seeing themselves as dedicated to the pursuit of creative, unalienated forms of experience, united by a profound hatred of bourgeois life and everything it stood for. Ideologically, they were about equally likely to be proponents of "art for art's sake" or social revolutionaries. Contemporary theorists are actually quite divided over how to evaluate their larger significance. Pierre Bourdieu, for example [2000], insisted that the promulgation of the idea of "art for art's sake," far from being depoliticizing, should be considered a significant accomplishment, as was any that managed to establish the autonomy of one particular field of human endeavor from the logic of the market. Colin Campbell (1991), on the other hand, argues that, insofar as bohemians actually were an avant-garde, they were really the vanguard of the market itself, or more precisely, of consumerism: their actual social function, much though they would have loathed to admit it, was to explore new forms of pleasure or aesthetic territory that could be commodified in the next generation.[2]

Campbell also echoes common wisdom that bohemia was almost exclusively inhabited by the children of the bourgeoisie, who had—temporarily, at least—rejected their families' money and privilege—and who, if they did not die young of dissipation, were likely to end up back on the board of father's company. One hears the same claim repeated to this day about activists and revolutionaries: most recently, about the "trust-fund babies" who supposedly dominate the global justice movement. In fact, in this case, Pierre Bourdieu (1993) has done the actual historical research and discovered that, in fact, a very large percentage of nineteenth-century bohemians were the children of peasants. Bohemia was a convergence of a certain number of children with bourgeois backgrounds in broad rejection of their parents' values, and a larger number of children of quite modest origins, often beneficiaries of new public educational systems, who discovered that simply attaining a bourgeois education was not enough to actually win oneself membership in the bourgeoisie. The remarkable thing is that this is consistently the demographic for vanguardist revolutionaries as well: one might think here of the meeting of Chou En Lai (rebellious son of Mandarins) and Mao Tse-Tung (child of peasants turned school librarian), or Che Guevara (son of Argentine doctors), and Fidel Castro (son of modest shopkeepers turned unemployed lawyer). It continues to be true of revolutionaries and globalization activists to this day.

In the nineteenth century, the idea of the political vanguard was used very widely and very loosely for anyone seen as exploring the path to a future, free society. Radical newspapers, for example, often called themselves "the Avant Garde." Peter Kropotkin, for instance, was a frequent contributor to a Swiss anarchist newspaper called *L'Avant Garde* in the 1880s, and there were periodicals of the same name (or their local equivalents) in France, Spain, Italy, and Argentina. It was Marx, really, who began to significantly change the idea by introducing the notion that the proletariat were the true revolutionary class—he didn't actually use the term "vanguard"—because they were the most oppressed or, as he put it "negated" by capitalism, and therefore had the least to lose by its abolition. In doing so, he ruled out the possibility that less alienated enclaves, whether of artists or the sort of artisans and independent producers who tended to form the backbone of anarchism, had anything significant to offer. We all know the results. The idea of a vanguard party dedicated to both organizing and providing an intellectual project for that most-oppressed class chosen as the agent of history, but also actually sparking the revolution through their willingness to employ violence, was first outlined by Lenin in 1902 in *What Is to Be Done?*; it has echoed endlessly, to the point where the SDS in the late 1960s could end up locked in furious debates over whether the Black Panther Party, as the leaders of its most oppressed element, should be considered the vanguard of the Movement. All this, in turn, had a curious effect on the artistic avant-garde who increasingly started to organize themselves like vanguard parties, beginning with the Dadaists and Futurists, publishing their own manifes-tos, communiqués, purging one another, and otherwise making themselves (sometimes quite intentional) parodies of revolutionary sects. (Note, howev-er, that these groups always defined themselves, like anarchists, by a certain form of practice rather than after some heroic founder.) The ultimate fusion came with the Surrealists and then, finally, the Situationist International, which on the one hand was the most systematic in trying to develop a theory of revolutionary action according to the spirit of bohemia, thinking about what it might actually mean to destroy the boundaries between art and life, but at the same time, in its own internal organization, displayed a kind of insane sectarianism full of so many splits, purges, and bitter denunciations that Guy Debord finally remarked that the only logical conclusion was for the International to be finally reduced to two members, one of whom would purge the other and then commit suicide (which is not all that far from what actually ended up happening).

Non-Alienated Production

The historical relations between political and artistic avant-gardes have been explored at endless length already (e.g., Poggioli 1968; Buck-Morss 2000; Kastiaficas 2004). For me, though, the really intriguing questions is: why is it that artists have so often been drawn to revolutionary politics to begin with? Because it does seem to be the case that, even in times and places when there is next to no other constituency for revolutionary change, the place one is most likely to find one is among artists, authors, and musicians; even more so, in fact, than among professional intellectuals. It seems to me the answer must have something to do with alienation. There would appear to be a direct link between the experience of first imagining things and then bringing them into being (individually or collectively)—that is, the experi-ence of certain forms of unalienated production—and the ability to imagine social alternatives; particularly, the possibility of a society itself premised on less alienated forms of creativity. Which would allow us to see the historical shift between seeing the vanguard as the relatively unalienated artists (or perhaps intellectuals) to seeing them as the representatives of the "most oppressed" in a new light. In fact, I would suggest, revolutionary coalitions always tend to consist of an alliance between a society's least alienated and its most oppressed. And this is less elitist a formulation than it might sound, because it also seems to be the case that actual revolutions tend to occur when these two categories come to overlap. That would, at any rate, explain why it almost always seems to be peasants and craftspeople—or alternately, newly proletarianized former peasants and craftspeople—who actually rise up and overthrow capitalist regimes, and not those inured to generations of wage-labor. Finally, I suspect this would also help explain the extraordinary importance of indigenous peoples' struggles in that planetary uprising usually referred to as the "anti-globalization" movement: such people tend to be simultaneously the very least alienated and most oppressed people on earth, and, once it is technologically possible to include them in revolutionary co-alitions, it is almost inevitable that they should take a leading role.

The role of indigenous peoples, in turn, leads us back to the role of ethnography as a possible model for the would-be non-vanguardist revolutionary intellectual—as well as some of its potential pitfalls. Obviously, what I am proposing would only work if it was, ultimately, a form of auto-ethnography, combined, perhaps, with a certain utopian extrapolation: a matter of teasing out the tacit logic or principles underlying certain forms of radical practice, and then, not only offering the analysis back to those communities, but using them to formulate new visions ("If one applied the same principles as you are applying to political organization to economics, might it not look something like this?"). Here too there are suggestive parallels in the history of radical artistic movements, which became movements precisely as they became their own critics (and, of course, the idea of self-criticism took on a very different, and more ominous, tone within Marxist politics). There are also intellectuals already trying to do precisely this sort of auto-ethnographic work (see, for example, Graeber & Shukaitis 2007). But I say all this not so much to provide models as to open up a field for discussion, first of all, by emphasizing that even the notion of vanguardism itself has a far more rich history, and full of alternative possibilities, than most of us would ever be given to expect.

Endnotes

1   I also should point out that I'm aware I'm being a bit hypocritical here by indulging in some of the same sort of sectarian reasoning I'm otherwise critiquing: there are schools of Marxism which are far more open-minded and tolerant, and democrati-

cally organized. There are anarchist groups which are insanely sectarian; Bakunin himself was hardly a model for democracy by any standards.

2   One might think of this as the Tom Franks version of history.

Bibliography

Bonald, Louis-Gabriel-Ambroise
1864 *Œuvres complètes de M. de Bonald.* Paris : J.P. Migne

Bourdieu, Pierre
1993 *The Field of Cultural Production: Essays on Art and Literature* (Randal Johnson, ed.). Cambridge, England: Polity Press.
2000 *Pascalian meditations* (Richard Nice, trans.). Cambridge: Polity Press.

Buck-Morss, Susan
2000 *Dreamworld and Catastrophe: The Passing of Mass Utopia in East and West.* Cambridge: MIT Press.

Campbell, Colin
1987 *The Romantic Ethic and the Spirit of Modern Consumerism.* Oxford: Blackwell.

Comte, Auguste
1852 *Catechisme Positiviste. ou Sommaire Exposition de la Religion Universelle en Onze Entretiens Systematiques entre une Femme et un Prêtre de l'Humanité.* Paris: Chez le Auteur.

Epstein, Barbara
2001 "Anarchism and the Anti-Globalization Movement." *Monthly Review* 53 (4), September 2001: 1–14.

Graeber, David and Stevphen Shukaitis, editors
2007 *Constituent Imagination: Militant Investigation, Collective Research.* Oakland: AK Press.

Katsiaficas, George
2004 "Aesthetic and Political Avant-Gardes." *Journal of Aesthetics & Protest* 3.

Maistre, Joseph Marie, comte de
1822 *Considerations sur la France.* Paris: J.B. Pélagaud & cie.

Poggioli, Renato
1968 *The Theory of the Avant-Garde.* Cambridge, MA: Harvard University Press.

Saint-Simon, Henri, comte de
1825 *Nouveau Christianisme: dialogues entre un conservateur et un novateur, primier dia-logue.* Paris: Bossange.

10

SOCIAL THEORY AS SCIENCE AND UTOPIA: OR, DOES THE PROSPECT OF A GENERAL SOCIOLOGICAL THEORY STILL MEAN ANYTHING IN AN AGE OF GLOBALIZATION?

I can address the organizers' questions from two possible vantages: as an anthropologist, or as a political activist who has been working for some years with the globalization movement (the so-called "anti-globalization movement"), which has been reformulating the whole idea of revolution in accord with changing global conditions. In what follows, I will try to do a little bit of both, by offering some reflections on the history of social theory in general and its changing relation to the prospects of social revolution.[1]

I'm taking this approach not just because it provides a useful point of entry, but because I believe there is an integral relation between the two—or, more specifically, between the revolutionary imagination and the idea that there is something I will call "social reality" that bears empirical investigation, and that, therefore, makes a scholarly discipline like sociology possible. This I think seems abundantly clear as soon as we seriously consider the historical beginnings of social science. Let me begin, then, with some brief notes on the history of comparative ethnography, before moving on to the origins of sociology itself.

ON SOCIAL REALITY

Some Notes on the History of Comparative Ethnography

It has become fashionable in recent years to see anthropology basically as a product of imperialism, and certainly, it was the creation of vast European empires that made it possible. However, there have been plenty of multicultural empires in human history, and none, as far as we know, had ever before produced a project for the systematic comparison of cultural difference. Even if we confine ourselves to the Western tradition itself, what evidence there is points, if anything, in the opposite direction. In the ancient world, one could make a case that something like anthropology was emerging in fifth-century Greece, where geographers like Hecataeus and historians like Herodotus were developing ideas about how customs and mores might be systematically compared. This was during a period in which the Greek world was not even politically unified, let alone the center of a vast multicultural empire. When such empires did arise shortly afterward, this sort of literature disappeared: neither the Hellenistic empires nor Rome produced anything resembling anthropology. The reasonable explanation would seem to be that fifth-century Greece was a period of political possibility: full of social experiments, revolutions, and utopian schemes. Comparing social orders was one way to discuss the potential range for political (that is, human) society. This clearly was not the case during the centuries of Roman rule. In fact, it would seem it was the very political fragmentation of fifth-century Greece which encouraged this kind of thought. Since the basic political unit was the city-state, a relatively small community, the space for political experiments was in fact wide open: new Greek colonies, and hence political units, were in fact being founded all the time, new constitutions being mulled and created, old regimes overthrown.

Similarly, I suspect that it would be possible to document at least a loose connection between ethnographic curiosity and a sense of political possibility over the last five hundred years of European history. One could start in the sixteenth century, which saw both the first statements of what was to become modern relativism in authors like Montaigne, and a sudden burst of utopian speculation and revolutionary movements. During the century that followed both the curiosity and the sense of possibility fell somewhat into retreat in most places, only to be suddenly revived together in the years leading up to the French Revolution. This was followed by another retreat during the reactionary years following Napoleon's defeat, and another, even stronger revival after the revolutions of 1848. It was the last period that saw the emergence of anthropology as a professional discipline.

I have elsewhere pointed to a cluster of ideas that tend to appear together: the very idea that one might "give power to the imagination," as the famous 1968 slogan had it, to imagine different social orders and try to bring them into being, itself leads to a need to recognize a substratum of resistant "reality" of some sort (which must then be investigated), along with sparking curiosity about just how different actually existing societies have been known to be. Imagination and reality are reverse sides of the same process; a conception in part inspired by Critical Realism's definition of "reality" as precisely that which can never be completely known and, hence, never entirely encompassed by imaginary models. It would at least make it easier to understand why so many of the most idealistic people in recent history have insisted on calling themselves "materialists," or why a commitment to some sort of materialism has so often accompanied the most daring utopian projects. Also, why it was that all three principles (revolution, reality, ethnography) came under attack simultaneously during the 1980s.

On Sociology and Wreckage

Turning to sociology, all this becomes, if anything, more clear because sociology is widely seen to have emerged, as a discipline, from the wreckage of the French Revolution. As Robert Nisbet pointed out half a century ago, almost all the great themes on which the discipline was established—community, authority, status, the sacred—were issues first singled out by reactionary critics of the Revolution like Bonald, Burke, or de Maistre, who argued these were precisely the social realities which Enlightenment thinkers had treated as so many bad ideas that could be simply brushed away, with catastrophic results. The themes were then developed more systematically by figures like Saint-Simon and Comte, who were grappling quite explicitly with the question of what went wrong, and trying to find some substitute for the principles of order and integration assumed to have existed in the Middle Ages. They have remained at the center of the discipline ever since.

The Revolution's troubles, the failure to transform basic institutions simply by changing the laws, were perceived to have revealed the existence of something that, while it was no longer seen as having been simply ordained by God or some similar external principle of authority, could no longer be seen as a simple creation or embodiment of individual or collective will. It seemed to resist attempts to reshape it, or at least throw them in unpredictable directions. In other words, this "something" had a consistency and logic of its own that had to be understood in its own right, and could be scientifically investigated. That object—something which could be said not to have really existed, as an object, or at least as quite that sort of object, before it became the resistant object of projects rooted in some kind of utopian imaginary—has remained the object of sociology ever since.

Owing to the peculiar history of the formation of disciplines, however, it was also seen as an object whose integrity, whose consistency and logic, had been at least to some degree shattered.

Here the key role was played by political economy (later economics) which split off from moral philosophy before sociology established its own, somewhat subordinate, domain. This allowed for the development of a very particular division of intellectual labor. Economics concerned itself with the functioning of markets and market behavior. Markets were assumed to be self-regulating. The object of economic science might have been constituted, as Polanyi so well documented, largely by state planning, by the imposition of an apparatus of laws and policies meant to create a create the field for certain sorts of interaction, but (as Polanyi also noted) almost as soon as the apparatus was in any sense up and running economic theorists appeared, employing all sorts of naturalistic metaphors to argue that this was indeed a functioning equilibrium system and a direct product of human nature that should be left largely to its own devices. Critically, too, economics staked out for itself the study of rationality, by identifying the term primarily with certain forms of calculating greed. Sociology, in contrast, could almost be said to be based on the study of precisely those "externalities" that have to pushed away from the purview of economics in order to be able to define the latter field in equilibrium terms to begin with. The first sociology departments were recruited largely from the staffs of social reform societies; by men who by definition believed the existing state of things to be inadequate (or if not generally, then at least among the popular classes); it has maintained itself largely because of a concern with "social problems": crime, divorce, poverty, religious conflict, etc. The assumption was always that something was most definitively not in equilibrium; something wasn't working that could have or should have been. Solidarity, consensus, authority, collective spirit, community, however defined, were incomplete or absent. And this was usually seen as part and parcel with some kind of crisis of rationality. Again, this is all very explicit in the works of most of the founding figures and has continued, if often more tacitly, to frame subsequent debate.

Now, the actual political positions of social theorists varied enormously. Revolutionaries like Marx were exceptional; liberal reformers like Durkheim or nationalists like Weber more the rule. But I would argue that the world that revolution ushered in—one in which it was assumed to be possible, on some level, to act on society as an object, to bring it more in accord with some utopian imaginary—ended up becoming permanent. Not only was the possibility of outright, battles-in-the-streets revolution seen as ever-present during most of this time, its dynamic became institutionalized in the structure of governments and related organizations, all of which saw society basically as a problem to be solved. This was the situation that allowed what I have been calling "social reality"(or what they were more likely to call "social realities") to continue to seem like something that obviously did exist and that they should care about—a self-evident object of study. Some might argue that all this is ultimately irrelevant, since whatever might have ultimately inspired social theorists to examine such matters, the point is what they came up with, and what they came up with was a relatively objective science of social explanation. But it's hard to find any significant social theorists, even in the nineteenth century, who actually believed that. What made Marx and Weber the most profound social thinkers of their age is precisely that they grappled most directly with the question of how to deal with the fact that an objective social science really wasn't possible—that the idea that it was was itself profoundly utopian. The solutions they came up with were very different (Marx arguing that theorizing about the world was itself a form of political action that could only contribute to either maintaining or transforming the object it was theorizing; Weber arguing that, while the questions we ask about the world can never be objective, our means of answering them can—but that before we will ever be able to accumulate objective knowledge, the questions will have changed), but they directly address the problem. One might even argue that it was the failure of sociologists like Durkheim to face up to their own ambivalent situation as researchers, closely tied to administrative circles, which drove them to effectively naturalize the problem by taking it down to the individual level—where individual, would-be economic actors (presumably motivated mainly by some form of self-interest) ended up facing "social facts" precisely as external, constraining realities. But this is a long argument.

There are two interesting corollaries to all this:

Curiously, the most powerful analyses of systems that do, effectively, what they are supposed to do have emerged from collapsed radical hopes: especially former Marxists, or others working in that critical tradition, who gradually gave up their faith that the system's internal contradictions would someday destroy it. Hence, figures like Baudrillard or Foucault provide models (if very different ones) of systems of power and domination that are, ultimately, ineluctable and all-encompassing—that is, which do in fact work.

It's also interesting to note that anthropology proved the great exception here—understandably, if my argument about the sources of ethnographic curiosity is substantially correct. At least, for most of the twentieth century, it did largely adopt equilibrium models and saw its object, whether social or cultural, as a series of small, self-contained systems which did, in fact, "function." And, as if to make the inversion perfect, this was complemented by a special branch of economics—development economics—to study economic systems that did not work.

QUESTIONS ABOUT GLOBALIZATION

If social reality only becomes an object (indeed, only becomes a reality) in the face of some imaginary which tries to shape it—of which the paradigm, I have argued, is revolution—then it makes it easier to understand why globalization has left sociology with such an "identity crisis." It is not just because the immediate onset of globalization saw what appeared to be strange and unprecedented realignments, with free-market economists suddenly posing as wild-eyed revolutionaries (by around 2000, *New York Times* op-ed writers were fervently insisting that Che Guevara, were he alive today, would certainly be a free-market reformer, just for the sheer joy of radical transformation). All that was the product of one giddy moment that faded almost immediately. It is because the theater for potential revolution, just like that of more modest projects of social reform, had always been the state. If utopian dreams were brought to bear on some stubborn social reality, it was always assumed—usually without even having to state it, so much was it the very basis of Left, Right, liberal, radical, and conservative thought—that this could only be accomplished through the coercive mechanisms of government. As Immanuel Wallerstein has been arguing for some years now, we seem to be witnessing the death of a kind of tacit agreement about the nature of politics that has existed since roughly the French Revolution. This has rested, he says, on three assumptions. The first is that social change is inevitable and, at least if properly managed, good. The second is that the appropriate mechanism to manage social change is the state. The third is that the state apparatus derives its legitimacy, its right to do so, from an entity referred to as "the people." In 1720, very few educated Europeans would have agreed with any of these statements. By 1820, just about everyone had to at least pay lip service. What's more, social theory as we know it developed almost entirely within this framework. It's only in recent decades, he notes, that we have seen significant portions of the global educated classes moving away from these positions. But as they do so, now that the state is not assumed as one's implicit point of reference from which to gaze down at stubborn realities, it is no longer clear what that "resistant object" is even supposed to be.

In this section, then, I will make two arguments. The first has to do with the inadequacy of our existing theoretical tools, particularly, the need for a renewal of historical sociology. Without this, we can't seriously begin to think about what is even happening in the world. Second, I want to suggest that rather than disappearing as a political horizon, revolutionary projects are being renewed and reconstituted along new lines (or, more accurately, perhaps, through the maturation of some previously subordinate revolutionary strands). This fact might itself point us toward a possible resolution, not only of the problem of how to constitute one's object under new conditions, but of how social theory might be organized itself.

Conceptualizing the Moment

The most striking thing revealed by sociology's identity crisis in the face of globalization is the remarkably weak state of historical sociology, whose major strands (Marxist and Weberian) seem to have largely disintegrated at exactly the moment we most need them.

Let me take one vivid example: the question of global citizenship.

This is an issue that comes up quite a lot nowadays: sometimes within the neoliberal framework and, even more, because it is a very common demand among new social movements calling for global freedom of movement. But what exactly would global citizenship mean? The most common objection to the idea is that any such notion would imply some kind of global state, and this is the last thing most of those calling for it would want to see. So, then, the question becomes how to theorize a citizenship apart from the state? This is often treated as a profound, perhaps insuperable problem. But, if one considers the matter historically, it is a bit odd that it should. Modern Western notions of citizenship and political freedoms are usually seen to derive from two traditions, one originating in ancient Athens, the other primarily stemming from Medieval England (where it tends to be traced back to the assertion of aristocratic privilege against the Crown in the Magna Carta, Petition of Right, etc., and then the gradual extension of these same rights to the rest of the population). In fact, there is no consensus among historians that either classical Athens or Medieval England were states at all—and, moreover, precisely for the reason that citizens' rights (in the first) and aristocratic privilege (in the second) were so strong.

In other words, our very ability to think about the present is hobbled by our lack of categories with which to talk about the past. If these were not states, or states in the classic sense, what were they? A theory of complex political entities that are not states is almost completely lacking. How could one talk about rights and responsibilities in the absence of a state? Again, it's hard to know where to start.

Such questions seem all the more pressing at a moment when many of these older forms—city-states, for example, or complex overlapping forms of sovereignty reminiscent of feudalism—seem to be reemerging. Here, it might be useful to consider the notion of the territorial nation-state, which so excited Europeans of the seventeenth century: a single state embracing a single people who spoke the same colloquial language, which was also the language of high culture and a national literature; an efficient bureaucracy chosen by merit and educated in that literature, administering a uniform system of laws. It seems to me this could best be seen as an attempt by European states to model themselves on China. The Chinese empire was, certainly, the only state that existed in the seventeenth century that in any way resembled this model; surely it did far more than anything that existed in Europe at the time. There was good reason for Leibniz to write that the Middle Kingdom should be sending missionaries to Europe rather than the other way around. One might argue that, until fairly recently, insofar as those national bourgeoisies who were creating modern capitalism had a political project, it was to transform their states into something resembling China, minus the emperor and claims to universality. They envisioned, instead, a series of small, equal states organized on essentially Chinese lines. Of course, through colonialism, this European version of the Chinese model ended up being imposed on pretty much every other country in the world, including—belatedly—China itself, providing the pretext for the creation of the interstate system of border controls which is perhaps colonialism's most lasting political legacy. This system of border controls, in turn, is hardly dissolving with globalization.

It has become popular, of course, to say that it is, to talk as if the growth of trade and migration are making national borders increasingly irrelevant. Look at the same situation in terms of the last five hundred years. It's easy to see that, while world trade has increased somewhat, overall migration rates are nothing like what they were one (let alone two or three) hundred years ago, and the only element that's entirely new here is the presence of the borders themselves. The modern "interstate system," which carves up the earth through thousands of highly patrolled and regulated borders, was only fully completed quite recently; and far from being eaten away by globalization, institutions like the IMF or WTO are entirely premised on it. The number of armed men patrolling the US border with Mexico has tripled or even quadrupled since the signing of NAFTA; before it, no one was even considering the idea of reinforcing the border with a giant wall.

On the other hand, the decline of the "Chinese model" has allowed phenomena to reemerge which would have looked, just fifty years ago, bizarrely antiquated: e.g., new zones of permanent low-intensity warfare, such as were typical of part of Renaissance Europe; the rise of mercantile city-states; the reemergence of essentially feudal relations starting in much of the former Communist world; the parcelization of sovereignty, whereby the elements we have come to think of as naturally combined in the state are instead broken up and distributed to different institutions on totally different geographical scales. A merchant in medieval Antwerp for example had to deal with the local government, criminal law, property law, and religious (what we'd now call "social") law all invested in radically different entities: a local feudal lord, the Pope, the Emperor. A merchant in contemporary Antwerp finds himself increasingly in much the same situation, even if the entities are now local government, the EU, and the WTO. Some even speak of "neo-Medievalism." Admittedly, this is a somewhat eccentric view, and it might well turn out to be completely misconceived. I am throwing it out mainly to illustrate the sort of theorizing that is currently both very much called for and largely absent.

Even the emphasis on those things which genuinely are new about the present moment—the emergence of a virtual sphere, as it's sometimes called—is difficult to theorize outside a larger historical context, which we probably won't really have until generations in the future. Industrial civilization has been around for such a brief moment of historical time that it's very difficult to perceive patterns in its development. Let me throw in one last question here, one that strikes me as very significant, though for some reason, it is almost never actually discussed. Is the current character of "globalization" the product of an unprecedented technological moment, or is it the result of a temporary slowing and involution of technological development? We seem to assume as a matter of course that technology is always leaping ahead in fundamental ways. It's not clear, of course, whether there can be said to be an objective measure in such matters. But I think it is possible at least to talk about the realization of popular expectations. In terms of cultural attitudes at least, it seems to me that the real difference between the first and second halves of the twentieth century is that, while almost all the technologies children in 1900 imagined would exist by 1950, but were the stuff of science fiction at the time—radios, airplanes, organ transplants, space rockets, skyscrapers, moving pictures, etc.—did in fact come into being more or less on schedule, pretty much none of the ones children born in 1950 or 1960 imagined would exist by 2000 (anti-gravity sleds, teleportation, force fields, cloning, death-rays, interplanetary travel, personal robot attendants) ever came about. It would be easy to imagine, when observing the crude special effects of 1950s science fiction movies, that their makers would be quite impressed by the remarkable effects of their contemporary equivalents. But, in reality, they almost certainly would not. Science fiction movies of the 1950s were often set in the year 2000. They assumed we'd be *doing* these things by now—actually exploring distant galaxies, not just developing ever more impressive ways to simulate it. Where, in earlier generations, science fiction projections seemed to regularly become reality a generation later, now they remain trapped on the screen—even if the screen images look increasingly realistic.

In the late 1960s, Alvin Toffler wrote a book called *Future Shock* in which he pointed out that in every recent decade, the fastest speed at which it was possible for human beings to travel had at least doubled, and that, taken over a longer time span, it appeared to be rising geometrically. Could conquest of the stars be far away? He proved an atrocious prophet. In fact, the top speed at which it was possible for human beings to travel stopped increasing almost the moment the book came out and has not changed since. True, we can now communicate instantly on the internet. Computer, imaging, and communications technology—along with medical technology—have been about the only kind that have been advancing at anything like the pace people once expected. But, even here, we have to remember how high those expectations have traditionally been. In the 1950s and 1960s, it was assumed by now we would have computers with whom we could carry on a conversation, or robots who could put away the dishes or walk the dog. It seems for the moment at least we have reached a point where disappointment with childhood dreams has become institutionalized. If they are realized, they are realized in a virtual realm, as simulations. Is it any wonder, then, that we are surrounded by philosophers telling us that everything is simulation and that nothing is really new?

Autonomy and Revolutionary Consensus

Clearly, national revolutions can no longer make the same difference they once did; and, on a global scale, it's entirely unclear what the equivalent of storming the Bastille or Winter Palace would even be. But there are those who argue that revolutions were never really national affairs. Immanuel Wallerstein has pointed out that even the French Revolution wasn't really a national revolution in its ultimate effects (it might well have had just as much transformative effect on Denmark as on France); the revolutions of 1848 occurred in numerous capitals, took power in none of them, and nonetheless managed to transform the world in profound ways; and this, he says, was even more true of the anti-state revolutions of 1968, which, he argued, reached Eastern Europe in 1989. These were all, he argues, world revolutions. If so, matters appear to have transformed even more radically over the last decade, in which a revolutionary strategy of permanent, open-ended global uprising (from Chiapas to Seattle, Genoa, and Argentina) has been so successful that it's now being answered with a doctrine of permanent, open-ended global war.

The revolutionary imaginary being adopted within the globalization movement finds its roots less in the Marxist tradition than the anarchist, which was always dedicated to starting to build a new world "within the shell of the old," and on prioritizing an ethics of organization and practice over a focus on strategies for seizing power. The aim is simultaneously to expose, delegitimize, and undermine mechanisms of global rule, while simultaneously creating spaces of autonomy which are, as Cindy Millstein puts it, "prefigurative," which themselves embody the viability of radical alternatives. It is a way of permanently invoking what Negri calls "constituent power." Mass direct actions like Seattle, Washington, Prague, or Genoa, aimed to do all this simultaneously, since their own directly democratic, leaderless organization was itself a vast social experiment, and for most participants, a dazzlingly successful one. At the same time, permanent enclaves can be established: from the autonomous municipalities of Chiapas to the occupied factories of Argentina. In such a strategy, one of the most constantly invoked words is "process." Unlike Marxist parties, which have always tended to demand ideological conformity combined with top-down, usually highly authoritarian, decision-making structures, anarchist-inspired revolutionary "networks" and "convergences" employ decision-making processes which assume that no ideological uniformity can or should be possible. Rather, these forms become ways of managing a diversity, even incommensurability, which is seen as a value in itself. The assumption is that this can be managed through a spirit of reasonableness and mutual compromise that emerges from commitment to shared projects of action. That is, anarchist-inspired groups tend to studiously avoid political arguments about the definition of reality, and assume that decision-making structures should concentrate instead on immediate questions of action in the present, on maintaining egalitarian process in doing so, and making those forms of process the main model of (or, better perhaps, elementary, germ-like template for) their vision for a just society. This is, in effect, a way of preserving diversity as a resource and a value at the same time: since, if one sees one's work essentially as practical problem-solving, then it is pretty obvious that ten people with diverse (even formally incommensurable) perspectives are more likely to be able to come up with a workable solution than ten people who all share exactly the same experience and point of view. What I am saying, then, is that it is precisely what most outside observers take to be the foolishness and naiveté of the movement (their apparent lack of a coherent ideology) has turned out to be a token of their most sophisticated accomplishment and contribution to revolutionary theory. It was not that the new movements lack ideology. As I have argued in the past, these new forms of organization, which presume and are ways of articulating a diversity of perspectives, *are* its ideology.

It seems to me this pragmatic model might have implications for social theory, and in particular, the problem of theoretical diversity. In the next and final section, I will try to illustrate what I think is at stake here.

CONCERNING REGULATORY PRINCIPLES

At the moment, social theory is even more fragmented than it has usually been and there's a good deal of debate as to whether this is a good or bad thing. Some degree of theoretical fragmentation seems inevitable, given the way the object (social reality) has been constituted, as a somewhat battered residual set off from economics. As a theoretically unified neoclassical economics has become increasingly dominant, to the point of becoming the effective ideology of rule for just about all the emerging institutions of global governance, and as economic versions of "rationality" have increasingly begun to colonize other disciplines, it is understandable that this diversity might seem like a strategic weakness by those who resist the current status quo.

Still, there's no particular reason to imagine that an intellectual united front against economism would demand any sort of ideological uniformity, any more than a political one would. Or even that it demands complete commensurability. For example: many have recognized that the most profound way to challenge the economistic world-view theoretically is through the development of alternative theories of action, which expose the inherently alienating version of reality promulgated by economism by instead focusing on creativity, and, specifically, on trying to locate the capacity to create new social forms. There have been a number of attempts in this direction, ranging from Hans Joas' work in the tradition of American pragmatism, to Alain Caillé's, which begins from the creation of new social relations in the gift, to my own attempt to rework some Marxian ideas of production as a value theory of action. It is not entirely clear, however, if all of these can be completely reconciled. It is also not entirely clear if this is a problem. Certainly, there are approaches out there that are utterly irreconcilable even in ontological terms, and these include some of the more interesting and productive ones. For instance, Actor Network Theory, which looks at "society" as an effect rather than a cause, cannot be squared with Critical Realism, which sees it as an emergent reality which cannot be entirely reduced to anything else. And my own argument earlier in this paper, about the mutual constitution of imagination and reality, probably can't be reconciled with either. But I don't think there is any reason this incommensurability cannot be seen as itself a value that allows pragmatic integration through a common project of action (the pursuit of some kind of truth, of certain values inextricable from that pursuit, etc.), which can be agreed on as what one might call a regulatory principle. What does seem certain is that, without something along these lines, we are likely to see even further dominance by the logic of the market.

In the Absence of Regulatory Principles

Let me explain precisely what I mean by this. The colonization of other fields by the logic of the market does not just occur on the overt level (i.e., with the promulgation of "rational choice" models, or other blatant forms of economism), but also on a level which seems entirely unconscious. In a surprising variety of ways, the most ostensibly radical critical theory has been known to anticipate later neoliberal arguments. Take, for example, the concept of "postmodernism." This is a tricky term, of course, because there were never many scholars willing to actually call themselves "postmodernists." But, in a way, this was precisely what made the term so powerful: "postmodernism" was not something anyone was proposing but a fait accompli that everyone simply had to accept. From the 1980s on, it has become common to be presented with a series of arguments which might be summarized, in caricature form, as something like this:

> 1) We now live in a Postmodern Age. The world has changed. No one is responsible, it simply happened as a result of inexorable processes. Neither can we do anything about it, but must simply adapt ourselves to new conditions.
> 2) One result of our postmodern condition is that schemes to change the world or human society through collective political action are no longer viable. Everything is broken up and fragmented. Anyway, such schemes will inevitably prove either impossible, or produce totalitarian nightmares.
> 3) While this might seem to leave little room for human agency in history, one need not despair completely. Legitimate political action can take place, provided it is on a personal level: through the fashioning of subversive identities, forms of creative consumption, and the like. Such action is itself political and potentially liberatory.

This is, as I say, a caricature: the actual arguments made in any particular theoretical tract are usually infinitely more complex. Still, they almost invariably share some version of these three themes. Compare them, then, to the arguments that began to be promulgated in the 1990s, in the popular media, about a phenomena referred to as "globalization":

> 1) We now live in the age of the Global Market. The world has changed. No one is responsible, it simply happened as the result of inexorable processes. Neither can we do anything about it, but must simply adapt ourselves to new conditions.
> 2) One result is that schemes aiming to change society through collective political action are no longer viable. Dreams of revolution have been proven impossible or, worse, bound to produce totalitarian nightmares. Even any idea of changing society through electoral politics must now be abandoned in the name of "competitiveness."

3) If this might seem to leave little room for democracy, one need not despair: market behavior, and particularly individual consumption decisions, *are* democracy; indeed, all the democracy we'll ever really need.

There is, of course, one enormous difference between the two arguments. The central claim of those who celebrated postmodernism is that we have entered a world in which all totalizing systems—science, humanity, nation, truth, and so forth—have all been shattered; where there are no longer any grand mechanisms for stitching together a world now broken into incommensurable fragments. One can no longer even imagine that there could be a single standard of value by which to measure everything. The neoliberals, on the other hand, are singing the praises of a global market which is, in fact, the single greatest and most monolithic system of measurement ever created, a totalizing system which would subordinate everything—every object, every piece of land, every human capacity or relationship—on the planet to a single standard of value.

It is becoming increasingly obvious that what those who celebrated postmodernism were describing was in large part simply the effects of this universal market system: which, like any totalizing system of value, tends to throw all others into doubt and disarray. The critical thing for present purposes is not so much to ask how they could fail to notice this, but to establish one simple truth: that it is absurd to pretend that one could really have an intellectual universe in which there is no principle of articulation between different perspectives whatsoever. Anyone who pretends to have eliminated such principles entirely will simply be opening the way to reintroducing the dominant ideology of the day in covert form. And this is precisely what much of the most epistemologically radical approaches have ended up doing: reintroducing the logic and spirit of the market (with its ethos of endless flux, choice, reinvention, etc.) in a different register. To do otherwise would require establishing some alternate principle of articulation.

Prefigurative Social Theory?

In the above, I have sketched out some very preliminary thoughts on what such a principle might be like. Rather than develop a detailed argument (this is hardly the place), let me end, then, by suggesting that there's no reason why social theory itself might not take on a certain "prefigurative" role: that is, embody, in its own organization, as an articulation of extremely diverse philosophies, a vision of what a more reasonable political order could possibly be like. I think it is possible. However, certain habits of thought would definitely have to change. In everyday practice, the way that different schools of thought interact does not even resemble market relations so much as the style of argument preferred by contending Marxist sects. We see all the same sectarian habits: of reducing other positions into hostile caricatures so as to be able to plug them into some prefab set of categories, each representing a type of ideological error; of treating minor differences as if they were moral chasms. There are profound historical reasons why this happened. The organization of intellectual schools or tendencies has always rather resembled that of vanguardist political parties (and also, in a way, avant-garde artistic movements); but this is, in part, because all three had their origins in the same place, in Saint-Simon and Comte, who differed merely on whether an artistic "avant-garde" or social scientists should form the priesthood of their new religions. In order to begin to unify the diverse strands of social thought in opposition to the hegemony of economism, it would be necessary, first of all, to overcome this pernicious history and formulate instead something like what I suggested at the end of the previous section: a collection of approaches to social reality which, while necessarily constituting that reality in relation to a certain utopian social imaginary, are united not in their aspiration to impose themselves as the only legitimate approach, as if they were so many sects trying to seize power, but rather, by their shared commitment to a project and ethics which begins with the refusal to do so. It is a daunting prospect. Sectarian habits are very deeply ingrained. But it is hardly impossible. Most of the best social research already adopts something like this attitude, at least implicitly. It is, again, more than anything else a matter of giving serious reflective thought to what we are already starting to do in practice.

Endnotes

1   This paper was originally presented at a conference in Paris between the 12th and 14th of June 2003, entitled *Perspectives d'une théorie sociologique générale à l'ère de la mondialisation* (Perspectives on a General Sociological Theory in the Era of Globalization), sponsored by Alain Caillé of the MAUSS group. The conference was intended as a kind of summit of social theorists, attended by such luminaries as Margaret Archer, Raymond Boudon, Shmuel Eisenstadt, Bruno Latour, Hans Joas, Anne Rawls, Saskia Sassen, and Alain Touraine. Inviting me was very much an act of generosity on Caillé's part and I still greatly appreciate it. The essays from the conference were later published in *Revue du MAUSS Semestrielle*, all without footnotes or bibliography. I have decided here to preserve it in its original published form. The first part of the title is the one chosen for the piece by the French

editors (Alain Caillé and Stephane Dufois). The second half is the original question the organizers posed to all participants in the conference.

11

THERE NEVER WAS A WEST: OR, DEMOCRACY EMERGES FROM THE SPACES IN BETWEEN

What follows emerges largely from my own experience of the alternative globalization movement, where issues of democracy have been very much at the center of debate. Anarchists in Europe or North America and indigenous organizations in the Global South have found themselves locked in remarkably similar arguments. Is "democracy" an inherently Western concept? Does it refer a form of governance (a mode of communal self-organization), or a form of government (one particular way of organizing a state apparatus)? Does democracy necessarily imply majority rule? Is representative democracy really democracy at all? Is the word permanently tainted by its origins in Athens, a militaristic, slave-owning society founded on the systematic repression of women? Or does what we now call "democracy" have any real historical connection to Athenian democracy in the first place? Is it possible for those trying to develop decentralized forms of consensus-based direct democracy to reclaim the word? If so, how will we ever convince the majority of people in the world that "democracy" has nothing to do with electing representatives? If not, if we instead accept the standard definition and start calling direct democracy something else, how can we say we're against democracy—a word with such universally positive associations?

These are arguments about words much more than they are arguments about practices. On questions of practice, in fact, there is a surprising degree of convergence; especially within the more radical elements of the movement. Whether one is talking with members of Zapatista communities in Chiapas, unemployed *piqueteros* in Argentina, Dutch squatters, or anti-eviction activists in South African townships, almost everyone agrees on the importance of horizontal, rather than vertical structures; the need for initiatives to rise up from relatively small, self-organized, autonomous groups rather than being conveyed downwards through chains of command; the rejection of permanent, named leadership structures; and the need to maintain some kind of mechanism—whether these be North American-style "facilitation," Zapatista-style women's and youth caucuses, or any of an endless variety of other possibilities—to ensure that the voices of those who would normally find themselves marginalized or excluded from traditional participatory mechanisms are heard. Some of the bitter conflicts of the past, for example, between partisans of majority voting versus partisans of consensus process, have been largely resolved, or perhaps more accurately seem increasingly irrelevant, as more and more social movements use full consensus only within smaller groups and adopt various forms of "modified consensus" for larger coalitions. Something is emerging. The problem is what to call it. Many of the key principles of the movement (self-organization, voluntary association, mutual aid, the refusal of state power) derive from the anarchist tradition. Still, many who embrace these ideas are reluctant, or flat-out refuse, to call themselves "anarchists." Similarly with democracy. My own approach has normally been to openly embrace both terms, to argue, in fact, that anarchism and democracy are—or should be—largely identical. However, as I say, there is no consensus on this issue, nor even a clear majority view.

It seems to me these are tactical, political questions more than anything else. The word "democracy" has meant any number of different things over the course of its history. When first coined, it referred to a system in which the citizens of a community made decisions by equal vote in a collective assembly. For most of its history, it referred to political disorder, rioting, lynching, and factional violence (in fact, the word had much the same associations as "anarchy" does today). Only quite recently has it become identified with a system in which the citizens of a state elect representatives to exercise state power in their name. Clearly there is no true essence to be discovered here. About the only thing these different referents have in common, perhaps, is that they involve some sense that political questions that are normally the concerns of a narrow elite are here thrown open to everyone, and that this is either a very good, or a very bad, thing. The term has always been so morally loaded that to write a dispassionate, disinterested history of democracy would almost be a contradiction in terms. Most scholars who want to maintain an appearance of disinterest avoid the word. Those who do make generalizations about democracy inevitably have some sort of axe to grind.

I certainly do. That is why I feel it only fair to the reader to make my own axes evident from the start. It seems to me that there's a reason why the word "democracy," no matter how consistently it is abused by tyrants and demagogues, still maintains its stubborn popular appeal. For most people, democracy is still identified with some notion of ordinary people collectively managing their own affairs. It already had this connotation in the nineteenth century, and it was for this reason that nineteenth-century politicians, who had earlier shunned the term, reluctantly began to adopt the term and refer to themselves as "democrats"—and, gradually, to patch together a history by which they could represent themselves as heirs to a tradition that traced back to ancient Athens. However, I will also assume—for no particular reason, or no particular scholarly reason, since these are not scholarly questions but moral and political ones—that the history of "democracy" should be treated as more than just the history of the word "democracy." If democracy is simply a matter of communities managing their own affairs through an open and relatively egalitarian process of public discussion, there is no reason why egalitarian forms of decision-making in rural communities in Africa or Brazil should not be at least as worthy of the name as the constitutional systems that govern most nation-states today—and, in many cases, probably a good deal more worthy.

In light of this, I will be making a series of related arguments and perhaps the best way to proceed would be to just set out them all out right away.

1) Almost everyone who writes on the subject assumes "democracy" is a "Western" concept that begins its history in ancient Athens. They also assume that what eighteenth- and nineteenth-century politicians began reviving in Western Europe and North America was essentially the same thing. Democracy is thus seen as something whose natural habitat is Western Europe and its English- or French-speaking settler colonies. Not one of these assumptions is justified. "Western civilization" is a particularly incoherent concept, but, insofar as it refers to anything, it refers to an intellectual tradition. This intellectual tradition is, overall, just as hostile to anything we would recognize as democracy as those of India, China, or Mesoamerica.

2) Democratic practices—processes of egalitarian decision-making—however, occur pretty much anywhere, and are not peculiar to any one given "civilization," culture, or tradition. They tend to crop up wherever human life goes on outside systematic structures of coercion.

3) The "democratic ideal" tends to emerge when, under certain historical circumstances, intellectuals and politicians, usually in some sense navigating their way between states and popular movements and popular practices, interrogate their own traditions—invariably, in dialogue with other ones—citing cases of past or present democratic practice to argue that their tradition has a fundamental kernel of democracy. I call these moments of "democratic refoundation." From the perspective of the intellectual traditions, they are also moments of recuperation, in which ideals and institutions that are often the product of incredibly

complicated forms of interaction between people of very different histories and traditions come to be represented as emerging from the logic of that intellectual tradition itself. Over the course of the nineteenth and twentieth centuries especially, such moments did not just occur in Europe, but almost everywhere.

4) The fact that this ideal is always founded on (at least partly) invented traditions does not mean it is inauthentic or illegitimate or, at least, more inauthentic or illegitimate than any other. The contradiction, however, is that this ideal was always based on the impossible dream of marrying democratic procedures or practices with the coercive mechanisms of the state. The result are not "Democracies" in any meaningful sense of the world but Republics with a few, usually fairly limited, democratic elements.

5) What we are experiencing today is not a crisis of democracy but rather a crisis of the state. In recent years, there has been a massive revival of interest in democratic practices and procedures within global social movements, but this has proceeded almost entirely outside of statist frameworks. The future of democracy lies precisely in this area.

Let me take these up in roughly the order I've presented them above. I'll start with the curious idea that democracy is somehow a "Western concept."

Part I: On the Incoherence Of the Notion of the "Western Tradition"

I'll begin, then, with a relatively easy target: Samuel P. Huntington's famous essay on the "Clash of Civilizations." Huntington is a professor of International Relations at Harvard, a classic Cold War intellectual, beloved of right-wing think tanks. In 1993, he published an essay arguing that, now that the Cold War was over, global conflicts would come to center on clashes between ancient cultural traditions. The argument was notable for promoting a certain notion of cultural humility. Drawing on the work of Arnold Toynbee, he urged Westerners to understand that theirs is just one civilization among many, that its values should in no way be assumed to be universal. Democracy in particular, he argued, is a distinctly Western idea and the West should abandon its efforts to impose it on the rest of the world:

> At a superficial level, much of Western culture has indeed permeated the rest of the world. At a more basic level, however, Western concepts differ fundamentally from those prevalent in other civilizations. Western ideas of individualism, liberalism, constitutionalism, human rights,

equality, liberty, the rule of law, democracy, free markets, the separation of church and state, often have little resonance in Islamic, Confucian, Japanese, Hindu, Buddhist, or Orthodox cultures. Western efforts to propagate such ideas produce instead a reaction against "human rights imperialism" and a reaffirmation of indigenous values, as can be seen in the support for religious fundamentalism by the younger generation in non-Western cultures. The very notion that there is a "universal civilization" is a Western idea, directly at odds with the particularism of most Asian societies and their emphasis on what distinguishes one people from another (1993: 120).

The list of Western concepts is fascinating from any number of angles. If taken literally, for instance, it would mean that "the West" only really took any kind of recognizable form in the nineteenth or even twentieth centuries, since in any previous one the overwhelming majority of "Westerners" would have rejected just about all these principles out of hand—if, indeed, they would have been able even to conceive of them. One can, if one likes, scratch around through the last two or three thousand years in different parts of Europe and find plausible forerunners to most of them. Many try. Fifth-century Athens usually provides a useful resource in this regard, provided one is willing to ignore, or at least skim over, almost everything that happened between then and perhaps 1215 AD, or maybe 1776. This is roughly the approach taken by most conventional textbooks. Huntington is a bit subtler. He treats Greece and Rome as a separate, "Classical civilization," which then splits off into Eastern (Greek) and Western (Latin) Christianity—and later, of course, Islam. When Western civilization begins, it is identical to Latin Christendom. After the upheavals of the Reformation and CounterReformation, however, the civilization loses its religious specificity and transforms into something broader and essentially secular. The results, however, are much the same as in conventional textbooks, since Huntington also insists that the Western tradition was all along "far more" the heir of the ideas of Classical civilization than its Orthodox or Islamic rivals.

Now there are a thousand ways one could attack Huntington's position. His list of "Western concepts" seems particularly arbitrary. Any number of concepts were adrift in Western Europe over the years, and many far more widely accepted. Why choose this list rather than some other? What are the criteria? Clearly, Huntington's immediate aim was to show that many ideas widely accepted in Western Europe and North America are likely to be viewed with suspicion in other quarters. But, even on this basis, could one not equally well assemble a completely different list: say, argue that "Western culture" is premised on science, industrialism, bureaucratic rationality, nationalism, racial theories, and an endless drive for geographic expansion, and then argue that the culmination of Western culture was the Third Reich? (Actually, some radical critics of the West would probably make precisely this argument.) Yet even after criticism, Huntington has been stubborn in sticking to more or less the same arbitrary list (e.g., 1996).

It seems to me the only way to understand why Huntington creates the list he does is to examine his use of the terms "culture" and "civilization." In fact, if one reads the text carefully, one finds that the phrases "Western culture" and "Western civilization" are used pretty much interchangeably. Each civilization has its own culture. Cultures, in turn, appear to consist primarily of "ideas," "concepts," and "values." In the Western case, these ideas appear to have once been tied to a particular sort of Christianity, but now have developed a basically geographic or national distribution, having set down roots in Western Europe and its English- and French-speaking settler colonies.[1] The other civilizations listed are—with the exception of Japan—not defined in geographic terms. They are still religions: the Islamic, Confucian, Buddhist, Hindu, and Orthodox Christian civilizations. This is already a bit confusing. Why should the West have stopped being primarily defined in religious terms around 1520 (despite the fact that most Westerners continue to call themselves "Christians"), while the others all remain so (despite the fact that most Chinese, for example, would certainly not call themselves "Confucians")? Presumably because, for Huntington to be consistent in this area, he would either have to exclude from the West certain groups he would prefer not to exclude (Catholics or Protestants, Jews, Deists, secular philosophers) or else provide some reason why the West can consist of a complex amalgam of faiths and philosophies while all the other civilizations cannot: despite the fact that if one examines the history of geographical units like India, or China (as opposed to made-up entities like Hinduism or Confucianism), a complex amalgam of faiths and philosophies is precisely what one finds.

It gets worse. In a later clarification called "What Makes the West Western" (1996), Huntington actually does claim that "pluralism" is one of the West's unique qualities:

> Western society historically has been highly pluralistic. What is distinctive about the West, as Karl Deutsch noted, "is the rise and persistence of diverse autonomous groups not based on blood relationship or marriage." Beginning in the sixth and seventh centuries these groups initially included monasteries, monastic orders, and guilds, but afterwards expanded in many areas of Europe to include a variety of other associations and societies (1996: 234).

He goes on to explain this diversity also included class pluralism (strong aristocracies), social pluralism (representative bodies), linguistic diversity, and so on. All this gradually set the stage, he says, for the unique complexity of Western civil society. Now, it would be easy to point out how ridiculous all this is. One could, for instance, remind the reader that China and India in fact had, for most of their histories, a great deal more religious pluralism than Western Europe;[2] that most Asian societies were marked by a dizzying variety of monastic orders, guilds, colleges, secret societies, sodalities, professional and civic groups; that none ever came up with such distinctly Western ways of enforcing uniformity as the war of extermination against heretics, the Inquisition, or the witch hunt. But the amazing thing is that what Huntington is doing here is trying to turn the very incoherence of his category into its defining feature. First, he describes Asian civilizations in such a way that they cannot, by definition, be plural; then, if one were to complain that people he lumps together as "the West" don't seem to have any common features at all—no common language, religion, philosophy, or mode of government—Huntington could simply reply that this pluralism *is* the West's defining feature. It is the perfect circular argument.

In most ways, Huntington's argument is just typical, old-fashioned Orientalism: European civilization is represented as inherently dynamic, "the East," at least tacitly, as stagnant, timeless, and monolithic. What I really want to draw attention to, however, is just how incoherent Huntington's notions of "civilization" and "culture" really are. The word "civilization," after all, can be used in two very different ways. It can be used to refer to a society in which people live in cities, in the way an archeologist might refer to the Indus Valley. Or it can mean refinement, accomplishment, cultural achievement. Culture has much the same double meaning. One can use the term in its anthropological sense, as referring to structures of feeling, symbolic codes that members of a given culture absorb in the course of growing up and which inform every aspect of their daily life: the way people talk, eat, marry, gesture, play music, and so on. To use Bourdieu's terminology, one could call this culture as habitus. Alternately, one can use the word to refer to what is also called "high culture": the best and most profound productions of some artistic, literary, or philosophical elite. Huntington's insistence on defining the West only by its most remarkable, valuable concepts—like freedom and human rights—suggests that, in either case, it's mainly the latter sense he has in mind. After all, if "culture" were to be defined in the anthropological sense, then clearly the most direct heirs to ancient Greeks would not be modern Englishmen and Frenchmen, but modern Greeks. Whereas, in Huntington's system, modern Greeks parted company with the

West over 1500 years ago, the moment they converted to the wrong form of Christianity.

In short, for the notion of "civilization," in the sense used by Huntington, to really make sense, civilizations have to be conceived basically as traditions of people reading one another's books. It is possible to say Napoleon or Disraeli are more heirs to Plato and Thucydides than a Greek shepherd of their day for one reason only: both men were more likely to have read Plato and Thucydides. Western culture is not just a collection of ideas; it is a collection of ideas that are taught in textbooks and discussed in lecture halls, cafés, or literary salons. If it were not, it would be hard to imagine how one could end up with a civilization that begins in ancient Greece, passes to ancient Rome, maintains a kind of half-life in the Medieval Catholic world, revives in the Italian renaissance, and then passes mainly to dwell in those countries bordering the North Atlantic. It would also be impossible to explain how, for most of their history, "Western concepts" like human rights and democracy existed only *in potentia*. We could say: this is a literary and philosophical tradition, a set of ideas first imagined in ancient Greece, then conveyed through books, lectures, and seminars over several thousand years, drifting as they did westward, until their liberal and democratic potential was fully realized in a small number of countries bordering the Atlantic a century or two ago. Once they became enshrined in new, democratic institutions, they began to worm their way into ordinary citizens' social and political common sense. Finally, their proponents saw them as having universal status and tried to impose them on the rest of the world. But here they hit their limits, because they cannot ultimately expand to areas where there are equally powerful, rival textual traditions—based in Koranic scholarship, or the teachings of the Buddha—that inculcate other concepts and values.

This position, at least, would be intellectually consistent. One might call it the Great Books theory of civilization. In a way, it's quite compelling. Being Western, one might say, has nothing to do with habitus. It is not about the deeply embodied understandings of the world one absorbs in childhood—that which makes certain people upper class Englishwomen, others Bavarian farm boys, or Italian kids from Brooklyn. The West is, rather, the literary-philosophical tradition into which all of them are initiated, mainly in adolescence—though, certainly, some elements of that tradition do, gradually, become part of everyone's common sense. The problem is that, if Huntington applied this model consistently, it would destroy his argument. If civilizations are not deeply embodied, why, then, should an upper class Peruvian woman or Bangladeshi farm boy not be able to take the same curriculum and become just as Western as anyone else? But this is precisely what Huntington is trying to deny.

As a result, he is forced to continually slip back and forth between the two meanings of "civilization" and the two meanings of "culture." Mostly, the West is defined by its loftiest ideals. But sometimes it's defined by its ongoing institutional structure—for example, all those early Medieval guilds and monastic orders, which do not seem to be inspired by readings of Plato and Aristotle, but cropped up all of their own accord. Sometimes Western individualism is treated as an abstract principle, usually suppressed, an idea preserved in ancient texts, but occasionally poking out its head in documents like the Magna Carta. Sometimes it is treated as a deeply embedded folk understanding, which will never make intuitive sense to those raised in a different cultural tradition.

Now, as I say, I chose Huntington largely because he's such an easy target. The argument in "The Clash of Civilizations" is unusually sloppy.[3] Critics have duly savaged most of what he's had to say about non-Western civilizations. The reader may, at this point, feel justified to wonder why I'm bothering to spend so much time on him. The reason is that, in part because they are so clumsy, Huntington's argument brings out the incoherence in assumptions that are shared by almost everyone. None of his critics, to my knowledge, have challenged the idea that there is an entity that can be referred to as "the West," that it can be treated simultaneously as a literary tradition originating in ancient Greece, and as the common sense culture of people who live in Western Europe and North America today. The assumption that concepts like individualism and democracy are somehow peculiar to it goes similarly unchallenged. All this is simply taken for granted as the grounds of debate. Some proceed to celebrate the West as the birthplace of freedom. Others denounce it as a source of imperial violence. But it's almost impossible to find a political, or philosophical, or social thinker on the left or the right who doubts one can say meaningful things about "the Western tradition" at all. Many of the most radical, in fact, seem to feel it is impossible to say meaningful things about anything else.[4]

Parenthetical Note: On the Slipperiness of the Western Eye

What I am suggesting is that the very notion of the West is founded on a constant blurring of the line between textual traditions and forms of everyday practice. To offer a particular vivid example: In the 1920s, a French philosopher named Lucien Lévy-Bruhl wrote a series of books proposing that many of the societies studied by anthropologists evinced a "pre-logical mentality" (1926, etc.). Where modern Westerners employ logico-experimental thought, he argued, primitives employ profoundly different principles. The whole argument need not be spelled out. Everything Lévy-Bruhl said about primitive logic was attacked almost immediately and his argument is now considered entirely discredited. What his critics did not, generally speaking, point out is that Lévy-Bruhl was comparing apples and oranges. Basically, what he did was assemble the most puzzling ritual statements or surprising reactions to unusual circumstances he could cull from the observations of European missionaries and colonial officials in Africa, New Guinea, and similar places, and try to extrapolate the logic. He then compared this material, not with similar material collected in France or some other Western country, but rather, with a completely idealized conception of how Westerners ought to behave, based on philosophical and scientific texts (buttressed, no doubt, by observations about the way philosophers and other academics act while discussing and arguing about such texts). The results are manifestly absurd—we all know that ordinary people do not in fact apply Aristotelian syllogisms and experimental methods to their daily affairs—but it is the special magic of this style of writing is that one is never forced to confront this.

Because, in fact, this style of writing is also extremely common. How does this magic work? Largely, by causing the reader to identify with a human being of unspecified qualities who's trying to solve a puzzle. One sees it in the Western philosophical tradition, especially starting with the works of Aristotle that, especially compared with similar works in other philosophical traditions (which rarely start from such decontextualized thinkers), give us the impression the universe was created yesterday, suggesting no prior knowledge is necessary. Even more, there is the tendency to show a commonsense narrator confronted with some kind of exotic practices—this is what makes it possible, for example for a contemporary German to read Tacitus' *Germania* and automatically identify with the perspective of the Italian narrator, rather than with his own ancestor,[5] or an Italian atheist to read an Anglican missionary's account of some ritual in Zimbabwe without ever having to think about that observer's dedication to bizarre tea rituals or the doctrine of transubstantiation. Hence, the entire history of the West can be framed as a story of "inventions" and "discoveries." Most of all, there is the fact that it is precisely when one actually begins to write a text to address these issues, as I am doing now, that one effectively becomes part of the canon and the tradition most comes to seem overwhelmingly inescapable.

More than anything else, the "Western individual" in Lévy-Bruhl, or for that matter most contemporary anthropologists, is more than anything else, precisely that featureless, rational observer, a disembodied eye, carefully scrubbed of any individual or social content, that we are supposed to pretend to be when writing in certain genres of prose. It has little relation to any human being who has ever existed, grown up, had loves and hatreds and commitments. It's a pure abstraction. Recognizing all of this creates a terrible problem for anthropologists: if the "Western individual" doesn't exist, then what precisely is our point of comparison?

It seems to me, though, it creates an even worse problem for anyone who wishes to see this figure as the bearer of "democracy," as well. If democracy is communal self-governance, the Western individual is an actor already purged of any ties to a community. While it is possible to imagine this relatively featureless, rational observer as the protagonist of certain forms of market economics, to make him (and he is, unless otherwise specified, presumed to be male) a democrat seems possible only if one defines democracy as itself a kind of market that actors enter with little more than a set of economic interests to pursue. This is, of course, the approach promoted by rational-choice theory, and, in a way, you could say it is already implicit in the predominant approach to democratic decision-making in the literature since Rousseau, which tends to see "deliberation" merely as the balancing of interests rather than a process through which subjects themselves are constituted, or even shaped (Manin 1994).[6] It is very difficult to see such an abstraction, divorced from any concrete community, entering into the kind of conversation and compromise required by anything but the most abstract form of democratic process, such as the periodic participation in elections.

World-Systems Reconfigured

The reader may feel entitled to ask: If "the West" is a meaningless category, how can we talk about such matters? It seems to me we need an entirely new set of categories. While this is hardly the place to develop them, I've suggested elsewhere (Graeber 2004) that there are a whole series of terms—starting with the West, but also including terms like "modernity"—that effectively substitute for thought. If one looks either at concentrations of urbanism, or literary-philosophical traditions, it becomes hard to avoid the impression that Eurasia was for most of its history divided into three main centers: an Eastern system centered on China, a South Asian one centered on what's now India, and a Western civilization that centered on what we now called "the Middle East," extending sometimes further, sometimes less, into the Mediterranean.[7] In world-system terms, for most of the Middle Ages, Europe and Africa both seem to have almost precisely the same relation with the core states of Mesopotamia and the Levant: they were classic economic peripheries, importing manufactures and supplying raw materials like gold and silver, and, significantly, large numbers of slaves. (After the revolt of African slaves in Basra from 868–883 CE, the Abbasid Caliphate seem to have began importing Europeans instead, as they were considered more docile.) Europe and Africa were, for most of this period, cultural peripheries as well. Islam resembles what was later to be called "the Western tradition" in so many ways—the intellectual efforts to fuse Judeo-Christian scripture with the categories of Greek philosophy, the literary emphasis on courtly love, the scientific rationalism, the legalism, puritanical monotheism, missionary impulse, the expansionist mercantile capitalism—even the periodic waves of fascination with "Eastern mysticism"—that only the deepest historical prejudice could have blinded European historians to the conclusion that, in fact, this *is* the Western tradition; that Islamicization was and continues to be a form of Westernization; that those who lived in the barbarian kingdoms of the European Middle Ages only came to resemble what we now call "the West" when they themselves became more like Islam.

If so, what we are used to calling "the rise of the West" is probably better thought of, in world-system terms, as the emergence of what Michel-Rolph Trouillot (2003) has called the "North Atlantic system," which gradually replaced the Mediterranean semi-periphery, and emerged as a world economy of its own, rivaling, and then gradually, slowly, painfully, incorporating the older world economy that had centered on the cosmopolitan societies of the Indian Ocean. This North Atlantic world-system was created through almost unimaginable catastrophe: the destruction of entire civilizations, mass enslavement, the death of at least a hundred million human beings. It also produced its own forms of cosmopolitanism, with endless fusions of African, Native American, and European traditions. Much of the history of the seaborne, North Atlantic proletariat is only beginning to be reconstructed (Gilroy 1993; Sakolsky & Koehnline 1993; Rediker 1981, 1990; Linebaugh and Rediker 2001; etc.), a history of mutinies, pirates, rebellions, defections, experimental communities, and every sort of Antinomian and populist idea, largely squelched in conventional accounts, much of it permanently lost, but which seems to have played a key role in many of the radical ideas that came to be referred to as "democracy." This is jumping ahead. For now, I just want to emphasize that rather than a history of "civilizations" developing through some Herderian or Hegelian process of internal unfolding, we are dealing with societies that are thoroughly entangled.

Part II: Democracy Was Not Invented

I began this essay by suggesting that one can write the history of democracy in two very different ways. Either one can write a history of the word "democracy," beginning with ancient Athens, or one can write a history of the sort of egalitarian decision-making procedures that in Athens came to be referred to as "democratic."

Normally, we tend to assume the two are effectively identical because common wisdom has it that democracy—much like, say, science, or philosophy—was invented in ancient Greece. On the face of it this seems an odd assertion. Egalitarian communities have existed throughout human history—many of them far more egalitarian than fifth-century Athens—and they each had some kind of procedure for coming to decisions in matters of collective importance. Often, this involved assembling everyone for discussions in which all members of the community, at least in theory, had equal say. Yet somehow, it is always assumed that these procedures could not have been, properly speaking, "democratic."

The main reason this argument seems to make intuitive sense is because in these other assemblies, things rarely actually came to a vote. Almost invariably, they used some form of consensus-finding. Now this is interesting in itself. If we accept the idea that a show of hands, or having everyone who supports a proposition stand on one side of the plaza and everyone against stand on the other, are not really such incredibly sophisticated ideas that some ancient genius had to "invent" them, then why are they so rarely employed? Why, instead, did communities invariably prefer the apparently much more difficult task of coming to unanimous decisions?

The explanation I would propose is this: it is much easier, in a face-to-face community, to figure out what most members of that community want to do, than to figure out how to change the minds of those who don't want to do it. Consensus decision-making is typical of societies where there would be no way to compel a minority to agree with a majority decision; either because there is no state with a monopoly of coercive force, or because the state has no interest in or does not tend to intervene in local decision-making. If there is no way to compel those who find a majority decision distasteful to go along with it, then the last thing one would want to do is to hold a vote: a public contest which someone will be seen to lose. Voting would be the most likely means to guarantee the sort of humiliations, resentments, and hatreds that ultimately lead the destruction of communities. As any activist who has gone through a facilitation training for a contemporary direct action group can tell you, consensus process is not the same as parliamentary debate and finding consensus in no way resembles voting. Rather, we are dealing with a process of compromise and synthesis meant to produce decisions that no one finds so violently objectionable that they are not willing to at least assent. That is to say two levels we are used to distinguishing—decision-making, and enforcement—are effectively collapsed here. It is not that everyone has to agree. Most forms of consensus include a variety of graded forms of disagreement. The point is to ensure that no one walks away feeling that their views have been totally ignored and, therefore, that even those who think the group came to a bad decision are willing to offer their passive acquiescence.

Majority democracy, we might say, can only emerge when two factors coincide:

(1) a feeling that people should have equal say in making group deci-
    sions, and
(2) a coercive apparatus capable of enforcing those decisions.

For most of human history, it has been extremely unusual to have both at the same time. Where egalitarian societies exist, it is also usually consid-ered wrong to impose systematic coercion. Where a machinery of coercion did exist, it did not even occur to those wielding it that they were enforcing any sort of popular will.

It is of obvious relevance that Ancient Greece was one of the most com-petitive societies known to history. It was a society that tended to make ev-erything into a public contest, from athletics to philosophy or tragic drama or just about anything else. So it might not seem entirely surprising they made political decision-making into a public contest as well. Even more cru-cial, though, was the fact that decisions were made by a populace in arms. Aristotle, in his *Politics*, remarks that the constitution of a Greek city-state will normally depend on the chief arm of its military: if this is cavalry, it will be an aristocracy, since horses are expensive. If hoplite infantry, it will be oli-garchic, as all could not afford the armor and training. If its power was based in the navy or light infantry, one can expect a democracy, as anyone can row, or use a sling. In other words, if a man is armed, then one pretty much has to take his opinions into account. One can see how this worked at its starkest in Xenophon's *Anabasis*, which tells the story of an army of Greek mercenar-ies who suddenly find themselves leaderless and lost in the middle of Persia. They elect new officers, and then hold a collective vote to decide what to do next. In a case like this, even if the vote was 60/40, everyone could see the balance of forces and what would happen if things actually came to blows. Every vote was, in a real sense, a conquest.

In other words, here too decision-making and the means of enforcement were effectively collapsed (or could be), but in a rather different way.

Roman legions could be similarly democratic; this was the main reason they were never allowed to enter the city of Rome. And, when Machiavelli revived the notion of a democratic republic at the dawn of the "modern" era, he immediately reverted to the notion of a populace in arms.

This in turn might help explain the term "democracy" itself, which ap-pears to have been coined as something of a slur by its elitist opponents: it literally means the "force" or even "violence" of the people. *Kratos*, not *archos*. The elitists who coined the term always considered democracy not too far from simple rioting or mob rule; though, of course, their solution was the permanent conquest of the people by someone else. Ironically, when they did manage to suppress democracy for this reason, which was usually, the result was that the only way the general populace's will was known was precisely through rioting, a practice that became quite institutionalized in, say, imperial Rome or eighteenth-century England.

One question that bears historical investigation is the degree to which such phenomena were in fact encouraged by the state. Here, I'm not referring to literal rioting, of course, but to what I would call the "ugly mirrors": institutions promoted or supported by elites that reinforced the sense that popular decision-making could only be violent, chaotic, and arbitrary "mob rule." I suspect that these are quite common to authoritarian regimes. Consider, for example, that while the defining public event in democratic Athens was the *agora*, the defining public event in authoritarian Rome was the circus, assemblies in which the plebs gathered to witness races, gladiatorial contests, and mass executions. Such games were sponsored either directly by the state, or more often, by particular members of the elite (Veyne 1976; Kyle 1998; Lomar and Cornell 2003). The fascinating thing about gladiatorial contests in particular, is that they did involve a kind of popular decision-making: lives would be taken, or spared, by popular acclaim. However, where the procedures of the Athenian *agora* were designed to maximize the dignity of the *demos* and the thoughtfulness of its deliberations—despite the underlying element of coercion, and its occasional capability of making terrifyingly bloodthirsty decisions—the Roman circus was almost exactly the opposite. It had more the air of regular, state-sponsored lynchings. Almost every quality normally ascribed to "the mob" by later writers hostile to democracy—the capriciousness, overt cruelty, factionalism (supporters of rival chariot teams would regularly do battle in the streets), hero worship, mad passions—all were not only tolerated, but actually encouraged, in the Roman amphitheatre. It was as if an authoritarian elite was trying to provide the public with constant nightmare images of the chaos that would ensue if they were to take power into their own hands.

My emphasis on the military origins of direct democracy is not meant to imply that popular assemblies in, say, Medieval cities or New England town meetings were not normally orderly and dignified procedures; though one suspects this was in part due to the fact that here, too, in actual practice, there was a certain baseline of consensus-seeking going on. Still, they seem to have done little to disabuse members of political elites of the idea that popular rule would more resemble the circuses and riots of imperial Rome and Byzantium. The authors of the Federalist Papers, like almost all other literate men of their day, took it for granted that what they called "democracy"—by which they meant, direct democracy, "pure democracy" as they sometimes put it—was in its nature the most unstable, tumultuous form of government, not to mention one which endangers the rights of minorities (the specific minority they had in mind in this case being the rich). It was only once the term "democracy" could be almost completely transformed to incorporate the principle of representation—a term which itself has a very curious history, since as Cornelius Castoriadis liked to point out (1991; Godbout 2005), it originally referred to representatives of the people before the *king*, internal ambassadors in fact, rather than those who wielded power in any sense themselves—that it was rehabilitated, in the eyes of well-born political theorists, and took on the meaning it has today. In the next section let me pass, however briefly, to how this came about.

Part III: On the Emergence of the "Democratic Ideal"

The remarkable thing is just how long it took. For the first three hundred years of the North Atlantic system, democracy continued to mean "the mob." This was true even in the "Age of Revolutions." In almost every case, the founders of what are now considered the first democratic constitutions in England, France, and the United States, rejected any suggestion that they were trying to introduce "democracy." As Francis Dupuis-Deri (1999, 2004) has observed:

> The founders of the modern electoral systems in the United States and France were overtly anti-democratic. This anti-democratism can be explained in part by their vast knowledge of the literary, philosophical and historical texts of Greco-Roman antiquity. Regarding political history, it was common for American and French political figures to see themselves as direct heirs to classical civilization and to believe that all through history, from Athens and Rome to Boston and Paris, the same political forces have faced off in eternal struggles. The founders sided with the historical republican forces against the aristocratic and democratic ones, and the Roman republic was the political model for both the Americans and the French, whereas Athenian democracy was a despised counter-model (Dupuis-Deri 2004: 120).

In the English-speaking world, for example, most educated people in the late eighteenth century were familiar with Athenian democracy largely through a translation of Thucydides by Thomas Hobbes. Their conclusion,

that democracy was unstable, tumultuous, prone to factionalism and dem-
agoguery, and marked by a strong tendency to turn into despotism, was
hardly surprising.

Most politicians, then, were hostile to anything that smacked of democracy precisely *because* they saw themselves as heirs to what we now call
"the Western tradition." The ideal of the Roman republic was enshrined,
for example, in the American constitution, whose framers were quite consciously trying to imitate Rome's "mixed constitution," balancing monarchical, aristocratic, and democratic elements. John Adams, for example, in his
Defense of the Constitution (1797) argued that truly egalitarian societies do
not exist; that every known human society has a supreme leader, an aristocracy (whether of wealth or a "natural aristocracy" of virtue) and a public, and
that the Roman Constitution was the most perfect in balancing the powers
of each. The American constitution was meant to reproduce this balance by
creating a powerful presidency, a senate to represent the wealthy, and a congress to represent the people—though the powers of the latter were largely
limited to ensuring popular control over the distribution of tax money. This
republican ideal lies at the basis of all "democratic" constitutions and to this
day many conservative thinkers in America like to point out that "America is
not a democracy: it's a republic."

On the other hand, as John Markoff notes, "those who called themselves
democrats at the tail end of the eighteenth century were likely to be very
suspicious of parliaments, downright hostile to competitive political parties,
critical of secret ballots, uninterested or even opposed to women's suffrage,
and sometimes tolerant of slavery" (1999: 661)—again, hardly surprising,
for those who wished to revive something along the lines of ancient Athens.

At the time, outright democrats of this sort—men like Tom Paine, for
instance—were considered a tiny minority of rabble-rousers even within
revolutionary regimes. Things only began to change over the course of the
next century. In the United States, as the franchise widened in the first decades of the nineteenth century, and politicians were increasingly forced to
seek the votes of small farmers and urban laborers, some began to adopt
the term. Andrew Jackson led the way. He started referring to himself as a
democrat in the 1820s. Within twenty years, almost all political parties, not
just populists but even the most conservative, began to follow suit. In France,
socialists began calling for "democracy" in the 1830s, with similar results:
within ten or fifteen years, the term was being used by even moderate and
conservative republicans forced to compete with them for the popular vote
(Dupuis-Deris 1999, 2004). The same period saw a dramatic reappraisal of
Athens, which—again starting in the 1820s—began to be represented as
embodying a noble ideal of public participation, rather than a nightmare of

violent crowd psychology (Saxonhouse 1993). This is not, however, because anyone, at this point, was endorsing Athenian-style direct democracy, even on the local level (in fact, one rather imagines it was precisely this fact that made the rehabilitation of Athens possible). For the most part, politicians simply began substituting the word "democracy" for "republic," without any change in meaning. I suspect the new positive appraisal of Athens had more to do with popular fascination with events in Greece at the time than any-thing else: specifically, the war of independence against the Ottoman Empire between 1821 and 1829. It was hard not see it as modern replay of the clash between the Persian Empire and Greek city-states narrated by Herodotus, a kind of founding text of the opposition between freedom-loving Europe and the despotic East; and, of course, changing one's frame of reference from Thucydides to Herodotus could only do Athens' image good.

When novelists like Victor Hugo and poets like Walt Whitman began touting democracy as a beautiful ideal—as they soon began to do—they were not, however, referring to word-games on the part of elites, but to the broader popular sentiment that had caused small farmers and urban laborers to look with favor on the term to begin with, even when the political elite was still largely using it as a term of abuse. The "democratic ideal," in other words, did not emerge from the Western literary-philosophical tradition. It was, rather, imposed on it. In fact, the notion that democracy was a distinct-ly "Western" ideal only came much later. For most of the nineteenth century, when Europeans defined themselves against "the East" or "the Orient," they did so precisely as "Europeans," not "Westerners."[8] With few exceptions, "the West" referred to the Americas. It was only in the 1890s, when Europeans began to see the United States as part of the same, coequal civilization, that many started using the term in its current sense (GoGwilt 1995; Martin & Wigan 1997: 49–62). Huntington's "Western civilization" comes even later: this notion was first developed in American universities in the years follow-ing World War I (Federici 1995: 67), at a time when German intellectuals were already locked in debate about whether they were part of the West at all. Over the course of the twentieth century, the concept of "Western civili-zation" proved perfectly tailored for an age that saw the gradual dissolution of colonial empires, since it managed to lump together the former colonial metropoles with their wealthiest and most powerful settler colonies, at the same time insisting on their shared moral and intellectual superiority, and abandoning any notion that they necessarily had a responsibility to "civilize" anybody else. The peculiar tension evident in phrases like "Western science," "Western freedoms," or "Western consumer goods"—do these reflect univer-sal truths that all human beings should recognize? or are they the products of one tradition among many?—would appear to stem directly from the ambiguities of the historical moment. The resulting formulation is, as I've noted, so riddled with contradictions that it's hard to see how it could have arisen except to fill a very particular historical need.

If you examine these terms more closely, however, it becomes obvious that all these "Western" objects are the products of endless entanglements. "Western science" was patched together out of discoveries made on many continents, and is now largely produced by non-Westerners. "Western consumer goods" were always drawn from materials taken from all over the world, many explicitly imitated Asian products, and nowadays, are all produced in China. Can we say the same of "Western freedoms"?

The reader can probably guess what my answer will be.

Part IV: Recuperation

In debates about the origins of capitalism, one of the main bones of contention is whether capitalism—or, alternately, industrial capitalism—emerged primarily within European societies, or whether it can only be understood in the context of a larger world-system connecting Europe and its overseas possessions, markets and sources of labor overseas. It is possible to have the argument, I think, because so many capitalist forms began so early—many could be said to already be present, at least in embryonic form, at the very dawn of European expansion. This can hardly be said for democracy. Even if one is willing to follow by-now accepted convention and identify republican forms of government with that word, democracy only emerges within centers of empire like England and France, and colonies like the United States, after the Atlantic system had existed for almost three hundred years.

Giovanni Arrighi, Iftikhar Ahmad, and Min-wen Shih (1997) have produced what's to my mind one of the more interesting responses to Huntington: a world-systemic analysis of European expansion, particularly in Asia, over the last several centuries. One of the most fascinating elements in their account is how, at exactly the same time as European powers came to start thinking themselves as "democratic"—in the 1830s, 1840s, and 1850s—those same powers began pursuing an intentional policy of supporting reactionary elites against those pushing for anything remotely resembling democratic reforms overseas. Great Britain was particularly flagrant in this regard: whether in its support for the Ottoman Empire against the rebellion of Egyptian governor Muhammed Ali after the Balta Limani Treaty of 1838, or in its support for the Qing imperial forces against the Taiping rebellion after the Nanjing Treaty of 1842. In either case, Britain first found some excuse to launch a military attack on one of the great Asian *ancien regimes*, defeated it militarily, imposed a commercially advantageous treaty, and then, almost immediately upon doing so, swung around to prop that same regime up against political rebels who clearly were closer to their own supposed "Western" values than the regime itself: in the first case a rebellion aiming to turn Egypt into something more like a modern nation-state, in the second, an egalitarian Christian movement calling for universal brotherhood. After the Great Rebellion of 1857 in India, Britain began employing the same strategy in her own colonies, self-consciously propping up "landed magnates and the petty rulers of 'native states' within its own Indian empire" (1997: 34). All of this was buttressed on the intellectual level by the development around the same time of Orientalist theories that argued that, in Asia, such authoritarian regimes were inevitable, and democratizing movements were unnatural or did not exist.[9]

> In sum, Huntington's claim that Western civilization is the bearer of a heritage of liberalism, constitutionalism, human rights, equality, liberty, the rule of law, democracy, free markets, and other similarly attractive ideals—all of which are said to have permeated other civilizations only superficially—rings false to anyone familiar with the Western record in Asia in the so-called age of nation-states. In this long list of ideals, it is hard to find a single one that was not denied in part or full by the leading Western powers of the epoch in their dealings either with the peoples they subjected to direct colonial rule or with the governments over which they sought to establish suzerainty. And conversely, it is just as hard to find a single one of those ideals that was not upheld by movements of national liberation in their struggle against the Western powers. In upholding these ideals, however, non-Western peoples and governments invariably combined them with ideals derived from their own civilizations in those spheres in which they had little to learn from the West (Arrighi, Ahmad, and Shih 1997: 25).

Actually, I think one could go much further. Opposition to European expansion in much of the world, even quite early on, appears to have been carried out in the name of "Western values" that the Europeans in question did not yet even have. Engseng Ho (2004: 222–24) for example draws our attention to the first known articulation of the notion of jihad against Europeans in the Indian Ocean: a book called *Gift of the Jihad Warriors in Matters Regarding the Portuguese*, written in 1574 by an Arab jurist named Zayn al-Din al Malibari and addressed to the Muslim sultan of the Deccan state of Bijapur. In it, the author makes a case that it is justified to wage war again the Portuguese specifically because they destroyed a tolerant, pluralistic society in which Muslims, Hindus, Christians, and Jews had always managed to coexist.

In the Muslim trading ecumene of the Indian Ocean, some of Huntington's values—a certain notion of liberty, a certain notion of equality, some very explicit ideas about freedom of trade and the rule of law—had long been considered important; others, such as religious tolerance, might well have become values as a result of Europeans coming onto the scene—if only by point of contrast. My real point is that one simply cannot lay any of these values down to the one particular moral, intellectual, or cultural tradition. They arise, for better or worse, from exactly this sort of interaction.

I also want to make another point, though. We are dealing with the work of a Muslim jurist, writing a book addressed to a South Indian king. The values of tolerance and mutual accommodation he wishes to defend— actually, these are our terms; he himself speaks of "kindness"—might have emerged from a complex intercultural space, outside the authority of any overarching state power, and they might have only crystallized, as values, in the face of those who wished to destroy that space. Yet, in order to write about them, to justify their defense, he was forced to deal with states and frame his argument in terms of a single literary-philosophical tradition: in this case, the legal tradition of Sunni Islam. There was an act of reincorporation. There inevitably must be, once one reenters the world of state power and textual authority. And, when later authors write about such ideas, they tend to represent matters as if the ideals emerged from that tradition, rather than from the spaces in between

So do historians. In a way, it's almost inevitable that they should do so, considering the nature of their source material. They are, after all, primarily students of textual traditions, and information about the spaces in between is often very difficult to come by. What's more, they are—at least when dealing with the "Western tradition"—writing, in large part, within the same literary tradition as their sources. This is what makes the real origins of democratic ideals—especially that popular enthusiasm for ideas of liberty and popular sovereignty that obliged politicians to adopt the term to begin with—so difficult to reconstruct. Recall here what I said earlier about the "slipperiness of the Western eye." The tradition has long had a tendency to describe alien societies as puzzles to be deciphered by a rational observer. As a result, descriptions of alien societies were often used, around this time, as a way of making a political point: whether contrasting European societies with the relative freedom of Native Americans, or the relative order of China. But they did not tend to acknowledge the degree to which they were themselves entangled with those societies and to which their own institutions were influenced by them. In fact, as any student of early anthropology knows, even authors who were themselves part Native American or part Chinese, or who had never set foot in Europe, would tend to write this way. As men or women of action, they would negotiate their way between worlds. When it came time to write about their experiences, they would become featureless abstractions. When it came time to write institutional histories, they referred back, almost invariably, to the Classical world.

The "Influence Debate"

In 1977, an historian of the Iroquois confederacy (himself a Native American and member of AIM, the American Indian Movement) wrote an essay proposing that certain elements of the US constitution—particularly its federal structure—were inspired in part by the League of Six Nations. He expanded on the argument in the 1980s with another historian, David Johansen (1982; Grinde and Johansen 1990), suggesting that, in a larger sense, what we now would consider America's democratic spirit was partly inspired by the example of Native Americans.

Some of the specific evidence they assembled was quite compelling. The idea of forming some sort of federation of colonies was indeed proposed by an Onondaga ambassador named Canassatego, exhausted by having to negotiate with so many separate colonies during negotiations over the Lancaster Treaty in 1744. The image he used to demonstrate the strength of union, a bundle of six arrows, still appears on the Seal of the Union of the United States (the number later increased to thirteen). Ben Franklin, present at the event, took up the idea and promoted it widely through his printing house over the next decade, and, in 1754, his efforts came to fruition with a conference in Albany, New York—with representatives of the Six Nations in attendance—that drew up what came to be known as the Albany Plan of Union. The plan was ultimately rejected both by British authorities and colonial parliaments, but it was clearly an important first step. More importantly, perhaps, proponents of what has come to be called the "influence theory" argued that the values of egalitarianism and personal freedom that marked so many Eastern Woodlands societies served as a broader inspiration for the equality and liberty promoted by colonial rebels. When Boston patriots triggered their revolution by dressing up as Mohawks and dumping British tea into the harbor, they were making a self-conscious statement of their model for individual liberty.

That Iroquois federal institutions might have had some influence on the US constitution was considered a completely unremarkable notion, when it was occasionally proposed in the nineteenth century. When it was proposed again in the 1980s it set off a political maelstrom. Many Native Americans strongly endorsed the idea, Congress passed a bill acknowledging it, and all sorts of right-wing commentators immediately pounced on it as an example of the worst sort of political correctness. At the same time, though, the argument met immediate and quite virulent opposition both from most professional historians considered authorities on the constitution and from anthropological experts on the Iroquois.

The actual debate ended up turning almost entirely on whether one could prove a direct relation between Iroquois institutions and the thinking of the framers of the constitution. Payne (1999), for example, noted that some New England colonists were discussing federal schemes before they were even aware of the League's existence; in a larger sense, they argued that proponents of the "influence theory" had essentially cooked the books by picking out every existing passage in the writings of colonial politicians that praised Iroquoian institutions, while ignoring hundreds of texts in which those same politicians denounced the Iroquois, and Indians in general, as ignorant murdering savages. Their opponents, they said, left the reader with the impression that explicit, textual proof of an Iroquoian influence on the constitution existed, and this was simply not the case. Even the Indians present at constitutional conventions appear to have been there to state grievances, not to offer advice. Invariably, when colonial politicians discussed the origins of their ideas, they looked to Classical, Biblical, or European examples: the book of Judges, the Achaean League, the Swiss Confederacy, the United Provinces of the Netherlands. Proponents of the influence theory, in turn, replied that this kind of linear thinking was simplistic: no one was claiming the Six Nations were the only or even primary model for American federalism, just one of many elements that went into the mix—and considering that it was the only functioning example of a federal system of which the colonists had any direct experience, to insist it had no influence whatever was simply bizarre. Indeed, some of the objections raised by anthropologists seem so odd—for example, Elisabeth Tooker's objection (1998) that, since the League worked by consensus and reserved an important place for women, and the US constitution used a majority system and only allowed men to vote, one could not possibly have served as inspiration for the other, or Dean Snow's remark (1994: 154) that such claims "muddle and denigrate the subtle and remarkable features of Iroquois government"—one can only conclude that Native American activist Vine Deloria probably did have a point in suggesting much of this was simply an effort by scholars to protect what they considered their turf—a matter of intellectual property rights (in Johansen 1998: 82).

The proprietary reaction is much clearer in some quarters. "This myth isn't just silly, it's destructive," wrote one contributor to *The New Republic*.

"Obviously Western civilization, beginning in Greece, had provided models of government much closer to the hearts of the Founding Fathers than this one. There was nothing to be gained by looking to the New World for inspiration" (Newman 1998: 18). If one is speaking of the immediate perceptions of many of the United States' "founding fathers," this may well be true, but if we are trying to understand the Iroquois influence on American *democracy*, then matters look quite different. As we've seen, the Constitution's framers did indeed identify with the classical tradition, but they were hostile to democracy for that very reason. They identified democracy with untrammeled liberty, equality, and, insofar as they were aware of Indian customs at all, they were likely to see them as objectionable for precisely the same reasons.

If one reexamines some of the mooted passages, this is precisely what one finds. John Adams, remember, had argued in his *Defense of the Constitution* that egalitarian societies do not exist; political power in every human society is divided between the monarchical, aristocratic, and democratic principles. He saw the Indians as resembling the ancient Germans in that "the democratical branch, in particular, is so determined, that real sovereignty resided in the body of the people," which, he said, worked well enough when one was dealing with populations scattered over a wide territory with no real concentrations of wealth, but, as the Goths found when they conquered the Roman empire, could only lead to confusion, instability, and strife as soon as such populations became more settled and have significant resources to administer (Adams: 296; see Levy 1999: 598; Payne 1999: 618). His observations are typical. Madison, even Jefferson, tended to describe Indians much as did John Locke, as exemplars of an individual liberty untrammeled by any form of state or systematic coercion—a condition made possible by the fact that Indian societies were not marked by significant divisions of property. They considered Native institutions obviously inappropriate for a society such as their own, which did.

Still, Enlightenment theory to the contrary, nations are not really created by the acts of wise lawgivers. Neither is democracy invented in texts; even if we are forced to rely on texts to divine its history. Actually, the men who wrote the Constitution were not only for the most part wealthy landowners, few had a great deal of experience in sitting down with a group of equals—at least, until they became involved in colonial congresses. Democratic practices tend to first get hammered out in places far from the purview of such men, and, if one sets out in search for which of their contemporaries had the most hands-on experience in such matters, the results are sometimes startling. One of the leading contemporary historians of European democracy, John Markoff, in an essay called "Where and When Was Democracy Invented?," remarks, at one point, very much in passing:

that leadership could derive from the consent of the led, rather than be bestowed by higher authority, would have been a likely experience of the crews of pirate vessels in the early modern Atlantic world. Pirate crews not only elected their captains, but were familiar with countervailing power (in the forms of the quartermaster and ship's council) and contractual relations of individual and collectivity (in the form of written ship's articles specifying shares of booty and rates of compensation for on-the-job injury) (Markoff 1999: 673n62).

As a matter of fact, the typical organization of eighteenth-century pirate ships, as reconstructed by historians like Marcus Rediker (2004: 60–82), appears to have been remarkably democratic. Captains were not only elected, they usually functioned much like Native American war chiefs: granted total power during chase or combat, they were otherwise were treated like ordinary crewmen. Those ships whose captains were granted more general powers also insisted on the crew's right to remove them at any time for cowardice, cruelty, or any other reason. In every case, ultimate power rested in a general assembly that often ruled on even the most minor matters, always, apparently, by majority show of hands.

All this might seem less surprising if one considers the pirates' origins. Pirates were generally mutineers, sailors often originally pressed into service against their will in port towns across the Atlantic, who had mutinied against tyrannical captains and "declared war against the whole world." They often became classic social bandits, wreaking vengeance against captains who abused their crews, and releasing or even rewarding those against whom they found no complaints. The make-up of crews was often extraordinarily heterogeneous. "Black Sam Bellamy's crew of 1717 was 'a Mix'd Multitude of all Country's,' including British, French, Dutch, Spanish, Swedish, Native American, African American, and two dozen Africans who had been liberated from a slave ship" (Rediker 2004: 53). In other words, we are dealing with a collection of people in which there was likely to be at least some first-hand knowledge of a very wide range of directly democratic institutions, ranging from Swedish *tings* to African village assemblies to Native American councils such as those from which the League of Six Nations itself developed, suddenly finding themselves forced to improvise some mode of self-government in the complete absence of any state. It was the perfect intercultural space of experiment. In fact, there was likely to be no more conducive ground for the development of new democratic institutions anywhere in the Atlantic world at the time.

I bring this up for two reasons. One is obvious. We have no evidence that democratic practices developed on Atlantic pirate ships in the early part of the eighteenth century had any influence, direct or indirect, on the evolution of democratic constitutions sixty or seventy years later. Nor could we. While accounts of pirates and their adventures circulated widely, having much the same popular appeal as they do today (and presumably, at the time, were likely to be at least a little more accurate than contemporary Hollywood versions), this would be about the very last influence a French, English, or colonial gentleman would ever have been willing to acknowledge. This is not to say that pirate practices were likely to have influenced democratic constitutions. Only that we would not know if they did. One can hardly imagine things would be too different with those they ordinarily referred to as "the American savages."

The other reason is that frontier societies in the Americas were probably more similar to pirate ships than we would be given to imagine. They might not have been as densely populated as pirate ships, or in as immediate need of constant cooperation, but they were spaces of intercultural improvisation, largely outside of the purview of states. Colin Calloway (1997; cf. Axtell 1985) has documented just how entangled the societies of settlers and natives often were, with settlers adopting Indian crops, clothes, medicines, customs, and styles of warfare; trading with them, often living side by side, sometimes intermarrying, and most of all, inspiring endless fears among the leaders of colonial communities and military units that their subordinates were absorbing Indian attitudes of equality and individual liberty. At the same time, as New England Puritan minister Cotton Mather, for example, was inveighing against pirates as a blaspheming scourge of mankind, he was also complaining that fellow colonists had begun to imitate Indian customs of child-rearing (for example, by abandoning corporal punishment), and increasingly forgetting the principles of proper discipline and "severity" in the governance of families for the "foolish indulgence" typical of Indians, whether in relations between masters and servants, men and women, or young and old (Calloway 1997: 192).[10] This was true most of all in communities, often made up of escaped slaves and servants who "became Indians," outside the control of colonial governments entirely (Sakolsky & Koehnline 1993), or island enclaves of what Linebaugh and Rediker (1991) have called "the Atlantic proletariat," the motley collection of freedmen, sailors, ships whores, renegades, Antinomians, and rebels that developed in the port cities of the North Atlantic world before the emergence of modern racism, and from whom much of the democratic impulse of the American—and other— revolutions seems to have first emerged. But it was true for ordinary settlers as well. The irony is that this was the real argument of Bruce Johansen's book *Forgotten Founders* (1982), which first kicked off the "influence debate"—an argument that largely ended up getting lost in all the sound and fury about the constitution: that ordinary Englishmen and Frenchmen settled in the colonies only began to think of themselves as "Americans," as a new sort of freedom-loving people, when they began to see themselves as more like Indians. And that this sense was inspired not primarily by the sort of romanticization at a distance one might encounter in texts by Jefferson or Adam Smith, but rather, by the actual experience of living in frontier societies that were essentially, as Calloway puts it, "amalgams." The colonists who came to America, in fact, found themselves in a unique situation: having largely fled the hierarchy and conformism of Europe, they found themselves confronted with an indigenous population far more dedicated to principles of equality and individualism than they had hitherto been able to imagine; and then proceeded to largely exterminate them, even while adopting many of their customs, habits, and attitudes.

I might add that during this period the Five Nations were something of an amalgam as well. Originally a collection of groups that had made a kind of contractual agreement with one another to create a way of mediating disputes and making peace, they became, during their period of expansion in the seventeenth century, an extraordinary jumble of peoples, with large proportions of the population war captives adopted into Iroquois families to replace family members who were dead. Missionaries in those days often complained that it was difficult to preach to Seneca in their own languages, because a majority were not completely fluent in it (Quain 1937). Even during the eighteenth century, for instance, while Canassatoga was an Onondaga sachem, the other main negotiator with the colonists, Swatane (called Schickallemy) was actually French—or, at least, born to French parents in what's now Canada. On all sides, then, borders were blurred. We are dealing with a graded succession of spaces of democratic improvisation, from the Puritan communities of New England with their town councils, to frontier communities, to the Iroquois themselves.

Traditions as Acts of Endless Refoundation

Let me try to pull some of the pieces together now.

Throughout this essay, I've been arguing that democratic *practice*, whether defined as procedures of egalitarian decision-making, or government by public discussion, tends to emerge from situations in which communities of one sort or another manage their own affairs outside the purview of the state. The absence of state power means the absence of any systematic mechanism of coercion to enforce decisions; this tends to result either in some form of consensus process, or, in the case of essentially military formations like Greek hoplites or pirate ships, sometimes a system of majority voting (since, in such cases, the results, if it did come down to a contest of force, are readily apparent). Democratic innovation, and the emergence of what might be called democratic values, has a tendency to spring from what I've called zones of cultural improvisation, usually also outside of the control of states, in which diverse sorts of people with different traditions and experiences are obliged to figure out some way to deal with one another. Frontier communities whether in Madagascar or Medieval Iceland, pirate ships, Indian Ocean trading communities, Native American confederations on the edge of European expansion, are all examples here.

All of this has very little to do with the great literary-philosophical traditions that tend to be seen as the pillars of great civilizations: indeed, with few exceptions, those traditions are overall explicitly hostile to democratic procedures and the sort of people that employ them.[11] Governing elites, in turn, have tended either to ignore these forms, or to try to stomp them out.[12]

At a certain point in time, however, first in the core states of the Atlantic system—notably England and France, the two that had the largest colonies in North America—this began to change. The creation of that system had been heralded by such unprecedented destruction that it allowed endless new improvisational spaces for the emerging "Atlantic proletariat." States, under pressure from social movements, began to institute reforms; eventually, those working in the elite literary tradition started seeking precedents for them. The result was the creation of representative systems modeled on the Roman Republic that then were later redubbed, under popular pressure, "democracies" and traced to Athens.

Actually, I would suggest that this process of democratic recuperation and refoundation was typical of a broader process that probably marks any civilizational tradition, but was at that time entering a phase of critical intensity. As European states expanded and the Atlantic system came to encompass the world, all sorts of global influences appear to have coalesced in European capitals, and to have been reabsorbed within the tradition that eventually came to be known as "Western." The actual genealogy of the elements that came together in the modern state, for example, is probably impossible to reconstruct—if only because the very process of recuperation tends to scrub away the more exotic elements in written accounts, or, if not, integrate them into familiar topoi of invention and discovery. Historians, who tend to rely almost exclusively on texts and pride themselves on exacting standards of evidence, therefore, often end up, as they did with the Iroquois influence theory, feeling it is their professional responsibility to act as if new ideas do emerge from within textual traditions. Let me throw out two examples:

African fetishism and the idea of the social contract. The Atlantic system, of course, began to take form in West Africa even before Columbus sailed to America. In a fascinating series of essays, William Pietz (1985, 1987, 1988) has described the life of the resulting coastal enclaves where Venetian, Dutch, Portuguese, and every other variety of European merchant and adventurer cohabited with African merchants and adventurers speaking dozens of different languages, a mix of Muslim, Catholic, Protestant, and a variety of ancestral religions. Trade, within these enclaves, was regulated by objects the Europeans came to refer to as "fetishes," and Pietz does much to elaborate the European merchants' theories of value and materiality to which this notion ultimately gave rise. More interesting, perhaps, is the African perspective. Insofar as it can be reconstructed, it appears strikingly similar to the kind of social contract theories developed by men like Thomas Hobbes in Europe at the same time (MacGaffey 1994; Graeber 2005). Essentially, fetishes were created by a series of contracting parties who wished to enter into ongoing economic relations with one another, and were accompanied by agreements on property rights and the rules of exchange; those violating them were to be destroyed by the objects' power. In other words, just as in Hobbes, social relations are created when a group of men agreed to create a sovereign power to threaten them with violence if they failed to respect their property rights and contractual obligations. Later, African texts even praised the fetish as preventing a war of all against all. Unfortunately, it's completely impossible to find evidence that Hobbes was aware of any of this: he lived most of his life in a port town and very likely had met traders familiar with such customs; but his political works contain no references to the African continent whatever.

China and the European nation-state. Over the course of the early Modern period, European elites gradually conceived the ideal of governments that ruled over uniform populations, speaking the same language, under a uniform system of law and administration; and eventually that this system also should be administered by a meritocratic elite whose training should consist largely in the study of literary classics in that nation's vernacular language. The odd thing is nothing approaching a precedent for a state of this sort existed anywhere in previous European history, though it almost exactly corresponded to the system Europeans believed to hold sway (and which to a large extent, did hold sway) in Imperial China.[13] Is there evidence for a Chinese "influence theory?" In this case, there is a little. The prestige of the Chinese government evidently being higher, in the eyes of European philosophers, than African merchants, such influences would not be entirely ignored.

From Leibniz's famous remark that the Chinese should really be sending missionaries to Europe rather than the other way around, to the
work of Montesquieu and Voltaire, one sees a succession of political
philosophers extolling Chinese institutions—as well as a popular fascination with Chinese art, gardens, fashions, and moral philosophy
(Lovejoy 1955)—at exactly the time that Absolutism took form; only
to fade away in the nineteenth century once China had become the
object of European imperial expansion. Obviously none of this constitutes proof that the modern nation-state is in any way of Chinese
inspiration. But considering the nature of the literary traditions we're
dealing with, even if it were true, this would be about as much proof as
we could ever expect to get.

So, is the modern nation-state really a Chinese model of administration,
adopted to channel and control democratic impulses derived largely from
the influence of Native American societies and the pressures of the Atlantic
proletariat, that ultimately came to be justified by a social contract theory
derived from Africa? Probably not. At least, this would no doubt be wildly
overstating things. But neither do I think it a coincidence either that democratic ideals of statecraft first emerged during a period in which the Atlantic
powers were at the center of vast global empires, and an endless confluence
of knowledge and influences, or that they eventually developed the theory
that those ideals sprang instead exclusively from their own "Western" civilization—despite the fact that, during the period in which Europeans had
not been at the center of global empires, they had developed nothing of the
kind.

Finally, I think it's important to emphasize that this process of recuperation is by no means limited to Europe. In fact, one of the striking things is
how quickly almost everyone else in the world began playing the same game.
To some degree, as the example of al Malibari suggests, it was probably happening in other parts of the world even before it began happening in Europe.
Of course, overseas movements only started using the word "democracy"
much later—but even in the Atlantic world, that term only came into common usage around the middle of the nineteenth century. It was also around
the middle of the nineteenth century—just as European powers began re-
cuperating notions of democracy for their own tradition—when Britain led
the way in a very self-conscious policy of suppressing anything that looked
like it might even have the potential to become a democratic, popular movement overseas. The ultimate response, in much of the colonial world, was
to begin playing the exact same game. Opponents to colonial rule scoured
their own literary-philosophical traditions for parallels to ancient Athens,

along with examining traditional communal decision-making forms in their hinterlands. As Steve Muhlenberger and Phil Payne (1993; Baechler 1985), for example, have documented, if one simply defines it as decision-making by public discussion, "democracy" is a fairly common phenomenon; examples can be found even under states and empires, if only, usually, in those places or domains of human activity in which the rulers of states and empires took little interest. Greek historians writing about India, for example, witnessed any number of polities they considered worthy of the name. Between 1911 and 1918, a number of Indian historians (K.P. Jayaswal, D.R. Bhandarkar, R.C. Majumdar)[14] began examining some of these sources, not only Greek accounts of Alexander's campaigns but also early Buddhist documents in Pali and early Hindu vocabularies and works of political theory. They discovered dozens of local equivalents to fifth-century Athens on South Asian soil: cities and political confederations in which all men formally classified as a warriors—which in some cases meant a very large proportion of adult males—were expected to make important decisions collectively, through public deliberation in communal assemblies. The literary sources of the time were mostly just as hostile to popular rule as Greek ones,[15] but, at least until around 400 AD, such polities definitely existed, and the deliberative mechanisms they employed continue to be employed, in everything from the governance of Buddhist monasteries to craft guilds, until the present day. It was possible, then, to say that the Indian, or even Hindu, tradition was always inherently democratic; and this became a strong argument for those seeking independence.

These early historians clearly overstated their case. After independence came the inevitable backlash. Historians began to point out that these "clan republics" were very limited democracies at best, that the overwhelming majority of the population—women, slaves, those defined as outsiders—were completely disenfranchised. Of course, all this was true of Athens as well, and historians have pointed that out at length. But it seems to me questions of authenticity are of at best secondary importance. Such traditions are always largely fabrications. To some degree, that's what traditions are: the continual process of their own fabrication. The point is that, in every case, what we have are political elites—or would-be political elites—identifying with a tradition of democracy in order to validate essentially republican forms of government. Also, not only was democracy not the special invention of "the West," neither was this process of recuperation and refoundation. True, elites in India started playing the game some sixty years later than those in England and France, but, historically, this is not a particularly long period of time. Rather than seeing Indian, or Malagasy, or Tswana, or Maya claims to being part of an inherently democratic tradition as an attempt to ape the

West, it seems to me we are looking at different aspects of the same planetary process: a crystallization of longstanding democratic practices in the formation of a global system, in which ideas were flying back and forth in all directions, and the gradual, usually grudging adoption of some by ruling elites.

The temptation to trace democracy to some particular cultural "origins," though, seems almost irresistible. Even serious scholars continue to indulge it. Let me return to Harvard to provide one final, to my mind particularly ironic, example: a collection of essays called *The Breakout: The Origins of Civilization* (M. Lamberg-Karlovsky 2000), put together by leading American symbolic archeologists.[16] The line of argument sets out from a suggestion by archeologist K.C. Chang, that early Chinese civilization was based on a fundamentally different sort of ideology than Egypt or Mesopotamia. It was essentially a continuation of the cosmos of earlier hunting societies, in which the monarch replaced the shaman as having an exclusive and personal connection with divine powers. The result was absolute authority. Chang was fascinated by the similarities between early China and the Classic Maya, as reconstructed through recently translated inscriptions: the "stratified universe with bird-perched cosmic tree and religious personnel interlinking the Upper, Middle, and Under Worlds," animal messengers, use of writing mainly for politics and ritual, veneration of ancestors, and so on (1988, 2000: 7). The states that emerged in the third millennium in the Middle East, in contrast, represented a kind of breakthrough to an alternate, more pluralistic model, that began when gods and their priesthoods came to be seen as independent from the state. Most of the resulting volume consists of speculations as to what this breakthrough really involved. C.C. Lamberg-Karlovsky argued that the key was the first appearance of notions of freedom and equality in ancient Mesopotamia, in royal doctrines which saw a social contract between the rulers of individual city-states and their subjects—which he calls a "breakout," and which most contributors agreed should be seen as "pointing the way towards Western Democracy" (122). In fact, the main topic of debate soon became who, or what, deserved the credit. Mason Hammond argued for "The Indo-European Origins of the Concept of a Democratic Society," saying that notions of democracy "did not reach Greece from contact with the Near East or Mesopotamia—where equity and justice were the gift of the ruler—but stemmed from an Indo-European concept of a social organization in which sovereignty might be said to rest, not with the chief, but with the council of elders and the assembly of arms-bearing males" (59). Gordon Willey, on the other hand, sees democratic urges as arising from the free market, which he thinks was more developed in Mesopotamia than China, and largely absent under Maya kingdoms, where rulers ruled by divine right "and there is no evidence of any counterbalancing power within the chiefdom or state that could have held him in check" (29).[17] Linda Schele, the foremost authority on the Classic Maya, concurs, adding that this shamanic cosmos "is still alive and functioning today" in "modern Maya communities" (54). Other scholars try to put in a good word for their own parts of the ancient world: Egypt, Israel, the Harappan civilization.

At times, these arguments seem almost comical parodies of the kind of logic I've been criticizing in historians: most obviously, the line of reasoning that assumes that, if there is no direct evidence for something, it can be treated as if it does not exist. This seems especially inappropriate when dealing with early antiquity, an enormous landscape on which archeology and linguistics can at best throw open a few tiny windows. For example: the fact that "primitive Celts and Germans" met in communal assemblies does not in itself prove that communal assemblies have an Indo-European origin— unless, that is, one can demonstrate that stateless societies speaking non-Indo-European languages at the time did not. In fact, the argument seems almost circular, since by "primitive," the author seems to mean "stateless" or "relatively egalitarian," and such societies almost by definition cannot be ruled autocratically, no matter what language people speak. Similarly, when characterizing the Classic Maya as lacking any form of "countervailing institutions" (Willey describes even the bloodthirsty Aztecs as less authoritarian, owing to their more developed markets), it doesn't seem to occur to any of the authors to wonder what ancient Rome or Medieval England might look like if they had to be reconstructed exclusively through ruined buildings and official statements carved in stone.

In fact, if my argument is right, what these authors are doing is searching for the origins of democracy precisely where they are least likely to find it: in the proclamations of the states that largely suppressed local forms of self-governance and collective deliberation, and the literary-philosophical traditions that justified their doing so. (This, at least, would help explain why, in Italy, Greece, and India alike, sovereign assemblies appear at the beginnings of written history and disappear quickly thereafter.) The fate of the Mayas is instructive here. Sometime in the late first millennium, Classic Maya civilization collapsed. Archeologists argue about the reasons; presumably they always will; but most theories assume popular rebellions played at least some role. By the time the Spaniards arrived six hundred years later, Mayan societies were thoroughly decentralized, with an endless variety of tiny city-states, some apparently with elected leaders. Conquest took much longer than it did in Peru and Mexico, and Maya communities have proved so consistently rebellious that, over the last five hundred years, there has been virtually no point during which at least some have not been in a state of armed insurrection. Most ironic of all, the current wave of the global justice movement was largely kicked off by the EZLN, or Zapatista Army of National Liberation, a group of largely Maya-speaking rebels in Chiapas, mostly drawn from *campesinos* who had resettled in new communities in the Lacandon rain forest. Their insurrection in 1994 was carried out explicitly in the name of democracy, by which they meant something much more like Athenian-style direct democracy than the republican forms of government that have since appropriated the name. The Zapatistas developed an elaborate system in which communal assemblies, operating on consensus, supplemented by women and youth caucuses to counterbalance the traditional dominance of adult males, are knitted together by councils with recallable delegates. They claim it to be rooted in, but a radicalization of, the way that Maya-speaking communities have governed themselves for thousands of years. We do know that most highland Maya communities have been governed by some kind of consensus system since we have records: that is, for at least five hundred years. While it's possible that nothing of the sort existed in rural communities during the Classic Maya heyday a little over thousand years ago, it seems rather unlikely.

Certainly, modern rebels make their own views on the Classic Maya clear enough. As a Chol-speaking Zapatista remarked to a friend of mine recently, pointing to the ruins of Palenque, "we managed to get rid of those guys. I don't suppose the Mexican government could be all that much of a challenge in comparison."

Part V: The Crisis of the State

We're finally back, then, where we began, with the rise of global movements calling for new forms of democracy. In a way, the main point of this piece has been to demonstrate that the Zapatistas are nothing unusual. They are speakers of a variety of Maya languages—Tzeltal, Tojalobal, Chol, Tzotzil, Mam—originally from communities traditionally allowed a certain degree of self-governance (largely so they could function as indigenous labor reserves for ranches and plantations located elsewhere), who had formed new largely multi-ethnic communities in newly opened lands in the Lacandon (Collier 1999; Ross 2000; Rus, Hernandez & Mattiace 2003). In other words, they inhabit a classic example of what I've been calling spaces of democratic improvisation, in which a jumbled amalgam of people, most with at least some initial experience of methods of communal self-governance, find themselves in new communities outside the immediate supervision of the state. Neither is there anything particularly new about the fact that they are at the fulcrum of a global play of influences: absorbing ideas from everywhere, and their own example having an enormous impact on social movements across the planet. The first Zapatista *encuentro* in 1996, for example, eventually led to the formation of an international network (People's Global Action, or PGA), based on principles of autonomy, horizontality, and direct democracy, that included such disparate groups as the Movimento dos Trabalhadores Rurais Sem Terra (MST) in Brazil; the Karnataka State Farmer's Association (KRSS), a Gandhian socialist direct action group in India; the Canadian Postal Workers' Union; and a whole host of anarchist collectives in Europe and the Americas, along with indigenous organizations on every continent. It was PGA, for instance, that put out the original call to action against the WTO meetings in Seattle in November 1999. Even more, the principles of Zapatismo, the rejection of vanguardism, the emphasis on creating viable alternatives in one's own community as a way of subverting the logic of global capital, has had an enormous influence on participants in social movements that, in some cases, are at best vaguely aware of the Zapatistas themselves and have certainly never heard of PGA. No doubt the growth of the Internet and global communications have allowed the process to proceed much faster than ever before, and allowed for more formal, explicit alliances; but this does not mean we are dealing with an entirely unprecedented phenomenon.

One might gauge the importance of the point by considering what happens when it's not born constantly in mind. Let me turn here to an author whose position is actually quite close to my own. In a book called *Cosmopolitanism* (2002), literary theorist Walter Mignolo provides a beautiful summary of just how much Kant's cosmopolitanism, or the UN discourse on human rights, was developed within a context of conquest and imperialism; then invokes Zapatista calls for democracy to counter an argument by Slavoj Žižek that Leftists need to temper their critiques of Eurocentrism in order to embrace democracy as "the true European legacy from ancient Greece onward" (1998: 1009). Mignolo writes:

> The Zapatistas have used the word democracy, although it has a different meaning for them than it has for the Mexican government. Democracy for the Zapatistas is not conceptualized in terms of European political philosophy but in terms of Maya social organization based on reciprocity, communal (instead of individual) values, the value of wisdom rather than epistemology, and so forth... The Zapatistas have no choice but to use the word that political hegemony imposed, though using that word does not mean bending to its mono-logic interpretation. Once democracy is singled out by the Zapatistas, it becomes a connector through which liberal concepts of democracy and indigenous concepts of reci-

procity and community social organization for the common good must
come to terms (Mignolo 2002: 180).

This is a nice idea. Mignolo calls it "border thinking." He proposes it
as a model for how to come up with a healthy, "critical cosmopolitanism,"
as opposed to the Eurocentric variety represented by Kant or Žižek. The
problem though, it seems to me, is that in doing so, Mignolo himself ends
up falling into a more modest version of the very essentializing discourse he's
trying to escape.

First of all, to say "the Zapatistas have no choice but to use the word"
democracy is simply untrue. Of course they have a choice. Other indige-
nous-based groups have made very different ones. The Aymara movement
in Bolivia, to select one fairly random example, chose to reject the word
"democracy" entirely, on the grounds that, in their people's historical experience, the name has only been used for systems imposed on them through
violence.[18] They therefore see their own traditions of egalitarian decision-
making as having nothing to do with democracy. The Zapatista decision
to embrace the term, it seems to me, was more than anything else a decision to reject anything that smacked of a politics of identity, and to appeal for allies, in Mexico and elsewhere, among those interested in a broader
conversation about forms of self-organization—in much the same way as
they also sought to begin a conversation with those interested in reexamin-
ing the meaning of words like "revolution." Second, Mignolo, not entirely
unlike Lévy-Bruhl, ends up producing yet another confrontation between
apples and oranges. He ends up contrasting Western theory and indigenous
practice. In fact, Zapatismo is not simply an emanation of traditional Maya
practices: its origins have to be sought in a prolonged confrontation between
those practices and, among other things, the ideas of local Maya intellectuals
(many, presumably, not entirely unfamiliar with the work of Kant), liberation theologists (who drew inspiration from prophetic texts written in ancient Palestine), and mestizo revolutionaries (who drew inspiration from the
works of Chairman Mao, who lived in China). Democracy, in turn, did not
emerge from anybody's discourse. It is as if simply taking the Western literary tradition as one's starting point—even for purposes of critique—means
authors like Mignolo always somehow end up trapped within it.

In reality, the "word that political hegemony imposed" is in this case
itself a fractured compromise. If it weren't, we would not have a Greek word
originally coined to describe a form of communal self-governance applied
to representative republics to begin with. It's exactly this contradiction the
Zapatistas were seizing on. In fact, it seems impossible to get rid of. Liberal
theorists (e.g., Sartori 1987: 279) do occasionally evince a desire to simply

brush aside Athenian democracy entirely, to declare it irrelevant and be done with it, but for ideological purposes, such a move would be simply inadmissible. After all, without Athens, there would be no way to claim that "the Western tradition" had anything inherently democratic about it. We would be left tracing back our political ideals to the totalitarian musings of Plato, or if not, perhaps, to admit there's really no such thing as "the West." In effect, liberal theorists have boxed themselves into a corner. Obviously, the Zapatistas are hardly the first revolutionaries to have seized on this contradiction; but their doing so has found an unusually powerful resonance, this time—in part, because this is a moment of a profound crisis of the state.

The Impossible Marriage

In its essence, I think, the contradiction is not simply one of language. It reflects something deeper. For the last two hundred years, democrats have been trying to graft ideals of popular self-governance onto the coercive apparatus of the state. In the end, the project is simply unworkable. States cannot, by their nature, ever truly be democratized. They are, after all, basically ways of organizing violence. The American Federalists were being quite realistic when they argued that democracy is inconsistent with a society based on inequalities of wealth; since, in order to protect wealth, one needs an apparatus of coercion to keep down the very "mob" that democracy would empower. Athens was a unique case in this respect because it was, in effect, transitional: there were certainly inequalities of wealth, even, arguably, a ruling class, but there was virtually no formal apparatus of coercion. Hence there's no consensus among scholars whether it can really be considered a state at all.

It's precisely when one considers the problem of the modern state's monopoly of coercive force that the whole pretense of democracy dissolves into a welter of contradictions. For example: while modern elites have largely put aside the earlier discourse of the "mob" as a murderous "great beast," the same imagery still pops back, in almost exactly the form it had in the sixteenth century, the moment anyone proposes democratizing some aspect of the apparatus of coercion. In the US, for example, advocates of the "fully informed jury movement," who point out that the Constitution actually allows juries to decide on questions of law, not just of evidence, are regularly denounced in the media as wishing to go back to the days of lynchings and "mob rule." It's no coincidence that the United States, a country that still prides itself on its democratic spirit, has also led the world in mythologizing, even deifying, its police.

Francis Dupuis-Deri (2002) has coined the term "political agoraphobia" to refer to the suspicion of public deliberation and decision-making that runs through the Western tradition, just as much in the works of Constant, Sieyés, or Madison as in Plato or Aristotle. I would add that even the most impressive accomplishments of the liberal state, its most genuinely democratic elements—for instance, its guarantees on freedom of speech and freedom of assembly—are premised on such agoraphobia. It is only once it becomes absolutely clear that public speech and assembly is no longer itself the medium of political decision-making, but at best an attempt to criticize, influence, or make suggestions to political decision-makers, that they can be treated as sacrosanct. Critically, this agorophobia is not just shared by politicians and professional journalists, but in large measure by the public itself. The reasons, I think, are not far to seek. While liberal democracies lack anything resembling the Athenian *agora*, they certainly do not lack equivalents to Roman circuses. The ugly mirror phenomenon, by which ruling elites encourage forms of popular participation that continually remind the public just how much they are unfit to rule, seems, in many modern states, to have been brought to a condition of unprecedented perfection. Consider here, for example, the view of human nature one might derive generalizing from the experience of driving to work on the highway, as opposed to the view one might derive from the experience of public transportation. Yet the American—or German—love affair with the car was the result of conscious policy decisions by political and corporate elites beginning in the 1930s. One could write a similar history of the television, or consumerism, or, as Polanyi long ago noted, "the market."

Jurists, meanwhile, have long been aware that the coercive nature of the state ensures that democratic constitutions are founded on a fundamental contradiction. Walter Benjamin (1978) summed it up nicely by pointing out that any legal order that claims a monopoly of the use of violence has to be founded by some power other than itself, which inevitably means by acts that were illegal according to whatever system of law came before. The legitimacy of a system of law, thus, necessarily rests on acts of criminal violence. American and French revolutionaries were, after all, by the law under which they grew up, guilty of high treason. Of course, sacred kings from Africa to Nepal have managed to solve this logical conundrum by placing themselves, like God, outside the system. But as political theorists from Agamben to Negri remind us, there is no obvious way for "the people" to exercise sovereignty in the same way. Both the right-wing solution (constitutional orders are founded by, and can be set aside by, inspired leaders—whether Founding Fathers, or Führers—who embody the popular will), and the left-wing solution (constitutional orders usually gain their legitimacy through violent popular revolutions) lead to endless practical contradictions. In fact, as sociologist Michael Mann has hinted (1999), much of the slaughter of the twen-

tieth century derives from some version of this contradiction. The demand
to simultaneously create a uniform apparatus of coercion within every piece
of land on the surface of the planet, and to maintain the pretense that the
legitimacy of that apparatus derives from "the people," has led to an endless
need to determine who, precisely, "the people" are supposed to be.

> In all the varied German law courts of the last eighty years—from
> Weimar to Nazi to communist DDR to the Bundesrepublik—the judg-
> es have used the same opening formula: "In Namen des Volkes," "In the
> Name of the People." American courts prefer the formula "The Case of
> the People versus X" (Mann 1999: 19).

In other words, "the people" must be evoked as the authority behind the
allocation of violence, despite the fact that any suggestion that the proceedings be in any way democratized is likely to be greeted with horror by all
concerned. Mann suggests that pragmatic efforts to work out this contradiction, to use the apparatus of violence to identify and constitute a "people"
that those maintaining that apparatus feel are worthy of being the source of
their authority, has been responsible for at least sixty million murders in the
twentieth century alone.

It is in this context that I might suggest that the anarchist solution—
that there really is no resolution to this paradox—is really not all that unreasonable. The democratic state was always a contradiction. Globalization has
simply exposed the rotten underpinnings, by creating the need for decision-
making structures on a planetary scale where any attempt to maintain the
pretense of popular sovereignty, let alone participation, would be obviously
absurd. The neo-liberal solution, of course, is to declare the market the only
form of public deliberation one really needs, and to restrict the state almost
exclusively to its coercive function. In this context, the Zapatista response—
to abandon the notion that revolution is a matter of seizing control over the
coercive apparatus of the state, and instead proposing to refound democracy
in the self-organization of autonomous communities—makes perfect sense.
This is the reason an otherwise obscure insurrection in southern Mexico
caused such a sensation in radical circles to begin with. Democracy, then, is
for the moment returning to the spaces in which it originated: the spaces in
between. Whether it can then proceed to engulf the world depends perhaps
less on what kind of theories we make about it, but on whether we honestly
believe that ordinary human beings, sitting down together in deliberative
bodies, would be capable of managing their own affairs as well as elites,
whose decisions are backed up by the power of weapons, are of managing
it for them—or even whether, even if they wouldn't, they have the right to

be allowed to try. For most of human history, faced with such questions, professional intellectuals have almost universally taken the side of the elites. It is rather my impression that, if it really comes down to it, the overwhelming majority are still seduced by the various ugly mirrors and have no real faith in the possibilities of popular democracy. But perhaps this too could change.

Endnotes

1 But not those that speak Spanish or Portuguese. It is not clear if Huntington has passed judgment on the Boers.

2 It was utterly unremarkable, for example, for a Ming court official to be a Taoist in his youth, become a Confucian in his middle years, and a Buddhist on retirement. It is hard to find parallels in the West even today.

3 Some of his statements are so outrageous (for example, the apparent claim that, unlike the West, traditions like Islam, Buddhism, and Confucianism do not claim universal truths, or that, unlike Islam, the Western tradition is based on an obsession with law) that one wonders how any serious scholar could possibly make them.

4 Actually, one often finds some of the authors who would otherwise be most hostile to Huntington going even further, and arguing that love, for example, is a "Western concept" and therefore cannot be used when speaking of people in Indonesia or Brazil.

5 Or a French person to read Posidonius' account of ancient Gaul and identify with the perspective of an ancient Greek (a person, who if he had actually met him, he would probably first think was some sort of Arab).

6 This is why Classical Greek philosophers are so suspicious of democracy, incidentally: because, they claimed, it doesn't teach goodness.

7 This conclusion is in world-systems terms hardly unprecedented: what I am describing corresponds to what David Wilkinson (1987) for example calls the "Central Civilization."

8 One reason this is often overlooked is that Hegel was among the first to use "the West" in its modern sense, and Marx often followed him in this. However, this usage was, at the time, extremely unusual.

9 One should probably throw in a small proviso here: Orientalism allowed colonial powers to make a distinction between rival civilizations, which were seen as hopelessly decadent and corrupt, and "savages," who insofar as they were not seen as hopelessly racially inferior, could be considered possible objects of a "civilizing mission." Hence Britain might have largely abandoned attempts to reform Indian institutions in the 1860s, but it took up the exact same rhetoric later in Africa.

Africa was thus in some ways relegated to the "savage slot" that had been the place of the West—that is, had been before Europeans decided they were themselves "Westerners."

10 "Though the first English planters in this country had usually a government and a discipline in their families and had a sufficient severity in it, yet, as if the climate had taught us to Indianize, the relaxation of it is now such that it is wholly laid aside, and a foolish indulgence to children is become an epidemical miscarriage of the country, and like to be attended with many evil consequences" (op. cit.).

11 Usually, one can pick out pro-democratic voices here and there, but they tend to be in a distinct minority. In ancient Greece, for instance, there would appear to be precisely three known authors who considered themselves democrats: Hippodamus, Protagoras, and Democritus. None of their works, however, have survived so their views are only known by citations in anti-democratic sources.

12 It's interesting to think about Athens itself in this regard. The results are admittedly a bit confusing: it was by far the most cosmopolitan of Greek cities (though foreigners were not allowed to vote), and historians have yet to come to consensus over whether it can be considered a state. The latter largely depends on whether one takes a Marxian or Weberian perspective: there was clearly a ruling class, if a very large one, but there was almost nothing in the way of an administrative apparatus.

13 Obviously the Chinese state was profoundly different in some ways as well: first of all it was a universalistic empire. But, Tooker to the contrary, one can borrow an idea without embracing every element.

14 Rather than pretend to be an expert on early-twentieth-century Indian scholarship, I'll just reproduce Muhlenberger's footnote: "K.P. Jayaswal, *Hindu Polity: A Constitutional History of India in Hindu Times* 2nd and enl. edn. (Bangalore, 1943), published first in article form in 1911–13; D.R. Bhandarkar, *Lectures on the Ancient History of India on the Period from 650 to 325 B.C.*, The Carmichael Lectures, 1918 (Calcutta, 1919); R.C. Majumdar. *Corporate Life in Ancient India*, (orig. written in 1918; cited here from the 3rd ed., Calcutta, 1969, as *Corporate Life*)."

15 I say "almost." Early Buddhism was quite sympathetic: particularly the Buddha himself. The Brahamanical tradition however is as one might expect uniformly hostile.

16 Most were in fact published in a journal called *Symbols*.

17 One is tempted to say this leaves us to choose between two theories for the origin of Huntington's "Western civilization," one neoliberal, one crypto-fascist. But this would probably be unfair. At least the authors here do treat the broad zone that later includes Islam as part of a "Western" bloc to which they attribute the origin of Western ideas of freedom: though it is hard to do otherwise, since virtually nothing is known of what was happening in Europe during this early period. Probably the most fascinating contribution is Gregory Possehl's essay on Harappan civiliza-

tion, the first urban civilizaion in India, which, as far as is presently known, seems to have lacked kingship and any sort of centralized state. The obvious question is what this has to say about the existence of early Indian "democracies" or "republics." Could it be, for instance, that the first two thousand years of South Asian history was really the story of the gradual erosion of more egalitarian political forms?

18   I am drawing here on a conversation with Nolasco Mamani, who, among other things, was the Aymara representative at the UN, in London during the European Social Forum 2004.

Bibliography

Adams, John
1797 *Defense of the Constitutions of Government of the United States of America, Against the Attack of M. Turgot in his Letter to Dr. Price,* Dated the Twenty-Second Day of March, 1778. Philadelphia: W. Cobbet.

Arrighi, Giovanni, Ahmad, Iftikhar, and Miin-wen Shih
1997 "Beyond Western Hegemonies." Paper presented at the XXI Meeting of the Social Science History Association, New Orleans, Louisiana, October 10–13, 1996. Available at: http: //fbc.binghamton.edu/gaht5.htm.

Arrighi, Giovanni, Po-Keung Hui, Ho-Fung Hung, and Mark Selden
2003 "Historical Capitalism, East and West." In *The Resurgence of East Asia: 500, 150, and 50 Year Perspectives* (G. Arrighi, T. Hamashita, and M. Selden, eds.). London: Routledge.

Axtell, James
1985 *The Invasion Within: The Contest of Cultures in Colonial North America.* Oxford: Oxford University Press.

Baechler, Jean
1985 *Démocraties.* Paris: Calmann-Lévy.

Benjamin, Walter
1978 "Critique of Violence." In *Reflections: Essays, Aphorisms, and Autobiographical Writings.* New York: Harcourt Brace Jovanovich.

Calloway, Colin
1997 *New Worlds For All: Indians, Europeans, and the Remaking of Early America.* Baltimore: Johns Hopkins.

Castoriadis, Cornelius
1991 *Philosophy, Politics, Autonomy: Essays in Political Philosophy.* New York: Oxford University Press.

Collier, George A. with Elizabeth Lowery Quaratiello
1999 *Basta! Land & The Zapatista Rebellion in Chiapas.* Revised Edition. Oakland: Food First Books.

Dever, William G.
2000 "How Was Ancient Israel Different?" In *The Breakout: The Origins of Civilization,* M. Lamber-Karlovsky, ed. Cambridge, MA: Harvard University Press.

Dupuis-Déri, Francis

1999 "L'Esprit Anti-Démocratique des Fondateurs des 'Démocraties' modernes." *Agone* 22: 95–113.

2002 "The Struggle Between Political Agoraphobia and Agoraphilia." Paper presented at the Massachusetts Institute of Technology, political science workshop.

2004 "The Political Power of Words: The Birth of Pro-Democratic Discourse in the Nineteenth Century in the United States and Canada." *Political Studies* 52: 118–134.

2005 "Anarchy in Political Philosophy." *Anarchist Studies*. Volume 13 no 1: 8–22.

Federici, Silvia, ed.

1995 *Enduring Western Civilization: The Construction of the Concept of Western Civilization and its "Others."* London: Praeger.

Gilroy, Paul

1993 *The Black Atlantic: Modernity and Double Consciousness*. Cambridge: Harvard University Press.

Godbout, Jacques

2005 "Pas de représentation sans représentativité?" *Revue du MAUSS Semestrielle* No. 26: 90–104.

GoGwilt, Chris

1995 "True West: The Changing Idea of the West from the 1880s to the 1920s." In *Western Civilization and its "Others"* (S. Federici, ed.). London: Praeger.

Graeber, David

2001 *Toward an Anthropological Theory of Value*. New York: Palgrave.

2004 *Fragments of an Anarchist Anthropology*. Chicago: University of Chicago Press.

2005 "Fetishism and Social Creativity, or Fetishes are Gods in Process of Construction." *Anthropological Theory*, Volume 5 no 4: 407–438. [Chapter 4 in this volume]

Grinde, Donald A.

1977 *The Iroquois and the Founding of the American Nation*. San Francisco: Indian Historian Press.

Grinde, Donald A., and Bruce E. Johansen

1990 *Exemplar of Liberty: Native America and the Evolution of Democracy*. Los Angeles: University of California Los Angeles.

1995. "Sauce for the Goose: Demand and Definitions for 'Proof' Regarding the Iroquois and Democracy." *William & Mary Quarterly* 53 (3): 628–635.

Hammond, Mason

2000. "The Indo-European Origins of the Concept of a Democratic Society." In *The Breakout: The Origins of Civilization* (M. Lamber-Karlovsky, ed.). Cambridge, MA: Harvard University Press.

Ho, Engseng

2004 "Empire Through Diasporic Eyes: A View From the Other Boat." *Comparative Studies in Society and History* 46(2): 210–246.

Huntington, Samuel P

1993 "The Clash of Civilizations." *Foreign Affairs* 72(3): 22–48.

1996 "The West: Unique, Not Universal." *Foreign Affairs* 75(1): 28–46.

Johansen, Bruce

1982 *Forgotten Founders: How the American Indian Helped Shape Democracy*. Boston: Harvard Common Press.

1998 *Debating Democracy: Native American Legacy of Freedom*. Santa Fe: Clear Light Publishers.

Kyle, Donald G.
1998 *Spectacles of Death in Ancient Rome*. New York: Routledge.

Lamberg-Karlovsky, C.C.
2000 "The Eastern 'Breakout' and the Mesopotamian Social Contract." In *The Breakout: The Origins of Civilization* (M. Lamber-Karlovsky, ed.). Cambridge, MA: Harvard University Press.

Lamberg-Karlovsky, Martha, ed.
2000 *The Breakout: The Origins of Civilization*. Peabody Museum Monographs. Cambridge: Harvard University Press.

Levy, Philip A.
1996 "Exemplars of Taking Liberties: The Iroquois Influence Thesis and the Problem of Evidence." *William & Mary Quarterly* 53(3): 587–604.

Lévy-Bruhl, Lucien
1986 [1926] *How Natives Think* (Lilian Clare, trans.). Salem: Ayer & Co.

Lewis, Martin W., and Kären E. Wigen
1997 *The Myth of Continents: A Critique of Metageography*. Berkeley: University of California Press.

Linebaugh, Peter
1991 *The London Hanged: Crime and Civil Society in the Eighteenth Century*. New York: Allen Lane, The Penguin Press.

Linebaugh, Peter, and Marcus Rediker
2000 *Many-Headed Hydra: Sailors, Slaves, Commoners, and the Hidden History of the Revolutionary Atlantic*. Boston: Beacon Press.

Lomar, Kathryn, and Tim Cornell, eds.
2003 *"Bread and Circuses": Euergetism and Municipal Patronage in Roman Italy*. London: Routledge.

Lovejoy, Arthur
1955. "The Chinese Origin of a Romanticism." In *Essays in the History of Ideas*. New York: George Braziller.

MacGaffey, Wyatt
1994 "African Objects and the Idea of the Fetish." *RES: Journal of Anthropology and Aesthetics* 25: 123–31.

Manin, Bernard
1994 "On Legitimacy and Political Deliberation." In *New French Thought: Political Philosophy* (M. Lilla, ed.). Princeton: Princeton University Press.

Mann, Michael
1999 "The Dark Side of Democracy: the Modern Tradition of Ethnic and Political Cleansing." *New Left Review* 235: 18–45.

Markoff, John
1995 *Waves of Democracy: Social Movements and Political Change*. Thousand Oaks: Pine Forge Press.
1999 "Where and When Was Democracy Invented?" *Comparative Studies in Society and History* 41(4): 660–690.

Mignolo, Walter D.

2002 "The Many Faces of Cosmo-polis: Border Thinking and Critical Cosmopolitanism." In *Cosmopolitanism* (C. Breckenridge, S. Pollock, H. Bhabha, and D. Chakrabarty, eds.). Durham: Duke University Press.

Muhlberger, Steven, and Phil Paine
1993 "Democracy's Place in World History." *Journal of World History* 4(1): 23–45.
1997 "Democracy in Ancient India." World History of Democracy site, http: //www. nipissingu.ca./department/history/histdem/, accessed November 22, 2004.

Negri, Antonio
1999 *Insurgencies: Constituent Power and the Modern State* (Maurizia Boscagli, trans.). Minneapolis: University of Minnesota Press.

Newman, Michael
1998 "Founding Feathers: The Iroquois and the Constitution." *The New Republic* 199(19): 17–21.

Ober, Josiah
1996 *The Athenian Revolution: Essays on Ancient Greek Democracy and Political Theory.* Princeton: Princeton University Press.

Ostrom, Elinor
1990 *Governing the Commons: The Evolution of Institutions for Collective Action.* Cambridge: Cambridge University Press.

Payne, Samuel B.
1997 "The Iroquois League, the Articles of the Confederation, and the Constitution." *William and Mary Quarterly* 53(3): 605–620.

Pietz, William
1985 "The Problem of the Fetish I." *RES: Journal of Anthropology and Aesthetics* 9: 5–17.
1987 "The Problem of the Fetish II: The Origin of the Fetish." *RES: Journal of Anthropology and Aesthetics* 13: 23–45.
1988 "The Problem of the Fetish IIIa: Bosman's Guinea and the Enlightenment Theory of Fetishism." *RES: Journal of Anthropology and Aesthetics* 16: 105–123.

Rediker, Marcus
1981 "'Under the Banner of King Death': The Social World of Anglo-American Pirates, 1716–1726." *William & Mary Quarterly*, 3rd series, 38(2): 203–227.
1987 *Between the Devil and the Deep Blue Sea: Merchant Seamen, Pirates, and the Anglo-American Maritime World, 1700–1750.* Cambridge: Cambridge University Press.
2004 *Villains of All Nations: Atlantic Pirates in the Golden Age.* Beacon Press: Boston.

Ross, John
2000. *The War Against Oblivion: The Zapatista Chronicles.* Monroe, ME: Common Courage Press.

Rus, Jan, Rosalva Aída Hernández Castillo, and Shannan L. Mattiace
2003 *Mayan Lives, Mayan Utopias: The Indigenous Peoples of Chiapas and the Zapatista Rebellion.* Lanham, MD: Rowman and Littlefield.

Sakolsky, Ron and James Koehnline, eds.
1993 *Gone to Croatan: The Origins of North American Dropout Culture.* Brooklyn, NY: Autonomedia.

Sartori, Giovanni
1987 *The Theory of Democracy Revisited.* Chatham, NJ: Chatham House.

Saxonhouse, Arlene W.

1993 "Athenian Democracy: Modern Mythmakers and Ancient Theorists." *PS: Political Science and Politics* (26)3: 486–490.

Snow, Dean R.
1994 *The Iroquois.* London: Blackwell.

Tooker, Elizabeth
1988 "The United States Constitution and the Iroquois League." *Ethnohistory* 35: 305–36.
1990 "Rejoinder to Johansen." *Ethnohistory* 37: 291–297.

Toynbee, Arnold
1934–1961 *A Study of History.* 12 volumes. New York: Oxford University Press.

Trouillot, Michel-Rolph
2003 *Global Transformations: Anthropology and the Modern World.* New York: Palgrave.

Veyne, Paul
1976 *Le Pain et Le Cirque: Sociologie Historique d'un Pluralisme Politique.* Paris: Editions du Seuil.

Wilkinson, David
1985 "Central Civilization." *Comparative Civilizations Review*, Fall 1985: 31–53.

Žižek, Slavoj
1998 "A Leftist Plea for Eurocentrism." *Critical Inquiry* 24: 989–1009.

12

ON THE PHENOMENOLOGY OF GIANT PUPPETS: BROKEN WINDOWS, IMAGINARY JARS OF URINE, AND THE COSMOLOGICAL ROLE OF THE POLICE IN AMERICAN CULTURE

What follows is an essay of interpretation. It is about direct action in North America, about the mass mobilizations organized by the so called "anti-globalization movement," and especially, about the war of images that has surrounded it. It begins with a simple observation. I think it's fair to say that if the average American knows just two things about these mobilizations, they are, first of all, that there are often people dressed in black who break windows; second, that they involve colorful giant puppets. I want to start by asking why these images in particular appear to have so struck the popular imagination. I also want to ask why it is that, of the two, American police seem to hate the puppets more. As many activists have observed, the forces of order in the United States seem to have a profound aversion to giant puppets. Often police strategies aim to destroy or capture them before they can even appear on the streets. As a result, a major concern for those planning actions soon became how to hide the puppets so they would not be destroyed in pre-emptive attacks. What's more, for many individual officers at least, the objection to puppets appeared to be not merely strategic, but personal, even visceral. Cops hate puppets. Activists are puzzled as to why.

To some degree this essay emerges from that puzzlement. It is written very much from the perspective of a participant. I have been involved in the global justice movement[1] for six years now, having helped organize and taken part in actions small and large, and I have spent a good deal of time wondering about such questions myself. If this were simply an essay on police psychology, of course, my involvement would put me at a significant disadvantage, since it makes it difficult to carry out detailed interviews with police. Granted, being active in the movement does afford frequent occasions for casual chats with cops. But they're not always the most enlightening. The only extended conversation I ever had with police officers on the subject of puppets, on the other hand, was carried out while I was handcuffed—which if nothing else makes it very difficult to take notes. At any rate, this essay is not so much about the particulars of police, or activist, psychology as about what the Annales school historians liked to call a "structure of the conjuncture": the peculiar—and endlessly shifting—symbolic interactions of state, capital, mass media, and oppositional movements that the globalization movement has sparked. Since any strategic planning must start from an understanding of such matters, those engaged in planning actions end up endlessly discussing the current state of this conjuncture. I see this essay, therefore, as a contribution to an ongoing conversation—one that is necessarily aesthetic, critical, ethical, and political all at the same time. I also see it as ultimately pursuing the movements' aims and aspirations in another form. To ask these questions—Why puppets? Why windows? Why do these images seem to have such mythic power? Why do representatives of the state react the way they do? What is the public's perception? What is the "public," anyway? How would it be possible to transform "the public" into something else?—is to begin to try to piece together the tacit rules of the game of symbolic warfare, from its elementary assumptions to the details of how the terms of engagement are negotiated in any given action, ultimately, to understand the stakes in new forms of revolutionary politics. I am myself personally convinced that such understandings are themselves revolutionary in their implications.

Hence, the unusual structure of this essay, in which an analysis of the symbolism of puppets leads to a discussion of police media strategies and, from there, to reflections on the very nature of violence and the state of international politics. It is an attempt to understand an historical moment from the perspective on someone very much situated inside it.

A Problematic

There is a widespread perception that events surrounding the WTO ministerial in Seattle in November 1999 marked the birth of a new movement in North America. It would probably be better to say that Seattle marked the moment when a much larger global movement—one which traces back at least to the Zapatista rebellion in 1994—made its first appearance on North American shores. Nonetheless, the actions in Seattle were widely considered a spectacular victory. They were quickly followed in 2000 and 2001 by a series of similar mobilizations in Washington, Prague, Québec City, and Genoa, growing in size, but facing increasing levels of state repression. September 11 and the subsequent "war on terror" changed the nature of the playing field, enabling governments to step up this repression quite dramatically, which became clear in the US with the extraordinary violence with which police tactics confronted protestors during the Free Trade Areas of the Americas summit in Miami in November 2003. Since then, the movement has largely been in a process of regrouping, though at the time of writing (summer 2006) there are increasing signs of a second wind.

The movement's disarray was not simply due to heightened levels of repression. Another reason, however paradoxical this may seem, was that it reached so many of its immediate goals so quickly. After Seattle, the WTO process froze in its tracks and has never really recovered. Most ambitious global trade schemes were scotched. The effects on political discourse were even more remarkable. In fact, the change was so dramatic that it has become difficult, for many, to even remember what public discourse was actually like in the years immediately before Seattle. In the late 1990s, "Washington consensus," as it was then called, simply had no significant challengers. In the US itself, politicians and journalists appeared to have come to unanimous agreement that radical "free market reforms" were the only possible approach to economic development, anywhere and everywhere. In the mainstream media, anyone who challenged the basic tenets of this faith was likely to be treated as if they were almost literally insane. Speaking as someone who became active in the first months of 2000, I can attest that, however exhilarated by what had happened at Seattle, most of us still felt it would take five or ten years to shatter these assumptions. In fact, it took less than two. By late 2001, it was commonplace to see even news journals that had just months before denounced protestors as so many ignorant children, declaring that we had won the war of ideas. Much as the movement against nuclear power discovered in the 1970s and early 1980s, the direct-action approach was so effective that short-term goals were reached almost immediately, forcing participants to scramble to redefine what the movement was actually about. Splits quickly developed between the "anti-corporates" and the "anti-capitalists." As anarchist ideas and forms of organization became increasingly important, unions and NGOs began to draw back. What's critical for present purposes is that all this became a problem largely because the initial movement was so successful in getting its message out.

I must, however, introduce one crucial qualification. This success applied only to the movement's *negative* message—what we were against. That organizations like the IMF, WTO, and World Bank were inherently unaccountable and undemocratic, that neoliberal policies were devastating the planet and throwing millions of human beings into death, poverty, hopelessness, and despair—all this, we found, was relatively easy to communicate. While mainstream media were never willing to quote our spokespeople or run the editorials we sent them, it wasn't long before accredited pundits and talking heads (encouraged by renegade economists like Joseph Stiglitz), began simply repeating the same things as if they'd made them up themselves. Admittedly, American newspaper columnists were not going to repeat the whole of the movement's arguments—they certainly were not willing to repeat anything that suggested these problems were ultimately rooted in the very nature of the state and capitalism. But the immediate message did get out.

Not so for what most in the movement were actually *for*. If there was one central inspiration to the global justice movement, it was the principle of direct action. This is a notion very much at the heart of the anarchist tradition and, in fact, most of the movement's central organizers—more and more as time went on—considered themselves anarchists, or at least, heavily influenced by anarchist ideas. They saw mass mobilizations not only as opportunities to expose the illegitimate, undemocratic nature of existing institutions, but as ways to do so in a form that itself demonstrated why such institutions were unnecessary, by providing a living example of genuine, direct democracy. The key word here is "process"—meaning, decision-making process. When members of the Direct Action Network or similar groups are considering whether to work with some other group, the first question that's likely to be asked is "what sort of process do they use?"—that is: Do they practice internal democracy? Do they vote or use consensus? Is there a formal leadership? Such questions are usually considered of much more immediate importance than questions of ideology.[2] Similarly, if one talks to someone fresh from a major mobilization and asks what she found most new and exciting about the experience, one is most likely to hear long descriptions of the organization of affinity groups, clusters, blockades, flying squads, spokescouncils, and network structures, or about the apparent miracle of consensus decision making in which one can see thousands of people coordinate their actions without any formal leadership structure. There is a technical term for all this: "prefigurative politics." Direct action is a form of resistance which, in its structure, is meant to prefigure the genuinely free society one wishes to create. Revolutionary action is not a form of self-sacrifice, a grim dedication to doing whatever it takes to achieve a future world of freedom. It is the defiant insistence on acting as if one is already free.

The positive message, then, was a new vision of democracy. In its ability to get it out before a larger public, though, the movement has been strikingly unsuccessful. Groups like the Direct Action Network have been fairly effective in disseminating its models of decision-making within activist circles (since they do, in fact, work remarkably well), but beyond those circles, they have had very little luck. Early attempts to provoke a public debate about the nature of democracy were invariably brushed aside by the mainstream media. As for the new forms of organization: readers of mainstream newspapers or TV viewers, even those who followed stories about the movement fairly assiduously, would have had little way to know that they existed.

Media Images

I do not want to leave the reader with the impression that many of those involved in the global justice movement see their main task as getting a message out through the media. It is a somewhat unusual feature of this new movement that large elements of it are openly hostile to any attempt to influence what they called "the corporate media," or even, in many cases, to engage with it at all. Companies like CNN or the Associated Press, they argue, are capitalist firms; it would be utterly naïve to imagine they would been willing to provide a friendly venue for anyone actively opposed to capitalism—let alone to carry anti-capitalist messages to the public. Some argue that, as a key element in the structure of power, the media apparatus should itself be considered an appropriate target for direct action. One of the greatest accomplishments of the movement, in fact, has been to develop an entirely new, alternative media network—Independent Media, an international, participatory, activist-driven, largely Internet-based media project that has, since Seattle, provided moment-to-moment coverage of large mobilizations in email, print, radio, and video forms.

All this is very much in the spirit of direct action. Nonetheless, there are always activists—even anarchists—who are willing to do more traditional media work. I myself can often be counted among them. During several mobilizations, I ended up spending much of my time preparing press conferences, attending meetings on daily spins and sound bites, and fielding calls from reporters. I have in fact been the object of severe opprobrium from certain hardcore anarchist circles as a result. Still, I think the anarchist critique is largely correct—especially in America. In my own experience, editors and most reporters in this country are inherently suspicious of protests, which they tend to see not as real news stories but as artificial events concocted to influence them.[3] They seem willing to cover such artificial events only when constituted by proper authorities. When they do cover activist events, they are very self-conscious about the dangers that they might be manipulated—particularly if they see protests as "violent." For journalists, there is an inherent dilemma here, because violence in itself is inherently newsworthy. A "violent" protest is far more likely to be covered; but, for that reason, the last thing journalists want to think of themselves as doing is allowing violent protestors to "hijack" the media to convey a message. The matter is further complicated by the fact that journalists have a fairly idiosyncratic definition of "violence": something like "damage to persons or property not authorized by properly constituted authorities." So, if even one protestor damages a Starbucks window, one can speak of "violent protests," but if police then proceed to attack everyone present with tazers, sticks, and plastic bullets, this cannot be described as violent. In these circumstances, it's hardly surprising that anarchist media teams mainly end up doing damage control.

One can now begin to understand the environment in which images of Black Bloc anarchists smashing windows, and colorful puppets, predominate media coverage. "Message" is largely off-limits. Almost every major mobilization has been accompanied by a day of public seminars in which radical intellectuals analyze the policies of the IMF, G8, and so on, and discuss possible alternatives. None, to my knowledge, have ever been covered by the corporate press. "Process" is complicated and difficult to capture visually; meetings are usually off-limits to reporters anyway. Still, the relative lack of attention to street blockades and street parties, lock-downs, banner drops, critical mass rides, and the like, is harder to explain. All these are dramatic, public, and often quite visually striking. Admittedly, since it is almost impossible to describe those engaged in such tactics as "violent," the fact that participants frequently end up gassed, beaten, pepper-sprayed, shot at with plastic bullets, and otherwise manhandled by police provides narrative dilemmas most journalists would (apparently) prefer to avoid.[4] But this alone does not seem an adequate explanation.[5]

We return, then, to my initial observation: that there would seem to be something compelling about the paired images of masked window-breakers and giant puppets. Why?

Well, if nothing else, the two do mark a kind of neat structural opposition. Anarchists in Black Bloc mean to render themselves anonymous and interchangeable, identifiable only by their political affinity, their willingness to engage in militant tactics, and their solidarity with one another. Hence, the uniform black-hooded sweatshirts and black bandanas worn as masks. The papier-mâché puppets used in actions are all unique and individual: they tend to be brightly painted, but otherwise to vary wildly in size, shape, and conception. So, on the one hand, one has faceless, black anonymous figures, all roughly the same; on the other polychrome goddesses and birds and pigs and politicians. One is a mass, anonymous, destructive, deadly serious; the other, a multiplicity of spectacular displays of whimsical creativity.

If the paired images seem somehow powerful, I would suggest, it is because their juxtaposition does, in fact, say something important about what direct action aims to achieve. Let me begin by considering property destruction. Such acts are anything but random. They tend to follow strict ethical guidelines: individual possessions are off-limits, for example, along with any commercial property that's the base of its owner's immediate livelihood.

Every possible precaution is to be taken to avoid harming actual human beings. The targets—often carefully researched in advance—are corporate facades, banks and mass retail outlets, government buildings, or other symbols of state power. When describing their strategic vision, anarchists tend to draw on Situationism (Debord and Vaneigem have always been the most popular French theorists in anarchist infoshops). Consumer capitalism renders us isolated passive spectators, our only relation to one another our shared fascination with an endless play of images that are, ultimately, representations of the very sense of wholeness and community we have lost. Property destruction, then, is an attempt to "break the spell," to divert and redefine. It is a direct assault upon the Spectacle. Consider here the words of the famous N30 Seattle Black Bloc communiqué, from the section entitled "On the Violence of Property":

> When we smash a window, we aim to destroy the thin veneer of legitimacy that surrounds private property rights. At the same time, we exorcise that set of violent and destructive social relationships which has been imbued in almost everything around us. By "destroying" private property, we convert its limited exchange value into an expanded use value. A storefront window becomes a vent to let some fresh air into the oppressive atmosphere of a retail outlet (at least until the police decide to tear-gas a nearby road blockade). A newspaper box becomes a tool for creating such vents or a small blockade for the reclamation of public space or an object to improve one's vantage point by standing on it. A dumpster becomes an obstruction to a phalanx of rioting cops and a source of heat and light. A building facade becomes a message board to record brainstorm ideas for a better world.
>
> After N30, many people will never see a shop window or a hammer the same way again. The potential uses of an entire cityscape have increased a thousand-fold. The number of broken windows pales in comparison to the number of broken spells—spells cast by a corporate hegemony to lull us into forgetfulness of all the violence committed in the name of private property rights and of all the potential of a society without them. Broken windows can be boarded up (with yet more waste of our forests) and eventually replaced, but the shattering of assumptions will hopefully persist for some time to come (in David & X 2002: 56).

Property destruction is a matter of taking an urban landscape full of endless corporate facades—and flashing imagery that seems immutable, permanent, monumental—and demonstrating just how fragile it really is. It is a literal shattering of illusions.

What then of puppets?

Again, they seem the perfect complement. Giant papier-mâché puppets are created by taking the most ephemeral of material—ideas, paper, wire mesh—and transforming it into something very like a monument, even if they are, at the same time, somewhat ridiculous. A giant puppet is the mockery of the idea of a monument[6], and of everything monuments represent: the inapproachability, monochrome solemnity, above all, the implication of permanence, the state's (itself ultimately somewhat ridiculous) attempt to turn its principle and history into eternal verities. If "property destruction" is meant to shatter the existing Spectacle, giant puppets, it seems to me, suggest the permanent capacity to create new ones.

In fact, from the perspective of the activists, it is again process—in this case, the process of production—that is really the point. There are brainstorming sessions to come up with themes and visions, organizing meetings; but, above all, the wires and frames lie on the floors of garages or yards or warehouses or similar quasi-industrial spaces for days, surrounded by buckets of paint and construction materials, almost never alone, with small teams in attendance, molding, painting, smoking, eating, playing music, arguing, wandering in and out. Everything is designed to be communal, egalitarian, expressive. The objects themselves are not expected to last. They are for the most part made of fairly delicate materials; few would withstand a heavy rainstorm; some are even self-consciously destroyed or set ablaze in the course of actions. In the absence of permanent storage facilities, they usually quickly start to fall apart.

As for the images: these are clearly meant to encompass, and hence constitute, a kind of universe. Normally, Puppetistas, as they sometimes call themselves, aim for a rough balance between positive and negative images. On the one hand, one might have the Giant Pig that represents the World Bank, on the other, a Giant Liberation Puppet whose arms can block an entire highway. Many of the most famous images identify marchers and the things they wear or carry: for instance, a giant bird puppet at A16 (the 2000 IMF/World Bank actions) was accompanied by hundreds of little birds on top of signs distributed to all and sundry. Similarly, Haymarket martyrs, Zapatistas, the Statue of Liberty, or a Liberation Monkeywrench might carry slogans identical to those carried on the signs, stickers, or T-shirts of those actually taking part in the action.

The most striking images, though, are often negative ones: the corporate control puppet at the 2000 democratic convention, operating both Bush and Gore like marionettes; a giant riot policeman who shoots out pepper spray; and endless effigies to be encompassed and ridiculed.

The mocking and destruction of effigies is, of course, one of the oldest and most familiar gestures of political protest. Often, such effigies are an explicit assault on monumentality. The fall of regimes is marked by the pulling down of statues. It was the (apparently staged) felling of the statue of Saddam Hussein in Baghdad that, in the minds of almost everyone, determined the moment of the actual end of his regime. Similarly, during George Bush's visit to England in 2004, protestors erected innumerable mock statues of Bush, large and small, just in order to pull them down again.

Still, the positive images are often treated with little more respect than the effigies.

Here is an extract from my early reflections on the subject, jotted down shortly after spending time in the Puppet Warehouse in Philadelphia before the Republican Convention in 2000, somewhat reedited:

> **(field notes extracts: July 31, 2000)**
> The question I keep asking myself is: why are these things even called "puppets?" Normally, one thinks of "puppets" as figures that move in response to the motions of some puppeteer. Most of these have few, if any, moving parts. These are more like moving statues, sometimes worn, sometimes carried. So in what sense are they "puppets?"
>
> These puppets are extremely visual, large, but also delicate and ephemeral. Usually they fall apart after a single action. This combination of huge size and lightness, it seems to me, makes them a bridge between words and reality; they are the point of transition; they represent the ability to start to make ideas real and take on solid form, to make our view of the world into something of equal physical bulk and greater spectacular power even than the engines of state violence that stand against it. The idea that they are extensions of our minds, words, may help explain the use of the term "puppets." They may not move around as an extension of some individual's will. But, if they did, this would somewhat contradict the emphasis on collective creativity. Insofar as they are characters in a drama, it is a drama with a collective author; insofar as they are manipulated, it is in a sense by everyone, in processions, often passed around from one activist to the next. Above all, they are meant to be emanations of a collective imagination. As such, for them either to become fully solid, or fully manipulable by a single individual, would contradict the point.

Puppets can be worn like costumes and in large actions, they are in fact continuous with costumes. Every major mobilization had its totem, or totems: the famous sea-turtles at Seattle, the birds and sharks at A16, the Dancing Skeletons at R2K (the Republican Convention in Philly), the caribou at Bush's inauguration, or for that matter the fragments of Picasso's *Guernica* designed for the protests against the upcoming Iraq invasion in 2003, designed so that they could each wander off and then all periodically combine together.

In fact, there's usually no clear line between puppets, costumes, banners and symbols, and simple props. Everything is designed to overlap and reinforce each other. Puppets tend to be surrounded by a much larger "carnival bloc," replete with clowns, stilt-walkers, jugglers, fire-breathers, unicyclists, Radical Cheerleaders, costumed kick-lines, or, often, entire marching bands—such as the Infernal Noise Brigade in Seattle or Hungry March Band in New York—that usually specialize in klezmer or circus music, in addition to the ubiquitous drums and whistles. The circus metaphor seems to sit particularly well with anarchists, presumably because circuses are collections of extreme individuals (one can't get much more individualistic than a collection of circus freaks) nonetheless engaged in a purely cooperative enterprise that also involves transgressing ordinary boundaries. Tony Blair's famous comment in 2004 that he was not about to be swayed by "some traveling anarchist circus" was not taken, by many, as an insult. There are in fact quite a number of explicitly anarchist circus troupes, their numbers only matched, perhaps, by that of various phony preachers. The connection is significant; for now, the critical thing is that every action will normally have its circus fringe, a collection of flying squads that circulate through the large street blockades to lift spirits, perform street theater, and also, critically, to try to defuse moments of tension or potential conflict. This latter is crucial. Since direct actions, unlike permitted marches, scrupulously avoid marshals or formal peacekeepers (who police will always try to co-opt), the puppet/circus squads often end up serving some of the same functions. Here is a first-hand account by members of one such affinity group from Chapel Hill ("Paper Hand Puppet Intervention") about how this might work itself out in practice.

> Burger and Zimmerman brought puppets to the explosive protests of the World Trade Organization in Seattle two years ago, where they joined a group that was blockading the building in which talks were being held. "People had linked arms," Zimmerman says. "The police had beaten and pepper-sprayed them already, and they threatened that they were coming back in five minutes to attack them again." But the protestors held their line, linking arms and crying, blinded by the pepper spray. Burger, Zimmerman and their friends came along—on stilts,

with clowns, a 40-foot puppet, and a belly dancer. They went up and down the line, leading the protesters in song. When the security van returned, they'd back the giant puppet up into its way. Somehow, this motley circus diffused the situation. "They couldn't bring themselves to attack this bunch of people who were now singing songs," Zimmerman says. Injecting humor and celebration into a grim situation, he says, is the essence of a puppet intervention (Cooks 2001).

For all the circus trappings, those most involved in making and deploying giant puppets will often insist that they are deeply serious. "Puppets are not cute, like muppets," insists Peter Schumann, the director of Bread and Puppet Theater—the group historically most responsible for popularizing the use of papier-mâché figures in political protest in the 1960s. "Puppets are effigies and gods and meaningful creatures."[7] Sometimes, they are literally so: as with the Maya gods that came to greet delegates at the WTO meetings in Cancun in September 2003. Always, they have a certain numinous quality.

Still, if giant puppets, generically, are gods, most are obviously, foolish, silly, ridiculous gods. It is as if the process of producing and displaying puppets becomes a way to both seize the power to make gods, and to make fun of it at the same time. Here, one seems to be striking against a profoundly anarchist sensibility. Within anarchism, one encounters a similar impulse at every point where one approaches the mythic or deeply meaningful. It appears to be operative in the doctrines of Zerzanites and similar Primitivists, who go about self-consciously creating myths (their own version of the Garden of Eden, the Fall, the coming Apocalypse) that seem to imply they want to see millions perish in a worldwide industrial collapse, or that imply they seek to abolish agriculture or even language—and who then bridle at the suggestion that they really do. It's clearly present in the writings of theorists like Peter Lamborn Wilson, whose meditations on the role of the sacred in revolutionary action are written under the persona of an insane Ismaili pederastic poet named Hakim Bey. It's even more clearly present among Pagan anarchist groups like Reclaiming, who since the anti-nuclear movement of the 1980s (Epstein 1991) have specialized in conducting what often seem like extravagant satires of pagan rituals that they nonetheless insist are real rituals that are really effective and which represent what they see as the deepest possible spiritual truths about the world.[8]

Puppets simply push this logic to a kind of extreme. The sacred here is, ultimately, the sheer power of creativity, of the imagination—or, perhaps more exactly, the power to bring the imagination into reality. This is, after all, the ultimate ideal of all revolutionary practice, to, as the 1968 slogan put

it, "give power to the imagination." But it is also as if the democratization of
the sacred can only be accomplished through a kind of burlesque. Hence, the
constant self-mockery, which, however, is never meant to genuinely undercut
the gravity and importance of what's being asserted, but rather, to imply the
ultimate recognition that, although gods are human creations, they are still
gods, and that taking this fact too seriously might prove dangerous.

Symbolic Warfare On the Part of the Police

Anarchists, as I've said, avoid designing their strategies around the media. The same cannot be said of the police.

It's obvious that the events of N30 in Seattle came as a surprise to most
in the American government. The Seattle police were clearly unprepared
for the sophisticated tactics adopted by the hundreds of affinity groups that
surrounded the hotel and, at least for the first day, effectively shut down the
meetings. The first impulse of many commanders appears to have been to
respect the non-violence of the actions.[9] It was only after 1 PM on the 30th,
after Madeleine Albright called the governor from inside the hotel demanding that he tell them to do whatever they had to do to break the blockade,
that police began a full-blown assault with tear gas, pepper spray, and con-
cussion grenades.[10] Even then, many seemed to hesitate, while others, when
they did enter the fray, descended into wild rampages, attacking and arresting scores of ordinary shoppers in Seattle's commercial district. In the end,
the governor was forced to call in the National Guard. While the media
pitched in by representing police actions as a response to Black Bloc actions
that began much later, having to bring in federal troops was an undeniable
spectacular symbolic defeat.

In the immediate aftermath of Seattle, law enforcement officials—on
the national and international level—appear to have begun a concerted effort to develop a new strategy. The details of such deliberations are, obviously, not available to the public. Nonetheless, judging by subsequent events,
it seems that their conclusion (unsurprisingly) was that the Seattle police had
not resorted to violence quickly or efficiently enough. The new strategy—
soon put into practice during subsequent actions in Washington, Windsor,
Philadelphia, Los Angeles, and Québec—appears to have been one of aggressive preemption. The problem of course was how to justify this against
a movement that was overwhelmingly non-violent, engaged in actions that
for the most part could not even be defined as criminal, and whose message
appeared to have at least potentially strong public appeal. [11]

One might phrase it this way. The events targeted by the movement—
trade summits, political conventions, IMF meetings—were largely symbolic

events. They were not, for the most part, venues for formal political decision-making, but junkets, self-celebratory rituals, and networking occasions
for some of the richest and most powerful people on earth. The effect of the
actions is normally not to shut down the meetings, but to create a sense of
siege. It might all be done in such a way as not to physically endanger anyone; the catapults might (as in Québec) only be hurling stuffed animals, but
the result is to produce meetings surrounded by mayhem, in which those
attending have to be escorted about by heavily armed security, the cocktail
parties are cancelled, and the celebrations, effectively, ruined. Nothing could
have been more effective in shattering the air of triumphant inevitability that
had surrounded such meetings in the 1990s. To imagine that the "forces of
order" would not respond aggressively would be naïve indeed. For them, the
non-violence of the blockaders was simply irrelevant. Or, to be more precise,
it was an issue only because it created a potential problem of public perception. This problem, however, was quite serious. How was one to represent
protestors as a threat to public safety, justifying extreme measures, if they did
not actually do anyone physical harm?

Here one should probably let events speak for themselves. If one looks
at what happened during the months immediately following Seattle, the first
thing one observes is a series of preemptive strikes, always aimed at threats
that (not unlike Iraq's weapons of mass destruction) never quite material-
ized:

April 2000, Washington DC

Hours before the protests against the IMF and World Bank are to begin
on April 15, police round up 600 marchers in a preemptive arrest and
seize the protesters' Convergence Center. Police Chief Charles Ramsey
loudly claims to have discovered a workshop for manufacturing molotov cocktails and homemade pepper spray inside. DC police later admit
no such workshop existed (really they'd found paint thinner used in
art projects and peppers being used for the manufacture of gazpacho);
however, the convergence center remains closed and much of the art
and many of the puppets inside are confiscated.

July 2000, Minneapolis

Days before a scheduled protest against the International Society of
Animal Geneticists, local police claim that activists had detonated a
cyanide bomb at a local McDonald's and might have their hands on
stolen explosives. The next day the DEA raids a house used by organizers, drags off the bloodied inhabitants, and confiscates their computers and boxes full of outreach materials. Police later admit there never

actually was a cyanide bomb and they had no reason to believe activists
were in possession of explosives.

August 2000, Philadelphia

Hours before the protests against the Republican Convention are to
begin, police, claiming to be acting on a tip, seize the warehouse where
the art, banners, and puppets used for the action are being prepared,
arresting all of the at least seventy-five activists discovered inside. Police
Chief John Timoney loudly claims to have discovered C4 explosives
and water balloons full of hydrochloric acid in the building. Police later
admit no explosives or acid were really found; the arrestees are however
not released until well after the actions are over. All of the puppets,
banners, art, and literature to be used in the protest are systematically
destroyed.

While it is possible that we are dealing with a remarkable series of honest
mistakes, this does look an awful lot like a series of attacks on the material activists were intending to use to get their message out to the public. Certainly
that's how the activists interpreted them—especially after Philadelphia.
Organizers planning the parallel protests against the Democratic Convention
in LA managed to obtain a restraining order barring police from attacking
their convergence center, but ever since, in the weeks before any major mobilization, a key issue is always how to hide and protect the puppets.

By Philadelphia, it became quite clear that the police had adopted a
very self-conscious media strategy. Their spokesmen would pepper each
daily press conference with wild accusations, well aware that the crime-desk
reporters assigned to cover them (who usually relied on good working relations with police for their livelihood) would normally uncritically reproduce
anything they said, and rarely consider it to merit a story if, afterwards, the
claims turned out to be false. I was working the phones for the activist media
team during much of this time and can attest that a large part of what we
ended up doing was coming up with responses to what we came to call "the
lie of the day." The first day, police announced that they had seized a van
full of poisonous snakes and reptiles that activists were intending to release
in the city center (they were later forced to admit that it actually belonged to
a pet store and had nothing to do with the protests). The second day, they
claimed that anarchists had splashed acid in an officer's face; this sent us
scrambling to figure out what might have actually happened. They dropped
the story immediately thereafter, but it would appear that if anything was
actually splashed on an officer, it was probably red paint that was actually
directed at a wall. On the third day we were accused of planting "dry ice
bombs" throughout the city. This, again, sent the anarchist media teams

scrambling to try to figure out precisely what dry ice bombs were (it turned out the police had apparently found the reference in a copy of the *Anarchist Cookbook*). Interestingly, this last story does not seem to have actually made the news: at this point, most reporters no longer were willing to reproduce the most dramatic claims by the authorities. The fact that the first two claims turned out to be false, however, along with the claims of acid and explosives in the puppet warehouse, or that Timoney appeared to have developed an intentional policy of lying to them, was never considered itself newsworthy. Neither, however, was the actual reason for the actions, that were meant to draw attention to the prison industrial complex (a phrase that we repeated endlessly to reporters, but never made it into a single news report)—presumably on the grounds that it would be unethical for reporters to allow violent protestors to "hijack" the media.

This same period began to see increasingly outlandish accounts of what had happened at Seattle. During the WTO protests themselves, I must emphasize, no one, including the Seattle police, had claimed anarchists had done anything more militant than break windows. That was the end of November 1999. In March 2000, less than three months later, a story in the *Boston Herald* reported that, in the weeks before an upcoming bio-tech conference, officers from Seattle had come to brief the local police on how to deal with "Seattle tactics," such as attacking police with "chunks of concrete, BB guns, wrist rockets, and large capacity squirt guns loaded with bleach and urine" (Martinez 2000). In June, *New York Times* reporter Nicole Christian, apparently relying on police sources in Detroit preparing for a trade protest across the Canadian border in Windsor, claimed that Seattle demonstrators had "hurled Molotov cocktails, rocks and excrement at delegates and police officers." On this occasion, after the New York Direct Action Network picketed their offices, the *Times* ended up having to run a retraction, admitting that according to Seattle authorities, no objects had been thrown at human beings.[12] Nonetheless, the account appears to have become canonical. Each time there is a new mobilization, stories invariably surface in local newspapers with the same list of "Seattle tactics"—a list that also appears to have become enshrined in training manuals distributed to street cops. Before the Miami Summit of the Americas in 2003, for example, circulars distributed to local businessmen and civic groups listed every one of these "Seattle tactics" as what they should expect to see on the streets once anarchists arrived:

> **Wrist Rockets**: larger hunter-type sling shots that they use to shoot steel ball bearings or large bolts. A very dangerous and deadly weapon.

Molotov Cocktails: many were thrown in Seattle and Quebec and caused extensive damage.

Crow Bars: to smash windows, cars, etc. They also pry up curbs, then break the cement into pieces that they can throw at police officers. This was done extensively in Seattle.

Squirt guns: filled with acid or urine.[13]

Again, according to local police's own accounts, none of these weapons or tactics had been used in Seattle and no one has produced any evidence they've been used in any subsequent US mobilization.[14] In Miami, the predictable result was that, by the time the first marches began, most of downtown lay shuttered and abandoned.

Miami, as the first major convergence in the new security climate after September 11, might be said to mark the full culmination of this approach, combining aggressive disinformation and preemptive attacks on activists. During the actions, the police chief—John Timoney again—had officers pouring out an endless series of accusations of activists hurling rocks, bottles, urine, and bags of feces at police. (Needless to say, despite ubiquitous video cameras and hundreds of arrests, no one was ever charged, let alone convicted, of assaulting an officer with any such substance, and no reporter managed to produce an image of an activist doing so.) Police strategy consisted almost entirely of raids and preemptive attacks on protestors, employing the full arsenal of old and newly developed "non-lethal" weaponry: tasers, pepper spray, plastic and rubber and wooden bullets, bean-bag bullets soaked in pepper spray, tear gas, and so on—and rules of engagement that allowed them to pretty much fire at anyone at will.

Here too, puppets were singled out. In the months before the summit, the Miami city council actually attempted to pass a law making the display of puppets illegal, on the grounds that they could be used to conceal bombs or other weapons (Koerner 2003). It failed, since it was patently unconstitutional, but the message got out. As a result, the Black Bloc in Miami actually ended up spending most of their time and energy protecting the puppets. Miami also provides a vivid example of the peculiar personal animus many police seem to have against large figures made of papier-mâché. According to one eyewitness report, after police routed protesters from Seaside Plaza, forcing them to abandon their puppets, officers spent the next half hour or so systematically attacking and destroying them: shooting, kicking, and ripping the remains; one even putting a giant puppet in his squad car with the head sticking out and driving so as to smash it against every sign and street post available.

Rallying the Troops

The Boston example is particularly striking because it indicates that there were elements in the Seattle police actually training other police in how to deal with violent tactics that official Seattle spokesmen were, simultaneously, denying had actually been employed. It's very difficult to know exactly what's going on here—even really, to figure out precisely who these endlessly cited "police intelligence" sources actually are. We seem to be entering a murky zone involving information being collected, concocted, and passed back and forth between a variety of federal police task forces, private security agencies, and allied right-wing think tanks, in such a way that the images become self-reinforcing and presumably, no one is quite sure what is and isn't true. However, it is easy to see how one of the main concerns in the wake of Seattle would be to ensure the reliability of one's troops. As commanders discovered in Seattle, officers used to considering themselves guardians of public safety frequently balk, or at least waver, when given orders to make a baton charge against a collection of non-violent sixteen-year-old white girls. These were, after all, the very sort of people they are ordinarily expected to protect. At least some of the imagery, then, appears to be designed specifically to appeal to the sensibility of ordinary street cops.

This at least would help to explain the otherwise peculiar emphasis on bodily fluids: the water-pistols full of bleach and urine, for example, or claims that officers were pelted with urine and excrement. This appears to be very much a police obsession. Certainly, it has next to nothing to do with anarchist sensibilities. When I've asked activists where they think such stories come from, most confess themselves deeply puzzled. One or two suggested that, when defending a besieged squat, sometimes buckets of human waste is one of the few things one has to throw. But none have ever heard of anyone actually transporting human waste to an action in order to hurl or shoot at police, or could suggest why anyone might want to. A brick, some point out, is unlikely to injure an officer in full riot gear; but it will certainly slow him down. But what would be the point of shooting urine at him? Yet images like this reemerge almost every time police attempt to justify a preemptive strike. In press conferences, they have been known to actually produce jars of urine and bags of feces that they claim to have discovered hidden in backpacks or activist convergence sites.[15]

It is hard to see these claims as making sense except within the peculiar economy of personal honor typical of any institution that, like the police, operates on an essentially military ethos. For police officers, the most legitimate justification for violence is an assault on one's personal dignity. To cover another person in shit and piss is obviously about as powerful an assault on their personal dignity as one can possibly make. We also seem to be dealing here with a self-conscious allusion to the famous image of 1960s protesters "spitting on soldiers in uniform" when they returned from Vietnam—one whose mythic power continues to resonate, not just in right-wing circles, to this day, despite the fact that there's little evidence that it ever happened.[16] It's almost as if someone decided to ratchet the image up a notch: "if spitting on a uniform is such an insult, what would be even worse?"

That there might have been some kind of coordination in this effort might be gleaned, too, from the fact that it was precisely around the time of the Democratic and Republican conventions in the summer of 2000 that mayors and police chiefs around America began regularly declaring, often in striking similar terms (and based on no evidence whatsoever) that anarchists were actually a bunch of "trust fund babies," who disguised their faces while breaking things so their wealthy parents wouldn't recognize them on TV—an accusation that soon became received wisdom among right-wing talk show hosts and law enforcement professionals across America.[17] The obvious message to the officer on the street appeared to be: "do not think of your assignment as having to protect a bunch of bankers and politicians who have contempt for you against protestors whose actual positions on economic issues you might well agree with; think of it, rather, as a chance to beat up on those bankers' and politicians' children." In a sense, one might say the message was perfectly calibrated to the level of repression required, since it suggests that, while force was appropriate, deadly force was not: if one were to actually maim or kill a protestor, one might well be killing the son or daughter of a senator or CEO, which would be likely to provoke a scandal.

Police are also apparently regularly warned that puppets might be used to conceal bombs or weapons.[18] If questioned on their attitudes towards puppets, this is how they are likely to respond. However, it's hard to imagine this alone could explain the level of personal vindictiveness witnessed in Miami and other actions—especially since police hacking puppets to pieces must have been aware that there was nothing hidden inside them. The antipathy seems to run far deeper. Many activists have speculated on the reasons:

> **David Corston-Knowles:** You have to bear in mind these are people who are trained to be paranoid. They really do have to ask themselves whether something so big and inscrutable might contain explosives, however absurd that might seem from a non-violent protester's perspective. Police view their jobs not just as law enforcement, but also as maintaining order. And they take that job very personally. Giant demonstrations and giant puppets aren't orderly. They are about creating something—a different society, a different way of looking at things— and creativity is fundamentally at odds with the status quo.

Daniel Lang: Well, one theory is that the cops just don't like being up-staged by someone putting on a bigger show. After all, normally *they're* the spectacle: they've got the blue uniforms, they've got the helicopters and horses and rows of shiny motorcycles. So maybe they just resent it when someone steals the show by coming up with something even bigger and even more visually striking. They want to take out the com-petition.

Yvonne Liu: It's because they're so big. Cops don't like things that tower over them. That's why they like to be on horses. Plus, puppets are silly and round and misshapen. Notice how much cops always have to maintain straight lines? They stand in straight lines, they always try to make you stand in straight lines... I think round misshapen things somehow offend them.

Max Uhlenbeck: Obviously, they hate to be reminded that they're pup-pets themselves.

I will return to this question shortly.

Analysis I: The Hollywood Movie Principle

From the point of view of security officials during this period, rallying the troops was presumably the easy part. The stickier problem was what to do with the fact that the bulk of the American public refused to see the global justice movement as a threat. The only survey I am aware of taken at the time that addressed the question—a Zogby America poll taken of TV viewers during the Republican convention in 2000—found that about a third claimed to feel "pride" when they saw images of protestors on TV, and less than 16% percent had an unqualified negative reaction (Reuters/Zogby 2000).[19] This was especially striking in a poll of television viewers, since TV coverage during the convention was unremittingly hostile, treating the events almost exclusively as potential security threats.

There is, I think, a simple explanation. I would propose to call it the Hollywood Movie Principle. Most Americans, in watching a dramatic con-frontation on TV, effectively ask themselves: "if this were a Hollywood mov-ie, who would be the good guys?" Presented with a contest between what appear to be a collection of idealistic kids who do not actually injure anyone, and a collection of heavily armed riot cops protecting trade bureaucrats and corporate CEOs, the answer is pretty obvious. Individual maverick cops can be movie heroes. Riot cops never are. In fact, in Hollywood movies, riot cops almost never appear; about the closest one can find to them are the Imperial Storm Troopers in *Star Wars*, who, like their leader Darth Vader, stand in

American popular culture as one of the most familiar archetypes of evil. This point is not lost on the anarchists, who have since A16 taken to regularly bringing recordings of the Imperial Storm Trooper music from *Star Wars* to blast from their ranks as soon as a line of riot cops starts advancing.

If so, the key problem for the forces of order became: what would it take to reverse this perception? How to cast protesters in the role of the villain?

In the immediate aftermath of Seattle, the focus was all on broken windows. As we've seen, this imagery certainly did strike some sort of chord. But in terms of creating a sense that decisive measures were required, efforts to make a national issue out of property destruction came to surprisingly little effect. In the terms of my analysis, this makes perfect sense. After all, in the moral economy of Hollywood, property destruction is at best a very minor peccadillo. In fact, if the popularity of the various *Terminators*, *Lethal Weapons*, or *Die Hards* and the like reveal anything, it is that most Americans seem to rather like the idea of property destruction. If they did not themselves harbor a certain hidden glee at the idea of someone smashing a branch of their local bank, or a McDonald's (not to mention police cars, shopping malls, and complex construction machinery), it's hard to imagine why they would so regularly pay money to watch idealistic do-gooders smashing and blowing them up for hours on end, always in ways which, through the magic of the movies—but also like the practice of the Black Bloc—tend to leave innocent bystanders entirely unharmed? Certainly, it's unlikely that there are significant numbers of Americans who have not, at some time or another, had a fantasy about smashing up their bank. In the land of demolition derbies and monster trucks, Black Bloc anarchists might be said to be living a hidden aspect of the American dream.

Obviously, these are just fantasies. Most working class Americans do not overtly approve of destroying a Starbucks facade; but, unlike the talking classes, neither do they see such activity as a threat to the nation, let alone anything requiring military-style repression.

Analysis II: Creative Destruction and the Privitization of Desire

One could even say that in a sense, the Black Bloc appear to be the latest avatars of an artistic/revolutionary tradition which runs at least through the Dadaists, Surrealists, and Situationists: one which tries to play off the contradictions of capitalism by turning its own destructive, leveling forces against it. Capitalist societies—and America in particular—are, in essence, potlatch societies. That is, they are built around the spectacular destruction of consumer goods.[20] They are societies that imagine themselves as built on something they call "the economy" which, in turn, is imagined as a nexus between "production" and "consumption," endlessly spitting out products and then destroying them again. Since it is all based on the principle of infinite expansion of industrial production—the very principle which the Black Bloc anarchists, mostly being highly ecologically conscious anti-capitalists, most vehemently oppose—all that stuff has to be constantly destroyed to make way for new products. But this, in turn, means inculcating a certain passion for or delight in the smashing and destruction of property that can very easily slip into a delight in the shattering of those structures of relation which make capitalism possible. It is a system that can only renew itself by cultivating a hidden pleasure at the prospect of its own destruction.[21]

Actually, one could well argue that there have been two strains in twentieth century artistic/revolutionary thought, and that both have been entangled in the—endlessly ambivalent—image of the potlatch. In the 1930s, for example, Georges Bataille became fascinated by Marcel Mauss' description of the spectacular destruction of property in Kwakiutl potlatches. It ultimately became the basis for his famous theory of "expenditure," of the creation of meaning through destruction that he felt was ultimately lacking under modern capitalism. There are endless ironies here. First of all, what Bataille and subsequent authors seized on was not, in fact, "the potlatch" at all, but a small number of very unusual potlatches held around the turn of the century, at a time when Kwakiutl population was rapidly declining and a simultaneous minor economic boom had left the region awash in an unprecedented number of consumer goods. Ordinary potlatches did not normally involve the destruction of property at all; they were simply occasions for aristocrats to lavish wealth on the community. If the image of Indians setting fire to thousands of blankets or other consumer goods proved captivating, in other words, it was not because it represented some fundamental truth about human society that consumer capitalism had forgotten, but rather because it reflected the ultimate truth of consumer capitalism itself. In 1937, Bataille teamed up with Roger Callois to found a reading group called "The College of Sociology" that expanded his insights into a general theory of the revolutionary festival, arguing that it was only by reclaiming the principle of the sacred and the power of myth embodied in popular festivals that effective revolutionary action would be possible. Similar ideas were developed in the 1950s by Henri Lefebvre, and within the Lettrist International, whose journal, edited by Guy Debord, was, significantly, entitled *Potlatch*.[22] Here there is, of course, a direct line from the Situationists, with their promulgation of art as a form of revolutionary direct action, to the punk movement and contemporary anarchism.

If Black Blocs embody one side of this tradition—capitalism's encouragement of a kind of fascination with consumerist destruction that can, ultimately, be turned back against capitalism itself—the puppets surely represent the other one, the recuperation of the sacred and unalienated experience in the collective festival. Radical puppeteers tend to be keenly aware that their art harkens back to the wickerwork giants and dragons, Gargantuas and Pantagruels of Medieval festivals. Even those who have not themselves read Rabelais or Bakhtin are likely to be familiar with the notion of the carnivalesque.[23] Convergences are regularly framed as "carnivals against capitalism" or "festivals of resistance." The base-line reference seems to be the late Medieval world immediately before the emergence of capitalism, particularly, the period after the Black Death when the sudden decline in population had the effect of putting unprecedented amounts of money into the hands of the laboring classes. Most of it ended up being poured into popular festivals of one sort or another, which themselves began to multiply until they took up large parts of the calendar year; what nowadays might be called events of "collective consumption," celebrations of carnality and rowdy pleasures and—if Bakhtin is to be believed—tacit attacks on the very principle of hierarchy. One might say that the first wave of capitalism, the Puritan Moment as it's sometimes called, had to begin with a concerted assault on this world, which was condemned by improving landlords and nascent capitalists as pagan, immoral, and utterly unconducive to the maintenance of labor discipline. Of course, a movement to abolish all moments of public festivity could not last forever: Cromwell's reign in England is reviled to this day on the grounds that he outlawed Christmas. More importantly, once moments of festive, collective consumption were eliminated, the nascent capitalism would be left with the obvious problem of how to sell its products, particularly in light of the need to constantly expand production. The end result was what I like to call a process of the privatization of desire: the creation of endless individual, familial, or semi-furtive forms of consumption—none of which, as we are so often reminded, could really be fully satisfying or else the whole logic of endless expansion wouldn't work. While one should hardly imagine that police strategists are fully cognizant of all this, the very existence of police is tied to a political cosmology which sees such forms of collective consumption as inherently disorderly, and (much like a Medieval carnival) always brimming with the possibility of violent insurrection. "Order" means that citizens should go home and watch TV.[24]

For police, then, what revolutionaries see as an eruption of the sacred through a re-creation of the popular festival is a "disorderly assembly"—and exactly the sort of thing they exist to disperse. However, since this sense of festival as threatening does not appear to resonate with large sectors of the TV audience, the police were forced to, as it were, change the script. What we've seen is a very calculated campaign of symbolic warfare, an attempt to eliminate images of colorful floats and puppets, and substitute images of bombs and hydrochloric acid—the very substances that, in police fantasies, are likely to actually lurk beneath the papier-mâché façade.

Analysis III: The Laws of War

To fully understand the place of puppets, though, I think one has to grapple with the question of rules of engagement.

I already touched on this question obliquely earlier when I suggested that, when politicians informed street cops that protestors were "trust fund babies," what they really meant to suggest was that they could be brutalized, but not maimed or killed, and that police tactics should be designed accordingly. From an ethnographer's perspective, one of the most puzzling things about direct action is to understand how these rules are actually negotiated. Certainly, rules exist. There are lines that cannot be crossed by the police without risk of major scandal, there are endless lines that cannot be crossed by activists. Yet each side acts as if it is playing a game whose rules it had worked out exclusively through its own internal processes, without any consultation with the other players. This could not ultimately be the case. I first began thinking about these questions after my experience in Philly during the Republican Convention in the summer of 2000. As I've said, I was working mainly with an activist media team. During the day of action, however, my job was to go out into the streets with a cell phone to report back to them what was actually happening. I ended up accompanying a column of Black Bloc'ers whose actions were originally meant as a diversion, to lure police away from street blockades in a different part of town. The police appear to have decided not to take the bait, and as a result, the Bloc briefly had their run of a wide stretch of downtown Philadelphia:

(based on field notes: Philadelphia, August 1, 2000)
Faced with a rapidly moving column of several hundred anarchists appearing out of nowhere, small groups of police would often abandon their cars, which the anarchists would then proceed to trash and spray-paint. A couple dozen police cars, one stretch limo, and numerous official buildings were hit in the course of the next hour or so. Eventually, reinforcements, in the form of police bicycle squads began to appear and before long there was a rough balance of forces. What followed at this point could only be described as an episode of some kind of nonviolent warfare. A few Black Bloc kids would try to shut down a bus by playing with valves in the back; a squad of bike cops would swoop in and grab

a few, cuffing them and locking their bikes together to create tiny fortresses in which to hold them. Once, a large mass of protesters appeared from another direction and the cops ended up besieged in their little bike fort, with Black Bloc'ers surrounding them, screaming insults, throwing paint bombs above their heads, doing everything but actually attacking them. On that occasion the Bloc wasn't quite able to snatch back their arrested comrades before police vans with reinforcements appeared to take them away; elsewhere, there were rumors of successful "unarrests." The police even suffered a casualty in that particular confrontation: one overweight cop, overwhelmed by the tension and stifling heat, collapsed and had to be carried off or revived with smelling salts.

It was obvious that both sides had worked out rules of engagement. Activists tended to work out their principles carefully in advance and, while there were certainly differences, say, between those who adopted classic non-violent civil disobedience rules (who had, for example, undergone nonviolence trainings) and the more militant anarchists I was with, all agree at least on the need to avoid directly causing harm to other human beings, or to damaging personal property or owner-operated "mom and pop" stores. The police of course could attack protesters more or less at will, but at this point at least, they seemed to feel they had to do so in such a way as to be fairly sure that none would be killed or that more than a handful required hospitalization—which, in the absence of very specific trainings and technologies, required a fair amount of constraint.

These basic rules applied throughout; however, over the course of the day, the tenor of events was constantly shifting. The Black Bloc confrontations were tense and angry; other areas were placid or somber ritual, drum circles or pagan spiral dances; others, full of music or ridiculous carnival. The Black Bloc column I was accompanying, for example, eventually converged with a series of others until there were almost a thousand anarchists rampaging through the center of the city. The district attorney's office was thoroughly paint-bombed. More police cars were destroyed. However it was all done quickly on the move. Larger and larger bike squads started followed our columns, splitting the Bloc and threatening to isolate smaller groups that could, then, be arrested. We were running faster and faster, dodging through alleys and parking lots.

Finally, the largest group descended on a plaza where a permitted rally was being held; this was assumed to be a safe space. In fact, it wasn't quite. Riot police soon began surrounding the plaza and cutting off routes of escape; it seemed like they were preparing for a mass arrest.

Such matters usually simply come down to numbers: it takes something like two officers in the field for every protester to carry off a mass arrest, probably three if the victims are trying to resist, and have some idea of how to go about it (i.e., know enough to link arms and try to keep a continuous line). In this situation the Black Bloc kids could be expected to know exactly what to do. The others, who thought they were attending a safe, permitted event, were mostly entirely unprepared, but could nonetheless be expected to follow their lead. On the other hand, they were trapped, they had no way to receive reinforcements, and the police were getting a constant flow of them. The mood was extremely tense. Activists who had earlier been conducting a teach-in and small rally against the prison industrial complex milled about uncomfortably around a giant poster-board as the Bloc, now reduced to a couple hundred black figures in bandanas and gas masks, formed a mini-spokescouncil, then faced off against the police lines at two different points where it seemed there might be a break in their lines (there usually is, when the police first begin to deploy); but to no avail.

I lingered on the plaza, chatting with a friend, Brad, who was complaining that he had lost his backpack and most of his worldly goods in the police raid on the puppet space that morning. We munched on apples—none of us had eaten all day—and watched as four performance artists on bicycles with papier-mâché goat heads, carrying a little sign saying "Goats With A Vote," began wading into the police lines to perform an acapella rap song. "You see what you can do with puppets?" laughed Brad. "No one else would ever be able to get away with that."

The Goats, as it turned out, were just the first wave. They were followed, ten minutes later, by a kind of "puppet intervention." Not with real puppets—the puppets had all been destroyed, and the musicians all arrested, at the warehouse earlier that morning. Instead, the Revolutionary Anarchist Clown Bloc appeared; led by two figures on high bicycles, blowing horns and kazoos, spreading streamers and confetti everywhere; alongside a large contingent of "Billionaires for Bush (or Gore)," dressed in high camp tuxedos and evening gowns. There were probably not more than thirty or forty of them in all but between them they immediately managed to change the tenor of the whole event, and to throw everything into confusion. The Billionaires started handing fake money to the police ("to thank them for suppressing dissent"). The clowns attacked the Billionaires with squeaky mallets. Unicycles appeared, and fire jugglers. In the ensuing confusion, cracks did appear in the police lines and just about everyone on the Plaza took advantage to form a wedge and burst out and to safety, with the Black Bloc leading the way.

Let's consider for a moment this idea of nonviolent warfare. How much of a metaphor is it really?

One could well make the argument that it is not a metaphor at all. Clausewitz notwithstanding, war has never been a pure contest of force with no rules. Just about all armed conflicts have had very complex and detailed sets of mutual understandings between the warring parties. (When total war does occur, its practitioners—Attila, Cortes—tend to be remembered a thousand years later for this very reason). There are always rules. As the Israeli military theorist Martin Van Creveld (1991) observes, if nothing else, in any armed conflict there will normally be:

- Rules for parlays and truces (this would include, for example, the sanctity of negotiators);
- Rules for how to surrender and how captives are to be treated;
- Rules for how to identify and deal with non-combatants (normally including medics);
- Rules for levels and types force allowable between combatants—which weapons or tactics are dishonorable or illegal (i.e., even when Hitler and Stalin were going at it, neither tried to assassinate the another or used chemical weapons).

Van Creveld emphasizes that such rules are actually necessary for any effective use of force, because to maintain an effective army, one needs to maintain a certain sense of honor and discipline, a sense of being the good guys. Without the rules, in other words, it would be impossible to maintain any real morale or command structure. An army which does not obey rules degenerates into a marauding band, and faced with a real army, marauding bands invariably lose. Van Creveld suggests there are probably other reasons why there must be rules: for instance, that violence is so intrinsically frightening that humans always immediately surround it with regulation. But one of the most interesting, because it brings home how much the battlefield is an extension of a larger political field, is that, without rules, it is impossible to know when you have won—since ultimately one needs to have both sides agree on this question.

Now consider the police. Police certainly see themselves soldiers of a sort. But insofar as they see themselves as fighting a war (the "war on crime"), they also know they are involved in a conflict in which victory is by definition impossible.

How does this affect the rules of engagement? On one level the answer is obvious. When it comes to levels of force, what sort of weapons or tactics one can use in what circumstances, police operate under enormous constraints—far more than any army. Some of these constraints remain tacit. Others are quite legal and explicit. Certainly, every time a policeman fires a gun, there must be an investigation. This is one of the reasons for the endless elaboration of "non-lethal" weapons—tasers, plastic bullets, pepper spray, and the like—for purposes of crowd control: they are not freighted with the same restrictions. On the other hand, when police are engaged in actions *not* deemed to involve potentially lethal force, and that are not meant to lead to a suspect's eventual criminal conviction, there are almost no constraints of what they can do—certainly none that can be enforced in any way.[25]

So in the last of Van Creveld's categories—the specific kinds of weapons that can be used in open combat, especially, the use of lethal force—there are endless constraints. As for the other rules, anyone who has been involved in direct action can testify to the fact that the police systematically violate all of them. Police regularly engage in practices which, in war, would be considered outrageous, or at the very least, utterly dishonorable. Police regularly arrest mediators. If members of an affinity group occupy a building, and one does not but instead acts as police liaison, it might well end up that the liaison is the only one who is actually arrested. If one does negotiate an agreement with the police, they will almost invariably violate it. Police frequently attack or arrest those they have earlier offered safe passage. They regularly target medics. If those carrying out an action in one part of a city try to create "green zones" or safe spaces in another—in other words, if they try to set up an area in which everyone agrees not to break the law or provoke the authorities, as a way to distinguish combatants and non-combatants—the police will almost invariably attack the green zone.

Why? There are various reasons. Some are obviously pragmatic: you don't have to come to an understanding about how to treat prisoners if you can arrest protesters, but protesters can't arrest you. But, in a broader sense, such behavior is a means of refusing any suggestion of equivalency—the kind that would simply be assumed if fighting another army in a conventional war. Police represent the state; the state has a monopoly of the legitimate use of violence within its borders: therefore, within that territory, police are by definition incommensurable with anyone else. This is essential to understanding what police actually are. Many sociological studies have pointed out that maybe six percent of the average police officer's time is spent on anything which can even remotely be considered "fighting crime." Police are a group of armed, lower-echelon government administrators, trained in the scientific application of physical force to aid in the resolution of administrative problems. They are bureaucrats with guns, and, whether they are guarding lost children, talking rowdy drunks out of bars, or supervising free concerts in the park, the one common feature of the kind of situation to which they're assigned is the possibility of having to impose "non-negotiated solutions backed up by the potential use of force."[26] The key term here, I think, is "non-negotiable." Police do not negotiate—at least when it comes to anything important—because that would imply equivalency. When they are forced to negotiate, they pretty much invariably break their word.[27]

In other words, police find themselves in a paradoxical position. Their job is to embody the state's monopoly on the use of coercive force; yet their freedom to employ that force is extremely limited. The refusal to treat the other side as honorable opponents, and, therefore, as equivalent in any way, seems to be the only way to maintain the principle of absolute incommensurability that representatives of the state must, by definition, maintain. This would appear to be the reason why, when restrictions on the use of force by police are removed, the results are catastrophic. Whenever you see wars that violate all the rules and involve horrific atrocities against civilians, they are invariably framed as "police actions."

Obviously, none of this actually answers the question of how rules of engagement are negotiated. But it does make it clear why it cannot be done directly. This seems particularly true in America. In many countries, from Italy to Madagascar, the rules of civil resistance can sometimes be worked quite explicitly, so that protest ends up becoming a kind of game in which the rules are clearly understood by each side. A good example is the famous *tute bianci* or "white overalls" tactics employed in Italy between 1999 and 2001, where protestors would fortify themselves with layers of padding and inflatable inner tubes and the like, and rush the barricades, at the same time pledging to do no harm to another human being. Participants often admitted to me that the rules were, for the most part, directly negotiated: "you can hit us as hard as you like as long as you hit us on the padding; we won't hit you but we'll try to plow through the barricades; let's see who wins!" In fact, matters had come to such a pass that negotiation was expected: before the G8 meetings in Genoa, when the government opted for a policy of violent repression, they were forced to bring in the LAPD to train Italian police in how *not* to interact with protesters, how *not* to allow either side to be effectively humanized in the eyes of the other.[28] In the United States, however, police appear to object to such negotiations on principle—unless, that is, protestors are actually trying to get arrested, and are willing to negotiate the terms.

Still, it's obvious that on some level, negotiation must take place. What's more, whatever level that is, it is the real level of power: since, after all, as always in politics, real power is not the power to win a contest, but the power to define the rules and stakes; not the power to win an argument, but the power to define what the argument is about. Here, it is clear that the power is not all on one side. Years of moral-political struggle, one might say, have created a situation in which the police, generally speaking, have to accept extreme restrictions on their use of force. This is much more true when dealing with people defined as "white," of course, but nonetheless it is a real limit on their ability to suppress dissent. The problem for those dedicated to the principle of direct action is that, while these rules of engagement—particularly the levels of force police are allowed to get away with—are under constant renegotiation, this process is expected to take place through institutions to which anarchists, on principle, object. Normally, one is expected to employ the language of "rights" or "police brutality," to pursue one's case though the courts—with the help of liberal NGOs and sympathetic politicians—but most of all, one is expected to do battle in "the court of public opinion." This, of course, means through the corporate media, since "the public" in this context is little more than its audience. Of course, for an anarchist, the very fact that human beings are organized into a "public," into a collection of atomized spectators, is precisely the problem. The solution for them is self-organization: they wish to see the public abandon their role as spectators and organize themselves into an endless and overlapping collection of directly democratic voluntary associations and communities. Yet, according to the language normally employed by the media and political classes, the moment members of the public begin to do this, the moment they self-organize in any way—say, by forming labor unions or political associations—they are no longer the public but "special interest groups" presumed by definition to be opposed to the public interest. (This helps explain why even peaceful protestors at permitted events expressing views shared by overwhelming majorities of Americans are nonetheless never described as members of "the public.")

Negotiation, then, is supposed to take place indirectly. Each side is supposed to make their case via the media—mainly, through precisely the kind of calculated symbolic warfare that the police, in America, are willing to play quite aggressively, but activists, and particularly anarchists, are increasingly unwilling to play at all. Anarchists and their allies are above all trying to circumvent this game. To some degree, they are trying to do so by creating their own media. To some degree, they are trying to do so by using the corporate media to convey images that they know are likely to alienate most suburban middle class viewers, but that they hope will galvanize potentially revolutionary constituencies: oppressed minorities, alienated adolescents, the working poor. Many Black Bloc anarchists were quite delighted, after Seattle, to see the media "sensationalizing" property destruction for this very reason. To some degree, too, they are trying to circumvent the game by trying to seize the power to renegotiate the terms of engagement on the field of battle. It's the latter, I think, that the police see as fundamentally unfair.

So Why Do Cops Hate Puppets?

Let's return, then, to the notion of a "puppet intervention."

In Philly, on the evening of the first, we organized a press conference in which one of the few puppetistas who escaped arrest that morning was given center stage. During the press conference and subsequent talks with the media, we all emphasized that the puppet crews were, effectively, our peacekeepers. One of their main jobs was to intervene to defuse situations of potential violence. If the police were really primarily concerned with maintaining public order, as they maintained, peacekeepers seemed a strange choice for a preemptive strike.

By now, it should be easy enough to see why police might not see things this way. This is not to say we were wrong to insist that the attack on the puppet warehouse was inspired by political motives, rather than a desire to protect the public.[29] It was. As we've seen, it appears, with its wild claims of acid and explosives, to have been part of a calculated campaign of symbolic warfare. At the same time, the *manner* in which puppets can be used to defuse situations of potential violence is completely different than, say, that employed by protest marshals. Police tend to appreciate the presence of marshals, since marshals are organized into a chain of command that police tend to immediately treat as a mere extension of their own—and which, as a result, often effectively becomes so. Unlike marshals, puppets cannot be used to convey orders. Rather, like the clowns and Billionaires, they aim to transform and redefine situations of potential conflict.

It might be helpful here to reflect on the nature of the violence—"force," if you like—that police represent. A former LAPD officer, writing about the Rodney King case, pointed out that on most of the occasions in which a citizen is severely beaten by police, it turns out that the victim was actually innocent of any crime. "Cops don't beat up burglars," he observed. If you want to cause the police to be violent, the surest way is to *challenge their right to define the situation*. This is not something a burglar is likely to do (Cooper 1991).[30] This of course makes perfect sense if we remember that police are, essentially, bureaucrats with guns. Bureaucratic procedures are all about questions of definition. Or, to be more precise, they are about the imposition of a narrow range of pre-established schema to a social reality that is, usually, infinitely more complex. A crowd can be either orderly or disorderly; a citizen can be white, black, Hispanic, or an Asian/Pacific Islander; a petitioner is or is not in possession of a valid photo ID: such simplistic rubrics can only be maintained in the absence of dialogue. Hence, the quintessential form of bureaucratic violence is the wielding of the truncheon when somebody "talks back."

I began by saying that this was to be an essay of interpretation. In fact, it has been just as much an essay about frustrated interpretation, about the limits of interpretation. Ultimately, I think this frustration can be traced back to the very nature of violence—bureaucratic or otherwise. Violence is in fact unique among forms of human action in that it holds out the possibility of affecting the actions of others about whom one understands nothing. Any other way one might wish to affect another's actions, one must at least have some idea who they think they are, what they want, what they think is going on. Interpretation is required, and that requires a certain degree of imaginative identification. Hit someone over the head hard enough, all this becomes irrelevant. Obviously, two parties locked in an equal contest of violence would usually do well to get inside each other's heads, but when access to violence becomes extremely unequal, the need vanishes. This is typically the case in situations of structural violence: of systemic inequality that is ultimately backed up by the threat of force. Structural violence always seems to create extremely lopsided structures of imagination. Gender is actually a telling example here. Women almost everywhere know a great deal about men's work, men's lives, and male experience; men are almost always not only ignorant about women's lives, they often react with indignation at the idea they should even try to imagine what being a woman might be like. The same is typically the case in most relations of clear subordination: masters and servants, employers and employees, rich and poor. The victims of structural violence invariably end up spending a great deal of time imagining what it is like for those who benefit from it; the opposite rarely occurs. One concomitant is that the victims often end up identifying with, and caring about, the beneficiaries of structural violence—which, next to the violence itself, is probably one of the most powerful forces guaranteeing the perpetuation of systems of inequality. Another is that violence, as we've seen, allows the possibility of cutting through the subtleties of constant mutual interpretation on which ordinary human relations are based.

The details of this play of imagination against structural violence are endlessly complicated and this is hardly the place to work out the full theoretical ramifications. For now, I only want to emphasize two crucial points.

The first is that the line of riot police is precisely the point where structural violence turns into the real thing. Therefore, it functions as a kind of wall against imaginative identification. Nonviolence training actually focuses on trying to break the barrier and teach activists how to constantly bear in mind what the cops are likely to be thinking, but, even here, we are usually dealing with thought on its most elemental, animalistic level ("a police officer will panic if he feels he is cornered," "never do anything that he might interpret as reaching towards a gun," etc.). For most anarchists, the existence of the imaginative wall is intensely frustrating, because anarchist morality is based on a moral imperative towards imaginative identification.[31] On many occasions, I have seen legal trainers having to remind activists that, whatever their inclinations, one should not engage in conversation with one's arresting officer, no matter how apparently open or interested they seem to be, because chances are they are simply fishing for information which will help in a conviction. And, during the actions themselves, one tends to hear endless dismayed speculation about what the cops must be thinking as they truncheon or tear gas nonviolent citizens—conversations which make clear, above all else, that no one really has the slightest idea. But this is precisely the police role. The point of military-style discipline is to make any individual officer's actual feelings or opinions not just impenetrable, but entirely irrelevant.

Obviously no wall is completely impenetrable. Given sufficient pressure, any will eventually begin to crumble. Most of those who help to organize mass actions are keenly aware that historically, when anarchists actually win, when civil resistance campaigns of any sort topple governments, it is usually at the point when the police refuse to fire on them. This is one reason why the image of police officers crying behind their gasmasks in Seattle was so important to them. Security officials seem to understand this principle as well. That's why they spent so much energy, in the months after Seattle, trying to rally their troops.

So this is the first point: the imaginative wall.

The second point is that this juxtaposition of imagination and violence reflects a much larger conflict between two principles of political action. One might even say, between two conceptions of political reality. The first—call it a political ontology of violence—assumes that the ultimate reality is one of forces, with "force" here largely a euphemism for various technologies of physical coercion. To be a "realist" in international relations, for example, has nothing to do with recognizing material realities—in fact, it is all about attributing "interests" to imaginary entities known as "nations"—but about willingness to accept the realities of violence. Nation-states are real because they can kill you. Violence here really is what defines situations. The other could be described as a political ontology of the imagination. It's not so much a matter of giving "power to the imagination" as recognizing that the imagination is the source of power in the first place (and here we might take note of the fact that, next to the Situationists, the French theorist one will encounter the most often in anarchist bookstores is Cornelius Castoriadis).[32] This is why imaginative powers are seen as suffused with the sacred. What anarchists regularly try to do is to level a systematic and continual challenge to the right of the police, and the authorities in general, to define the situation. They do it by proposing endless alternative frameworks—or, more precisely, by insisting on the power to switch frameworks whenever they like. Puppets are the very embodiment of this power.

What this means in the streets is that activists are trying to effectively collapse the political, negotiating process into the structure of the action itself. To win the contest, as it were, by continually changing the definition of what is the field, what are the rules, what are the stakes—and to do so on the field itself.[33] A situation that is sort of like nonviolent warfare becomes a situation that is sort of like a circus, or a theatrical performance, or a religious ritual, and might equally well slip back at any time. Of course, from the point of view of the police, this is simply cheating. Protesters who alternate between throwing paint balls over their heads, and breaking into song-and-dance numbers, are not fighting fair. But, as we've seen, the police aren't fighting fair either. They systematically violate all the laws of combat. They systematically violate agreements. They have to, as a matter of principle, since to do otherwise would be to admit the existence of a situation of dual power: it would be to deny the absolute incommensurability of the state.

In a way, what we are confronting here is the familiar paradox of constituent power. As various German and Italian theorists are fond of reminding us, since no system can create itself (i.e., any God capable of instituting a moral order cannot be bound by that morality), any legal/political order can only be created by some force to which that legality does not apply.[34] In modern Euro-American history, this has meant that the legitimacy of constitutions ultimately harkens back to some kind of popular revolution: at precisely the point, in my terms, where the politics of force meets the politics of imagination. Now, of course, revolution is precisely what the people with the puppets feel they are ultimately about—even if they are trying to do so with an absolute minimum of actual violence. But it seems to me that what really provokes the most violent reactions on the part of the forces of order is precisely the attempt to make constituent power—the power of popular imagination to create new institutional forms—present not just in brief flashes, but continually. To permanently challenge the authorities' ability to define the situation. The insistence that the rules of engagement, as it were, can be constantly renegotiated on the field of battle—that you can constantly change the narrative in the middle of the story—is, in this light, just one aspect of a much larger phenomenon. It also explains why anarchists hate to think of themselves as having to rely in any way on the good offices of even well-meaning corporate media or liberal NGO groups—and even their frequent hostility to would-be benefactors, who nonetheless demand, as a prerequisite to their help, the right to place anarchists within their own pre-set narrative frameworks. Direct action is, by definition, unmediated. It is about cutting through all such frameworks and bringing the power of definition into the streets. Obviously, under ordinary conditions—that is, outside of those magical moments when the police actually do refuse to fire—there is only a very limited degree to which one can actually do this. In the meantime, moral-political struggle in the "courts of public opinion" —as well of the courts of law—would seem unavoidable. Some anarchists deny this. Others grudgingly accept it. All cling to direct action as the ultimate ideal.

This, I think, makes it easier to see why giant puppets, that are so extraordinarily creative but at the same time so intentionally ephemeral, that make a mockery of the very idea of the eternal verities that monuments are meant to represent, can so easily become the symbol of this attempt to seize the power of social creativity, the power to recreate and redefine institutions.[35] Why, as a result, they can end up standing in for everything—the new forms of organization, the emphasis on democratic process—that standard media portrayals of the movement make disappear. They embody the permanence of revolution. From the perspective of the "forces of order," this is precisely what makes them both ridiculous and somehow demonic. From the perspective of many anarchists, this is precisely what makes them both ridiculous and somehow divine.[36]

Some Very Tenuous Conclusions

This essay thus ends where it should perhaps have begun, with the need to thoroughly rethink the idea of "revolution." While most of those engaged with the politics of direct action think of themselves as, in some sense, revolutionaries, few, at this point are operating within the classic revolutionary framework where revolutionary organizing is designed to build towards a violent, apocalyptic confrontation with the state. Even fewer see revolution as a matter of seizing state power and transforming society through its mechanisms. On the other hand, neither are they simply interested in a strategy of "engaged withdrawal" (as in Virno's "revolutionary exodus"), and the founding of new, autonomous communities (Virno & Hardt 1996). In a way, one might say the politics of direct action, by trying to create alternative forms of organization in the very teeth of state power, means to explore a middle ground precisely between these two alternatives. Anyway, we are dealing with a new synthesis that, I think, is not yet entirely worked out.

If nothing else, some of the theoretical frameworks proposed in this essay provide an interesting vantage on the current historical moment. Consider the notion of "the war on terror." Many have spoken with some dismay of the notion of permanent war that seems to be implied. In fact, while the twentieth century could be described as one of permanent war—almost the entire period between 1914 and 1991 was spent either fighting or preparing for world wars of one kind or another—it is not at all clear whether the twenty-first could be described in the same terms. It might be better to say that what the United States is attempting to impose on the world is not really a war at all. It has, of course, become a truism that, as nuclear weapons proliferate, declared wars between states no longer occur, and all conflicts come to be framed as "police actions." Still, it is also critical to bear in mind that police actions have their own, very distinctive, qualities. Police see themselves as engaged in a war largely without rules, against an opponent without honor, towards whom one is therefore not obliged to act honorably, but in which victory is ultimately impossible.

States have a strong tendency to define their relation to their people in terms of an unwinnable war of some sort or another. The American state has been one of the most flagrant in this regard: in recent decades we have seen a war on poverty degenerate into a war on crime, then a war on drugs (which was extended internationally), and finally, now, a war on terror. But, as this sequence makes clear, the latter is not really a war at all but an attempt to extend this same, internal logic to the entire globe. It is an attempt to declare a kind of diffuse global police state. In the final analysis, I suspect the panic reaction on the part of the state was really more a reaction to the success of an ongoing, if subtle, global anti-capitalist uprising than to the threat of Osama bin Laden (though the latter certainly provided the ultimate convenient excuse): it's just that on a global scale as well, moral-political struggle has created rules of engagement which make it very difficult for the US to strike out directly at those against whom it would most like to strike out.[37]

To put it somewhat glibly: just as the form of violence most appropriate for a political ontology based in the imagination is revolution, so is the form of imagination most appropriate for a political ontology based in violence, precisely, terror. One might add that the Bushes and Bin Ladens are working quite in tandem in this regard (it is significant, I think, that if al-Qaeda does harbor some gigantic utopian vision—a reunification of the old Islamic Indian Ocean Diaspora? a restoration of the Caliphate?—they haven't told us much about it).

Still, this is no doubt a bit simplistic. To understand the American regime as a global structure, and at the same time to understand its contradictions, I think one must return to the cosmological role of the police in American culture. It is a peculiar characteristic of life in the United States that most American citizens, who over the course of the day can normally be expected to try to avoid any circumstance that might lead them to have to deal with police or police affairs, can also normally be expected to go home and spend hours watching dramas that invite them to see the world from a policeman's point of view. This was not always so. It's actually quite difficult to identify an American movie from before the 1960s where a policeman was a sympathetic hero. Over the course of the 1960s, however, police abruptly took the place previously held by cowboys in American entertainment.[38] The timing seems hardly insignificant. Neither does the fact that, by now, cinematic and TV images of American police are being relentlessly exported to every corner of the world, at the same time as their flesh and blood equivalents. What I would emphasize here though is that both are characterized by an extra-legal impunity which, paradoxically, makes them able to embody a kind of constituent power turned against itself. The Hollywood cop, like the cowboy, is a lone maverick who breaks all the rules (this is permissible, even necessary, since he is always dealing with dishonorable opponents). In fact, it is usually precisely the maverick cop who engages in the endless property destruction which provides so much of the pleasure of Hollywood action films. In other words, police can be heroes in such movies largely because they are the only figures who can systematically ignore the law. It is constituent power turned on itself, of course, because cops, on screen or in reality, are not trying to create (or constitute) anything. They are simply maintaining the status quo.

In one sense, this is the most clever ideological displacement of all—the perfect complement to the aforementioned privatization of (consumer) desire. Insofar as the popular festival endures, it has become pure spectacle, with the role of Master of the Potlatch granted to the very figure who, in real life, is in charge of ensuring that any actual outbreaks of popular festive behavior are forcibly suppressed.

Like any ideological formula, however, this one is extraordinarily unstable, riddled with contradictions—as the initial difficulties of the US police in suppressing the globalization movement so vividly attest. It seems to me it is best seen as a way of managing a situation of extreme alienation and insecurity that itself can only be maintained by systematic coercion. Faced with anything that remotely resembles creative, non-alienated experience, it tends to look as ridiculous as a deodorant commercial during a time of national disaster. But then, I am an anarchist. The anarchist problem remains how to bring that sort of experience, and the imaginative power that lies behind it, into the daily lives of those outside the small, autonomous bubbles we anarchists have already created. This is a continual problem, but there seems to me every reason to believe that, were it possible, the power of the police cosmology, and with it, the power of the police themselves, would simply melt away.

Endnotes

1   I'm adopting here the name most commonly employed by participants in North America. Most firmly reject the term "anti-globalization." I have in the past proposed simply "globalization movement," but some find this confusing. In Europe, the terms "alternative-" or "alter-globalization" are often used, but these have yet to be widely adopted in the US.

2   Obviously, this assumes that the groups in question are broadly on the same page; if a group were overtly racist or sexist no one would ask about their internal decision-making process. The point is that questions of process are far more important than the kind of sectarian affiliations that had so dominated radical politics in the past: i.e., Anarcho-Syndicalists versus Social Ecologists, or Platformists, etc. Sometimes these factors do enter in. But, even then, the objections are likely to be raised in process terms.

3   That policy can be summed up by the *New York Times*' senior news editor, Bill Borders, who, when challenged by FAIR, a media watchdog group, to explain why the *Times* provided almost no coverage of 2000's inauguration protests (the second largest inaugural protests in American history), replied that they did not consider the protests themselves to be a news story, but "a staged event," "designed to be covered," and therefore "not genuine news" (FAIR 2001). FAIR, needless to say, replied by asking in what sense the inaugural parade itself was any different.

4   One effect of the peculiar definition of violence adopted by the American media is that Gandhian tactics do not, generally speaking, work in the US. One of the aims of non-violent civil disobedience is to reveal the inherent violence of the state, to demonstrate that it is prepared to brutalize even dissidents who could not possibly be the source of physical harm. Since the 1960s, however, the US media has simply refused to represent authorized police activity of any sort as violent. In the several years immediately preceding Seattle, for instance, forest activists on the West Coast had developed lockdown techniques by which they immobilized their arms in concrete-reinforced PVC tubing, making them at once obviously harmless and very difficult to remove. It was a classic Gandhian strategy. The police response was to develop what can only be described as torture techniques: rubbing pepper spray in the eyes of incapacitated activists. When even that didn't cause a media furor (in fact, courts upheld the practice), many concluded Gandhian tactics simply didn't work in America. It is significant that a large number of the Black Bloc anarchists in Seattle, who rejected the lockdown strategy and opted for more mobile and aggressive tactics, were precisely forest activists who had been involved in tree-sits and lockdowns in the past.

5   Those with puppets have been attacked and arrested frequently as well, but, to my knowledge, the corporate media has never reported this.

6   I owe the phrase to Ilana Gershon.

7   Similar themes recur in many interviews with radical puppeteers. This is from
    Mattyboy of the Spiral Q Puppet Theater in Philadelphia: "OK, I'm 23. I've lost
    13 friends to AIDS. This is wartime, it's a plague. This is the only way for me
    to deal with it. With puppets I create my own mythology. I bring them back as
    gods and goddesses" (Freid 1997). One illustrated volume on Bread & Puppet is
    actually called *Rehearsing with Gods: Photographs and Essays on the Bread & Puppet
    Theater* (Simon & Estrin 2004).

8   The Pagan Bloc has been a regular fixture in large-scale actions since Seattle, and,
    unlike the Quakers and other Christian proponents of civil disobedience, was will-
    ing, ultimately, to recognize Black Bloc practice as a form of non-violence and even
    to form a tacit alliance with them.

9   Videographers documented police commanders on the first day reassuring activ-
    ists that the Seattle police "had never attacked non-violent protestors and never
    would." Within hours the same commanders had completely reversed course.

10 The best source I've found on these events is in Boski (2002).

11 Blocking a street is in fact technically not even a crime, but an "infraction" or "vio-
    lation": the legal equivalent of jaywalking, or a parking ticket. If one violates such
    ordinances for non-political purposes one can normally expect to receive some kind
    of ticket, but certainly, not to be taken to a station or to spend the night in jail.

12 *New York Times*, June 6, Corrections, A2. The original story was significantly
    entitled, "Detroit Defends Get-Tough Stance" (Christian 2000). The correction
    reads: "An article on Sunday about plans for protests in Detroit and in Windsor,
    Ontario, against an inter-American meeting being held in Windsor through today
    referred incorrectly to the protests last November at the World Trade Organization
    meeting in Seattle. The Seattle protests were primarily peaceful. The authorities
    there said that any objects thrown were aimed at property, not people. No protes-
    tors were accused of throwing objects, including rocks and Molotov cocktails, at
    delegates or police."

13 This document was transcribed and widely circulated on activist listservs at the
    time. According to one story in the *Miami Herald* (Fleischman 2003), it derived
    from "retired DEA agent Tom Cash, 63, now senior managing director for Kroll
    Inc., an international security and business consulting firm." Cash in turn claimed
    to derive his information from "police intelligence" sources.

14 A number of Molotovs were thrown during the FTAA summit in Québec City,
    apparently all by Québec City residents. But francophone Canada has a very dif-
    ferent tradition of militancy.

15 One has to wonder where they actually get these things. A typical example from
    my own experience comes from the World Economic Forum protests in New York
    in early 2002. Police at one point attacked a group of protestors, who were part of
    a crowd waiting to begin a permitted march, when they observed them distribut-

ing large plexiglass posters that were designed to double as shields. Several were dragged off and arrested. Police later circulated several different stories explaining the reasons for the attack, but the one they eventually fixed on was a claim that the arrestees were preparing to attack the nearby Plaza Hotel. They claimed to have discovered "lead pipes and jars full of urine" on their persons—though in this case they did not actually produce the evidence. This is a case on which I have some first-hand knowledge, since I knew the arrestees and had been standing a few feet away from them when it happened. They were, in fact, undergraduate students from a small New England liberal arts college who had agreed to have their preparations and training before the march video-taped by a team of reporters from ABC Nightline (the reporters, unfortunately, were not actually there at the time). A less likely group of thugs would have been hard to imagine. Needless to say, they were startled and confused to discover police were claiming that they had come to the march equipped with jars of urine. In such cases, claims that urine or excrement were involved is considered, by activists, instant and absolute proof that the police had planted the evidence.

16   There is also no clear evidence that 1960s protestors spat on soldiers any more than early feminists actually burned bras. At least, no one has managed to come up with a contemporary reference to such an act. The story seems to have emerged in the late 1970s or early 1980s, and, as the recent documentary *Sir! No Sir!* nicely demonstrates, the only veteran who has publicly claimed this happened to him is likely to be lying.

17   I have been unable to trace who first publicly announced such claims, though my memory from the time was that they were voiced almost simultaneously from Mayor Riordan of Los Angeles and a Philadelphia Democratic Party official, during the preparations for those cities' respective primaries. The claim was obviously also meant to appeal to conservative stereotypes of liberals as members of a "cultural elite"—but it had surprisingly wide influence. As Stevphen Shukaitis (2005) has pointed out, it has been reproduced even by sympathetic voices in the NGO community. While I have not conducted systematic surveys of the socio-economic background of anarchists in the course of my own research, I can rely on six years of personal experience to say that, in fact, "trust fund babies" in the movement are extremely rare. Any major city is likely to have one or two, often prominent simply because of their access to resources, but I myself know at least two or three anarchists from military families for every one equipped with a trust fund.

18   One common fear is that wooden dowels used in their construction could be detached and used as cudgels, or to break windows.

19   "In a Zogby America survey of 1,004 adults, 32.9% said they were proud of the protesters, while another 31.2% said they were wary. Another 13.2% said they were sympathetic and 15.7% irritated and 6.9% said they were unsure." Considering the almost uniform hostility of the coverage, the fact that a third of the audience

were nonetheless "proud," and that less than one in six were sure their reaction was negative, is quite remarkable.

20 Probably the destruction of productive capacity as well, which must be endlessly renewed.

21 It might be significant here that the United States' main exports to the rest of the world consist of Hollywood action movies and personal computers. If you think about it, they form a kind of complementary pair to the brick-through-window/giant puppet set I've been describing. Or, rather, the brick/puppet set might be considered a kind of subversive, desublimated reflection of them—the first involving paeans to property destruction, the second, the endless ability to create new, but ephemeral, insubstantial imagery in the place of older, more permanent forms.

22 Some of this history is retold, and the story brought forward to Reclaim the Streets and the current carnivals against capitalism. See Grindon (2006).

23 For one good example of such reflections, see *Wise Fool Puppet Intervention* (n.d.). Wise Fool traces its art more back to Medieval mystery plays than festivals, but it provides a nice historical perspective.

24 Where they will normally turn on shows which take the perspective of the same police in charge of getting them off the streets to begin with. More on this later.

25 See Bitner (1990) for a good summary of police sociology's understanding of these constraints and the general issue of "discretion." Since most Americans assume that police are normally engaged in preventing or investigating crimes, they assume that police conduct is freighted with endless bureaucratic restraints. In fact, one of the great discoveries of police sociology is that police spend a surprisingly small percentage of their time on criminal matters.

26 Bittner's phrase. See also Neocleus (2000).

27 Consider here the fact that "police negotiators" are generally employed in hostage situations. In other words, in order to actually get the police to negotiate, one has to literally be holding a gun to someone's head. In such situations police can hardly be expected to honor their promises: in fact, they could well argue they are morally obliged not to.

28 Organizers at Genoa uniformly spoke of their shock during the actions when all the police commanders, whose cell phone numbers they had assembled, suddenly refused to answer calls from activists.

29 I have yet to hear of a passing pedestrian or other member of "the public" who was injured by even the rowdiest anarchist tactics; in any large-scale action, large numbers of passing pedestrians are likely to end up gassed, injured, or arrested by police.

30 I have developed these themes in much greater detail elsewhere (Graeber 2006).

31 Peter Kropotkin (1909, 1924), still probably the most famous anarchist thinker to have developed an explicit ethical theory, argued that all morality is founded on

the imagination. Most contemporary anarchists would appear to follow him on this, at least implicitly.

32 Particularly his *Imaginary Institution of Society* (1987). Again, this is a theme that I can only fully develop elsewhere, but one could describe the history of left-wing thought since the end of the eighteenth century as revolving around the assumption that creativity and imagination were the fundamental ontological principles. This is obvious in the case of Romanticism, but equally true of Marx—who insisted, in his famous comparison of architects and bees that it was precisely the role of imagination in production that made humans different from animals. Marx, in turn, was elaborating on perspectives already current in the worker's movement of his day. This helps explain, I think, the notorious affinity that avant-garde artists have always felt with revolutionary politics. Rightwing thought has always tended to accuse the Left of naiveté in refusing to take account of the importance of the "means of destruction," arguing that ignoring the fundamental role of violence in defining human relations can only end up producing pernicious effects.

33 One might draw an analogy here to the collapse of levels typical of consensus decision-making. One way to think of consensus process is an attempt to merge the process of deliberation with the process of enforcement. If one does not have a separate mechanism of coercion that can force a minority to comply with a majority decision, majority voting is clearly unadvisable—the process of finding consensus is meant to produce outcomes that do not need a separate mechanism of enforcement, because compliance has already been guaranteed within the process of decision-making itself.

34 I am referring here, of course, to Carl Schmitt and Walter Benjamin, and more recently, to Toni Negri and Giorgio Agamben.

35 The T-shirt of the Arts in Action collective, which actually makes many of these puppets, features a quote from Brecht: "We see art not as a mirror to hold up to reality but as a hammer with which to shape it."

36 It is interesting to observe that there is a longstanding tradition in American thought that sees creativity as inherently anti-social, and therefore, demonic. It emerges particularly strongly in racial ideologies. This however is properly the subject for another essay.

37 The fact that almost all the principal figures involved in the repression of protest in America ended up as "security consultants" in Baghdad after the American conquest of Iraq seems rather telling here. Of course, they rapidly discovered their usual tactics were not particularly effective against opponents who really *were* violent—capable, for example, of dealing with IMF and World Bank officials by actually blowing them up.

38 Clint Eastwood, of course, in his shift from Spaghetti Western to Dirty Harry, was the very avatar of the transformation. The moment cop movies rose to prominence, cowboy movies effectively disappeared.

Bibliography

Bitner, Egon
1990 *Aspects of Police Work*. Boston: Northeastern University Press.

Boski, Joseph
2002 "The Costs of Global Governance: Security and International Meetings since WTO Seattle." Paper Presented at the CYBER Conference, Globalization: Governance and Inequality, May 31–June 1, 2002, Ventura California.

Castoriadis, Cornelius
1987 *The Imaginary Institution of Society* (Kathleen Blamey, trans.). Cambridge: Polity Press.

Christian, Nicole
2000 "Detroit Defends Get-Tough Stance." *New York Times*, June 4, 2000, A6.

Cooks, Ristin
2001 "Puppet Masters: Paper Hand Puppet Intervention Brings Its Brand of Political Theater Back to Chapel Hill" *Independent Ontline*, August 8, 2001, http: //indy-week.com/durham/2001-08-08/ae.html, accessed June 2004.

Cooper, Marc
1991 "Dum Da Dum-Dum." *Village Voice*, April 16, 1991, 28–33.

Creveld, Martin Van
1991 *The Transformation of War*. New York, Free Press.

David and X
2002 *The Black Bloc Papers*, compiled by David and X of the Green Mountain Anarchist Collective. Baltimore: Black Clover Press.

Epstein, Barbara
1991 *Political Protest and Cultural Revolution: Non-violent Direct Action in the 1970s and 1980s*. Berkeley: University of California Press.

FAIR (Fairness and Accuracy In Reporting)
2001 "ACTIVISM UPDATE: New York Times Responds on Inauguration Criticism." News release, February 22, 2001.

Fleischman, Joan
2003 "Trade Protesters Mean Business, Analyst Warns." *Miami Herald*, October 1, 2003.

Freid, Daisy
1997 "The Puppets Are Coming." *Philadelphia Citypaper*, January 16–23, 1997.

Graeber, David
2006 "Beyond Power/Knowledge: an Exploration of the Relation of Power, Ignorance, and Stupidity." Malinowski Memorial Lecture, London School of Economics. May 25. Available at http: //www.lse.ac.uk/collections/LSEPublicLecturesAndEvents/pdf/20060525-Graeber.pdf.

Grindon, Gavin
2006 "The Breath of the Possible." In *Constituent Imagination: Militant Investigation, Collective Research* (David Graeber and Stevphen Shukaitis, eds.). Oakland: AK Press.

Koerner, Brendan I,

2003 "Can Miami Really Ban Giant Puppets?" *Slate*, Nov. 12, 2003. http: //www.slate. com/id/2091139/.

Kropotkin, Peter

1909 *Anarchist Morality*. London: Freedom Office.

1924 *Ethics, Origin and Development*. (Authorized translation from the Russian, by Louis S. Friedland and Joseph R. Piroshnikoff.) New York: The Dial Press.

Martinez, José

2000 "Police Prep for Protests over Biotech Conference at Hynes." *Saturday Boston Herald*, March 4 2000.

Neocleus, Mark

2000 *The Fabrication of Social Order: A Critical Theory of Police Power*. London: Pluto Press.

Reuters/Zogby

2000 "Convention Protests Bring Mixed Reactions," Newswire: Monday August 21 2000 4:45 PM ET.

Shukaitis, Stevphen

2005 "Space, Imagination // Rupture: The Cognitive Architecture of Utopian Political Thought in the Global Justice Movement." *University of Sussex Journal of Contemporary History* 8.

Simon, Ronald T., & Marc Estrin

2004 *Rehearsing with Gods: Photographs and Essays on the Bread & Puppet Theater*. White River Junction, VT.: Chelsea Green Pub. Co.

Virno, Paolo, and Michael Hardt, eds.

1996 *Radical Thought in Italy: A Potential Politics*. Minneapolis, MN: University of Minnesota Press.

Wise Fool Puppet Intervention

n.d. "History of Radical Puppetry," www.zeitgeist.net/wfca/radpup.htm. Accessed July 15, 2007.

INDEX

Friends of AK Press

Help sustain our vital project!

AK Press is a worker-run collective that publishes and distributes radical books, audio/visual media, and other materials. We're small: a dozen individuals who work long hours for short money, because we believe in what we do. We're anarchists, which is reflected both in the books we publish and in the way we organize our business: without bosses.

AK Press publishes the finest books, CDs, and DVDs from the anarchist and radical traditions—currently about 18 to 20 per year. Joining The Friends of AK Press is a way in which you can directly help us to keep the wheels rolling and these important projects coming.

As ever, money is tight as we do not rely on outside funding. We need your help to make and keep these crucial materials available. Friends pay a minimum (of course we have no objection to larger sums!) of $25 per month ($30 for international shipping), for a minimum three month period. Money received goes directly into our publishing funds. In return, Friends automatically receive (for the duration of their membership), as they appear, one FREE copy of EVERY new AK Press title. Secondly, they are also entitled to a 10% discount on EVERYTHING featured in the AK Press distribution catalog—or on our website—on ANY and EVERY order. We also have a program where individuals or groups can sponsor a whole book.

PLEASE CONTACT US FOR MORE DETAILS:

AK Press
674-A 23rd Street
Oakland, CA 94612
akpress@akpress.org
www.akpress.org

AK Press
PO Box 12766
Edinburgh, Scotland EH8, 9YE
ak@akedin.demon.co.uk
www.akuk.com